SpringBoard®

English Language Arts

Grade
9

ABOUT THE COLLEGE BOARD

The College Board is a mission-driven not-for-profit organization that connects students to college success and opportunity. Founded in 1900, the College Board was created to expand access to higher education. Today, the membership association is made up of more than 5,900 of the nation's leading educational institutions and is dedicated to promoting excellence and equity in education. Each year, the College Board helps more than seven million students prepare for a successful transition to college through programs and services in college readiness and college success— including the SAT® and the Advanced Placement Program®. The organization also serves the education community through research and advocacy on behalf of students, educators and schools.

For further information, visit www.collegeboard.com.

ISBN: 1-4573-0221-7
ISBN: 978-1-4573-0221-3

2 3 4 5 6 7 8   14 15 16 17 18 19
Printed in the United States of America

ACKNOWLEDGMENTS

The College Board gratefully acknowledges the outstanding work of the classroom teachers and writers who have been integral to the development of this revised program. The end product is testimony to their expertise, understanding of student learning needs, and dedication to rigorous and accessible English Language Arts instruction.

Pat Bishop
Writing Coach (Retired)
Hillsborough Schools
Tampa, Florida

Julie Manley
English Teacher
Bellevue School District 405
Bellevue, Washington

Susie Challancin
English Teacher
Bellevue School District 405
Bellevue, Washington

Le'Andra Myers
English Teacher
Pasco School District
Pasco, Washington

Bryant Crisp
English Teacher
Charlotte Mecklenburg Schools
Charlotte, North Carolina

Stephanie Sharpe
English Teacher
Hillsborough Schools
Tampa, Florida

Paul DeMaret
English Teacher
Poudre School District
Fort Collins, Colorado

Susan Van Doren
English Teacher
Douglas County School District
Minden, Nevada

Michelle Lewis
Curriculum Coordinator
Spokane Public Schools
Spokane, Washington

SPRINGBOARD ENGLISH LANGUAGE ARTS DEVELOPMENT

Betty Barnett
Executive Director
Content Development

Doug Waugh
Senior Director
Product Management

Joely Negedly
Instructional Specialist

Nina Wooldridge
Senior Director
Professional Development

JoEllen Victoreen
Senior Instructional Specialist

RESEARCH AND PLANNING ADVISORS

We also wish to thank the members of our SpringBoard Advisory Council and the many educators who gave generously of their time and their ideas as we conducted research for both the print and online programs. Your suggestions and reactions to ideas helped immeasurably as we planned the revisions. We gratefully acknowledge the teachers and administrators in the following districts.

ABC Unified
Cerritos, California

Albuquerque Public Schools
Albuquerque, New Mexico

Amarillo School District
Amarillo, Texas

Bellevue School District 405
Bellevue, Washington

Broward County Public Schools
Ft. Lauderdale, Florida

Clark County School District
Las Vegas, Nevada

District School Board of Collier
County
Collier County, Florida

Denver Public Schools
Denver, Colorado

Frisco ISD
Frisco, Texas

Garland ISD
Garland, Texas

Gilbert Unified School District
Gilbert, Arizona

Grand Prairie ISD
Grand Prairie, Texas

Hillsborough County Public Schools
Tampa, Florida

Hobbs Municipal Schools
Hobbs, New Mexico

Houston Independent School District
Houston, Texas

Irving Independent School District
Irving, Texas

Kenton County School District
Fort Wright, Kentucky

Lee County Public Schools
Fort Myers, Florida

Newton County Schools
Covington, Georgia

Noblesville Schools
Noblesville, Indiana

Oakland Unified School District
Oakland, California

Orange County Public Schools
Orlando, Florida

School District of Palm Beach County
Palm Beach, Florida

Peninsula School District
Gig Harbor, Washington

Polk County Public Schools
Bartow, Florida

Quakertown Community School
District
Quakertown, Pennsylvania

Rio Rancho Public Schools
Rio Rancho, New Mexico

Ronan School District
Ronan, Montana

St. Vrain School District
Longmont, Colorado

Scottsdale Public Schools
Phoenix, Arizona

Seminole County Public Schools
Sanford, Florida

Southwest ISD
San Antonio, Texas

Spokane Public Schools
Spokane, Washington

Spring ISD
Houston, Texas

Volusia County Schools
DeLand, Florida

Contents

Unit 1 **Coming of Age**

Activities

Unit 2 Defining Style

Activities

Unit 3 Coming of Age in Changing Times

Unit 4 Exploring Poetic Voices

Activities

Unit 5 Coming of Age on Stage

Activities

*Texts not included in these materials.

To the Student

Welcome to the SpringBoard program. The College Board publishes SpringBoard to help you acquire the knowledge and skills that you will need to be prepared for rigorous English Language Arts coursework. Developing proficient reading, writing, language, and speaking and listening skills is important to your success in school, in college, and in a career. Preparing you to develop these skills is the primary purpose of this program.

As you complete middle school and prepare for high school, these skills will also be valuable if you decide to take an Advanced Placement course or another college-level course. Not every student will take an Advanced Placement course in high school, but through SpringBoard you can acquire the knowledge and skills you will need to be successful if you do decide to enroll in AP Literature or AP Language Arts.

We hope you will discover how SpringBoard can help you achieve high academic standards, reach your learning goals, and prepare you for success in your study of literature and language arts. This program has been created with you in mind: the content you need to learn, the tools to help you learn, and the critical thinking skills that help you build confidence in your ability to succeed academically.

STANDARDS-BASED LEARNING

This SpringBoard edition was developed to help you achieve the expectations of being college and career ready. Rigorous standards outline what you should learn in English Language Arts in each grade. See pages xiii-xvi for the complete standards for Grade 9.

The SpringBoard program provides instruction and realistic activities that help you achieve the learning expected by rigorous college and career readiness standards. With this program, you will focus on developing the following skills:

- Close reading and analysis of texts
- Effective communication in collaborative discussions in which you use your textual analysis to share ideas and make decisions with peers
- Fluency in writing narratives, explanations, and arguments based on purpose and audience
- Vocabulary and language skills
- Reading and interpreting film while comparing it to a related print version
- Media literacy.

By learning these skills, you will enhance your ability to understand and analyze any challenging text, to write with clarity and voice, to speak and listen in order to communicate and work effectively with others, and to view media with a critical intelligence.

LEARNING STRATEGIES

Some tools to help you learn are built into every lesson. At the beginning of each activity, you will see suggested learning strategies. Each of these strategies is explained in full in the Resources section of your book. These strategies range from **close reading** and **marking** texts to drafting and revising written work. You will also encounter collaborative strategies in speaking and listening like **debate** and **Socratic Seminar**. Finally, SpringBoard uses a variety of pre-AP strategies like **SOAPSTone** and **TP-CASTT** to help you deeply analyze text; collect evidence for your writing; and critically think about issues, ideas, and concepts. As you learn to use each strategy, you will decide which strategies work best for you.

AP CONNECTIONS

When you reach high school, you may have an opportunity to take Advanced Placement (AP) classes or other rigorous courses. When the time comes to make that decision, we want you to be equipped with the kind of higher-order thinking skills, knowledge, and behaviors necessary to be successful in AP classes and beyond. You will see connections to AP in the texts that you read, the strategies you use, and the writing tasks throughout the material. Having connections to AP Language and Literature will help you:

- Close read a text to determine literary elements.

- Write with an attention to textual evidence and chose organizational patterns.

- Identify and write rhetorical appeals.

- Understand strong relationships among author's purpose, use of literary/stylistic devices, and desired effect.

- Analyze and synthesize information from a variety of texts to respond to an AP style prompt.

- Write to interpret, evaluate, and negotiate differing critical perspectives in literature.

THE SPRINGBOARD DIFFERENCE

SpringBoard is different because it provides instruction with hands-on participation that involves you and your classmates in daily discussions and analysis of what you're reading and learning. You will have an opportunity to:

- Discuss and **collaborate** with your peers to explore and express your ideas

- Explore multiple perspectives by reading a **variety of texts** that introduce you to different ways of thinking, writing, and communicating

- Examine writing from the perspective of a **reader and writer** and learn techniques that good writers use to communicate their message effectively

- Gain a **deep understanding** of topics, enabling you to apply your learning to new and varied situations

- Take **ownership** of your learning by choosing strategies that work for you

- **Reflect** on your growth as a reader, writer, speaker, and listener and showcase your best work in a working portfolio.

HIGH SCHOOL AT A GLANCE
Grade 9

Investigating the thematic concept of **coming of age**. you will read Harper Lee's novel *To Kill a Mockingbird*, informational articles about college; short stories by Poe and Collier; historical articles about segregation; poetry by Wordsworth, Neruda, and Cardiff; and Shakespeare's *Romeo and Juliet*. From your reading, you will gather evidence from texts and incorporate it in written and oral responses, including a presentation using multiple forms of media.

You will encounter more varied and complex writing in this grade as you write in a variety of modes including argumentative, informational, and narrative writing.

Film texts are a large part of Grade 9 activities. In Unit 2, you will study a film director's style and analyze how style is evident in the transformation of print texts to films. In Unit 5, you will *study Romeo and Juliet* and analyze how key scenes are represented in multiple film versions as well as the print text.

Grade 10

In this grade, you will explore the thematic concept of **culture**. Texts include Chinua Achebe's *Things Fall Apart*, Sophocles' *Antigone*, Susan B. Anthony's "On Women's Right to Vote," and the Nobel Prize acceptance speeches of Alexander Solzhenitsyn and Elie Wiesel.

You will be challenged to use evidence from these texts in both your written and oral responses. For example, you will study the extent to which one's culture influences one's worldview, and incorporate textual evidence in a written argument. Research plays a role as you investigate the Ibo culture represented in *Things Fall Apart* and present your findings in a collaborative presentation with digital media.

Film texts play a role when you analyze the degree of objectivity and subjectivity present in documentary films while also gathering evidence about environmental issues.

Grade 11

In this grade, you will explore the concept of the **American Dream**. You will read foundational U.S. documents such as Lincoln's Second Inaugural Address and The Declaration of Independence, essays by Thoreau and Emerson, poetry by Hughes and Whitman, Arthur Miller's drama *The Crucible*, and Zora Neale Hurston's *Their Eyes Were Watching God*. These texts will help you gather evidence to incorporate in an informative essay defining what it means to be an American and a synthesis essay that argues whether or not America still provides access to the American Dream.

You will compare both print and film versions of *The Crucible*, and study various features of news outlets while working collaboratively to create your own news outlet.

Grade 12

Your SpringBoard journey ends in Grade 12 when you study literary theory and move beyond reader response to apply multiple perspectives to complex texts. You will encounter Baldwin's "Stranger in The Village," Orwell's "Shooting an Elephant," Shakespeare's *Othello* and Shaw's *Pygmalion*. Throughout the level, you will learn and apply the theories of Archetypal, Marxist, Feminist, Historical, Cultural, and Reader Response Criticism.

Rigorous reading and writing tasks synthesize your learning throughout this course. Research and film texts go hand in hand in your study of Shakespeare. You will research and analyze the ways in which historical contexts have influenced performances of *Othello* and compare multiple film versions of the drama.

PERFORMANCE PORTFOLIO

One way to introduce yourself is through your writing. You are unique as a writer, and how and what you write is a way of showing yourself. When you collect your writing assignments over a period of time, you can see how your writing skills are changing as you learn new writing techniques.

Presenting yourself through a portfolio also provides direction as you revisit, revise, and reflect on your work throughout the year. Your teacher will guide you as you include items in your portfolio that illustrate a wide range of work, including examples of reading, writing, oral literacy, and collaborative activities. As you progress through the course, you will have opportunities to revisit prior work, revise it based on new learning, and reflect on the learning strategies and activities that help you be successful. The portfolio:

- Gives you a place to feature your work and a means to share it with others.

- Provides an organized, focused way to view your progress throughout the year.

- Allows you to reflect on the new skills and strategies you are learning.

- Enables you to measure your growth as a reader, writer, speaker, and performer.

- Encourages you to revise pieces of work to incorporate new skills.

Strong portfolios will include a variety of work from each unit, such as first drafts, final drafts, quickwrites, notes, reading logs, audio and video examples, and graphics that represent a wide variety of genre, forms, and media created for a variety of purposes.

We hope you enjoy the SpringBoard program as you explore your own and others' ideas about becoming effective readers, writers, and communicators.

College and Career Readiness Standards

READING STANDARDS FOR LITERATURE

Key Ideas and Details

1. Cite strong and thorough textual evidence to support analysis of what the text says explicitly as well as inferences drawn from the text.
2. Determine a theme or central idea of a text and analyze in detail its development over the course of the text including how it emerges and is shaped and refined by specific details; provide an objective summary of the text.
3. Analyze how complex characters (e.g., those with multiple or conflicting motivations) develop over the course of a text, interact with other characters, and advance the plot or develop the theme.

Craft and Structure

4. Determine the meaning of words and phrases as they are used in the text, including figurative and connotative meanings; analyze the cumulative impact of specific word choices on meaning and tone (e.g., how the language evokes a sense of time and place; how it sets a formal or informal tone).
5. Analyze how an author's choices concerning how to structure a text, order events within it (e.g., parallel plots), and manipulate time (e.g., pacing, flashbacks) create such effects as mystery, tension, or surprise.
6. Analyze a particular point of view or cultural experience reflected in a work of literature from outside the United States, drawing on a wide reading of world literature.

Integration of Knowledge and Ideas

7. Analyze the representation of a subject or a key scene in two different artistic mediums, including what is emphasized or absent in each treatment (e.g., Auden's "Musée des Beaux Arts" and Breughel's *Landscape with the Fall of Icarus*).
8. (Not applicable to literature)
9. Analyze how an author draws on and transforms source material in a specific work (e.g., how Shakespeare treats a theme or topic from Ovid or the Bible or how a later author draws on a play by Shakespeare).

Range of Reading and Level of Text Complexity

10. By the end of Grade 9, read and comprehend literature, including stories, dramas, and poems, in the grades 9-10 text complexity band proficiently, with scaffolding as needed at the high end of the range.

By the end of grade 10, read and comprehend literature, including stories, dramas, a and poems, at the high end of the grades 9–10 text complexity band independently and proficiently.

READING STANDARDS FOR INFORMATIONAL TEXT

Key Ideas and Details

1. Cite strong and thorough textual evidence to support analysis of what the text says explicitly as well as inferences drawn from the text.
2. Determine a central idea of a text and analyze its development over the course of the text, including how it emerges and is shaped and refined by specific details; provide an objective summary of the text.
3. Analyze how the author unfolds an analysis or series of ideas or events, including the order in which the points are made, how they are introduced and developed, and the connections that are drawn between them.

Craft and Structure

4. Determine the meaning of words and phrases as they are used in a text, including figurative, connotative, and technical meanings; analyze the cumulative impact of specific word choices on meaning and tone (e.g., how the language of a court opinion differs from that of a newspaper).
5. Analyze in detail how an author's ideas or claims are developed and refined by particular sentences, paragraphs, or larger portions of a text (e.g., a section or chapter).
6. Determine an author's point of view or purpose in a text and analyze how an author use rhetoric to advance that point of view or purpose.

Integration of Knowledge and Ideas

7. Analyze various accounts of a subject told in different mediums (e.g., a person's life story in both print and multimedia), determining which details are emphasized in each account.
8. Delineate and evaluate the argument and specific claims in a text, assessing whether the reasoning is valid and the evidence is relevant and sufficient; identify false statements and fallacious reasoning.
9. Analyze seminal U.S. documents of historical and literary significance (e.g., Washington's Farewell Address, the Gettysburg Address, Roosevelt's Four Freedoms speech, King's "Letter from Birmingham Jail"), including how they address related themes and concepts.

Range of Reading and Level of Text Complexity

10. By the end of grade 9, read and comprehend literary nonfiction in the grades 9–10 text complexity band proficiently, with scaffolding as needed at the high end of the range.

    By the end of grade 10, read and comprehend literary nonfiction at the high end of the grades 9–10 text complexity band independently and proficiently.

WRITING STANDARDS

Text Types and Purposes

1. Write arguments to support claims in an analysis of substantive topics or texts, using valid reasoning and relevant and sufficient evidence.

   a. Introduce precise claim(s), distinguish the claim(s) from alternate or opposing claims, and create an organization that establishes clear relationships among claims(s), counterclaims, reasons, and evidence.

   b. Develop claim(s) and counterclaims fairly, supplying evidence for each while pointing out the strengths and limitations of both in a manner that anticipates the audience's knowledge level and concerns.

   c. Use words, phrases, and clauses to link the major sections of the text, create cohesion, and clarify the relationships between claim(s) and reasons.

   d. Establish and maintain a formal style and objective tone while attending to the norms and conventions of the discipline in which they are writing.

   e. Provide a concluding statement or section that follows from and supports the argument presented.

2. Write informative/explanatory texts to examine and convey complex ideas, concepts, and information clearly and accurately through the effective selection, organization, and analysis of content.

   a. Introduce a topic; organize complex ideas, concepts, and information to make important connections and distinctions; include formatting (e.g., headings), graphics (e.g., figures tables), and multimedia when useful to aiding comprehension.

   b. Develop the topic with well-chosen, relevant, and sufficient facts, extended definitions, concrete details, quotations, or other information and examples appropriate to the audience's knowledge of the topic.

   c. Use appropriate and varied transitions to link the major sections of the text, create cohesion, and clarify the relationships among complex ideas and concepts.

   d. Use precise language and domain-specific vocabulary to manage the complexity of the topic.

   e. Establish and maintain a formal style and objective tone while attending to the norms and conventions of the discipline in which they are writing.

   f. Provide a concluding statement or section that follows from and supports the information or explanation presented (e.g., articulating implications or the significance of the topic).

3. Write narratives to develop real or imagined experiences or events using effective technique, well-chosen details, and well-structured event sequences.

   a. Engage and orient the reader by setting out a problem, situation, or observation, establishing one or multiple point(s) of view, and introducing a narrator and/or characters; create a smooth progression of experiences or events.

   b. Use narrative techniques, such as dialogue, pacing, description, reflection, and multiple plot lines, to develop experiences, events, and/or characters.

   c. Use a variety of techniques to sequence events so that they build on one another to create a coherent whole.

   d. Use precise words and phrases, telling details, and sensory language to convey the action and convey a vivid picture of the experiences, events, setting, and/or characters.

   e. Provide a conclusion that follows from and reflects on what is experienced, observed, or resolved over the course of the narrative.

Production and Distribution of Writing

4. Produce clear and coherent writing in which the development, organization, and style are appropriate to task, purpose, and audience. (Grade-specific expectations for writing types are defined in standards 1–3 above.)

5. Develop and strengthen writing as needed by planning, revising, editing, rewriting, or trying a new approach, focusing on addressing what is most significant for a specific purpose and audience. (Editing for conventions should demonstrate command of Language standards 1–3 up to and including grades 9–10 on page 54.)

6. Use technology, including the Internet, to produce, publish, and update individual or shared writing products, taking advantage of technology's capacity to link to other information and to display information flexibly and dynamically.

7. Conduct short as well as more sustained research projects to answer a question (including a self-generated question) or solve a problem; narrow or broaden the inquiry when appropriate; synthesize multiple sources on the subject, demonstrating understanding of the subject under investigation.

8. Gather relevant information from multiple authoritative print and digital sources, using advanced searches effectively; assess the usefulness of each source in answering the research question; integrate information into the text selectively to maintain the flow of ideas, avoiding plagiarism and following a standard format for citation.

9. Draw evidence from literary or informational texts to support analysis, reflection, and research.
   a. Apply grades 9–10 reading standards to literature (e.g., "Analyze how an author draws on and transforms source material in a specific work [e.g., how Shakespeare treats a theme or topic from Ovid or the Bible or how a later author draws on a play by Shakespeare]").
   b. Apply grades 9–10 reading standards to literary nonfiction (e.g., "Delineate and evaluate the argument and specific claims in a text, assessing whether the reasoning is valid and the evidence is relevant and sufficient; identify false statements and fallacious reasoning").

Range of Writing

10. Write routinely over extended time frames (time for research, reflection, and revision) and shorter time frames (a single sitting or a day or two) for a range of discipline-specific tasks, purposes, and audiences.

SPEAKING AND LISTENING STANDARDS

1. Initiate and participate effectively in a range of collaborative discussions (one-on-one, in groups, and teacher-led) with diverse partners on grades 9–10 *topics, texts, and issues*, building on others' ideas and expressing their own clearly and persuasively.
   a. Come to discussions prepared, having read and researched material under study; explicitly draw on that preparation by referring to evidence from texts and other research on the topic or issue to stimulate a thoughtful, well-reasoned exchange of ideas.
   b. Work with peers to set rules for collegial discussions and decision-making (e.g., informal consensus, taking votes on key idles, presentation of alternate views), clear goals and deadlines, and individual roles as needed.
   c. Propel conversations by posing and responding to questions that relate the current discussion to broader themes or larger ideas; actively incorporate others into the discussion; and clarify, verify, or challenge ideas and conclusions.
   d. Respond thoughtfully to diverse perspectives, summarize points of agreement and disagreement, and, when warranted, qualify or justify their own views and understanding and make new connections in light of the evidence and reasoning presented.

2. Integrate multiple sources of information presented in diverse media or formats (e.g., visually, quantitatively, orally) evaluating the credibility and accuracy of each source.

3. Evaluate a speaker's point of view, reasoning, and use of evidence and rhetoric, identifying any fallacious reasoning or exaggerated or distorted evidence.

Presentation of Knowledge and Ideas

4. Present information, findings, and supporting evidence clearly, concisely, and logically such that listeners can follow the line of reasoning and the organization, development, substance, and style are appropriate to purpose, audience, and task.

5. Make strategic use of digital media (e.g., textual, graphical, audio, visual, and interactive elements) in presentations to enhance understanding of findings, reasoning, and evidence and to add interest.

6. Adapt speech to a variety of contexts and tasks, demonstrating command of formal English when indicated or appropriate.

LANGUAGE STANDARDS

Conventions of Standard English

1. Demonstrate command of the conventions of standard English grammar and usage when writing or speaking.
   a. Use parallel structure.
   b. Use various types of phrases (noun, verb, adjectival, adverbial, participial, prepositional, absolute) and clauses (independent, dependent; noun, relative, adverbial) to convey specific meanings and add variety and interest to writing or presentations.
2. Demonstrate command of the conventions of standard English capitalization, punctuation, and spelling when writing.
   a. Use a semicolon (and perhaps a conjunctive adverb) to link two or more closely related independent clauses.
   b. Use a colon to introduce a list or quotation.
   c. Spell correctly.

Knowledge of Language

3. Apply knowledge of language to understand how language functions in different contexts, to make effective choices for meaning or style, and to comprehend more fully when reading or listening.
   a. Write and edit work so that it conforms to the guidelines in a style manual (e.g., *MLA Handbook*, Turabian's *Manual for Writers*) appropriate for the discipline and writing type.

4. Determine or clarify the meaning of unknown and multiple-meaning words and phrases based on grades 9–10 reading and content, choosing flexibly from a range of strategies.
   a. Use context (e.g., the overall meaning of a sentence, paragraph, or text; a word's position or function in a sentence) as a clue to the meaning of a word or phrase.
   b. Identify and correctly use patterns of word changes that indicate different meanings or parts of speech (e.g., *analyze, analysis, analytical, advocate, advocacy*).

   c. Consult general and specialized reference materials (e.g., dictionaries, glossaries, thesauruses), both print and digital, to find the pronunciation of a word or determine or clarify its precise meaning, its part of speech, or its etymology.
   d. Verify the preliminary determination of the meaning of a word or phrase (e.g., by checking the inferred meaning in context or in a dictionary).

5. Demonstrate understanding of figurative language, word relationships, and nuances in word meanings.
   a. Interpret figures of speech (e.g., euphemism, oxymoron) in context and analyze their role in the text.
   b. Analyze nuances in the meaning of words with similar denotations.
6. Acquire and use accurately general academic and domain-specific words and phrases, sufficient for reading, writing, speaking, and listening at the college and career readiness level; demonstrate independence in gathering vocabulary knowledge when considering a word or phrase important to comprehension or expression.

Coming of Age

Visual Prompt: What comes to mind when you hear the phrase "coming of age"?

Unit Overview

Ninth grade marks many important transitions, beginning the experiences of becoming an adult. In this unit, you will explore the theme of "coming of age" and examine how writers in a variety of texts use stylistic choices to create the voices of characters who are going through life-changing experiences. Along the way, you will study a novel independently, conduct interviews, analyze arguments regarding the value of post-secondary education, and examine the complex relationship between an author's purpose, his or her audience, and the ways in which he or she appeals to readers. By the end of the unit, your academic "coming of age" will be marked by a heightened understanding of voice, appeals, and persuasive techniques.

Coming of Age

GOALS:

- To understand the concept of coming of age
- To identify diction, syntax, imagery, and tone—and to understand the way they work together to convey an author's or speaker's voice
- To incorporate voice effectively in writing
- To analyze and use rhetorical appeals and evidence to present an argument to an audience
- To support an inference or claim using valid reasoning and relevant and sufficient evidence

ACADEMIC VOCABULARY

strategize
inference
denotation
connotation
transcript
claim
counterclaim
analogy

Literary Terms

voice
tone
narrative
narrator
anaphora
diction
juxtaposition
prose
rhetorical appeals
logos
ethos
pathos

Contents

Activities

Language and Writer's Craft

• Parallel Structure (1.4)

• Clauses (1.14)

Previewing the Unit

My Notes

Learning Targets
- Preview the big ideas and the vocabulary for the unit.
- Identify and anaylze the skills and knowledge needed to complete Embedded Assessment 1 successfully.

Making Connections
As you read about coming of age, you will learn about voice and style, the characteristics that make a writer's or speaker's work distinctive. You will evaluate texts and make inferences based on textual evidence. Then you will conduct an interview and write an interview narrative in which you capture the voice of the interviewee.

Essential Questions
Based on your current knowledge, write answers to these questions in the My Notes space.
1. What does it mean to "come of age"?
2. How are rhetorical appeals used to influence an audience?

Developing Vocabulary
Go back to the Contents page and use a QHT strategy to analyze and evaluate your knowledge of the Academic Vocabulary and Literary Terms for the unit. As a reminder, use the "Q" to identify words you do not know, an "H" for words you have heard and might be able to identify, and a "T" for words you know well enough to teach to someone else.

ACADEMIC VOCABULARY
To **strategize** is to plan the actions you will take to complete a task. Think about how this verb relates to the **strategies** you use to unpack the Embedded Assessment or the **strategic** thinking you use to solve problems.

Unpacking Embedded Assessment 1
Read the following assignment for Embedded Assessment 1 and summarize the major elements in your Reader/Writer Notebook.

> Your assignment is to interview a person who has attended a post-secondary institution (i.e., a two- or four-year college, a training or vocational school, the military). From that interview, you will write a narrative that effectively portrays the voice of the interviewee while revealing how the experience contributed to his or her coming of age.

Summarize in your own words what you will need to know for this assessment. With your class, create a graphic organizer that represents the skills and knowledge you will need to accomplish this task and **strategize** how you will complete the assignment. To help you complete your graphic organizer, be sure to review the criteria in the Scoring Guide on page 55.

INDEPENDENT READING LINK
For independent reading during this unit, you may want to choose biographies or autobiographies about people of interest to you. As you study the first part of this unit, apply the strategies and information you learn to your independent reading.

Talking About Voice

Learning Targets
- Identify and analyze how a writer's use of language creates a distinct voice.
- Cite textual evidence of voice to support inferences about a speaker.

Creating Voice

1. **Quickwrite:** When you think of pizza, what comes to mind? Write a paragraph describing pizza and showing your attitude toward it. You will come back to this later.

If several different people were asked to describe pizza, you might expect to get a variety of responses. Even though the subject would be the same, the descriptions might be quite different because each person uses a different **voice**. Voice is a result of a writer's or speaker's use of language, and it may be so unique that it's almost like a fingerprint: a sign of the writer's or speaker's identity. This fingerprint results from three central aspects of how language is used in the text.

- **Diction**—Word choice intended to convey a certain effect
- **Syntax**—Sentence structure; the arrangement of words and the order of grammatical elements in a sentence
- **Imagery**—The words or phrases, including specific details and figurative language, that a writer uses to represent persons, objects, actions, feelings, and ideas descriptively by appealing to the senses

Experienced writers choose language carefully knowing that readers draw conclusions or **inferences** based on their diction, imagery, and syntax.

2. Following is one person's description of pizza. What inferences can you draw about Speaker 1 based upon the speaker's voice? Write your inferences in the graphic organizer that follows. Cite details of the speaker's voice that led you to that conclusion.

Speaker 1: Eating pizza is rather like embarking on a transcontinental excursion. You embark on the journey without being quite certain of what you will encounter. A well-made pizza contains the aromatic essence of fresh basil, oregano, and garlic that beckon invitingly. Once you bite into a perfectly sliced piece of pizza, your taste buds awaken and celebrate. When properly prepared, pizza is an extraordinary culinary creation.

Literary Terms
Voice is a writer's (or speaker's) distinctive use of language to express ideas as well as his or her persona.
Tone is a writer's or speaker's attitude toward the subject. Tone is conveyed through the person's choice of words and detail.

ACADEMIC VOCABULARY
To **infer** or to make an **inference** is to come to a conclusion about ideas or information not directly stated. You infer something based on reasoning and evidence (details).

WORD CONNECTIONS
Roots and Affixes

The word *syntax* contains the Greek prefix *syn-*, which means "together," and the root *-tax-*, meaning "arrangement" or "order."
The prefix *syn-* is found in words like *synthesis*, *synonym*, and *synchronize*. The root *-tax-* occurs in *taxonomy* and *taxidermy*.

Talking About Voice

Speakers	Inferences About the Speaker (What might you infer about the speaker's age, status, preferences?)	Diction (What word choices does the speaker make? Formal or informal?)	Syntax (Are the sentences short, long, simple, complex?)	Imagery (What words and phrases include sensory details to create images?)	Tone (What can you conclude about the speaker's attitude toward the subject?)
Speaker 1					
Speaker 2					
Speaker 3					

3. Inferences are justifiable only if they can be supported by textual evidence. Discuss your conclusions about Speaker 1 with another set of partners, comparing the annotations and the inferences you have drawn based upon them. Evaluate how supportable the inferences are based on the evidence you can provide to support your inferences. Rank each of your inferences from "strongly supported by evidence" to "somewhat supported by evidence."

Be prepared to justify your inferences—and your rankings—by explaining how the textual evidence supports your conclusions.

4. Now read the remaining speakers' descriptions with a partner, highlighting and annotating each passage for the diction, syntax, and imagery that contribute to the voice and tone. Write your annotations in the graphic organizer on the previous page to capture your responses.

Speaker 2: It's yummy. I like it when the cheese is really gooey. My mom makes it for dinner on the weekends. When it's too hot, I have to wait for it to cool. Mom says if I don't wait I will burn my tongue. I like the way pizza smells. When I smell pizza cooking it always makes me want to eat it right up!

Inference about the speaker:_____

Speaker 3: As long as not one speck of gross disgusting animal flesh comes anywhere near my pizza, I can eat it. I prefer pizza with mushrooms, tomatoes, and spinach. Goat cheese is especially nice too. A thin whole-wheat crust topped with imported cheese and organic vegetables makes a satisfying meal.

Inference about the speaker:_____

Speaker 4: Pizza is, like, one of the basic food groups, right? I mean, dude, who doesn't eat pizza? Me and my friends order it like every day. We usually get pepperoni, and it's great when they are, like, covering the whole top! Dude, hot steamy pizza dripping with cheese and loaded with pepperoni is awesome.

Inference about the speaker:_____

Group Discussion Norms

During this course, you will participate in discussions with partners and in groups. All members of a group need to communicate effectively as speakers and listeners. To make collaborative discussions productive:

- Prepare for discussions. This preparation may mean doing research, reading assigned texts, or completing analyses of texts so that you are ready to share ideas.

- Organize your thoughts and speak clearly. Listen with an open mind to the viewpoints of others, posing and responding to questions to help broaden discussions and make new connections based on evidence and reasoning shared within the group.

- Establish rules for collegial discussions, including hearing the views of all group members and deciding how to settle disagreements on next steps. To foster meaningful discussion, ask questions to clarify understanding and listen attentively to other group members' responses.

- If your group is charged with creating a group project, establish clear goals for the project, responsibilities for individual roles for project tasks, and deadlines for each part of the project.

- Be aware of nonverbal communication such as eye contact, body posture, head nods, hand gestures, and vocal cues.

My Notes

Narrative Voices

My Notes

_____

_____

_____

_____

_____

_____

Literary Terms

A **narrative** tells a story about
a series of events that includes
character development,
plot structure, and theme.
A narrative can be a work of
fiction or nonfiction. A **narrator**
is the person telling the story
and is often the protagonist or
main character of the story.

_____

_____

_____

_____

_____

_____

_____

_____

_____

_____

_____

_____

_____

Learning Targets

- Apply a strategy for active reading and note-taking.
- Interpret writers' choices that create voice, engage readers, and suggest meanings.

Introducing the Strategy: Double-Entry Journal

A **double-entry journal** is a note-taking strategy for actively reading a text. In your journal, you can connect your own experiences to those of the characters, share your opinions about what is happening, trace the development of the characters, and comment on the writer's choices that create the voice of the narrator.

A double-entry journal can be used with any reading. In this unit, you will be reading texts written in a **narrative** structure. As you read these narratives, use the format below as a model for recording notes in a double-entry journal. In the left column ("Trigger Text"), copy or summarize passages that trigger your thoughts in some way, citing the page number with the quotation. In the right column, write your thoughts about the passage or some element of the narrative (character, plot, theme).

If you are having trouble thinking of what to write, try using these stems:

- I really like / dislike this part because . . .
- I wonder why . . . ?
- The diction / imagery creates a tone of . . .
- This quote shows the narrator's / character's voice by . . .
- I predict that . . .
- This reminds me of the time when I . . .
- If it was me, I would . . .

Trigger Text (The book says . . .)	Analysis / Question / Opinion (I say . . .)

Before Reading

1. In the following scene from *Speak*, the **narrator**, Melinda, is dealing with a new experience: the first day of high school. As you read, highlight quotes in the text that make you think; then, use the My Notes section and the sentence stems above to write a variety of responses to the text. Be prepared to discuss your responses after reading the text.

ABOUT THE AUTHOR

Born in 1961, Laurie Halse Anderson always loved reading and writing. Even as a child, she made up stories and wrote for fun. As an adult, she did freelance reporting until she began publishing her work. Her novel *Speak*, which won numerous awards and was a best seller, was made into a movie. In 2009, she won the Margaret A. Edwards Award for *Catalyst, Fever 1793*, and *Speak*. She continues to write historical fiction, like *Chains*, and young adult novels, like *Wintergirls*. She says she is inspired by her readers, who write to her with comments or come to her readings.

Novel

From Speak

by Laurie Halse Anderson

Spotlight

1 I find my locker after social studies. The lock sticks a little, but I open it. I dive into the stream of fourth-period lunch students and swim down the hall to the cafeteria.

2 I know enough not to bring lunch on the first day of high school. There is no way of telling what the acceptable fashion will be. Brown bags—humble testament to suburbia, or terminal geek gear? Insulated lunch bags—hip way to save the planet, or sign of an over involved mother? Buying is the only solution. And it gives me time to scan the cafeteria for a friendly face or an inconspicuous corner.

3 The hot lunch is turkey with reconstituted dried mashed potatoes and gravy, a damp green vegetable, and a cookie. I'm not sure how to order anything else, so I just slide my tray along and let the lunch drones fill it. This eight-foot senior in front of me somehow gets three cheeseburgers, French fries, and two Ho-Hos without saying a word. Some sort of Morse code with his eyes, maybe. Must study this further. I follow the Basketball Pole into the cafeteria.

4 I see a few friends—people I used to think were my friends—but they look away. Think fast, think fast. There's that new girl, Heather, reading by the window. I could sit across from her. Or I could crawl behind a trash can. Or maybe I could dump my lunch straight into the trash and keep moving right on out the door.

My Notes

GRAMMAR & USAGE
Dashes

Writers use **dashes** to emphasize certain content. Note how Anderson uses dashes to call attention to the different types of lunch bags.

WORD CONNECTIONS

Roots and Affixes

The word **protagonist** has a form of the Greek prefix *proto-*, which means "first," and the Greek root *-agon-*, which means "contest" or "struggle."

The prefix *proto-* is also found in these words: *prototype*, *protozoa*, and *protocol*.

The root *-agon-* is also found in *agony*.

KEY IDEAS AND DETAILS

Melinda (the protagonist) has a vivid inner voice. What is significant, then, about the fact that she never actually speaks in this passage?

GRAMMAR & USAGE

Compound Sentences

A compound sentence is one that has two independent clauses joined by a coordinating conjunction. Example: "The lock sticks a little, but I open it."

5   The Basketball Pole waves to a table of friends. Of course. The basketball team. They all swear at him—a bizarre greeting practiced by athletic boys with zits. He smiles and throws a Ho-Ho. I try to scoot around him.

6   Thwap! A lump of potatoes and gravy hits me square in the center of my chest. All conversation stops as the entire lunchroom gawks, my face burning into their retinas. I will be forever known as "that girl who got nailed by potatoes the first day." The Basketball Pole apologizes and says something else, but four hundred people explode in laughter and I can't read lips. I ditch my tray and bolt for the door.

7   I motor so fast out of the lunchroom the track coach would draft me for varsity if he were around. But no, Mr. Neck has cafeteria duty. And Mr. Neck has no use for girls who can run the one hundred in under ten seconds, unless they're willing to do it while holding on to a football.

8   Mr. Neck: "We meet again."

9   Me:

10   Would he listen to "I need to go home and change," or "Did you see what that bozo did"? Not a chance. I keep my mouth shut.

11   Mr. Neck: "Where do you think you're going?"

12   Me:

13   It is easier not to say anything. Shut your trap, button your lip, can it. All that crap you hear on TV about communication and expressing feelings is a lie. Nobody really wants to hear what you have to say.

14   Mr. Neck makes a note in his book. "I knew you were trouble the first time I saw you. I've taught here for twenty-four years and I can tell what's going on in a kid's head just by looking in their eyes. No more warnings. You just earned a demerit for wandering the halls without a pass."

My Notes

_____
_____
_____
_____
_____
_____
_____
_____
_____
_____

After Reading

Choose four of your responses, making sure you choose a variety of types, and record them below. Exchange with a partner and write responses to each other's comments, explaining your own reaction to the trigger text or how you feel about your partner's response. Did you see things the same way or differently? Why?

Trigger Text (The book says . . .)	Analysis / Question / Opinion (I say . . .)	Responses to Comments

Check Your Understanding

Anderson was 38 when *Speak* was published, yet she captures a teen girl's voice through her diction, syntax, and imagery. To explore how, choose three quotes you think sound particularly authentic, and write a response in a double-entry journal that explains how the quotes contribute to the narrator's teen voice. What inferences can you draw about the character of Melinda based on these quotes?

My Notes

_____

_____

_____

_____

_____

_____

_____

_____

_____

Language and Writer's Craft: Parallel Structure

GRAMMAR & USAGE
Parallel Structure

Parallel structure consists of two or more words, phrases, or clauses that are similar in length and grammatical form. A **phrase** is a group of related words that together function as a single part of speech; examples include prepositional phrases, participial phrases, infinitive phrases, and gerund phrases. See the Grammar Handbook for additional information on phrases. A **clause** is a group of words containing both a subject and a predicate. A clause can be dependent or independent. A *dependent clause* has both a subject and a verb but cannot stand alone as a sentence. An *independent clause* can stand alone as a complete sentence.

Learning Targets

- Identify parallel structure.
- Identify and revise instances of faulty parallelism.
- Use parallel structure in writing.

Syntax and Parallel Structure

Whether creating narratives or other forms or writing, writers use sentence structure (syntax) to create the effects they want. Using **parallelism** is one way of creating balanced sentence structure by creating a series at the word, phrase, or clause level.

- Words: simple nouns, pronouns, adjectives, adverbs, gerunds; e.g., "My guinea pig eats *nuts*, *seeds*, and *lettuce leaves*."
- Phrases: prepositional phrases (prepositions followed by nouns); e.g., "My cat raced *in the door, onto the table*, and *into my lap*."
- Clauses: parallel subject and verb; e.g., "*We swept the floor, we dusted the mantle*, and *we cooked a hot meal* to welcome our guests."

1. Look at the sentences below that use parallel structure (from the Gettysburg Address by Abraham Lincoln). Identify and highlight the parts that can be described as parallel.
   - "But, in a larger sense, we cannot dedicate, we cannot consecrate, we cannot hallow this ground."
   - ". . . government of the people, by the people, for the people shall not perish from the earth."

2. Which of the sentences above uses parallel prepositional phrases and which uses parallel clauses?

My Notes

_____

_____

_____

_____

_____

_____

_____

_____

_____

_____

_____

Parallel structure means using the same pattern of words in a series or in a compound structure to show that two or more ideas have the same level of importance. Just as importantly, this syntax creates balanced sentences that are powerful in their effect on readers and listeners.

Parallel structure is typical of powerful speeches. Following are more examples; these sentences are from Abraham Lincoln's second inaugural address:

- "To strengthen, perpetuate, and extend this interest [slavery] was the object for which the insurgents would rend the Union, even by war . . ."

- "With malice toward none; with charity for all; with firmness in the right, as God gives us to see the right, let us strive on to finish the work we are in . . ."

3. Describe the parallelism used in the previous examples (as parallelism with words, phrases, or clauses).

4. Mark the parallelism in the sentences below from John F. Kennedy's Inaugural Address.

"The torch has been passed to a new generation of Americans— born in this century, tempered by war, disciplined by a hard and bitter peace, proud of our ancient heritage ...."

"Let every nation know, whether it wishes us well or ill, that we shall pay any price, bear any burden, meet any hardship, support any friend, oppose any foe, to assure the survival and the success of liberty."

5. Martin Luther King, in his "I Have a Dream" speech, takes parallelism one step further to create a memorable form of repetition called **anaphora**. How would you describe this form of parallelism?

"Now is the time to make real the promises of democracy. Now is the time to rise from the dark and desolate valley of segregation to the sunlit path of racial justice. Now is the time to lift our nation from the quicksands of racial injustice to the solid rock of brotherhood. Now is the time to make justice a reality for all of God's children."

When similar elements do not have the same form, they are said to have **faulty parallelism.** Faulty parallelism can easily be detected by looking for the pattern; it can be corrected by repeating the pattern.

Check Your Understanding

Rewrite the following sentences with correct parallelism. Use the My Notes space or separate paper.

1. Mary likes hiking, to swim, and to ride a bicycle.

2. The teacher said that he was a good student because he took good notes, he studied for tests early, and his labs were completed carefully.

3. The coach told the players that they should get a lot of sleep, that they should not eat too much, and to do some warm-up exercises before the game.

4. The dictionary can be used for these purposes: to find word meanings, pronunciations, correct spellings, and looking up irregular verbs.

My Notes

Literary Terms
Anaphora is the repetition of the same word or group of words at the beginnings of two or more clauses or lines.

Defining Experiences

pick

ACADEMIC VOCABULARY
It is always important to know
the **denotation**, or precise
meaning, of a word, but often the
connotations, or associations and
emotional overtones attached,
help the reader make important
inferences about meaning.

Literary Terms
Diction refers to a writer's
word choices, which often
convey voice and tone.

My Notes

Learning Targets

- Explain how a writer creates effects through the connotations of words and images.
- Use textual details to support interpretive claims.

Before Reading

Writers choose words both for their literal meanings (their dictionary definitions, or **denotations**) and for their implied meanings (their emotional associations, or **connotations**).

Writers create their intended effects through particular connotations—the associations or images readers connect with certain words. Some words provoke strong positive or negative associations. These reactions are central to how we, as readers, draw inferences about the tone, the characters, and the meaning of a text.

1. Consider the following sentence from "Spotlight":"I dive into the stream of fourth-period lunch students and swim down the hall to the cafeteria." What connotations do the images of diving into and swimming through other students have here?

2. Rewrite the sentence, trying to keep the same denotative meaning, but changing the connotations to make them neutral.

3. Now consider what is conveyed by Anderson's **diction** (particularly the verbs) in this sentence.

   "I ditch my tray and bolt for the door."

   Based on the verbs, what inferences might you draw about the speaker's feelings in this moment?

4. Now revise Anderson's sentence to be more neutral.

During Reading

5. In "Marigolds," the narrator describes a key incident that had an impact on her "coming of age." As you read, highlight the text for examples of diction, syntax, and imagery that create the narrator's voice. Use the My Notes space to annotate the connotative effect of word choices, and explain the inferences they lead you to make regarding the tone, character, or significance of the event.

ABOUT THE AUTHOR

Eugenia Collier (b. 1928) grew up and continues to live in Baltimore. Retired now, she taught English at several universities. She has published two collections of short stories, a play, and many scholarly works. Her noteworthy and award-winning story "Marigolds" powerfully captures the moment of the narrator's coming of age.

Literary Terms

Juxtaposition is the arrangement of two or more things for the purpose of comparison.

Short Story

Marigolds

by Eugenia Collier

My Notes

1   When I think of the home town of my youth, all that I seem to remember is dust—the brown, crumbly dust of late summer—arid, sterile dust that gets into the eyes and makes them water, gets into the throat and between the toes of bare brown feet. I don't know why I should remember only the dust. Surely there must have been lush green lawns and paved streets under leafy shade trees somewhere in town; but memory is an abstract painting—it does not present things as they are, but rather as they *feel*. And so, when I think of that time and that place, I remember only the dry September of the dirt roads and grassless yards of the shantytown where I lived. And one other thing I remember, another incongruency[1] of memory—a brilliant splash of sunny yellow against the dust—Miss Lottie's marigolds.

2   Whenever the memory of those marigolds flashes across my mind, a strange nostalgia comes with it and remains long after the picture has faded. I feel again the chaotic emotions of adolescence, illusive as smoke, yet as real as the potted geranium before me now. Joy and rage and wild animal gladness and shame become tangled together in the multicolored skein of fourteen-going-on-fifteen as I recall that devastating moment when I was suddenly more woman than child, years ago in Miss Lottie's yard. I think of those marigolds at the strangest times; I remember them vividly now as I desperately pass away the time. . . .

3   I suppose that futile waiting was the sorrowful background music of our impoverished little community when I was young. The Depression that gripped the nation was no new thing to us, for the black workers of rural Maryland had always been depressed. I don't know what it was that we were waiting for; certainly not for the prosperity that was "just around the corner," for those were white folks' words, which we never believed. Nor did we wait for hard work and thrift to pay off in shining success, as the American Dream promised, for we knew better than that, too.

KEY IDEAS AND DETAILS
Writers manipulate time through the use of flashback. What textual evidence can you point to that indicates the use of flashback?

KEY IDEAS AND DETAILS
In the first paragraph, what two images does the narrator juxtapose for contrast? What are the connotations of these juxtaposed images?

---

[1] **incongruency:** something that is not appropriate or fitting

Defining Experiences

WORD
CONNECTIONS

Roots and Affixes

The word *amorphous* has the Greek root *-morph-*, meaning "shape" or "form." The root comes from Morpheus, the god of sleep—or shaper of dreams. The Greek prefix *a-* means "not" or "without."

KEY IDEAS AND DETAILS
Notice that in paragraph 8, the narrator uses **foreshadowing**. What is the effect of this hinting at events to come? Highlight other hints or foreshadowing provided by the narrator.

My Notes

Perhaps we waited for a miracle, amorphous[2] in concept but necessary if one were to have the grit to rise before dawn each day and labor in the white man's vineyard until after dark, or to wander about in the September dust offering some meager share of bread. But God was chary[3] with miracles in those days, and so we waited—and waited.

4 We children, of course, were only vaguely aware of the extent of our poverty. Having no radios, few newspapers, and no magazines, we were somewhat unaware of the world outside our community. Nowadays we would be called culturally deprived and people would write books and hold conferences about us. In those days everybody we knew was just as hungry and ill clad as we were. Poverty was the cage in which we all were trapped, and our hatred of it was still the vague, undirected restlessness of the zoo-bred flamingo who knows that nature created him to fly free.

5 As I think of those days I feel most poignantly the tag end of summer, the bright, dry times when we began to have a sense of shortening days and the imminence of the cold.

6 By the time I was fourteen, my brother Joey and I were the only children left at our house, the older ones having left home for early marriage or the lure of the city, and the two babies having been sent to relatives who might care for them better than we. Joey was three years younger than I, and a boy, and therefore vastly inferior. Each morning our mother and father trudged wearily down the dirt road and around the bend, she to her domestic job, he to his daily unsuccessful quest for work. After our few chores around the tumbledown shanty, Joey and I were free to run wild in the sun with other children similarly situated.

7 For the most part, those days are ill-defined in my memory, running together and combining like a fresh watercolor painting left out in the rain. I remember squatting in the road drawing a picture in the dust, a picture which Joey gleefully erased with one sweep of his dirty foot. I remember fishing for minnows in a muddy creek and watching sadly as they eluded my cupped hands, while Joey laughed uproariously. And I remember, that year, a strange restlessness of body and of spirit, a feeling that something old and familiar was ending, and something unknown and therefore terrifying was beginning.

8 One day returns to me with special clarity for some reason, perhaps because it was the beginning of the experience that in some inexplicable[2] way marked the end of innocence. I was loafing under the great oak tree in our yard, deep in some reverie which I have now forgotten, except that it involved some secret, secret thoughts of one of the Harris boys across the yard. Joey and a bunch of kids were bored now with the old tire suspended from an oak limb, which had kept them entertained for a while.

9 "Hey, Lizabeth," Joey yelled. He never talked when he could yell. "Hey, Lizabeth, let's go somewhere."

10 I came reluctantly from my private world. "Where you want to go? What you want to do?"

---

[2] **amorphous:** without shape or form
[3] **chary:** ungenerous, wary
[4] **inexplicable:** unable to be explained or understood

11 The truth was that we were becoming tired of the formlessness of our summer days. The idleness whose prospect had seemed so beautiful during the busy days of spring now had degenerated to an almost desperate effort to fill up the empty midday hours.

12 "Let's go see can we find some locusts on the hill," someone suggested.

13 Joey was scornful. "Ain't no more locusts there. Y'all got 'em all while they was still green."

14 The argument that followed was brief and not really worth the effort. Hunting locust trees wasn't fun anymore by now.

15 "Tell you what," said Joey finally, his eyes sparkling. "Let's us go over to Miss Lottie's."

16 The idea caught on at once, for annoying Miss Lottie was always fun. I was still child enough to scamper along with the group over rickety fences and through bushes that tore our already raggedy clothes, back to where Miss Lottie lived. I think now that we must have made a tragicomic spectacle, five or six kids of different ages, each of us clad in only one garment—the girls in faded dresses that were too long or too short, the boys in patchy pants, their sweaty brown chests gleaming in the hot sun. A little cloud of dust followed our thin legs and bare feet as we tramped over the barren land.

GRAMMAR & USAGE
Subjunctive Verbs
Formal diction sometimes requires the use of the **subjunctive** form of the verb to express a doubt, a wish, a possibility, or a situation contrary to fact. It is often used in a clause beginning with the word *if*. For example, "If I were rich..." uses the subjunctive to state something that is not fact.

The narrator in "Marigolds" uses the subjunctive to express a wish or possibility in this clause:

"... if one **were** to have the grit to rise before dawn each day ..."

When using subjunctive mood in your own writing, be sure to use the verb form correctly. Using the example above, "If I **was** rich" would be an incorrect verb form.

My Notes

_____
_____
_____
_____
_____
_____
_____
_____
_____
_____
_____
_____

Defining Experiences

My Notes

KEY IDEAS AND DETAILS
How does the narrator's diction help contrast John Burke's typical behavior with how he acts when annoyed by the children?

KEY IDEAS AND DETAILS
In Paragraph 22, why are the marigolds so important to Miss Lottie, and why do the children hate them?

17   When Miss Lottie's house came into view we stopped, ostensibly[5] to plan our strategy, but actually to reinforce our courage. Miss Lottie's house was the most ramshackle of all our ramshackle homes. The sun and rain had long since faded its rickety frame siding from white to a sullen gray. The boards themselves seemed to remain upright not from being nailed together but rather from leaning together, like a house that a child might have constructed from cards. A brisk wind might have blown it down, and the fact that it was still standing implied a kind of enchantment that was stronger than the elements. There it stood and as far as I know is standing yet—a gray, rotting thing with no porch, no shutters, no steps, set on a cramped lot with no grass, not even any weeds—a monument to decay.

18   In front of the house in a squeaky rocking chair sat Miss Lottie's son, John Burke, completing the impression of decay. John Burke was what was known as queer-headed. Black and ageless, he sat rocking day in and day out in a mindless stupor, lulled by the monotonous squeak-squawk of the chair. A battered hat atop his shaggy head shaded him from the sun. Usually John Burke was totally unaware of everything outside his quiet dream world. But if you disturbed him, if you intruded upon his fantasies, he would become enraged, strike out at you, and curse at you in some strange enchanted language which only he could understand. We children made a game of thinking of ways to disturb John Burke and then to elude his violent retribution.

19   But our real fun and our real fear lay in Miss Lottie herself. Miss Lottie seemed to be at least a hundred years old. Her big frame still held traces of the tall, powerful woman she must have been in youth, although it was now bent and drawn. Her smooth skin was a dark reddish brown, and her face had Indian-like features and the stern stoicism that one associates with Indian faces. Miss Lottie didn't like intruders either, especially children. She never left her yard, and nobody ever visited her. We never knew how she managed those necessities which depend on human interaction— how she ate, for example, or even whether she ate. When we were tiny children, we thought Miss Lottie was a witch and we made up tales that we half believed ourselves about her exploits. We were far too sophisticated now, of course, to believe the witch nonsense. But old fears have a way of clinging like cobwebs, and so when we sighted the tumbledown shack, we had to stop to reinforce our nerves.

20   "Look, there she is," I whispered, forgetting that Miss Lottie could not possibly have heard me from that distance. "She's fooling with them crazy flowers."

21   "Yeh, look at 'er."

22   Miss Lottie's marigolds were perhaps the strangest part of the picture. Certainly they did not fit in with the crumbling decay of the rest of her yard. Beyond the dusty brown yard, in front of the sorry gray house, rose suddenly and shockingly a dazzling strip of bright blossoms, clumped together in enormous mounds, warm and passionate and sun-golden. The old black witch-woman worked on them all summer, every summer, down on her creaky knees, weeding and cultivating and arranging, while the house crumbled and John Burke rocked. For some perverse reason, we children hated those marigolds. They interfered with the perfect ugliness of the place; they were too beautiful; they said too much that we could not understand; they did not make sense. There was something in the vigor with which the old woman destroyed the weeds that intimidated us. It should have been a comical sight—the old woman with the man's hat on her cropped white head, leaning over the bright mounds, her big backside in the air—but it wasn't comical, it was something we could not name. We had to annoy her by

---

[5] **ostensibly:** for the pretended reason

whizzing a pebble into her flowers or by yelling a dirty word, then dancing away from her rage, reveling in our youth and mocking her age. Actually, I think it was the flowers we wanted to destroy, but nobody had the nerve to try it, not even Joey, who was usually fool enough to try anything.

23 "Y'all git some stones," commanded Joey now and was met with instant giggling obedience as everyone except me began to gather pebbles from the dusty ground. "Come on, Lizabeth."

24 I just stood there peering through the bushes, torn between wanting to join the fun and feeling that it was all a bit silly.

25 "You scared, Lizabeth?"

26 I cursed and spat on the ground—my favorite gesture of phony bravado. "Y'all children get the stones, I'll show you how to use 'em."

27 I said before that we children were not consciously aware of how thick were the bars of our cage. I wonder now, though, whether we were not more aware of it than I thought. Perhaps we had some dim notion of what we were, and how little chance we had of being anything else. Otherwise, why would we have been so preoccupied with destruction? Anyway, the pebbles were collected quickly, and everybody looked at me to begin the fun.

28 "Come on, y'all."

29 We crept to the edge of the bushes that bordered the narrow road in front of Miss Lottie's place. She was working placidly, kneeling over the flowers, her dark hand plunged into the golden mound. Suddenly zing—an expertly aimed stone cut the head off one of the blossoms.

30 "Who out there?" Miss Lottie's backside came down and her head came up as her sharp eyes searched the bushes. "You better git!"

31 We had crouched down out of sight in the bushes, where we stifled the giggles that insisted on coming. Miss Lottie gazed warily across the road for a moment, then cautiously returned to her weeding. Zing—Joey sent a pebble into the blooms, and another marigold was beheaded.

32 Miss Lottie was enraged now. She began struggling to her feet, leaning on a rickety cane and shouting. "Y'all git! Go on home!" Then the rest of the kids let loose with their pebbles, storming the flowers and laughing wildly and senselessly at Miss Lottie's impotent rage. She shook her stick at us and started shakily toward the road crying, "Git 'long! John Burke! John Burke, come help!"

33 Then I lost my head entirely, mad with the power of inciting such rage, and ran out of the bushes in the storm of pebbles, straight toward Miss Lottie, chanting madly, "Old witch, fell in a ditch, picked up a penny and thought she was rich!" The children screamed with delight, dropped their pebbles, and joined the crazy dance, swarming around Miss Lottie like bees and chanting, "Old lady witch!" while she screamed curses at us. The madness lasted only a moment, for John Burke, startled at last, lurched out of his chair, and we dashed for the bushes just as Miss Lottie's cane went whizzing at my head.

My Notes

KEY IDEAS AND DETAILS
Describe the internal conflict going on in the narrator, Lizabeth. Find textual evidence to support your statement.

Defining Experiences

34   I did not join the merriment when the kids gathered again under the oak in our bare yard. Suddenly I was ashamed, and I did not like being ashamed. The child in me sulked and said it was all in fun, but the woman in me flinched at the thought of the malicious attack that I had led. The mood lasted all afternoon. When we ate the beans and rice that was supper that night, I did not notice my father's silence, for he was always silent these days, nor did I notice my mother's absence, for she always worked until well into evening. Joey and I had a particularly bitter argument after supper; his exuberance[6] got on my nerves. Finally I stretched out upon the pallet in the room we shared and fell into a fitful doze. When I awoke, somewhere in the middle of the night, my mother had returned, and I vaguely listened to the conversation that was audible through the thin walls that separated our rooms. At first I heard no words, only voices. My mother's voice was like a cool, dark room in summer—peaceful, soothing, quiet. I loved to listen to it; it made things seem all right somehow. But my father's voice cut through hers, shattering the peace.

35   "Twenty-two years, Maybelle, twenty-two years," he was saying, "and I got nothing for you, nothing, nothing."

36   "It's all right, honey, you'll get something. Everybody out of work now, you know that."

37   "It ain't right. Ain't no man ought to eat his woman's food year in and year out, and see his children running wild. Ain't nothing right about that."

38   "Honey, you took good care of us when you had it. Ain't nobody got nothing nowadays."

39   "I ain't talking about nobody else, I'm talking about *me*. God knows I try." My mother said something I could not hear, and my father cried out louder, "What must a man do, tell me that?"

40   "Look, we ain't starving. I get paid every week, and Mrs. Ellis is real nice about giving me things. She gonna let me have Mr. Ellis's old coat for you this winter—"

41   "Damn Mr. Ellis's coat! And damn his money! You think I want white folks' leavings? Damn, Maybelle"—and suddenly he sobbed, loudly and painfully, and cried helplessly and hopelessly in the dark night. I had never heard a man cry before. I did not know men ever cried. I covered my ears with my hand but could not cut off the sound of my father's harsh, painful, despairing sobs. My father was a strong man who could whisk a child upon his shoulders and go singing through the house. My father whittled toys for us, and laughed so loud that the great oak seemed to laugh with him, and taught us how to fish and hunt rabbits. How could it be that my father was crying? But the sobs went on, unstifled, finally quieting until I could hear my mother's voice, deep and rich, humming softly as she used to hum to a frightened child.

42   The world had lost its boundary lines. My mother, who was small and soft, was now the strength of the family; my father, who was the rock on which the family had been built, was sobbing like the tiniest child. Everything was suddenly out of tune, like a broken accordion. Where did I fit into this crazy picture? I do not now remember my thoughts, only a feeling of great bewilderment and fear.

---

[6] **exuberance:** extreme good cheer or high spirits

43 Long after the sobbing and humming had stopped, I lay on the pallet, still as stone with my hands over my ears, wishing that I too could cry and be comforted. The night was silent now except for the sound of the crickets and of Joey's soft breathing. But the room was too crowded with fear to allow me to sleep, and finally, feeling the terrible aloneness of 4 A.M., I decided to awaken Joey.

44 "Ouch! What's the matter with you? What you want?" he demanded disagreeably when I had pinched and slapped him awake.

45 "Come on, wake up."

46 "What for? Go 'way."

47 I was lost for a reasonable reply. I could not say, "I'm scared and I don't want to be alone," so I merely said, "I'm going out. If you want to come, come on."

48 The promise of adventure awoke him. "Going out now? Where to, Lizabeth? What you going to do?"

49 I was pulling my dress over my head. Until now I had not thought of going out. "Just come on," I replied tersely

50 I was out the window and halfway down the road before Joey caught up with me.

51 "Wait, Lizabeth, where you going?"

52 I was running as if the Furies[7] were after me, as perhaps they were—running silently and furiously until I came to where I had half known I was headed: to Miss Lottie's yard.

53 The half-dawn light was more eerie than complete darkness, and in it the old house was like the ruin that my world had become—foul and crumbling, a grotesque caricature. It looked haunted, but I was not afraid, because I was haunted too.

54 "Lizabeth, you lost your mind?" panted Joey.

55 I had indeed lost my mind, for all the smoldering emotions of that summer swelled in me and burst—the great need for my mother who was never there, the hopelessness of our poverty and degradation, the bewilderment of being neither child nor woman and yet both at once, the fear unleashed by my father's tears. And these feelings combined in one great impulse toward destruction.

56 "Lizabeth!"

57 I leaped furiously into the mounds of marigolds and pulled madly, trampling and pulling and destroying the perfect yellow blooms. The fresh smell of early morning and of dew-soaked marigolds spurred me on as I went tearing and mangling and sobbing while Joey tugged my dress or my waist crying, "Lizabeth, stop, please stop!"

58 And then I was sitting in the ruined little garden among the uprooted and ruined flowers, crying and crying, and it was too late to undo what I had done. Joey was sitting beside me, silent and frightened, not knowing what to say. Then, "Lizabeth, look."

My Notes

KEY IDEAS AND DETAILS
What can you infer from the text as to Lizabeth's reasons for her final act of destruction?

---

[7] **Furies:** in classical mythology, three spirits of revenge who pursued and punished wrongdoers.

Defining Experiences

KEY IDEAS AND DETAILS
Paragraph 60 is especially
rich in juxtaposition. Examine
the diction and imagery and
show your understanding of
juxtaposition by identifying
two images or words set up
for comparison.

59 I opened my swollen eyes and saw in front of me a pair of large, calloused feet; my gaze lifted to the swollen legs, the age-distorted body clad in a tight cotton nightdress, and then the shadowed Indian face surrounded by stubby white hair. And there was no rage in the face now, now that the garden was destroyed and there was nothing any longer to be protected.

60 "M-miss Lottie!" I scrambled to my feet and just stood there and stared at her, and that was the moment when childhood faded and womanhood began. That violent, crazy act was the last act of childhood. For as I gazed at the immobile face with the sad, weary eyes, I gazed upon a kind of reality which is hidden to childhood. The witch was no longer a witch but only a broken old woman who had dared to create beauty in the midst of ugliness and sterility. She had been born in squalor and lived in it all her life. Now at the end of that life she had nothing except a falling-down hut, a wrecked body, and John Burke, the mindless son of her passion. Whatever verve there was left in her, whatever was of love and beauty and joy that had not been squeezed out by life, had been there in the marigolds she had so tenderly cared for.

61 Of course I could not express the things that I knew about Miss Lottie as I stood there awkward and ashamed. The years have put words to the things I knew in that moment, and as I look back upon it, I know that that moment marked the end of innocence. Innocence involves an unseeing acceptance of things at face value, an ignorance of the area below the surface. In that humiliating moment I had looked beyond myself and into the depths of another person. This was the beginning of compassion, and one cannot have both compassion and innocence.

62 The years have taken me worlds away from that time and that place, from the dust and squalor of our lives, and from the bright thing that I destroyed in a blind, childish striking out at God knows what. Miss Lottie died long ago and many years have passed since I last saw her hut, completely barren at last, for despite my wild contrition[1] she never planted marigolds again. Yet, there are times when the image of those passionate yellow mounds returns with a painful poignancy. For one does not have to be ignorant and poor to find that his life is as barren as the dusty yards of our town. And I too have planted marigolds.

After Reading

6. Go back to your notes and annotations, and quote from the story examples of diction and imagery that convey Lizabeth's distinctive voice in "Marigolds." Use the graphic organizer on the next page to record your examples.

[1] **contrition:** sorrow or remorse for one's wrongs

Diction and imagery that convey voice:	
Opening	
First encounter with Miss Lottie	
Overheard conversation	
Final act of destruction	
Closing	

My Notes

Defining Experiences

Check Your Understanding

Writing Prompt: Describe the voice of the narrator. Then, explain how the writer's diction and imagery create this voice. You might also mention other literary elements, such as juxtaposition, that contribute to the narrator's voice or point of view. Be sure to:

- Begin with a clear thesis for your position.
- Include multiple direct quotations to support your claim, and punctuate them correctly.
- Include transitions and a concluding statement.

Learning How to Interview

Learning Targets
- Develop effective open-ended interview questions.
- Reproduce another person's voice through direct and indirect quotations in writing.

Interviewing: First Steps
For Embedded Assessment 1, you will be writing an interview narrative. To prepare for the interview, you will first practice your interview skills by interviewing a partner. You will then draft an introduction and present your partner to your classmates.

1. The first (and very important piece) of information you need is your partner's name:_____.

2. Write four questions that you could ask to learn important information about your partner.

    •

    •

    •

    •

3. When you interview someone, it is important to ask open-ended questions. Open-ended questions or statements require more than a simple "yes" or "no" response. They give your interviewee an opportunity to provide insight and explanation. In the question pairs below, circle the open-ended question or statement.

    a. Explain some of the best parts of playing soccer.

       Do you like playing soccer?

    b. As the youngest child in your family, do you think you get your own way?

       What are the advantages and disadvantages of being the youngest child in your family?

4. Revise each of the following to be an open-ended question.

    Is it fun to be in the band?

    Revision:

    Have you always lived in this town?

    Revision:

LEARNING STRATEGIES:
Brainstorming, Note-taking, Drafting

GRAMMAR & USAGE
Direct and Indirect Quotations

A **direct quotation** represents a person's exact words. These words are enclosed in quotation marks.

Example: Mr. Neck said, "I knew you were trouble the first time I saw you."

An **indirect quotation** reports what someone said but restates it in your own language. Quotation marks are not used with indirect quotations.

Example: I was about to bolt through the door when Mr. Neck asked me where I was going.

Transform the following direct quotation into an indirect quotation:

Mr. Neck: "I knew you were trouble the first time I saw you."

My Notes

_____

_____

_____

_____

_____

_____

_____

_____

Learning How to Interview

5. Look back at the four questions you wrote. Make sure they are open-ended questions or statements. If they are not, revise them as you write them in the question boxes below. Leave the answer boxes empty for now.

Question 1:	Answer:
Question 2:	Answer:
Question 3:	Answer:
Question 4:	Answer:

6. Now interview your partner. While your partner is answering, take notes in the answer boxes above. Try to write down some parts of the answer exactly, using quotation marks to show you are quoting your partner word for word (a **direct quotation**), as opposed to paraphrasing him or her (an **indirect quotation**).

7. Prepare to introduce your partner to the class. Look back over your interview notes and highlight the parts that best capture your partner's voice and convey a sense of who she or he is. Be sure to include **direct** and **indirect quotations** in your introduction.

The hardest part of any presentation can be the beginning. Here are some ways you might begin your introduction (your partner's name goes in the blank):

- I would like to introduce _____.

- I would like you all to meet _____.

- This is my new friend _____.

Write the opening of your introduction:

8. The other challenging part of any presentation is the closing. Sometimes people do not know how to end the introduction, so they say "That's it," or "I'm done." Don't end your introduction that way! You want to end your introduction on a strong note that encourages the rest of your class to get to know your partner.

You might end your introduction like this:

- I enjoyed getting to talk to _____ because

  _____.

- _____ is an interesting person and I'm glad I got the

  chance to meet my partner because _____.

Write the ending of your introduction:

My Notes

Learning How to Interview

9. Introductions are a natural situation in which to use **parallel structure**. For example, a person might say, "He likes listening to hip-hop, watching football, and playing video games." Review your introduction and find a place where you can revise it to incorporate an example of parallel structure. Then, write your introduction on a separate sheet of paper. Use the opener you already wrote, include the information from your notes that you highlighted, and then finish with the closing you wrote. Be sure your introduction shows respect for your partner.

Introducing Your Partner

10. Practice presenting your partner by reading your introduction aloud while standing next to your partner. When you introduce your partner, you may use your written introduction, but try not to rely on it the whole time. Avoid hiding behind your paper.

As you practice, make sure your introduction meets the following expectations:

- The introduction has a clear opening and an effective conclusion.
- The introduction includes a mixture of direct and indirect quotations.
- The introduction features at least one effective example of parallel structure.
- The introduction effectively captures your partner's voice and conveys his or her personality to your classmates.

Check Your Understanding

In two different colors, highlight the direct and indirect quotations you used in your introduction. Then annotate your script to explain why you chose to use the direct quotations you included—and not the ones you only cited indirectly. Also annotate the sentence where you used parallel structure and explain what makes it parallel.

Conversations with Characters

Learning Targets
- Analyze the diction, syntax, and imagery by which an author creates the voice of a narrator.
- Write open-ended questions to prepare for an interview.

LEARNING STRATEGIES:
Brainstorming, Generating Questions, Sharing and Responding

Exploring Coming of Age

1. What does it mean to "come of age"? Use the web organizer below or create one to explore different aspects of what coming of age involves. Consider the different texts you have read in class and your independent reading: What did the characters learn about the world? About themselves? How did they grow as a result of their experiences?

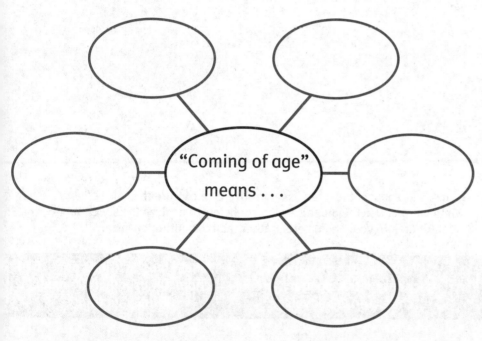

2. Now imagine that you are interviewing a character from "Marigolds." You could choose Miss Lottie and tell about the destruction of her flowers from her point of view. Another option is to have the narrator tell the story of the overheard conversation between her parents and explain its significance.

On the next page, write five open-ended questions you would ask either of these characters. These questions should push the character to reflect on the significance of key events revealed in the narrative—what he or she learned about himself or herself or about the world.

INDEPENDENT READING LINK
Independent Reading
Identify the coming-of-age elements in the narratives you are reading independently. Make a list of the key events that contribute to the main character's coming of age. As practice for the upcoming interview narrative, write a brief interview with the main character.

My Notes

Conversations with Characters

My Notes

Interview Questions

1.

2.

3.

4.

5.

3. One major goal of the interview narrative is to capture the voice of your interviewee. Use the graphic organizer below to analyze the style that contributes to your character's (rather than the author's) voice.

How would you describe the voice of your character?	What features of language (diction, syntax, imagery, etc.) characterize her voice?	What kinds of things does the character usually talk about? With what tone?

4. Now, use the space below to draft an interview with the character. Answer the questions from the character's perspective and voice, using details from the text to develop your answers. Try to integrate direct and indirect quotations in your interview narrative. If you do not have enough space here, use your Reader/ Writer Notebook to write your interview narrative.

Interview with _____

My Notes

Check Your Understanding

With your partner, annotate at least five of the choices you have made that help to recreate the voice of your interviewee. Explain why you made these choices.

Two Versions of One Narrative

LEARNING STRATEGIES:
Graphic Organizer, Shared
Reading, Discussion Groups,
Role Playing, RAFT

Literary Terms

Prose is ordinary written or spoken language using sentences and paragraphs without deliberate or regular meter or rhyme; in contrast, poetry is written in lines and stanzas.

My Notes

Learning Targets

- Compare and contrast language and content in two texts in different genres.
- Explain how a writer's choices regarding language and content construct the meaning of a text.
- Construct interview questions appropriate to a particular audience and topic.
- Draft an account of an interview narrative.

Before Reading

You will read two texts about the same incident by the same author, Luis Rodriquez. Both texts tell the true story of the time when the writer and his brother were beaten up by a group of much older boys. One version is a poem; the other is **prose**. These texts are examples of *nonfiction narrative*. Nonfiction narratives have the same elements as fictional stories, but they are based on actual characters and events.

1. What do you notice about the difference in the two titles? What can you infer about the different focus of each version based on these titles? How might the two versions be different based on the differences between poetry and prose?

During Reading

2. As you read the two texts, mark the key features of the voice that lead to inferences you can make about the speakers. Take notes by creating the graphic organizers below in your Reader/Writer Notebook.

Prose Version: "Always Running"

Diction	Imagery	Syntax	Inferences About the Speaker Based on Voice

Poetry Version: "'Race' Politics"

Diction	Imagery	Syntax	Inferences About the Speaker Based on Voice

ABOUT THE AUTHOR
Award-winning author Luis Rodriguez was born near the U.S.-Mexico border. He is a leading Chicano writer and is best known for his memoir of gang life in Los Angeles, *Always Running*. Rodriguez left the gang life in his late teens and has since worked in many jobs, from bus driver to newspaper reporter and community activist. He has developed many outreach programs to assist teens throughout the country. He continues to write both poetry and narrative works and is a co-organizer of the Chicago Poetry Festival.

Memoir

from **Always Running**

by Luis J. Rodriguez

My Notes
_____
_____
_____
_____
_____
_____
_____
_____
_____
_____

KEY IDEAS AND DETAILS
Like any narrative, this text introduces the setting, the characters, and the conflict. What is the important connection among all three of these elements?

KEY IDEAS AND DETAILS
How does the description in paragraphs 4–7 of the bullies, their words, and their actions shape your perceptions of them? Of Rano?

1   One day, my mother asked Rano and me to go to the grocery store. We decided to go across the railroad tracks into South Gate. In those days, South Gate was an Anglo neighborhood, filled with the families of workers from the auto plant and other nearby industry. Like Lynnwood or Huntington Park, it was forbidden territory for the people of Watts.

2   My brother insisted we go. I don't know what possessed him, but then I never did. It was useless to argue; he'd force me anyway. He was nine then, I was six. So without ceremony, we started over the tracks, climbing over discarded¹ market carts and tore-up sofas, across Alameda Street, into South Gate: all-white, all-American.

3   We entered the first small corner grocery store we found. Everything was cool at first. We bought some bread, milk, soup cans and candy. We each walked out with a bag filled with food. We barely got a few feet, though, when five teenagers on bikes approached. We tried not to pay any attention and proceeded to our side of the tracks. But the youths pulled up in front of us. While two of them stood nearby on their bikes, three of them jumped off theirs and walked over to us.

4   "What do we got here?" one of the boys said. "Spics to order—maybe with some beans?"

5   He pushed me to the ground; the groceries splattered onto the asphalt. I felt melted gum and chips of broken beer bottle on my lips and cheek. Then somebody picked me up and held me while the two others seized my brother, tossed his groceries out, and pounded on him. They punched him in the face, in the stomach, then his face again, cutting his lip, causing him to vomit.

---

¹ **discarded:** thrown away as useless

Two Versions of One Narrative

My Notes

KEY IDEAS AND DETAILS
How does the description in paragraphs 8–10 shape your perception of the narrator's relationship to his brother? Of his decision to write this piece?

6 I remember the shrill[2], maddening laughter of one of the kids on a bike, this laughing like a raven's wail, a harsh wind's shriek, a laugh that I would hear in countless beatings thereafter. I watched the others take turns on my brother, this terror of a brother, and he doubled over, had blood and spew on his shirt, and tears down his face. I wanted to do something, but they held me and I just looked on, as every strike against Rano opened me up inside.

7 They finally let my brother go and he slid to the ground, like a rotten banana squeezed out of its peeling. They threw us back over the tracks. In the sunset I could see the Watts Towers, shimmers of 70,000 pieces of broken bottles, sea shells, ceramic and metal on spiraling points puncturing the heavens, which reflected back the rays of a falling sun. My brother and I then picked ourselves up, saw the teenagers take off, still laughing, still talking about those stupid greasers who dared to cross over to South Gate.

8 Up until then my brother had never shown any emotion to me other than disdain. He had never asked me anything, unless it was a demand, an expectation, an obligation[3] to be his throwaway boy-doll. But for this once he looked at me, tears welled in his eyes, blood streamed from several cuts—lips and cheeks swollen.

9 "Swear—you got to swear—you'll never tell anybody how I cried," he said.

10 I suppose I did promise. It was his one last thing to hold onto, his rep as someone who could take a belt whipping, who could take a beating in the neighborhood and still go back risking more—it was this pathetic plea from the pavement I remember. I must have promised.

---

[2] **shrill:** high-pitched and sharp
[3] **obligation:** a duty

Poetry

"*Race*" POLITICS

by Luis J. Rodriguez

My brother and I
—shopping for *la jefita*—
decided to get the "good food"
over on the other side
5 of the tracks.

We dared each other.
Laughed a little.
Thought about it.
Said, what's the big deal.
10 Thought about that.
Decided we were men,
not boys.
Decided we should go wherever
we damn wanted to.

15 Oh, my brother—now he was bad.
Tough dude. Afraid of nothing.
I was afraid of him.

So there we go,
climbing over
20 the iron and wood ties,
over discarded sofas
        and bent-up market carts,
over a weed-and-dirt road,
into a place called South Gate
25 —all white. All American.

We entered the forbidden
narrow line of hate,
imposed,
transposed,
30 supposed,
a line of power/powerlessness
full of meaning,
meaning nothing—
those lines that crisscross

KEY IDEAS AND DETAILS
Luis Rodriguez uses
fragments for effect. Point
out several fragments, and
explain the different effects
they create in the poem.

KEY IDEAS AND DETAILS
How does Rodriguez's use
of repetition affect tone?
How does he combine this
repetition with specific
sensory details for effect?

GRAMMAR & USAGE
Reciprocal Pronouns

Rodriguez uses "each other"
when he speaks of himself
and his brother in line 6.
Each other and *one another*
are reciprocal pronouns.
When you write, use *each
other* to refer to two people
and *one another* to refer to
three or more.

Two Versions of One Narrative

My Notes

35   the abdomen of this land,

that strangle you

in your days, in your nights.

When you dream.

There we were, two Mexicans,

40   six and nine—from Watts no less.

Oh, this was plenty reason

to hate us.

Plenty reason to run up behind us.

Five teenagers on bikes.

45   Plenty reason to knock

the groceries out from our arms—

a splattering heap of soup

cans, bread and candy.

Plenty reason to hold me down

50   on the hot asphalt; melted gum,

and chips of broken

beer bottle on my lips

and cheek.

Plenty reason to get my brother

55   by the throat, taking turns

punching him in the face,

cutting his lower lip,

punching, him vomiting.

Punching until swollen and dark blue

60   he slid from their grasp

like a rotten banana from its peeling.

When they had enough, they threw us back,

dirty and lacerated;

back to Watts, its towers shiny

65   across the orange-red sky.

My brother then forced me

to promise not to tell anybody

how he cried.

He forced me to swear to God,

70   to Jesus Christ, to our long-dead

Indian Grandmother—

keepers of our meddling souls.

After Reading

3. Use the graphic organizer below to collect details from *Always Running* that indicate differences in the way the prose story is told compared to the poetic version of "'Race' Politics." Then discuss which components of coming of age are present in the two texts. Which voice do you think is more effective? Which is easier to visualize and understand? Why? Which version do you think is more powerful? Why?

Additions	What details or language have been added?	What is the effect of these changes?
Deletions	What details or language have been removed?	What is the effect of these changes?
Alterations	What is the effect of these changes?	What is the effect of these changes?

Identifying Parallel Structure

4. Rodriguez uses parallel structure in his poem. He uses prepositional phrases in line 20–24 ("climbing over / the iron and wood ties / over discarded sofas / and bent-up market carts, / over a weed-and-dirt road . . ."), and again to end the poem ("to God / to Jesus Christ, to our long-dead Indian Grandmother . . ."). Use the My Notes space to describe the effect he creates with his use of parallel structure.

Two Versions of One Narrative

Introducing the Strategy: RAFT

RAFT is commonly considered a writing strategy. The letters stand for Role, Audience, Format, and Topic. Although RAFT can be used as a tool to analyze texts, it is most often used to generate and create ideas by asking writers to think about the role, audience, format, and topic of a text they want to write.

5. Now imagine the story is being told by a different narrator. Use the RAFT strategy to come up with different possible voices you could use to describe the same incident. Working with your discussion group members, brainstorm some possibilities in each category of the chart.

Role	Audience
Format	Topic

6. **Group Discussion:** With your group, review the group discussion norms on page 7. Then choose several combinations from the preceding graphic organizer and discuss how the writer's or speaker's diction, syntax, and imagery would likely change based on a different audience, situation, and purpose. What sorts of details would be added, deleted, or altered?

7. Next, choose the voice of one of the characters and practice answering interview questions. With a partner, role-play how the interview might sound. First, one of you can ask questions while the other answers in the voice of one of the characters. The interviewee should try to maintain the voice of the character by keeping word choice, language, and culture in mind. Then, switch roles.

Here are some possible questions to help you get started. Ask additional follow-up questions. Remember that good interview questions are open-ended—they cannot be answered with a simple "yes" or "no."

Q: Can you tell me what happened today outside the grocery store?

A:

Q: Who would you say is mostly to blame for the incident and why?

A:

Q: If you could go back and change the incident, what would you do differently and why?

A:

Q: What is one way this incident could possibly end up having a positive outcome?

A:

Q: What did you learn from this incident?

A:

Writing Prompt: Construct an account of the incident appropriate to one of the scenarios from your RAFT chart. Be sure to:

- Craft a voice and provide information appropriate to your context.
- Begin with a statement that indicates your context.
- Incorporate some direct quotations from your "interview."

Check Your Understanding

How does changing the speaker, audience, or format influence the telling of an incident?

My Notes

Reading an Interview Narrative

LEARNING STRATEGIES:
Visual Prompt, SOAPSTone,
Marking the Text

Learning Targets

- Analyze how the relationship between a writer, the target audience, and the writer's purpose informs a writer's choices.
- Analyze the intended effect of descriptive narrative on readers' perspectives.

Before Reading

You have written an interview in a Q and A transcript format, but an interview narrative does more: it tells a story. An interview narrative contains certain elements that are common to all narratives.

- It has a **plot**—a sequence of events with a beginning, a middle, and an end.
- It features **characters** who are developed using various techniques of characterization (appearance, words, and actions).
- It has a **setting**.
- There is a central **conflict**, if not several, that may or may not be resolved.
- It is told from a particular **point of view**, or several, which affects how readers think and feel about the story.
- It has a **theme** or themes—a main message about life.

1. Examine a photograph of Chuck Liddell and consider the title of the article. What inferences might you draw regarding Liddell based on the article's title, the photo, and the photo caption?

2. Based on the photograph(s) you saw, write down several sentences describing Liddell's physical appearance that you might include if you were the writer.

-

-

-

-

My Notes

During Reading

3. As you read, notice whether Brian O'Connor, the writer, makes similar choices, and consider whether his choices support or challenge your inferences about Liddell and the article's tone. Consider ways in which O'Connor labels Liddell, captures his voice, considers a significant incident in his life, and conveys the significance to the reader—all through the narrative structure.

Nonfiction

WMDs

by Brian O'Connor, *Men's Fitness*

1 WHO IS THE NEW AMERICAN FIGHTER? For starters, he resembles Chuck Liddell: With a thick coil of a neck and a close-cropped Mohawk, the Ultimate Fighting Championship's (UFC) light-heavyweight title-holder looks like a Marine who'd take great delight in clearing a mosh pit. And that Chinese calligraphy tattooed on the side of his head? Obviously his threshold for pain far surpasses that of the average Joe—and Jim, Bill, and Bob combined.

2 And that's helpful when you work inside an octagonal cage for a living. As a mixed martial artist (the technical term for Ultimate Fighting Championship competitors), Liddell, aka "The Iceman," combines fisticuffs, kickboxing, wrestling, and choke holds to either knock out his opponent or force him to "tap out," indicating a submission. In any other context, of course, this behavior would pass for felonious assault, so being within arm's length of Liddell for a day imparts a clarifying effect. Here's a man not only capable of kneeing you in the ribs until you're coughing blood, but who'd enjoy doing it. Or he could deliver a flying kick to your face that floors you, or land a haymaker with such ferocity that your brain trickles out your nose. Yes, the clarity is unmistakable: You are not a fighter, and Chuck Liddell is.

3 But then you start talking with Chuck Liddell, and that clarity becomes clouded. You discover he grew up in sunny, sleepy Santa Barbara, Calif., and he has a degree in accounting with a minor in business from Cal Poly San Luis Obispo. And then you learn that nearly 80% of the Ultimate Fighters have at least some college education, if not degrees. Many are communications grads, engineers, and computer programmers who come from farms and middle-class suburbs. In that respect, they are just like you. "If I weren't fighting, I'd be in the business world," says the 37-year-old Liddell. "I did well in school, was the captain of the wrestling team and the football team, and always got along well with people, so I'm sure I would have gotten a job in the real world. I probably wouldn't have liked that, though."

4 And then it becomes clear that Liddell, like most professional fighters, has made a decision: to reject the life of the suit and the cubicle and revert to the most primal of instincts. And somewhere in the balance, he's maximizing his youthful exuberance and finding his own sense of manhood.

5 "After the Spike TV show began airing, my career and the sport and the fan base changed," says Liddell, whose $1 million purses have bought him a mansion and a Ferrari. "People accepted us and became more educated about what we do. I get noticed everywhere now, and it's surprising who recognizes me—like this one 50-year-old lady who had a tattoo of my face on her shoulder. It's gotten a lot crazier."

KEY IDEAS AND DETAILS
Most interview narratives include a mixture of examples of the three character description categories (appearance, actions, and speech). Mark the descriptions in the text that show Liddell to the reader. What can you infer about Liddell based on these descriptions?

GRAMMAR & USAGE
Subjunctive Mood

Writers use the subjunctive form of a verb to express a doubt, a wish, a possibility, or a situation contrary to fact. Chuck Liddell uses the subjunctive in this sentence: "If I weren't fighting, I'd be in the business world." Notice the verb. Be careful to use the correct tense in your own writing when you use the subjunctive.

Reading an Interview Narrative

My Notes

KEY IDEAS AND DETAILS
Where does O'Connor shift from explanation to narrative in his interview write-up? Why is it effective to combine different writing types here?

KEY IDEAS AND DETAILS
O'Connor shifts between what two points of view during this interview? Why might he be doing so? How effective is this strategy?

6 During the hour we linger in Muggs, dozens of men drift into the bar, all somehow not working on a Wednesday at 1 p.m., and none of them drinking. Liddell politely tries to step toward the front door, but that's not going to happen. The owner would like to snap a few photos; one guy has his buddy Sean on the phone—"Chuck, can you talk to him?" "Hey, can you sign this for me?" Liddell diplomatically obliges. The sound of backslapping and the hushed murmur of awe and deference fill the air.

7 Eventually we escape in a hired SUV that takes us to Manhattan's Peninsula Hotel before shuttling us to a taping of *Late Night With Conan O'Brien* and then The *Wiseguy Show* on Sirius Satellite Radio . . .

8 The SUV stops and **Liddell** exits toward the gilded entrance . . . where a small pack of fans congregate. He calmly signs autographs, gloves, and posters . . . It occurs to me that the Chinese calligraphy tattooed on his head, which **Liddell** translates as "place of peace and prosperity" is a self-fulfilling prophecy. He is living in the moment.

9 In a few weeks, he'll return to his grueling training schedule, walking a wheelbarrow filled with 150 pounds of concrete up and down a steep San Luis Obispo driveway. And when he returns to the octagon to do battle with his next opponent, a college degree might seem inconsequential, but it's not. He's defending against multiple disciplines from competitors who have grown up on MMA—from Japan, Britain, Eastern Europe, and Canada—guys who are helping the sport evolve and adding new martial-arts disciplines into the mix. And they're gunning for him. "Fighting is like chess, and boxing is like checkers" says **Liddell**. "You have to defend against guys who are coming at you with all sorts of new tactics, new martial arts. You must be aware on different levels."

10 In many ways, then, **Liddell's** job isn't unlike yours. You're competing in a global economy against younger guys looking to supplant you. As the world changes, so change is what a man must do to survive. **Chuck Liddell** has made his choice . . .

After Reading

4. O'Connor uses several examples of parallel structure in his article. Reread paragraph 2 and note where O'Connor has used parallel structure. Which examples are the most or least effective? Why? Is he using words, phrases, or clauses? What type is each?

5. Also reread paragraph 8 to identify uses of parallel structure. How does he use parallel structure there? How does that use help create style?

Introducing the Strategy: SOAPSTone

SOAPSTone stands for Speaker, Occasion, Audience, Purpose, Subject, and Tone. It is both a reading and a writing tool for analyzing the relationship between a writer, his or her purpose, and the target audience of the text. SOAPSTone guides you in asking questions to analyze a text or to plan for writing a composition. The questions are as follows:

- Who is the speaker? The speaker (or writer) is the voice that tells the story.

- What is the occasion? The occasion is the time and place of the story; it is the context that prompted the writing.

- Who is the audience? The audience is the person or persons to whom the piece is directed.

- What is the purpose? The purpose is the reason behind the text or what the writer wants the audience to think as a result of reading the text.

- What is the subject? The subject is the focus of the text.

- What is the tone? The tone is the speaker's (or writer's) attitude toward the topic.

6. Once you have read and marked the interview narrative, conduct a SOAPSTone analysis of the article using the graphic organizer on the next page.

My Notes

Reading an Interview Narrative

SOAPSTone	Analysis	Textual Support
Speaker: What does the reader know about the writer?		
Occasion: What are the circumstances surrounding this text?		
Audience: **Who is the target audience?**		
Purpose: Why did the author write this text?		
Subject: What is the topic?		
Tone: What is the author's tone, or attitude, towards the subject?		

Check Your Understanding

Explain how O'Connor creates a narrative rather than a simple interview. How does he make it a story? How does he use details and his voice as a writer to appeal to his target audience?

Examining the Art of Questioning

Learning Targets
- Transform an interview transcript into a narrative.
- Develop criteria for carefully crafting questions, including follow-up questions.
- Sequence questions to improve logical flow in an interview.

Before Reading

1. You have just read an article about Chuck Liddell, who was interviewed by the writer of the article. On the next page, you will read a **transcript** by a different writer of an interview with Chuck Liddell. How do you think a transcript is different from an article?

During Reading

2. As you read the transcript, note the interviewer's choices and whether they are effective. How could you do better?

3. As you read each question, annotate the text as follows:
   - Label each question as an open-ended or a closed question. Focus on the question itself, rather than on the answer. Not every interviewee will generously answer a closed question with an extended response.
   - Evaluate each question on a scale of 1–3 in terms of its effectiveness. Keep in mind the goals of the interview you will soon be conducting (to explore the significance of the person's college experience—how it contributed to his or her coming of age and becoming successful).

   1 = I learned a lot about the person from the answer elicited by this question.

   2 = I learned something about the person, but I wanted to learn more.

   3 = I did not learn very much about the person from the answer elicited by this question.

LEARNING STRATEGIES:
SOAPSTone, Manipulatives, Rearranging

ACADEMIC VOCABULARY
A **transcript** is a written copy or record of a conversation that takes place between two or more people. It can be used as the basis for creating an interview narrative.

My Notes

Interview Transcript

Chuck Liddell

By Steven Yaccino

Chuck "the Iceman" Liddell still lives in the town of his alma mater. That's right: This trained lethal weapon earned a B.A. in accounting at Cal Poly before claiming the Ultimate Fighting Championship light heavyweight title in 2005. He's since become a mixed martial arts superstar, appearing on an episode of HBO's *Entourage* and authoring the memoir *Iceman: My Fighting Life*. Here, Liddell revisits his Cal Poly days, back when he juggled priorities and drank a lot of caffeine.

Occupation: UFC fighter

Grew up: Santa Barbara, Calif.

College attended: California Polytechnic State University, San Luis Obispo

Major: Accounting

Graduation year: 1995

Nickname: The Iceman. My trainer called me that because I don't get nervous before fights.

Favorite drink / midnight snack: Mountain Dew was my favorite drink through college; it kept me up studying for a lot of tests. Also, any kind of candy.

How and why did you choose your major?
I was just good at it. Numbers have always come easy to me. When you came in as a freshman at Cal Poly, you had to declare a major. After about three years, I thought about changing it to construction management, because I was doing construction over the summers, or to PE. Originally, PE was the major I wanted, but my grandparents didn't see it as a real major. They saw it as I was going to be a PE teacher: They didn't realize that at Cal Poly, it was only two classes away from being pre-med. They didn't see that as looking for a real job. I think being a PE coach is a real job, but that's just me.

Were you a part of any activities like sports, music, clubs, or theater?
I played football my first year, and I wrestled for all five. You start football before school starts, and when you're done with football, wrestling has already started. Then when you're done with wrestling, there are three or four weeks and you're back into spring ball. And then you have a half of a summer and you're back into summer football.

It was just a little much. Plus, I was trying to cut weight for wrestling and trying to put on weight for football. It got to the point where I had to make a decision about where I wanted to be. I think I made the right decision with what I ended up doing.

Do you keep in touch with any of your college friends?
Yeah, a bunch of them. I still live in San Luis Obispo, so there's a bunch of us still here. Up until a couple years ago, my best friend in college lived a block away from me.

Were you a bookworm or a slacker?
I was the guy that would cram for everything, so I guess I was a bit of a slacker. I was a procrastinator. I spent a lot of all-nighters getting ready for tests.

Did you have a role model when you were in college?
Not really. I just kind of learned stuff on my own.

What was the biggest obstacle you overcame in college?
The biggest thing was balancing working out, competing, and academics to graduate. And also working in the summers to try and save money.

What did you like most and least about your school?
I love the town. It's a small town; it's beautiful here. I like visiting big cities, but I don't do well there for long periods of time.

Tell us one way in which college changed you.
I grew up while I was in college. I learned how to take care of myself. I learned how to prioritize things. I learned how to get things done.

If you could go back, what about college would you do differently?
I might have cared a little more about my grades. I ended up with a 3.1, but I could have easily done a lot better. I just didn't care too much.

I had a class where I was actually tutoring two kids from the wrestling team, but I got a C because I didn't do any of the homework. The teacher said if I turned in my homework on the day of the final, she'd give me my A or else she was going to give me a C. The guys I was tutoring gave me the homework to copy, and I copied four of them and said forget it: I'll take the C. Stuff like that. Not that it matters too much. I mean, I graduated.

What was your favorite hangout spot?
I used to bar-tend in college at a cool place. It was called Brubeck's. I worked probably six or seven days a week. We'd get a lot of different people there; it was a lot of fun.

Which schools did you apply to?
U of C-Berkeley, Cal Poly, and other West Coast schools. I went with Cal Poly because I wanted to wrestle and play football.

Did you get into all of them?
I got into all the schools I applied to except Cal Poly. I guess they lost my application. I never got a rejection or an acceptance. I either messed up on the application or it just didn't get through. My coach had to get me in. They have a way for a lot of teams to get you into the school. I don't know how it worked exactly, but I had the grades and SATs to get into my major.

My Notes

KEY IDEAS AND DETAILS
Notice how Liddell speaks. Look for examples of parallel structure in his responses.

Examining the Art of Questioning

After Reading

4. Now write down the five questions you thought were least effective (you probably gave them a 3) in the left-hand column below. With a partner, revise the questions to make them more open and effective. You might add a follow-up question to do so. **Follow-up questions** do exactly what the name implies: They follow up on something the interviewee has said. For example:

Q: What was the best thing that happened to you in college?

A: I guess when I got a "D" in my physics class.

Follow-up Q: That doesn't sound like a very good thing. Why was it the best thing that happened to you?

You might not have anticipated the answer to that question, but pursuing the topic could lead to some interesting information about your interviewee. You should be flexible about your planned questions and allow for follow-up questions. Here are a few ways you could follow up on an answer:

- Why do you think that?
- That sounds interesting. Could you tell me more about it?
- What happened next?
- How has that influenced your life?

Original Question	Revision or Follow-up Q

5. Now that you have finished reading the interview transcript, look carefully at the order of the questions. Does the sequence of questions create a logical flow? If not, what order would flow better? Be prepared to justify your choices.

Check Your Understanding

For Embedded Assessment 1, you will write your own interview narrative. You will create interview questions, conduct an interview, and record answers to draft a transcript much like the one you have just analyzed. Write a reflection on strategies you can use to plan for your interview and ask effective questions.

My Notes

Transforming the Transcript

Learning Targets

- Examine and transform an interview transcript into a narrative.
- Compare and evaluate two approaches to establishing point of view and focus in an interview narrative, and choose which best fits purpose and audience.

Before Reading

1. Narratives are typically written from the first-person or third-person point of view. Consider the two student essay excerpts that follow. As you read each, circle personal pronouns; highlight the sentences that integrate quotes and speaker tags such as "she says," or "she explains," to describe the speaker's voice; and underline any descriptive information. In the My Notes section, summarize the main idea of each passage and indicate the point of view.

Excerpt 1

As we begin the interview, Mrs. Gamer appears stressed, but includes her enthusiastic commentary and gesticulations nonetheless. It seems almost as if she's performing a play as she constructs her answers, and after all, she originally planned to pursue film studies. Upon questioning about her friend group, this vivacious pseudo-actress begins rambling off an extensive list of names, describing her old group in a dramatic whisper as "low drama, high impact." She continues on to outline her favorite classes, revealing a pattern: "A class on Chaucer with Dr. Ganim; Baroque Art with Dr. Pelzel; American Art and Architecture with Dr. Carrott…," she tells me. Her explanation for her favorite teacher is "because he loved Pedro Almodóvar just as much as I did." It is from these statements that the picture of a budding librarian emerges. But there is another trend accompanying the conversation: Mrs. Gamer was not the A student she makes herself out to be. On being asked what her study habits were like, she stares at me with a bewildered, gaping expression. "Study habits?" she intones gently.

Excerpt 2

Before she graduated from high school, Ruth took many steps to prepare herself for college. She remembers, "I always studied and worked hard; I had an after-school job and saved earnings to travel and go to college." A step she took to prepare herself was taking the PSAT and SAT exams. Ruth knew she wanted to study abroad and go far away for college. She applied to CU Boulder, University of Northern Colorado, Wittenberg University, Ithaca College, and Gettysburg College. She was accepted into all of these colleges, except for Gettysburg, and chose to attend Wittenberg. After considering the schools she chose, she recalled, "My main reason for attending Wittenberg was to please my dad. He really wanted me to attend a small Lutheran school, and because he was paying for my tuition, I thought it was the right thing to do." While at Wittenberg, Ruth played on the school's varsity lacrosse team, met her future husband, and studied hard. "I was a very balanced student," she recalls. "I knew I had to keep my priorities straight—and that's what I did." But she was restless, despite being well prepared. "I always felt that there was something bigger and better waiting ahead for me," she explains.

2. With your group members, discuss the strengths and weaknesses of these two approaches. How is the pacing different in the two excerpts? As readers, which do you prefer? Why? Which best allows the writer to capture the voice of the interviewee? How?

Writing Prompt: Transform the "Chuck Liddell" transcript from Activity 1.10 into an interview narrative using the point of view and narrative approach you have decided on and including the quotes you have selected from the transcript. Be sure to:

- Include the three descriptive techniques (appearance, speech, and actions) and focus on a key incident.
- Organize your narrative in a logical and/or chronological order.
- Vary your approach as you integrate quotes.

Look back at the "Chuck Liddell" interview transcript in Activity 1.10, and decide on a few questions that link together logically and / or chronologically. Then decide on which parts of the answers most vividly capture Liddell's voice, highlighting the words, phrases, or clauses you wish to include as direct quotations.

You may have to role-play and imagine being the interviewer if you choose to use first person and to focus on the interview itself. Whether you use first- or third-person, you will need to make inferences based on "WMDs" to add details regarding how Liddell would have been looking, acting, and speaking as he answered the questions.

Check Your Understanding

Review Activity 1.4 on parallel structure, as well as examples of parallelism used in the various texts in this unit. Consider, for example, how Brian O'Connor uses three examples of this technique in Paragraph 2 of "WMDs." Revise your draft to include at least three examples of parallel structure.

Annotate your draft, identifying where you have used the three descriptive techniques, direct and indirect quotations, and parallel structure. If you have used all of these successfully, you are ready to write your own interview narrative.

Planning an Interview

LEARNING STRATEGIES:
Brainstorming, Generating
Questions, Writer's Checklist

My Notes

Learning Target
• Plan and prepare to conduct an effective interview.

Planning an Interview

For Embedded Assessment 1, you will conduct an interview and write a narrative in which you present that interview. You have probably noticed that conducting an interview takes a good deal of planning. You need to begin planning now for the interview you will conduct.

The focus of your interview will be to find out about a person's overall experience during college and to discover at least one important incident during that time that influenced the interviewee's coming of age.

Step One

Make a list of people you might be able to interview. Include only people with whom you could have a face-to-face meeting before the assignment is due.

Name of Person I Might Be Able to Interview	Why I Would Like to Interview This Person About His or Her Experience in College

Step Two

Contact the people on your list to schedule your interview with one of them. Let the person know why you are conducting the interview and that some portions of it may be shared with your classmates.

Step Three

Write the details of your appointment:
• I have arranged to interview:

• Date the interview is scheduled:

• Time:

• Place:

Step Four

Brainstorm a list of questions and possible follow-up questions you might ask during the interview. Keep in mind the focus of your interview as you think of potential questions.

1.

2.

3.

4.

5.

6.

Step Five

Now exchange questions with a classmate. Have your classmate evaluate your questions. As you read your classmate's questions, suggest revisions, follow-up questions, or shifts in order.

Remember, you probably will not ask all these questions. Once your conversation begins to flow, you will ask follow-up questions. It is important, though, to walk into your interview with a list of questions to start the interview and to keep it going.

Step Six

With your group members, preview the "Writer's Checklist" for the interview narrative. Identify those skills you have specifically addressed in this unit.

Writing and Presenting an Interview Narrative

Assignment

Your assignment is to interview a person who has attended a post-secondary institution (i.e., a two- or four-year college, a training or vocational school, the military) and to write an interview narrative that effectively portrays the voice of the interviewee while revealing how the experience contributed to his or her coming of age.

Planning: Plan and conduct the interview.

- Have you arranged a time and place to meet with your interviewee?
- Are you satisfied with the list of questions you might ask? If not, revise them.
- Have you considered recording the interview? Or will you simply take hand-written notes, or both? Have you asked permission to record the interview?
- How will you set up the interview as a conversation rather than an interrogation?
- What will you do to remind yourself to ask good follow-up questions rather than simply sticking to the questions on your list?
- What question(s) will you ask to get your interviewee to describe in depth at least one specific coming-of-age incident from his or her college experience.
- When you feel that you have adequate information, you can begin to draw the interview to a close. Remember to take good notes and to thank the interviewee.

Prewriting: Prepare to write the interview narrative.

- How will you make time to read over your notes and add to, delete, or refine them as the basis for your interview narrative?
- What quotes or descriptions of the person will you use to give a vivid picture and create an authentic voice?

Drafting: Decide how to structure your interview narrative.

- What will you include in the introduction?
- Have you included information about the person's experiences in general and those related to college in particular?
- Have you used vivid and precise imagery, carefully chosen diction, and a mix of direct and indirect quotations to convey a sense of the interviewee's voice?

Revising and Editing for Publication: Review and revise to make your work the best it can be.

- Have you carefully transformed your questions and answers into a narrative?
- Have you arranged to share your draft with a partner or with your writing group?
- Have you consulted the Scoring Guide and the activities to prepare for revising your draft?
- Did you use your available resources (e.g., spell check, dictionaries, Writer's Checklist) to edit for conventions and prepare your narrative for publication?

Reflection

A successful interview can be a rewarding experience for both the interviewer and the interviewee. What did you learn that you did not expect to learn, and how would you evaluate the experience for both you and your interviewee?

SCORING GUIDE

Scoring Criteria	Exemplary	Proficient	Emerging	Incomplete
Ideas	The narrative • insightfully describes one or more college incidents that influenced the interviewee's coming of age • uses vivid examples of character description • develops an engaging and authentic character and presents that person's unique point of view.	The narrative • describes an incident from the person's college experience clearly and effectively • includes examples of character description • develops the character and presents the person's point of view.	The narrative • does not describe an incident using essential details about the person's college experience • includes only one or two examples of character description • develops some aspects of character but does not provide a clear point of view.	The narrative • does not contain essential details to establish an incident from the person's college experience • does not contain examples of character description • does not develop the character or the person's point of view
Structure	The narrative • follows the structure of the genre with well-sequenced events • clearly orients the reader and uses effective transitions to link ideas and events • demonstrates a consistent point of view.	The narrative • follows the structure of the genre with a sequence of events • orients the reader and uses transitions for coherence • uses a mostly consistent point of view.	The narrative • follows some structure of the genre • presents disconnected events with limited coherence • contains a point of view that is not appropriate for the focus of the narrative.	The narrative • does not follow the structure of the genre • includes few if any events and no coherence • contains inconsistent and confusing points of view.
Use of Language	The narrative • purposefully uses descriptive language, telling details, and vivid imagery to convey a strong sense of the intereviewee's voice • smoothly embeds direct and indirect quotations • demonstrates error-free spelling and use of standard English conventions.	The narrative • uses descriptive language and telling details to present the interviewee's voice • embeds some direct and/or indirect quotations • demonstrates general command of conventions and spelling; minor errors do not interfere with meaning.	The narrative • uses limited descriptive language or details to portray the voice of the interviewee • contains one or no embedded quotations • demonstrates limited command of conventions and spelling; errors interfere with meaning.	The narrative • uses no descriptive language or details to portray the voice of the interviewee • contains no embedded quotations • contains numerous errors in grammar and conventions that interfere with meaning.

Previewing Embedded Assessment 2 and Preparing to Write an Argument

My Notes

Learning Targets

* Identify the knowledge and skills needed to complete Embedded Assessment 2 successfully and reflect on prior learning that supports the knowledge and skills needed.
* Examine the essential elements of an argument.

Making Connections

In the first part of this unit, you studied voice, coming of age, and narratives in both fictional and nonfictional forms. For independent reading, you have been reading a variety of narratives. Now, you will shift your focus from narrative texts to texts that are persuasive in nature. You will review the rhetorical appeals of ethos, pathos, and logos and the way they work together with types of evidence to support the claim in an argument.

Essential Questions

Now that you have read texts and explored the concept of "coming of age," how would you change your answer to the first essential question that asks, "What does it mean to 'come of age'?"

Developing Vocabulary

Look back at the vocabulary that you have studied in the first part of this unit. Which terms do you know really well and can use effectively in class discussions and in your writing? Which terms do you need to learn more about or practice using more frequently?

Unpacking Embedded Assessment 2

Read the assignment for Embedded Assessment 2: Writing an Argumentative Essay. What knowledge must you have (what do you need to know) to succeed on Embedded Assessment 2? What skills must you have (what must you be able to do)?

> Your assignment is to write an essay of argumentation about the value of a college education. Your essay must be organized as an argument in which you assert a precise claim, support it with reasons and evidence, and acknowledge and refute counterclaims fairly.

In your own words, summarize what you will need to know to complete this assessment successfully. With your class, create a graphic organizer to represent the skills and knowledge you will need to complete the tasks identified in the Embedded Assessment.

INDEPENDENT READING LINK

Choose the argument that you plan to write about for Embedded Assessment 2, and for the rest of this unit read a variety of informational articles and other texts on the subject of your argument.

An **argument** is a discussion in which reasons are put forward in support of and against a claim. A written argument must meet several conditions in order to be a valid argument and not merely an effort to persuade.

1. The central claim needs to be debatable.
2. The claim must be supported by evidence.
3. The writer needs to address the opposition by acknowledging counterclaims and the evidence supporting them.

With these conditions in mind, consider the following elements of an effective argument.

- **Introduction and Claim:** an opening that grabs the reader's attention while informing the reader of the **claim,** which is a clear and straightforward statement of the writer's belief about the topic of the argument.
- **Supporting paragraphs:** the *reasons* offered in support of a claim, supported by different types of evidence.
- **Concession and / or Refutation:** restatements of valid **counterclaims** made by the opposing side (concessions) or the writer's arguments against those opposing viewpoints (refutations), explaining why the writer's position is more valid.
- **Conclusion / Call to Action:** closing statements restating the major arguments in defense of a thesis (the claim) with a final challenge to the reader to take action.

An argument has three major purposes:

- To change a reader's or listener's point of view
- To ask the reader or listener to take an action.
- To gain acceptance for the writer's ideas about a problem or issue

1. **Discussion Group:** Form a group of three or four students to share information. For Embedded Assessment 1, you wrote an interview narrative about a person who had attended college. What did you learn about the benefits of post-secondary education from your interviewee? What claims did your interviewee make? Use the space below and the My Notes space to write 3–5 benefits of college described by each person you interviewed. Describe the benefit, and add a direct quotation from the interviewee about that benefit.

> **ACADEMIC VOCABULARY**
> In an argument, a **claim** is a thesis statement describing the position the writer is taking on an issue. A **counterclaim** is a position taken by someone with an opposing viewpoint.

My Notes

Previewing Embedded Assessment 2 and Preparing to Write an Argument

My Notes

2. You will next watch a short video called "Five Ways Ed Pays," produced by the College Board (http://advocacy.collegeboard.org/five-ways-ed-pays/home. As you watch this video, take notes on the reasons given in support of the central claim. Be as specific as possible, and include quotes from the narrator as you record evidence in support of each reason.

Reason	Support / Evidence
Greater Wealth	
More Security	
Better Health	
Close Family	
Stronger Community	

3. Which of these reasons seem the most and which seem the least persuasive? Why?

Language and Writer's Craft: Clauses

Learning Targets
- Identify and analyze the effect of independent and dependent clauses.
- Effectively integrate adverbial and adjectival clauses into writing.

Creating Meaningful Text

When you read a text that "speaks" to you, what is it about the text that is meaningful? Is it the language the writer uses? Is it the ideas presented? Is it the way the writer has crafted the sentences?

Writers use sentence structure and elements within sentences to create specific effects. For example, read the following quotation:

> "Don't tell me the moon is shining; show me the glint of light on broken glass."
> —*Anton Chekhov*

This sentence is made up of two independent clauses (so it is a compound sentence). The independent clauses in a compound sentence are often connected with a comma and a coordinating conjunction (such as *and, or, but, yet, nor, for,* and *so*).

1. Reread Chekhov's quotation, but replace the semicolon with a comma and a coordinating conjunction. Is the effect the same? Explain why or why not.

Clauses may also be used adverbially or adjectivally.

Adverbial: An adverbial clause is a dependent clause that functions as an adverb. It modifies a verb, adjective, or adverb in another clause in the sentence. The writer can place the adverbial clause in different parts of the sentence, depending on where it best adds the desired effect. An adverb clause begins with a subordinating conjunction (such as *if, when, although, because, as*).
Example: *"Although the world is full of suffering,* it is full also of the overcoming of it." (Helen Keller)

Adjectival: An adjectival clause is a dependent clause that is used as an adjective in a sentence. Since an adjectival clause modifies a noun or pronoun, it cannot be moved around. That is, it should be as close as possible to the noun or pronoun it modifies. An adjectival clause generally begins with a relative pronoun (*that, which, who, whom, whose*).
Example: "The means by which we live have outdistanced the ends *for which we live.*" (Martin Luther King, Jr.)

LEARNING STRATEGIES:
Discussion Groups

GRAMMAR & USAGE
Clauses

A **clause** is a group of words with both a subject and verb. If the clause can stand alone as a complete sentence, it is an **independent clause**. If the clause does not form a complete idea, it is a **dependent clause**.

My Notes

_____
_____
_____
_____
_____
_____
_____
_____
_____
_____
_____
_____
_____
_____
_____
_____
_____
_____
_____
_____

Language and Writer's Craft: Clauses

My Notes

2. Read the following quotations. Analyze the structure of each sentence, and describe why you think the writers chose to punctuate their sentences as they did.

"You rely on a sentence to say more than the denotation and the connotation; you revel in the smoke that the words send up." —*Toni Morrison*

"Most writers regard the truth as their most valuable possession, and therefore are most economical in its use."—*Mark Twain*

"Don't try to figure out what other people want to hear from you; figure out what you have to say. It's the one and only thing you have to offer."—*Barbara Kingsolver*

Writing Prompt: With your writing group, write your own quotations about writing. Write at least three quotations. You will share your sentences with the class. Be sure to:

- Use vivid words and analogies.
- Integrate phrases and clauses into your sentences, using coordinating conjunctions as needed.
- Punctuate your sentences correctly.

Building an Argument

Learning Targets

- Evaluate how reasons support a claim.
- Examine and select appropriate evidence to support a persuasive claim.

The following quotations are all about education. Several of them use an **analogy** to explain education's importance. An analogy might be figurative or literal.

In a **figurative analogy** (such as a metaphor or simile), the two things being compared are generally unlike except for one shared characteristic. Such analogies are weak as evidence. In a **literal analogy**, however, the two things are similar in significant ways. For example, judges often rule based on similar previous rulings (case precedents), historians compare current events to previous historical examples, and critics often compare similar things.

1. With your discussion group, analyze each analogy by writing a paraphrase or explanation of the quote. Then, consider what each analogy suggests regarding education, and evaluate how insightful you think it is. Finally, discuss whether the analogy is figurative or literal.

   "Education is not the filling of a bucket but the lighting of a fire." —*William Butler Yeats*

   "The highest result of education is tolerance." —*Helen Keller*

   "Education is the most powerful weapon which you can use to change the world." —*Nelson Mandela*

   "Education is our passport to the future, for tomorrow belongs to the people who prepare for it today." —*Malcolm X*

   "Prejudices, it is well known, are most difficult to eradicate from the heart whose soil has never been loosened or fertilized by education; they grow there, firm as weeds among stones." —*Charlotte Bronte*

> **LEARNING STRATEGIES:**
> Discussion Groups, Paraphrasing, Visual Prompt, Drafting

> **ACADEMIC VOCABULARY**
> An **analogy** is a comparison between two things for the purpose of drawing conclusions on one based on its similarities to the other.

> **My Notes**
> _____
> _____
> _____
> _____
> _____
> _____
> _____
> _____
> _____

> **WORD CONNECTIONS**
> Word Patterns
> Words that are related to *analogy* are *analogue* and *analogous*. *Analogy* and *analogue* are both nouns, while *analogous* is an adjective. *Analogue* means something that is similar to another thing (e.g., soy burger is an analogue for a hamburger). *Analogous* describes two or more things that are similar or comparable (e.g., a computer is analogous to a brain).

Building an Argument

2. Based on your discussion, which of the analogies most appeals to you? Why?

3. What kinds of analogies are shown in these quotations? How effective might each be as evidence to support a claim about education?

4. Compare your response to those of the other members of your discussion group. Which do you think is most persuasive and why?

Before Reading

5. In the video "Five Ways Ed Pays," greater wealth was given as one of the benefits of a college education. How would your career choices and potential earnings be affected by having a college degree?

During Reading

6. You will next read an informational text on the financial benefits of a college education. As you read, identify the claim and highlight evidence that supports that claim.

Informational Text

New school year, old story: Education pays

Wondering if your studies will pay off? Recent data from the U.S. Bureau of Labor Statistics (BLS) suggest that they will. As past studies have shown, as workers' level of education increases, their earnings rise and unemployment rates fall.

The chart groups workers' earnings and unemployment by their highest level of educational attainment. Workers with a bachelor's degree, for example, earned about $415 more a week than workers whose highest level of education is a high school diploma. And the rate of unemployment for workers with a bachelor's degree was about half that of those with no education beyond high school.

For students in graduate school, the payoff for a degree might be even greater. Workers with a professional degree, such as lawyers and physicians, earned about $612 more a week than did workers with

a bachelor's degree—and over $1,000 more per week than workers who have a high school diploma as their highest level of education. Plus, at 2.4 percent, the unemployment rate for workers with a professional degree was also the lowest of any education level.

The numbers in the chart below are medians—meaning that half of all workers earned more than that amount, and half earned less. As the chart indicates, postponing work for school can pay off. But there are some financial drawbacks. Students often forego a full-time paycheck while they are in school. And when estimating the financial benefit of additional education, students who take out loans to pay for school should consider the amount they will be obligated to repay.

Data come from a special supplement to the BLS Current Population Survey. www.bls.gov / CPS.

Unemployment rates and earnings for full-time wage and salary workers ages 25 and older, by educational attainment, 2011

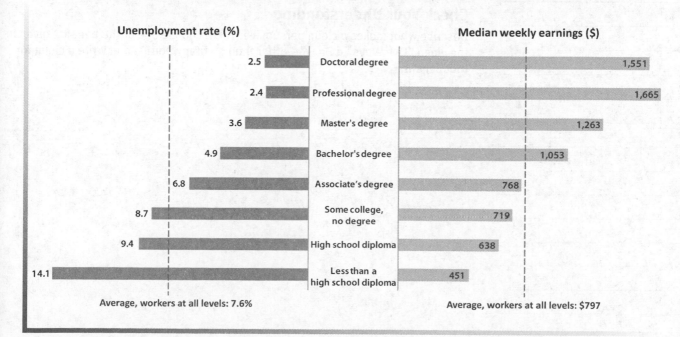

Building an Argument

After Reading

7. What claim does this article make?

8. How does the article support the claim?

9. What is the source of this information? How do you view this source? Do you think the data cited are reliable?

10. How does the presentation of data in a chart aid the reader?

Check Your Understanding

Describe what makes a claim persuasive. Then, choose one of the benefits given in the video "Five Ways Ed Pays"—other than greater wealth—and write a claim for that benefit.

Using Rhetorical Appeals

Learning Targets
- Identify and analyze the effectiveness of the use of logos, ethos, and pathos in texts.
- Explain how a writer or speaker uses rhetoric to advance his or her purpose.

Elements of Rhetoric

Rhetoric is the use of words to persuade, either in writing or speech. Aristotle defined rhetoric as "the ability, in each particular case, to see the available means of persuasion." He described three main types of rhetoric: *logos, ethos,* and *pathos*. Authors and speakers use **rhetorical appeals** in their arguments to persuade the intended audience that their claims are right.

The Rhetorical Triangle

Together, these rhetorical appeals are central to understanding how writers and speakers appeal to their audiences and persuade them to accept their messages. It is helpful to think of them as three points of a triangle.

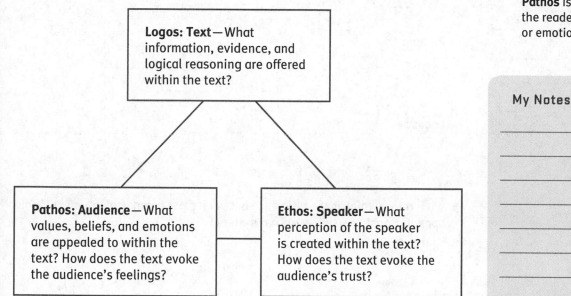

Logos: Text—What information, evidence, and logical reasoning are offered within the text?

Pathos: Audience—What values, beliefs, and emotions are appealed to within the text? How does the text evoke the audience's feelings?

Ethos: Speaker—What perception of the speaker is created within the text? How does the text evoke the audience's trust?

Literary Terms
Rhetorical appeals are emotional, ethical, and logical appeals used to persuade an audience to agree with the writer or speaker.
Logos is a rhetorical appeal to reason or logic.
Ethos is a rhetorical appeal that focuses on the character or qualifications of the speaker.
Pathos is a rhetorical appeal to the reader's or listener's senses or emotions.

My Notes

Using Rhetorical Appeals

**WORD
CONNECTIONS**

Roots and Affixes

The word *pathos* includes the
Greek root *-path-*, which comes
from the Greek word meaning
"suffering." This root also
occurs in these English words:
pathetic, sympathy, apathy, and
empathy.

My Notes

Before Reading

1. Read the following examples and then write the part of the triangle in which
   each would fit.

   a. In "Five Ways Ed Pays," consider the claims about having a "closer family"
      accompanied by images of parents with their children.

   b. The "more wealth" section of the "Five Ways Ed Pays" video relies on
      statistics regarding income as the basis for attending college.

   c. "Five Ways Ed Pays" uses several different narrators in the voice-over to
      make the message feel familiar and trustworthy to viewers.

2. Now, write your own example for each part of the rhetorical triangle.

   Ethos:

   Pathos:

   Logos:

3. What do you think is the difference between persuasion and argument? Which
   appeals might be used for each purpose?

4. Which part of the rhetorical triangle should be emphasized if you want to
   convince your audience of the validity of your claim?

During Reading

5. As you read the following speech, mark the text for examples of logos, ethos,
   and pathos.

Speech

REMARKS BY THE PRESIDENT IN A NATIONAL ADDRESS TO

AMERICA'S
Schoolchildren

By President Barack Obama
Wakefield High School, Arlington, Virginia, September 8, 2009

1 … I know that for many of you, today is the first day of school. And for those of you in kindergarten, or starting middle or high school, it's your first day in a new school, so it's understandable if you're a little nervous. I imagine there are some seniors out there who are feeling pretty good right now with just one more year to go. And no matter what grade you're in, some of you are probably wishing it were still summer and you could've stayed in bed just a little bit longer this morning.

2 I know that feeling. When I was young, my family lived overseas. I lived in Indonesia for a few years. And my mother, she didn't have the money to send me where all the American kids went to school, but she thought it was important for me to keep up with an American education. So she decided to teach me extra lessons herself, Monday through Friday. But because she had to go to work, the only time she could do it was at 4:30 in the morning.

3 Now, as you might imagine, I wasn't too happy about getting up that early. And a lot of times, I'd fall asleep right there at the kitchen table. But whenever I'd complain, my mother would just give me one of those looks and she'd say, "This is no picnic for me either, buster."

4 So I know that some of you are still adjusting to being back at school. But I'm here today because I have something important to discuss with you. I'm here because I want to talk with you about your education and what's expected of all of you in this new school year.

5 Now, I've given a lot of speeches about education. And I've talked about responsibility a lot. I've talked about teachers' responsibility for inspiring students and pushing you to learn. I've talked about your parents' responsibility for making sure you stay on track, and you get your homework done, and don't spend every waking hour in front of the TV or with the Xbox. I've talked a lot about your government's responsibility for setting high standards, and supporting teachers and principals, and turning around schools that aren't working, where students aren't getting the opportunities that they deserve.

6 But at the end of the day, we can have the most dedicated teachers, the most supportive parents, the best schools in the world—and none of it will make a difference, none of it will matter unless all of you fulfill your responsibilities, unless you show up to those schools, unless you pay attention to those teachers, unless you listen to your parents and grandparents and other adults and put in the hard work it takes to succeed. That's what I want to focus on today: the responsibility each of you has for your education.

GRAMMAR & USAGE
Commas

Commas help clarify meaning. When a phrase or a clause is not essential (nonrestrictive) to the meaning of a sentence, set it off with commas. However, If It Is essential (restrictive), do not use commas. Look at these examples of nonrestrictive phrases:

Adverbial phrase: "So she decided to teach me extra lessons herself, **Monday through Friday.**"

Participial phrase: "And for those of you in kindergarten, or **starting middle or high school**, . . ."

The commas indicate that the information in these phrases is additional but not necessary. In your writing, use commas to make clear the distinction between restrictive and nonrestrictive phrases.

KEY IDEAS AND DETAILS
The president begins his speech with statements about the audience's feelings and then a story about his own childhood. Why does he begin his speech in this way?

My Notes

Using Rhetorical Appeals

KEY IDEAS AND DETAILS
Can you identify an explicit
thesis for the speech? How
do paragraphs 7 and 8 define
the purpose of the President's
speech?

KEY IDEAS AND DETAILS
What is the appeal of these
hypothetical situations? Is it
logos, ethos, or pathos?

KEY IDEAS AND DETAILS
In paragraphs 7–12, what
does the speech focus on?
What reasons are offered in
support of the claim offered at
the end of paragraph 6?

My Notes

_____

_____

_____

_____

_____

_____

_____

_____

KEY IDEAS AND DETAILS
What type of appeal is most
prominent in paragraphs
13–16? Why might the
speaker choose to include his
own personal story here?

_____

_____

_____

_____

_____

_____

_____

7   I want to start with the responsibility you have to yourself. Every single one of you has something that you're good at. Every single one of you has something to offer. And you have a responsibility to yourself to discover what that is. That's the opportunity an education can provide.

8   Maybe you could be a great writer—maybe even good enough to write a book or articles in a newspaper—but you might not know it until you write that English paper—that English class paper that's assigned to you. Maybe you could be an innovator or an inventor—maybe even good enough to come up with the next iPhone or the new medicine or vaccine—but you might not know it until you do your project for your science class. Maybe you could be a mayor or a senator or a Supreme Court justice—but you might not know that until you join student government or the debate team.

9   And no matter what you want to do with your life, I guarantee that you'll need an education to do it. You want to be a doctor, or a teacher, or a police officer? You want to be a nurse or an architect, a lawyer or a member of our military? You're going to need a good education for every single one of those careers. You cannot drop out of school and just drop into a good job. You've got to train for it and work for it and learn for it.

10   And this isn't just important for your own life and your own future. What you make of your education will decide nothing less than the future of this country. The future of America depends on you. What you're learning in school today will determine whether we as a nation can meet our greatest challenges in the future.

11   You'll need the knowledge and problem-solving skills you learn in science and math to cure diseases like cancer and AIDS, and to develop new energy technologies and protect our environment. You'll need the insights and critical-thinking skills you gain in history and social studies to fight poverty and homelessness, crime and discrimination, and make our nation more fair and more free. You'll need the creativity and ingenuity you develop in all your classes to build new companies that will create new jobs and boost our economy.

12   We need every single one of you to develop your talents and your skills and your intellect so you can help us old folks solve our most difficult problems. If you don't do that—if you quit on school—you're not just quitting on yourself, you're quitting on your country.

13   Now, I know it's not always easy to do well in school. I know a lot of you have challenges in your lives right now that can make it hard to focus on your schoolwork.

14   I get it. I know what it's like. My father left my family when I was two years old, and I was raised by a single mom who had to work and who struggled at times to pay the bills and wasn't always able to give us the things that other kids had. There were times when I missed having a father in my life. There were times when I was lonely and I felt like I didn't fit in.

15   So I wasn't always as focused as I should have been on school, and I did some things I'm not proud of, and I got in more trouble than I should have. And my life could have easily taken a turn for the worse.

16 But I was—I was lucky. I got a lot of second chances, and I had the opportunity to go to college and law school and follow my dreams. My wife, our First Lady Michelle Obama, she has a similar story. Neither of her parents had gone to college, and they didn't have a lot of money. But they worked hard, and she worked hard, so that she could go to the best schools in this country.

17 Some of you might not have those advantages. Maybe you don't have adults in your life who give you the support that you need. Maybe someone in your family has lost their job and there's not enough money to go around. Maybe you live in a neighborhood where you don't feel safe, or have friends who are pressuring you to do things you know aren't right.

18 But at the end of the day, the circumstances of your life—what you look like, where you come from, how much money you have, what you've got going on at home—none of that is an excuse for neglecting your homework or having a bad attitude in school. That's no excuse for talking back to your teacher, or cutting class, or dropping out of school. There is no excuse for not trying. Where you are right now doesn't have to determine where you'll end up. No one's written your destiny for you, because here in America, you write your own destiny. You make your own future.

19 That's what young people like you are doing every day, all across America.

20 Young people like Jazmin Perez, from Roma, Texas. Jazmin didn't speak English when she first started school. Neither of her parents had gone to college. But she worked hard, earned good grades, and got a scholarship to Brown University—is now in graduate school, studying public health, on her way to becoming Dr. Jazmin Perez.

21 I'm thinking about Andoni Schultz, from Los Altos, California, who's fought brain cancer since he was three. He's had to endure all sorts of treatments and surgeries, one of which affected his memory, so it took him much longer—hundreds of extra hours—to do his schoolwork. But he never fell behind. He's headed to college this fall.

22 And then there's Shantell Steve, from my hometown of Chicago, Illinois. Even when bouncing from foster home to foster home in the toughest neighborhoods in the city, she managed to get a job at a local health care center, start a program to keep young people out of gangs, and she's on track to graduate high school with honors and go on to college.

23 And Jazmin, Andoni, and Shantell aren't any different from any of you. They face challenges in their lives just like you do. In some cases they've got it a lot worse off than many of you. But they refused to give up. They chose to take responsibility for their lives, for their education, and set goals for themselves. And I expect all of you to do the same.

24 That's why today I'm calling on each of you to set your own goals for your education—and do everything you can to meet them. Your goal can be something as simple as doing all your homework, paying attention in class, or spending some time each day reading a book. Maybe you'll decide to get involved in an extracurricular activity, or volunteer in your community. Maybe you'll decide to stand up for kids who are being teased or bullied because of who they are or how they look, because you believe, like I do, that all young people deserve a safe environment to study and learn. Maybe you'll decide to take better care of yourself so you can be more ready to learn. And along those lines, by the way, I hope all of you are washing your hands a lot, and that you stay home from school when you don't feel well, so we can keep people from getting the flu this fall and winter.

KEY IDEAS AND DETAILS
In paragraphs 18–24, what does the president do to overcome potential resistance by his audience? Does this approach rely more on logos or on pathos? Explain.

My Notes

_____

_____

_____

_____

_____

_____

_____

_____

_____

_____

_____

KEY IDEAS AND DETAILS
The president uses the word *maybe* eleven times in this speech, including three times in paragraph 24. Find the two other paragraphs where he uses it multiple times. What do these paragraphs have in common? Why would he use this approach so often with this audience? How does this use of parallelism affect the rhetoric?

_____

_____

_____

Using Rhetorical Appeals

KEY IDEAS AND DETAILS
In paragraph 26, the president
seems to shoot down the
dreams many students might
have. How does that link to
what follows in paragraphs
27–33? Is it logical to use
Rowling and Jordan to prove
his point? Why or why not?

My Notes

_____

_____

_____

_____

_____

_____

_____

_____

_____

_____

_____

_____

_____

_____

_____

_____

_____

KEY IDEAS AND DETAILS
How does the president use
pathos in paragraphs 32–35?
Underline sentences designed
to motivate the audience
using emotions rather than
logic.

_____

_____

_____

_____

_____

25 But whatever you resolve to do, I want you to commit to it. I want you to really work at it.

26 I know that sometimes you get that sense from TV that you can be rich and successful without any hard work—that your ticket to success is through rapping or basketball or being a reality TV star. Chances are you're not going to be any of those things.

27 The truth is, being successful is hard. You won't love every subject that you study. You won't click with every teacher that you have. Not every homework assignment will seem completely relevant to your life right at this minute. And you won't necessarily succeed at everything the first time you try.

28 That's okay. Some of the most successful people in the world are the ones who've had the most failures. J.K. Rowling's—who wrote Harry Potter—her first Harry Potter book was rejected 12 times before it was finally published. Michael Jordan was cut from his high school basketball team. He lost hundreds of games and missed thousands of shots during his career. But he once said, "I have failed over and over and over again in my life. And that's why I succeed."

29 These people succeeded because they understood that you can't let your failures define you—you have to let your failures teach you. You have to let them show you what to do differently the next time. So if you get into trouble, that doesn't mean you're a troublemaker, it means you need to try harder to act right. If you get a bad grade, that doesn't mean you're stupid, it just means you need to spend more time studying.

30 No one's born being good at all things. You become good at things through hard work. You're not a varsity athlete the first time you play a new sport. You don't hit every note the first time you sing a song. You've got to practice. The same principle applies to your schoolwork. You might have to do a math problem a few times before you get it right. You might have to read something a few times before you understand it. You definitely have to do a few drafts of a paper before it's good enough to hand in.

31 Don't be afraid to ask questions. Don't be afraid to ask for help when you need it. I do that every day. Asking for help isn't a sign of weakness, it's a sign of strength because it shows you have the courage to admit when you don't know something, and that then allows you to learn something new. So find an adult that you trust—a parent, a grandparent or teacher, a coach or a counselor—and ask them to help you stay on track to meet your goals.

32 And even when you're struggling, even when you're discouraged, and you feel like other people have given up on you, don't ever give up on yourself, because when you give up on yourself, you give up on your country.

33 The story of America isn't about people who quit when things got tough. It's about people who kept going, who tried harder, who loved their country too much to do anything less than their best. It's the story of students who sat where you sit 250 years ago, and went on to wage a revolution and they founded this nation. Young people. Students who sat where you sit 75 years ago who overcame a Depression and won a world war; who fought for civil rights and put a man on the moon. Students who sat where you sit 20 years ago who founded Google and Twitter and Facebook and changed the way we communicate with each other.

34 So today, I want to ask all of you, what's your contribution going to be? What problems are you going to solve? What discoveries will you make? What will a President who comes here in 20 or 50 or 100 years say about what all of you did for this country?

35 Now, your families, your teachers, and I are doing everything we can to make sure you have the education you need to answer these questions. I'm working hard to fix up your classrooms and get you the books and the equipment and the computers you need to learn. But you've got to do your part, too. So I expect all of you to get serious this year. I expect you to put your best effort into everything you do. I expect great things from each of you. So don't let us down. Don't let your family down or your country down. Most of all, don't let yourself down. Make us all proud.

36 Thank you very much, everybody. God bless you. God bless America. Thank you.

Introducing the Strategy: SMELL

SMELL is an acronym for Sender, Message, Emotional strategies, Logical strategies, and Language. This strategy is useful for analyzing a persuasive speech or essay by asking five essential questions:

- What is the sender-receiver relationship? Who are the images and language meant to attract? Describe the speaker (or writer) of the text.
- What is the message? Summarize the thesis of the text.
- What is the desired effect of the emotional strategies?
- What logic is being used? How does it (or its absence) affect the message? Consider the logic of images as well as words.
- What does the language of the text describe? How does it affect the meaning and effectiveness of the writing? Consider the language of images as well as words.

After Reading

6. Use the SMELL strategy to analyze how President Obama uses the different rhetorical appeals to persuade his audience. Using the graphic organizer on the next page, write answers to the five questions. Include specific quotes and textual evidence you noted while reading the speech.

KEY IDEAS AND DETAILS
A **rhetorical question** is one that is asked for effect or one for which the answer is obvious. Highlight examples the president uses.

My Notes

Using Rhetorical Appeals

Sender-Receiver Relationship: Who are the senders (speaker / writer) and receivers (audience) of the message, and what is their relationship (consider what different audiences the text may be addressing)? How does the sender attempt to establish his / her *ethos*?

Message: What is a literal summary of the content? What is the meaning / significance of this information?

Emotional Strategies: What emotional appeals (*pathos*) are included? What seems to be their desired effect?

Logical Strategies: What logical arguments / appeals (*logos*) are included? What is their effect?

Language: What specific language supports the message? How does it affect the text's effectiveness? Consider both images (if appropriate) and actual words. What is the speaker's voice in the text?

My Notes

Check Your Understanding

Writing Prompt: Some politicians have called for increasing the number of college graduates. Write an introduction and at least two to three paragraphs supporting a claim that we either need or do not need more college graduates. Be sure to:

• Orient the reader and set out the problem.
• Sequence relevant evidence from your experiences or what you have read to support the claim, using ethos and logos to engage the reader.
• Use transitions and parallel structure for coherence.

Targeting Your Audience

Learning Targets

- Identify different types of evidence and their purposes.
- Select evidence, appeals, and techniques specifically to reach a target audience.

LEARNING STRATEGIES:
Discussion Groups,
Brainstorming, Graphic
Organizer, KWHL Chart

Connecting with an Audience

To make an argument compelling, writers and speakers use a variety of reasons and evidence that they think will convince their audience to agree with them. Knowing the audience helps the writer or speaker decide what reasons and evidence to use.

1. With your group members, review the texts you have read in this unit and identify examples of the different types of evidence used. Then craft an explanation of the purpose of each as a tool of persuasion.

A. Type of Evidence / Support	B. Example from Class Readings / Viewings	C. Used to . . . (logos, ethos, pathos? In what way?)
Facts and Statistics: Numbers drawn from surveys, studies or observation, as well as pieces of commonly accepted information about the world		
Analogy (figurative or literal): Comparison between two unlike things to support conclusions about one based on similarities to the other		
Personal Experience / Anecdote: A true story that describes a person's experience relative to the topic		
Illustrative Example (brief or extended): Description of a specific experience or example to support the validity of a generalization		

Targeting Your Audience

A. Type of Evidence / Support	B. Example from Class Readings / Viewings	C. Used to . . . (logos, ethos, pathos? In what way?)
Expert / Personal Testimony: The use of a person's words or conclusions to support a claim, whether the person is like the audience or is distinguished by his or her expertise		
Hypothetical Case: Use of a "what if" or possible scenario in order to challenge the audience to consider its implications		

My Notes

2. List each text you cited, and then describe the target audience for that text.

Text 1:

Text 2:

Text 3:

Before Reading

3. **Quickwrite:** When you are writing to a friend (text message, email, note, etc.), how do you tailor the language you use? If you were writing to your teacher, how would you change your language?

During Reading

4. You will next read an editorial about the value of taking college courses for credit while in high school. As you read, identify the audience for this editorial.

Editorial

An *Early Start* on College

More Minnesota teens should use dual-credit enrollment

January 14, 2012, *StarTribune*

Taking advanced, dual-enrollment classes made a big difference in Paj Ntaub Lee's life.

Her Hmong immigrant parents didn't encourage her to go to college; they thought graduating from high school, then getting married or finding a job would be enough for their child.

But her exposure to college and higher-level courses while at Johnson High School in St. Paul set her on a path to graduate from St. Olaf College in Northfield.

Her experience should be shared by more Minnesota students, and the Legislature should expand the programs that make that possible.

Participating in any of the state's dual-credit programs can prepare more students for college work, save money and increase postsecondary graduation rates. Taking more-challenging classes can also open educational doors for not only the highest-performing students, but for kids across the academic spectrum.

Those are the conclusions of a recent study conducted by the Center for School Change (CSC) at Macalester College. Minnesota students can participate in one of five dual-credit options—Advanced Placement or International Baccalaureate classes, postsecondary options, concurrent enrollment programs or Project Lead the Way, which allows students to take courses in technical and scientific areas.

Each program allows students to earn college credit while still in high school.

The study showed that the programs are increasing in popularity— between 2001 and 2006, about 38,000 state students took AP or IB exams, and an average of about 5,500 students a year participated in postsecondary options during those years. Concurrent enrollment increased from 17,581 to 21,184 between 2008 and 2010.

A 2010 Minnesota State Colleges and Universities report showed that 53 percent of those who enrolled in a Minnesota public college within two years of graduation had to take at least one remedial course.

My Notes

KEY IDEAS AND DETAILS
What is the central claim in this editorial? How does the writer introduce it?

KEY IDEAS AND DETAILS
The CSC study is used as evidence in this editorial. What claim does it support? How effective is it as a source to support the editorial's central claims?

Targeting Your Audience

KEY IDEAS AND DETAILS
What call to action is offered in the editorial? Does the article effectively motivate you as a ninth grader to take action? Why or why not?

KEY IDEAS AND DETAILS
How does the conclusion support the central claim and convince readers to believe the writer's evidence?

My Notes

But if more students take advantage of dual-credit options, more will be prepared for college and other postsecondary level work. That will reduce the need for remedial courses and save money for students, families and taxpayers.

To expand the options to include more students, the CSC report rightly recommends that the Legislature change the statutes to allow ninth- and tenth-graders to participate and to allow colleges and universities to advertise about the savings.

Paj Ntaub Lee now works for the CSC and helped do the research for the center's report. She's a supporter—and a good example of why more Minnesota students should take advantage of dual-credit options.

After Reading

5. The *StarTribune* editorial addresses multiple audiences. In the space below, identify each audience. Use quotes you highlighted to show how each audience is referenced or directly addressed in the text.

6. How effective is this piece at appealing to high school students? Why? What types of evidence and which rhetorical appeals are effective for high school students?

Writing Prompt: Go back to the writing you did in response to the writing prompt about how to increase the number of college graduates (Activity 1.16). Evaluate your work based on your additional analyses of audience, claims, and evidence. Be sure to:

- Revise to clearly address your audience.
- Evaluate the types of evidence you include and revise to strengthen evidence as needed.
- Revise the language to clarify rhetorical appeals.

Evaluating Claims and Reasoning

Learning Targets

- Identify counterclaims and refutations in an argument.
- Analyze conclusions to an argument.
- Describe counterclaims and refutations in writing.

Before Reading

1. **Quickwrite:** Explain the difference between a formal and an informal writing style.

During Reading

Argumentative writing uses a **formal** writing style. Formal writing can be of any type, such as descriptive, analytical, or critical. It is typically based on facts and follows a plan for developing the content. It also is characterized by correct grammar, clear language, and the avoidance of any type of slang.

When writing an argument, you not only need to state your own claim, but you also need to address counterclaims and the evidence supporting them.

2. As you read the following two texts, mark the text to identify the elements of an argument, including the central claim and evidence as well as counterclaims and evidence. Who is the audience for each text?

My Notes

Evaluating Claims and Reasoning

KEY IDEAS AND DETAILS
What background details does the writer provide to set up the claim?

KEY IDEAS AND DETAILS
What are the major points in this opinion piece?

KEY IDEAS AND DETAILS
Where does the writer bring up the counterclaim, and how does he develop it?

Opinion

Why College Isn't for Everyone

By Richard Vedder , April 09, 2012

A person who compares the annual earnings of college and high school graduates would no doubt conclude that higher education is a good investment—the present value of the college earnings premium (the better part of $1 million) seemingly far outdistances college costs, yielding a high rate of return. But for many, attending college is unequivocally not the right decision on purely economic grounds.

First of all, college graduates on average are smarter and have better work habits than high school graduates. Those who graduated from college were better students in high school, for example. Thus, at least a portion of the earnings premium associated with college has nothing to do with college per se, but rather with other traits.

Second, a goodly proportion (more than 40 percent) of those attending four-year colleges full-time fail to graduate, even within six years. At some colleges, the dropout rate is strikingly higher. While college students sometimes still gain marketable skills from partial attendance, others end up taking jobs that are often given to high school graduates, making little more money but having college debts and some lost earnings accrued while unsuccessfully pursing a degree.

Third, not everyone is average. A non-swimmer trying to cross a stream that on average is three feet deep might drown because part of the stream is seven feet in depth. The same kind of thing sometimes happens to college graduates too entranced by statistics on averages. Earnings vary considerably between the graduates of different schools, and within schools, earnings differ a great deal between majors. Accounting, computer science, and engineering majors, for example, almost always make more than those majoring in education, social work, or ethnic studies.

Fourth, the number of new college graduates far exceeds the growth in the number of technical, managerial, and professional jobs where graduates traditionally have gravitated. As a consequence, we have a new phenomenon: underemployed college graduates doing jobs historically performed by those with much less education. We have, for example, more than 100,000 janitors with college degrees, and 16,000 degree-holding parking lot attendants.

Does this mean no one should go to college? Of course not. First of all, college is more than training for a career, and many might benefit from the social and non-purely academic aspects of advanced schooling, even if the rate of return on college as a financial investment is low. Second, high school students with certain attributes are far less likely to drop out of school, and are likely to equal or excel the average statistics.

Students who do well in high school and on college entrance exams are much more likely to graduate. Those going to private schools may pay more in tuition, but they also have lower dropout rates. Those majoring in some subjects, such as education or one of the humanities, can sometimes improve their job situation by double majoring or earning a minor in, say, economics.

As a general rule, I would say graduates in the top quarter of their class at a high-quality high school should go on to a four-year degree program, while those in the bottom quarter of their class at a high school with a mediocre educational reputation should not (opting instead for alternative methods of credentialing and training).

Those in between should consider perhaps doing a two-year program and then transferring to a four-year school. There are, of course, exceptions to this rule, but it is important for us to keep in mind that college is not for everyone.

Opinion

Actually, College Is Very Much Worth It

By Andrew J. Rotherham
May 19, 2011

Lately it's become fashionable—especially among the highly credentialed—to question whether it's really "worth it" to go to college. A recent report from the Harvard Graduate School of Education proposed deemphasizing college as the primary goal of our education system in favor of "multiple pathways" for students. Earlier this month, New York Magazine devoted almost 4,000 words to profiling venture capitalists (and college graduates) James Altucher and Peter Thiel and their efforts to convince Americans that they'd be better off skipping college. Thiel is even creating a $100,000 fellowship for young people who agree to delay going to college in favor of an internship.

Make no mistake, there is widespread dissatisfaction with higher education. According to a new survey released by the Pew Research Center, only 40 percent of Americans felt that colleges provided an "excellent" or "good" value for the money. At the same time, 86 percent of college graduates still felt the investment was a good one for them.

To understand these competing views, you have to juggle a few different ideas at once. First, there are plenty of problems with higher education—poor quality, even at brand-name schools, and out-of-control costs are two of the biggest. College presidents themselves shared some of these concerns and others with the Pew researchers. Second, it's true: College isn't for everyone. There are plenty of rewarding and important jobs and careers that do not require college. And due to the sluggish economy, there may in fact be more graduates than the current job market needs, or a temporary "college bubble." Jobs for recent grads are harder to find, and salaries are lower, but that won't last forever. And in spite of all of this, the data make clear that getting a college education is still a good idea—college graduates earn more, and are more likely to have a job in the first place—and is especially important for some Americans.

My Notes

KEY IDEAS AND DETAILS
What background details does the writer provide to set up the claim?

Evaluating Claims and Reasoning

Anti-college sentiment is nothing new. Mark Twain admonished us not to let schooling interfere with education, and we've always celebrated the maverick who blazes their own path. These days, it's Facebook founder Mark Zuckerberg, Microsoft's Bill Gates, or Apple's Steve Jobs—all college dropouts—who are held up as evidence of why all that time sitting in class is better spent elsewhere. Perhaps, but it's also worth remembering that their companies are bursting with college graduates. And what about all the people who didn't finish college and are not at the helm of a wildly successful venture?

Nobody spends a lot of time highlighting their stories, but let's not lose sight of what happens to them. According to the Bureau of Labor Statistics, in 2010, the median weekly earnings for someone with some college but no degree were $712, compared to $1038 for a college graduate. That's almost $17,000 over the course of a year and there is an even bigger divide for those with less education. College graduates are also more likely to be in jobs with better benefits, further widening the divide. Meanwhile, in 2010, the unemployment rate was 9.2 percent for those with only some college and more than 10 percent for those with just a high school degree, but it was 5.4 percent for college graduates. The economic gaps between college completers and those with less education are getting larger, too.

It's also odd to talk down college—which is the most effective social mobility strategy we have—at the very time Americans are becoming concerned about income inequality. Ron Haskins of the Brookings Institution found that without a college degree, only 14 percent of Americans from the bottom fifth of parental income reach the top two-fifths. But if they complete college, 41 percent of this same group can then expect to make it to the top two-fifths. Haskins' data also shows the extent to which debates like this are a luxury of the privileged, because their children enjoy much more of a safety net and the risks are different for them. In other words, children from low-income families gain more by going to college than children of the wealthy lose by not going.

So here's the key takeaway: Education gives you choices. Assuming you don't pile up mountains of debt that constrain your career options (and that outcome is avoidable) or go to a school where just fogging a mirror is good enough to get a diploma, there are not a lot of downsides to going to college. The stories of entrepreneurs who bootstrapped themselves are exciting but most of us are not a Gates or Zuckerberg. So before heeding the advice of the college naysayers, make sure you understand the stakes and the odds. Or, here's a good rule of thumb instead: When people who worked hard to achieve something that has benefitted them start telling you that it's really not all that important or useful—beware.

Disclosure: I'm a member of the Visiting Committee for the Harvard Graduate School of Education.

KEY IDEAS AND DETAILS
What are the major points in this opinion piece?

After Reading

3. Compare the claims made by each of these two writers. Evaluate the reasons and evidence used by each writer. What is relevant and convincing?

For each text, write the claim and its supporting evidence in the following chart.

"Why College Isn't for Everyone"	"Actually, College Is Very Much Worth It"
Claim:	Claim:
Evidence:	Evidence:
Counterclaims:	Counterclaims:
Evidence:	Evidence:

Evaluating Claims and Reasoning

4. Which writer presents the more convincing argument? Why? Cite evidence to support your conclusion.

5. What elements, if any, do you think are missing from either of these pieces? Explain.

6. Why do you think Andrew J. Rotherham disclosed at the end of his article that he is a member of an educational group? How does this disclosure affect your perception of his argument?

Conclusion/Call to Action

An argument contains a conclusion that often restates the primary claim and tries to convince the reader to take an action.

7. What is the call to action in each of these pieces?

Check Your Understanding

Writing Prompt: Go back to the work you did on revising your argument about how to increase the number of college graduates (Activity 1.16). Revise as needed to address counterclaims and refutations, as well as to add a conclusion / call to action. Be sure to:

- Address counterclaims clearly and fairly.
- Evaluate and refute the evidence for counterclaims.
- Revise language for formal style and coherence.

Writing an Argumentative Essay

Assignment

Your assignment is to write an essay of argumentation about the value of a college education. Your essay must be organized as an argument in which you assert a precise claim, suport it with reasons and evidence, and acknowledge and refute counterclaims fairly.

Planning: Make a plan for researching your topic and collecting evidence.

- What is your claim? Is it clear? What information do you need to support it?
- How will you use in your essay the articles you have been reading independently?
- How will you expand upon the articles in this unit by doing further research?
- How will you evaluate whether you have enough information to write your draft?
- How will you consider your audience and determine the reasons and evidence that will best convince them to support your argument?

Prewriting: Prepare to write the essay draft.

- How will you make time to read your notes and add to, delete, or refine them as the basis for your argument?
- What quotations will you use as evidence?
- What information do you have to address counterclaims?

Drafting: Decide how to structure your essay.

- What will you include in the introduction? How will you describe your claim?
- Have you used vivid and precise language, carefully chosen diction, and formal style?
- Have you acknowledged and addressed counterclaims?
- Have you written a strong conclusion with a call to action?

Revising and Editing for Publication: Review and revise to make your work the best it can be.

- Have you arranged to share your draft with a partner or with your writing group?
- Have you consulted the Scoring Guide and the activities to prepare for revising your draft?
- Did you use your available resources (e.g., spell check, dictionaries, Writer's Checklist) to edit for conventions and prepare your narrative for publication?

Reflection

Write an honest evaluation of your argument. Describe how you think it was effective (or not). What would you do differently next time to improve your argument?

My Notes

Technology TIP:

After writing and revising your argument, you might consider presenting it in a different medium. For example, could you use technology to transform your argument into a video? Or could you support your written argument with illustrations or charts?

Writing an Argumentative Essay

SCORING GUIDE

Scoring Criteria	Exemplary	Proficient	Emerging	Incomplete
Ideas	The essay • includes a well-developed introduction and background, a clear explanation of the issue, a claim, and a thesis statement • presents body paragraphs that strongly support the central claim with relevant details • summarizes counterclaims and clearly refutes them with relevant reasoning and evidence • concludes by summarizing the main points and providing logical suggestions for change.	The essay • includes an introduction with some background details, an explanation of the issue, a claim, and a thesis statement • presents body paragraphs that support the central claim but may not fully develop all evidence and paragraphs • summarizes and acknowledges counterclaims and offers some evidence to refute them • concludes by summarizing the main points and offering some suggestions for change.	The essay • states the thesis but does not adequately explain the problem or provide background details • includes some body paragraphs, but they are not developed and do not provide relevant evidence or details • describes some counterclaims, but they are vague and are not clearly refuted • concludes by repeating main topics rather than restating them and ends without a suggestion for change.	The essay • states a vague or unclear thesis • contains few paragraphs with ideas that are poorly developed or not developed at all • provides vague or no descriptions of counterclaims and refutations • concludes without summarizing main points or suggesting change.
Structure	The essay • follows a clear structure with a logical progression of ideas • showcases central points and uses effective transitions.	The essay • follows a clear structure with a logical progression of ideas • develops central points and uses transitions.	The essay • demonstrates an awkward progression of ideas • spends too much time on some irrelevant details and uses few transitions.	The essay • does not follow a logical organization • includes some details, but the writing lacks clear direction and uses no transitions.
Use of Language	The essay • uses a formal writing style • smoothly integrates credible source material into the text (with accurate citations) • demonstrates correct spelling and excellent command of standard English conventions.	The essay • uses a formal writing style • integrates credible source material into the text (with accurate citations) • demonstrates correct spelling and general command of standard English conventions.	The essay • mixes informal and formal writing styles • integrates some source material (citations may be missing or inaccurate) • includes some incorrect spelling and grammatical weaknesses that interfere with meaning.	The essay • uses incorrect sentence structures • does not include source material citations • includes several errors in spelling and grammatical weaknesses that interfere with meaning.

Defining Style

Visual Prompt: What kind of story might this photograph inspire?

Unit Overview

Through the ages, stories were passed from generation to generation, sometimes orally and sometimes in writing. Sometime between 1830 and 1835, Edgar Allan Poe began to write structured stories for magazines. His story structure provided the format that characterizes the short story genre today. Poe believed that a story should be short enough to be read in one sitting and that it should contain a single line of action with a limited number of characters, build to a climactic moment, and then quickly reach resolution. Poe's influence on storytelling is still felt today.

Defining Style

GOALS:

- To identify specific elements of an author's style
- To review and analyze elements of fiction and write a short story
- To analyze syntactical structure and use clauses to achieve specific effects
- To develop close reading skills
- To identify cinematic techniques and analyze their effects

ACADEMIC VOCABULARY
verify
commentary
textual commentary
textual evidence

Literary Terms
style
symbol
figurative language
literal language
tone
irony
allusions
imagery
cinematic techniques
main idea
theme
biography
autobiography
mood

Contents

Activities

Texts not included in these materials.

Previewing the Unit

My Notes

Learning Targets
- Connect prior knowledge to the genre of short story.
- Analyze the skills and knowledge needed to complete Embedded Assessment 1 successfully.

Making Connections

In this unit, you will build on your experiences reading and writing short stories. You will study elements of short stories, not only to write your own original stories, but also to understand how to analyze and write about literature. As you study poetry, short stories, and film, you will analyze the elements that make up a writer's or director's style. You will also examine the ways in which directors of visual media manipulate their audiences' reactions through the unique stylistic choices they make in creating their products.

Essential Questions

Based on your current knowledge, write your answers to these questions.

1. What makes a good story?

2. What are the elements of a style analysis?

Developing Vocabulary

Look at the list of Academic Vocabulary and Literary Terms on the Contents page. Use a QHT or other strategy to analyze and evaluate your knowledge of those words. Use your Reader/Writer Notebook to make notes about meanings you know already. Add to your notes as you study this unit and gain greater understanding of each of these words.

Unpacking Embedded Assessment 1

Read the following assignment for Embedded Assessment 1:

> Your assignment is to write an original narrative from real or imagined experiences or events. Your story must include a variety of narrative techniques—such as foreshadowing, point of view, figurative language, imagery, symbolism, and/or irony—as well as and effective details and a well-structured sequence of events.

With your class, create a graphic organizer to identify the skills and knowledge you will need to accomplish this task and plan how you will acquire them to complete the assignment. To help you complete your graphic organizer, be sure to review the criteria in the Scoring Guide on page 127.

INDEPENDENT READING LINK
The focus of this unit is on short stories. As you begin your study of the unit, choose three to four short stories to read independently. Make a plan for reading in which you decide which authors and kinds of stories you like, as well as a regular time you will set aside for reading. To get started thinking about the short story genre and the idea of style, answer the Essential Questions on this page.

Genre Study: Reviewing the Elements of a Story

Learning Targets
- Identify the elements of a short story and place them on a plot diagram.
- Make a plan for my independent reading during this unit.
- Create characters and conflicts for an original short story.

Elements of a Short Story/Narrative

A short story is a form of **narrative**. Narratives include made-up stories—fiction—as well as real-life stories—nonfiction. A short story is a work of fiction, and this genre includes certain literary elements.

Work with a partner and brainstorm in the My Notes section a list of elements of a plot. As a class, you will create a complete list of the literary terms associated with creating and analyzing the plot of any narrative.

Elements of Plot

After discussing the meanings of terms about plot, place the elements of plot that you identified in the appropriate place on the blank story diagram below.

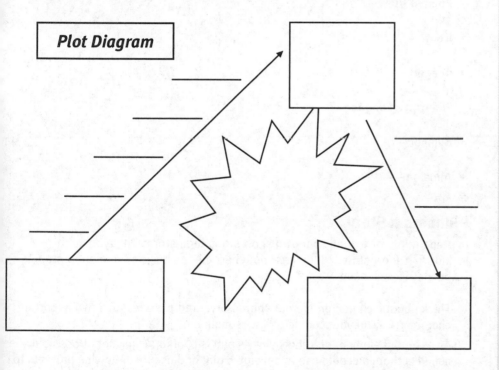

Plot Diagram

LEARNING STRATEGIES:
Graphic Organizer, Marking the Text, Rereading

My Notes

Genre Study: Reviewing the Elements of a Story

ACADEMIC VOCABULARY
To **verify** is to prove or confirm that something is true.

WORD CONNECTIONS

Roots and Affixes

The word *irony* has the Greek root *eiron*, referring to someone who, in speaking, conceals true thoughts or feelings.

My Notes

You may have brainstormed these additional elements of short stories. With your partner, discuss and then **verify** definitions using appropriate references, such as a dictionary.

Characters—

Main character or **protagonist—**

Minor characters—

Theme—

Literary elements:

- **Point of View—**

- **Irony—**

- **Imagery—**

- **Figurative Language—**

- **Symbol—**

- **Allusion—**

Planning a Story

In preparation for writing your own short story, brainstorm what you might include in a short story. Your ideas could become the basis of your short story for Embedded Assessment 1.

1. Think about a character for your short story. Create a name and two important characteristics of your character's personality.

2. An essential element of a short story's plot is conflict. Think about possible conflicts that you could use to develop a plot and use the following prompts to to think about both an internal and external conflict for your character.

    Character Name:

    Characteristic 1:

    Characteristic 2:

    External conflict: _____ versus _____

    Internal conflict: _____

Experimenting with Point of View

Learning Targets
- Identify and discuss the effect of the point of view from which a story is told.
- Choose an appropriate point of view for an original short story.

LEARNING STRATEGIES:
Close Reading, Rearranging

Comparing Points of View
Examine and discuss the differences among the following three points of view:

First Person:

Third-Person Limited:

Third-Person Omniscient:

Determine which point of view is modeled in the passages below. Then try to define the important characteristics of that point of view.

1. I ran into my ex-girlfriend Lisa. I did not want to see her again. She always wants to get back with me, and I just want to move on.

2. John was pained to see Lisa coming around the corner. He worried that she might still want to get back together.

3. John ran into Lisa at the convenience store. He mistook her good humor and friendliness as a desire to get back together with him. Lisa smiled at John, happy to tell him that she was newly engaged.

Now, use your understanding of point of view to transform each excerpt on the next page into the other two points of view. Work in pairs to discuss and transform the texts.

- After you and your partner have transformed each passage, take turns reading your rewrites to each other.
- Provide feedback to each other by studying the rewrites and answering this question: What parts of the response make it the correct point of view?

My Notes

WORD
CONNECTIONS

Roots and Affixes
The word **omniscient** has two Latin roots: *omni-*, meaning "all" or "everything," and *-sci-*, meaning "knowing" or "knowledge."

The root *omni-* also occurs in *omnivorous* and *omnipotent*.

The root *sci-* occurs in *science*, *conscious*, *conscience*, and *conscientious*.

Experimenting with Point of View

Excerpt 1

Third-Person Limited: The city skyline covered the horizon. From the balcony of her high-priced apartment that she shared with Jake, Sarah looked out and wondered if she was happy. Something seemed to be missing. Jake looked over to her, and Sarah looked away quickly, hoping that she had not given away her private thoughts.

First Person:

Third-Person Omniscient:

Excerpt 2

Third-Person Omniscient:

The robber looked over his potential prey for the evening. They all seemed like easy marks to him. *Who would it be*, he wondered. Feeling someone's eyes on her pocketbook, Jane held it closer to her body. She would not be robbed again, after that last time.

First Person:

Third-Person Limited:

Check Your Understanding

Point of view is an element of style that authors consciously choose. With another student, answer the following questions regarding point of view.

- Which point of view gives the most information about the actions and feelings of the characters? Why?
- Which is most limited? Why?
- Why would an author choose to tell a story in first person? In third-person limited? In third-person omniscient?

Writing a Short Story

Writing Prompt: Return to the conflicts and characters that you created in Activity 2.2. Write an opening to a story that presents the character, the conflict (s), and/or the setting using the point of view that you think would be best to narrate the story. Be sure to include the following:

- a central conflict that will drive the events of the story and develop the character
- an internal or external conflict for the main character
- a consistent point of view
- an introduction to the main character through description of appearance, actions and voice

Once you have written the opening, return to the plot diagram and use it to outline a plan of rising action for your story. What sequence of events could occur to move your character to the climax of the story?

My Notes

Language and Writer's Craft: Writer's Style

GRAMMAR & USAGE
Punctuation

Note the semicolon in the third sentence of Poe's opening. Poe uses a semicolon to join two *independent clauses*. A *semicolon* may also be used to join elements of a series when items in the series already have commas.

My Notes

_____
_____
_____
_____
_____
_____
_____
_____
_____
_____
_____
_____
_____
_____
_____
_____
_____
_____
_____
_____
_____
_____
_____
_____
_____
_____
_____
_____
_____
_____

Learning Targets
- Make inferences about the effect a writer achieves by using specific sentence types and patterns.
- Emulate an author's style by writing a story opener in that style.

Writer's Style

As you remember from Unit 1, a writer's style or voice is created by elements such as *diction, syntax,* and *imagery,* as well as *point of view.* Review these elements to be sure you understand and can define them.

Certain stories grab the reader's attention and never let go until the story ends. Read the opening paragraph from "The Gift of the Magi" by O. Henry from this unit.

- Circle the **images** that stand out in the passage.
- Underline the **sentence fragments,** and annotate the text to describe what effect the author creates with these fragments.

"One dollar and eighty-seven cents. That was all. And sixty cents of it was in pennies.

Pennies saved one and two at a time by bulldozing the grocer and the vegetable man and the butcher until one's cheeks burned with the silent imputation of parsimony that such close dealing implied. Three times Della counted it. One dollar and eighty-seven cents. And the next day would be Christmas."

In contrast, examine the opening of the short story, "The Cask of Amontillado," which you will be reading soon. After reading this passage, think about the effect of the **diction,** the **syntax,** and the **point of view.** What impression of the narrator does Edgar Allan Poe create?

"The thousand injuries of Fortunato I had borne as I best could, but when he ventured upon insult, I vowed revenge. You, who so well know the nature of my soul, will not suppose, however, that I gave utterance to a threat. At length I would be avenged; this was a point definitively settled—but the very definitiveness with which it was resolved precluded the idea of risk."

Notice how the syntax affects the pacing of the action. Which story seems to set a faster pace or seems to set the action of the story in motion more quickly?

Poe uses long compound and complex sentences, while O. Henry uses sentence fragments for effect. A **sentence fragment** is a group of words that is grammatically incomplete and cannot stand alone. Writers change their sentence structure—their use of phrases, clauses, and different types of sentences—to create certain effects.

Emulating a Writer's Style

Every writer has a unique **style**. You will develop your own style as you develop your writing skills. One way to begin experimenting with style is to emulate another writer. To **emulate** a writer is to imitate the writer's style, including how he or she constructs sentences. For example, here is an emulation of Edgar Allan Poe's opening paragraph from the preceding page.

> The deliberate rudeness of Lydia I had suffered silently, but when her actions bordered on bullying, I promised myself payback. You, who know my cautious, careful manner, do not think, however, that I indicated anything about my plans to Lydia. Eventually, I would get revenge, this I knew—but I would do so without any risk of blame.

Writing Prompt: Choose one of the short story opening paragraphs in this activity and emulate that writer's style to write an original story opening. Be sure to do the following:

- Emulate the style of the author you chose.
- Introduce a character, a setting, and/or a conflict in the opening.
- Vary your sentence types to create an effect (or to affect the pacing of the narrative).

Check Your Understanding

After you have completed your emulation of a story opening, reflect on your opening by asking and answering these questions:

a. What effect did I intend to create?

b. How do the sentences of my story opening achieve that effect?

c. Does the story opening represent the style of the writer I am trying to emulate?

Remember that a story's beginning, the exposition, has several purposes:
- To describe the setting
- To introduce the characters and/or narrator telling the story
- To introduce the conflict in the story and set the plot in motion

Revise your story opening based on your reflection, and expand your opening to include more elements of story exposition. You may want to begin outlining the rising action. What events might come next in the story? Do your revision and expansion of the original emulation change the style?

Next, share your revised story opening with a partner or small group. Does your story opening include effective elements of exposition and a variety of sentences types?

Literary Terms
Style refers to the distinctive way a writer uses language, characterized by elements of diction, syntax, imagery, organization, and so on.

INDEPENDENT READING LINK
As you read the short stories you have chosen, make notes about the writer's style for each story, based on what you have learned about authors' styles thus far. Examine the story opening for ideas about writing your own story.

My Notes

_____
_____
_____
_____
_____
_____
_____
_____
_____
_____
_____
_____
_____
_____
_____
_____
_____
_____
_____

The Meaning of Imagery and Symbols

LEARNING STRATEGIES:
Close Reading, Marking the Text, Diffusing, Summarizing, Oral Reading, Quickwrite, Peer Editing

Literary Terms

A **symbol** is anything (any object, animal, event, person, or place) that represents itself but also stands for something else on a figurative level.

Literary Terms

Figurative language refers to the use of words to describe one thing in terms of another. In contrast to figurative language, **literal language** uses the exact meanings, or *denotations*, of words. For example, "ice" and "fire" have specific literal meanings, but Frost also uses these words figuratively, or *connotatively*.

My Notes

_____

_____

_____

_____

_____

_____

_____

_____

_____

_____

_____

_____

_____

_____

Learning Targets

- Identify the imagery and symbols that writers use as a way to infer a writer's purpose and interpret meaning.
- Write an interpretive statement about meaning in a text by analyzing and synthesizing information.

Before Reading

In your review of literary elements in Activity 2.2, you discussed imagery and **symbol**. Think about those words as you answer these questions.

1. When you see the words "fire" and "ice," what *literal images* come to mind? Brainstorm with your class a list of the ideas, objects, or events that you associate with these two words.

2. Now, with a partner, make meaning of the common *figurative associations* as presented in the sentences below:
   - "Her icy stare let me know just how she felt."
   - "He acted so cold to me that I knew he was still angry."
   - "His face was red and flushed with the heat of his anger."
   - "The fierce fire in her eyes made her attitude clear."

When images are used figuratively rather than literally, they are being used symbolically, that is, the image represents itself but also stands for something more abstract. What do the images of fire and ice represent or symbolize in the sentences above?

During Reading

3. Writers may use symbols to help readers recognize a theme. Now that you have discussed the literal associations and figurative associations of the words *fire* and *ice*, consider the title of the poem "Fire and Ice." Think of the literal and figurative associations of these words, and predict what the poem will be about.

4. First, read the poem silently. Pay close attention to the punctuation marks that signal ends of sentences.

5. With a partner, take turns reading the poem aloud to each other. Read the poem so that you stop only at the end of each sentence, not each line.

6. As your partner reads the poem to you, circle the words associated with the two major images.

ABOUT THE AUTHOR
Robert Frost (1874–1963) was one of America's most popular twentieth-century poets. For much of his life, he lived on a farm in New Hampshire and wrote poems about farm life and the New England landscape. His apparently simple poems, however, have many layers of meaning.

Fire and Ice

by Robert Frost

Some say the world will end in fire,
Some say in ice.
From what I've tasted of desire
I hold with those who favor fire.

But if it had to perish twice,
I think I know enough of hate
To know that for destruction ice
Is also great
And would suffice.

My Notes

KEY IDEAS AND DETAILS
In Line 3, the speaker says "I've tasted of desire." Is this statement **literal** or **figurative**? Why?

After Reading

7. Using the words and phrases that you circled, discuss and analyze the purpose of the imagery and symbols in the poem with your partner. Annotate the text in the My Notes space.

Check Your Understanding

Learning to write an interpretive statement is an important step toward learning how to communicate your understandings. As you analyze and synthesize information, you must learn how to put the ideas of text into your own words. In one sentence, state what the poem is about by answering this question: What is Robert Frost saying about human emotions in "Fire and Ice"? You might use this sentence frame to guide your writing:

In _____, _____ suggests that _____

    (title of text)   *(author)*   *(purpose/meaning/main idea)*

WORD CONNECTIONS

Multiple Meanings

Many words have multiple meanings, and alert readers must determine a word's meaning by its context. Several meanings of "hold" as a verb include "to have or keep," "to support," "to detain," "to agree," "to resist."

Which definition best matches Frost's use of "hold" in the context of Line 4, "I hold with those who favor fire"?

Shared Gifts: Introducing Irony

Literary Terms

Tone is a writer's (or speaker's) attitude toward a subject, character, or audience. Tone can be serious, humorous, sarcastic, indignant, objective, etc. **Irony** occurs when something turns out to be quite different from what is expected.

My Notes

_____

_____

_____

_____

_____

_____

_____

_____

_____

Literary Terms

Allusions are references that writers make to a well-known person, event, or place from history, music, art, or another literary work. Writers make these references to draw comparisons, create imagery, establish humor, or reinforce emotions. The three main categories of allusions are biblical, mythological, and historical/topical.

Learning Targets

- Explain how images signify the literal and symbolic importance of objects to the development of characters.
- Explain how situational irony contributes to the theme of "The Gift of the Magi."

Before Reading

1. Review all you know about the elements of short stories, including point of view, character, theme, imagery, and symbolism. You should already be familiar with these terms. In addition, think about what you know about the following terms:

   - **Tone:** A writer's diction and imagery help create the tone. Irony is one common literary tone. To be able to recognize an author's tone, especially if the author is using an ironic tone, is a key factor in understanding an author's purpose or meaning. If you miss the irony, you miss the meaning.

   - **Irony:** This occurs when what is expected turns out to be quite different from what actually happens; one common form of irony is called *situational irony*. Writers use situational irony as a way to contradict the expectations of the characters or the reader.

Introducing the Strategy: Diffusing

To diffuse a text means to read a passage, note unfamiliar words, and then use context clues, dictionaries, or other resources to discover meaning for the unfamiliar words.

During Reading

2. Read the first four paragraphs of the story, and highlight any words you do not know. Try to figure out the meaning by using the context or by checking reference works. Write synonyms above the words you have highlighted. Notice that definitions for some words are footnoted for you. Practice diffusing by writing the definition or a synonym above the highlighted word.

3. Words you do not know might be references to people, places, or events in the Bible, mythology, or history. These **allusions** might be important to understanding the story. Highlight words that you think are allusions to the Bible or to historical people, places, or events. Be prepared to discuss the significance of these allusions to the meaning of the story.

4. As you read "The Gift of the Magi," you will see guided reading questions labeled **Key Ideas and Details**. As you read each chunk of the story, use the My Notes space to respond to the questions and cite textual details to support your answers.

To determine theme, you must consider how all elements work together within a story and what ideas about life these elements present. Also, keep these points in mind when writing the theme of a story:

A THEME IS NOT:

- A "topic" (such as love or sacrifice)
- A summary, such as "Two people sell their valuables to show their love for each other."
- A moral; e.g., "If you love someone, you will do anything for him or her."

A THEME IS:

- A general statement about life; e.g., "People show their love for each other by making sacrifices."

Based on these examples, why is the sentence above an appropriate general statement about, or theme of, "The Gift of the Magi"?

Check Your Understanding

O. Henry develops the theme in "The Gift of the Magi" by creating an ironic situation. Remember that writers use situational irony as a way to contradict the expectations of the characters or the reader. Think about the **situational irony** in this story:

- What unexpected events and results surround the watch chain and the combs?
- When Jim and Della realize what each has done for the other, how do they react?
- Why does O. Henry allude to the Youngs as "magi"?

Write a thematic statement that shows how irony is used to reinforce the theme of the story.

Writing Prompt: Review the short story to find the spot in the story where Della gets her hair cut at Madame Sofronie's. Use this "unseen scene" as an inspiration to write your own scene in which you imagine what the two characters might be doing and saying as the haircutting progresses. Or you may want to imagine the scene in which Jim sells his watch to buy the combs for Della. Be sure to:

- Use description and details to create a setting and situation.
- Set up the conflict, introduce characters and their perspectives for the reader.
- Create dialogue that creates a vivid picture of the characters and conflict.

My Notes

INDEPENDENT READING LINK
Demonstrate your understanding of a short story you have read independently by applying the SIFT strategy.

Close Reading of a Short Story

LEARNING STRATEGIES:
Rereading, Diffusing, Close
Reading, Marking the Text,
Visualizing, Drafting, Discussion
Groups

My Notes

Learning Targets

- Analyze the stylistic elements of foreshadowing, point of view, and imagery to interpret author's purpose.
- Apply the stylistic use of foreshadowing, point of view, and imagery in my own writing.

Before Reading

1. One technique that writers use to create suspense and anticipate the events of the story is **foreshadowing**. Writers use foreshadowing to give hints to the reader. As readers pay close attention to details and make connections to events and characters, they develop the ability to recognize these hints and how they create a sense of tension in the story. Sometimes, though, these hints are easy to spot only after reading the complete narrative and then rereading it.

   Describe your understanding of foreshadowing, and give one or two examples from texts you have read.

Introducing the Strategy: Questioning the Text

Another complex skill that successful readers practice is asking questions about the text. Readers can actively involve themselves with the text by asking three levels of questions:

- **Level 1, Literal**—Literal questions can be answered by referring back to the text or consulting references.

  EXAMPLE: *What is "Coney Island"?*

- **Level 2, Interpretive**—Interpretive questions call for inferences; answers cannot be found directly in the text; however textual evidence points to and supports your answers.

  EXAMPLE: *Why does the narrator call this young couple "the wisest"?*

- **Level 3, Universal**—Universal questions go beyond the text. What are the larger issues or ideas raised by the text?

  EXAMPLE: *Why are some people motivated to make sacrifices for others?*

ACADEMIC VOCABULARY
Textual evidence consists
of details, quotations, and
examples from a text that
support the analysis or argument
presented. It is the information
that supports or proves an
interpretation or claim.

During Reading

2. As you read the short story "The Stolen Party," which starts on the next page, think about how your expectations for an event may not be the same as what actually happens.

3. As you read each chunk of "The Stolen Party," use the My Notes space (1) to identify the level of each question and (2) to respond to the questions and cite **textual evidence**, or details, to support your answers.

ABOUT THE AUTHOR
Liliana Heker (b. 1943) is an Argentine journalist who also writes fiction. She has received a number of literary prizes in her country. In "The Stolen Party," Heker presents the events of a party through the eyes of a child.

Short Story

The Stolen Party

by Liliana Heker

Translated by Alberto Manguel

Chunk 1

As soon as she arrived she went straight to the kitchen to see if the monkey was there. It was: what a relief! She wouldn't have liked to admit that her mother had been right. Monkeys at a birthday? her mother had sneered. Get away with you, believing any nonsense you're told! She was cross, but not because of the monkey, the girl thought; it's just because of the party.

"I don't like you going," she told her. "It's a rich people's party."

"Rich people go to Heaven too," said the girl, who studied religion at school.

"Get away with Heaven,' said the mother.

The girl didn't approve of the way her mother spoke. She was barely nine, and one of the best in her class.

"I'm going because I've been invited," she said. "And I've been invited because Luciana is my friend. So there."

"Ah yes, your friend," her mother grumbled. She paused. "Listen, Rosaura,"[2] she said at last. "That one's not your friend. You know what you are to them? The maid's daughter, that's what."

Rosaura blinked hard: she wasn't going to cry. Then she yelled: "Shut up! You know nothing about being friends!"

Every afternoon she used to go to Luciana's house and they would both finish their homework while Rosaura's mother did the cleaning. They had their tea in the kitchen and they told each other secrets. Rosaura loved everything in the big house, and she also loved the people who lived there.

"I'm going because it will be the most lovely party in the whole world, Luciana told me it would. There will be a magician, and he will bring a monkey and everything."

The mother swung around to take a good look at her child, and pompously[3] put her hands on her hips.

---

[1] **Luciana** (Lū syə´nə)
[2] **Rosaura** (Rō sah´rə)
[3] **pompously** (pom'pəs lē) in a self-important way

KEY IDEAS AND DETAILS
What is the name of the main character?
What do you know about her?

GRAMMAR &USAGE
Reciprocal Pronouns
Heker uses the reciprocal pronoun *each other* in this sentence: "They had their tea in the kitchen and they told *each other* secrets." Use *each other* to describe interactions between two people and *one another* for three or more.

Close Reading of a Short Story

KEY IDEAS AND DETAILS
After reading Chunk 1, explain why Rosaura's mother seems so negative about her attending the birthday party. What textual details point to an answer?

KEY IDEAS AND DETAILS
How is it that Rosaura feels special at Luciana's birthday party?

KEY IDEAS AND DETAILS
After reading Chunks 1 and 2, can you identify the **point of view** of this story? Give specific details that help you define the point of view. In My Notes, write a brief explanation that defines the point of view of this story.

KEY IDEAS AND DETAILS
What is the attitude of the girl with the bow toward Rosaura?

My Notes

_____
_____
_____
_____
_____
_____
_____
_____
_____
_____
_____
_____
_____
_____
_____
_____
_____

Monkeys at a birthday? her mother had sneered. *Get away with you, believing any nonsense you're told!*

Rosaura was deeply offended. She thought it unfair of her mother to accuse other people of being liars simply because they were rich. Rosaura too wanted to be rich, of course. If one day she managed to live in a beautiful palace, would her mother stop loving her? She felt very sad. She wanted to go to that party more than anything else in the world.

"I'll die if I don't go," she whispered, almost without moving her lips.

Chunk 2
And she wasn't sure whether she had been heard, but on the morning of the party she discovered that her mother had starched her Christmas dress. And in the afternoon, after washing her hair, her mother rinsed it in apple vinegar so that it would be all nice and shiny. Before going out, Rosaura admired herself in the mirror, with her white dress and glossy hair, and thought she looked terribly pretty.

Senora Ines[4] also seemed to notice. As soon as she saw her, she said: "How lovely you look today, Rosaura."

Rosaura gave her starched skirt a light toss with her hands and walked into the party with a firm step. She said hello to Luciana and asked about the monkey. Luciana put on a secretive look and whispered into Rosaura's ear: "He's in the kitchen. But don't tell anyone, because it's a surprise."

Rosaura wanted to make sure. Carefully she entered the kitchen and there she saw it deep in thought, inside its cage. It looked so funny that the girl stood there for a while, watching it, and later, every so often, she would slip out of the party unseen and go and admire it. Rosaura was the only one allowed into the kitchen. Senora Ines had said: "You yes, but not the others, they're much too boisterous, they might break something." Rosaura had never broken anything. She even managed the jug of orange juice, carrying it from the kitchen into the dining room. She held it carefully and didn't spill a single drop. And Senora Ines had said: "Are you sure you can manage a jug as big as that?" Of course she could manage. She wasn't a butterfingers, like the others. Like that blonde girl with the bow in her hair. As soon as she saw Rosaura, the girl with the bow had said:

Chunk 3
"And you? Who are you?"

"I'm a friend of Luciana," said Rosaura.

"No," said the girl with the bow, "you are not a friend of Luciana because I'm her cousin and I know all her friends. And I don't know you."

"So what," said Rosaura. "I come here every afternoon with my mother and we do our homework together."

"You and your mother do your homework together?" asked the girl, laughing.

---

[4] **Señora Ines** (se nyōr'ā ē nes´)

"I and Luciana do our homework together," said Rosaura, very seriously.

The girl with the bow shrugged her shoulders.

"That's not being friends," she said. "Do you go to school together?"

"No."

"So where do you know her from?" said the girl, getting impatient.

Rosaura remembered her mother's words perfectly. She took a deep breath.

"I'm the daughter of the employee," she said.

Her mother had said very clearly: "If someone asks, you say you're the daughter of the employee; that's all." She also told her to add "And proud of it." But Rosaura thought that never in her life would she dare say something of the sort.

"What employee?" said the girl with the bow. "Employee in a shop?"

"No," said Rosaura angrily. "My mother doesn't sell anything in any shop, so there."

"So how come she's an employee?" said the girl with the bow.

Just then Señora Ines arrived saying shh shh, and asked Rosaura if she wouldn't mind helping serve out the hot dogs, as she knew the house so much better than the others.

"See?" said Rosaura to the girl with the bow, and when no one was looking she kicked her in the shin.

Chunk 4

Apart from the girl with the bow, all the others were delightful. The one she liked best was Luciana, with her golden birthday crown; and then the boys. Rosaura won the sack race, and nobody managed to catch her when they played tag. When they split into two teams to play charades, all the boys wanted her for their side. Rosaura felt she had never been so happy in all her life.

But the best was still to come. The best came after Luciana blew out the candles. First the cake. Señora Ines had asked her to help pass the cake around, and Rosaura had enjoyed the task immensely, because everyone called out to her, shouting "Me, me!" Rosaura remembered a story in which there was a queen who had the power of life or death over her subjects. She had always loved that, having the power of life or death. To Luciana and the boys she gave the largest pieces, and to the girl with the bow she gave a slice so thin one could see through it.

After the cake came the magician, tall and bony, with a fine red cape. A true magician: he could untie handkerchiefs by blowing on them and make a chain with links that had no openings. He could guess what cards were pulled out from a pack, and the monkey was his assistant. He called the monkey "partner."

"Let's see here, partner," he would say, "Turn over a card." And, "Don't run away, partner: time to work now."

The final trick was wonderful. One of the children had to hold the monkey in his arms and the magician said he would make him disappear.

"What, the boy?" they all shouted.

GRAMMAR & USAGE
Punctuating Dialogue
Note that punctuation such as periods, question marks, and commas are incorporated within quotation marks when writing dialogue.

KEY IDEAS AND DETAILS
Rosaura is delighted and proud to serve the orange juice, the hot dogs, and the cake. How do these actions establish Senora Ines's attitude toward Rosaura, and how might they foreshadow events to come?

My Notes

KEY IDEAS AND DETAILS
So far, what is the effect of the point of view the author has chosen for this story? How is this point of view limited?

GRAMMAR & USAGE
Clauses

Independent and **subordinate clauses** can be combined in a variety of ways with coordinating and subordinating conjunctions to form **compound** and **complex** sentences that express relationships among ideas.

Example: Rosaura won the sack race [**independent clause**], and [**coordinating conjunction**] nobody managed to catch her [**independent clause**] when [**subordinating conjunction**] they played tag [**subordinate clause**].

This sentence, with two independent clauses and one dependent clause, is a **compound-complex** sentence.

KEY IDEAS AND DETAILS
What does Rosaura expect at the end of the party? Why does she expect this? How is this an example of situational irony?

My Notes

_____

_____

_____

_____

_____

_____

_____

_____

_____

"No, the monkey!" shouted the magician.

Rosaura thought that this was truly the most amusing party in the whole world.

The magician asked a small fat boy to come and help, but the small fat boy got frightened almost at once and dropped the monkey on the floor. The magician picked him up carefully, whispered something in his ear, and the monkey nodded almost as if he understood.

"You mustn't be so unmanly, my friend," the magician said to the fat boy.

"What's unmanly?" said the fat boy.

The magician turned around as if to look for spies.

"A sissy," said the magician. "Go sit down."

Then he stared at all the faces, one by one. Rosaura felt her heart tremble.

"You, with the Spanish eyes," said the magician. And everyone saw that he was pointing at her.

She wasn't afraid. Neither holding the monkey, nor when the magician made him vanish; not even when, at the end the magician flung his red cape over Rosaura's head and uttered a few magic words …and the monkey reappeared, chattering happily, in her arms. The children clapped furiously. And before Rosaura returned to her seat, the magician said:

"Thank you very much, my little countess."

She was so pleased with the compliment that a while later, when her mother came to fetch her, that was the first thing she told her.

Chunk 5
"I helped the magician and he said to me, 'Thank you very much, my little countess.'"

It was strange because up to then Rosaura had thought that she was angry with her mother. All along Rosaura had imagined that she would say to her: "See that the monkey wasn't a lie?" But instead she was so thrilled that she told her mother all about the wonderful magician.

Her mother tapped her on the head and said: "So now we're a countess!"

But one could see that she was beaming.

And now they both stood in the entrance, because a moment ago Señora Ines, smiling, had said: "Please wait here a second."

Her mother suddenly seemed worried.

"What is it?" she asked Rosaura.

"What is what?" said Rosaura. "It's nothing; she just wants to get the presents for those who are leaving, see?"

She pointed at the fat boy and at a girl with pigtails who were also waiting there, next to their mothers. And she explained about the presents. She knew, because she had been watching those who left before her. When one of the girls was about to leave, Señora Ines would give her a bracelet. When a boy left, Señora Ines gave him a yo-yo.

Rosaura preferred the yo-yo because it sparkled, but she didn't mention that to her mother. Her mother might have said: "So why don't you ask for one, you blockhead?" That's what her mother was like. Rosaura didn't feel like explaining that she'd be horribly ashamed to be the odd one out. Instead she said:

"I was the best-behaved at the party."

And she said no more because Señora Ines came out into the hall with two bags, one pink and one blue.

First she went up to the fat boy, gave him a yo-yo out of the blue bag, and the fat boy left with his mother. Then she went up to the girl and gave her a bracelet out of the pink bag, and the girl with the pigtails left as well.

Finally she came up to Rosaura and her mother. She had a big smile on her face and Rosaura liked that. Señora Ines looked down at her, then looked up at her mother, and then said something that made Rosaura proud:

"What a marvelous daughter you have, Herminia."[5]

Chunk 6

For an instant, Rosaura thought that she'd give her two presents: the bracelet and the yo-yo. Señora Ines bent down as if about to look for something. Rosaura also leaned forward, stretching out her arm. But she never completed the movement.

Señora Ines didn't look in the pink bag. Nor did she look in the blue bag. Instead she rummaged[6] in her purse. In her hand appeared two bills.

"You really and truly earned this," she said handing them over. "Thank you for all your help, my pet."

Rosaura felt her arms stiffen, stick close to her body, and then she noticed her mother's hand on her shoulder. Instinctively she pressed herself against her mother's body. That was all. Except her eyes. Rosaura's eyes had a cold, clear look that fixed itself on Señora Ines's face.

Señora Ines, motionless, stood there with her hand outstretched. As if she didn't dare draw it back. As if the slightest change might shatter an infinitely[7] delicate balance.

[5] **Herminia** (er mē nyā')
[6] **rummaged** (rum'ijd) searched thoroughly by moving things about
[7] **infinitely** (in'fə nit lē) endlessly

My Notes

_____

_____

_____

_____

_____

_____

_____

KEY IDEAS AND DETAILS
Looking back at the events of the story, what incidents foreshadow Senora's Ines's final action?

_____

_____

_____

_____

_____

_____

_____

_____

KEY IDEAS AND DETAILS
Think about the tone of this story. How is the ironic tone similar to the tone of "The Gift of the Magi"? How is it different?

_____

_____

_____

_____

_____

_____

Close Reading of a Short Story

After Reading

4. Before proceeding, review your responses to the "Key Ideas and Details" questions within your group. Compare your labeling of the level of each question. Notice that these questions get at the meaning of the story.

5. Like the **images** of the combs and watch in "The Gift of the Magi," this story has a central image that may be used symbolically. Identify the image that is introduced at the beginning, appears in the middle, and ends the story.

6. Respond to this interpretive question: How can this image be interpreted as symbolic?

Literary Terms

Imagery is the descriptive or figurative language used to create **images** or pictures in a reader's mind.

Check Your Understanding

After you have studied the plot, point of view, imagery, and symbols in "The Stolen Party," write a theme statement for this story. After each group member reads his or her theme statement to the group, give feedback to each group member by considering these points:

- Is the theme statement a complete statement?
- Does the statement avoid merely summarizing the story?
- Does the statement avoid making a moral out of the story?

Quickwrite: Now that you have read two short stories, think about the essential question "What makes a good story?" Write a brief definition of "a good story." Pair with a partner and share your definitions.

Language and Writer's Craft: Sentence Types

In this story, the author varies sentence structure to create specific effects. Dialogue consists primarily of simple sentences, and the narration in the last two paragraphs makes use of sentence fragments. Reread this sentence from Chunk 4 of "The Stolen Party."

To Luciana and the boys she gave the largest pieces, and to the girl with the bow she gave a slice so thin one could see through it.

This sentence is **compound-complex** because it has two **independent clauses** and a **dependent clause**. Write each clause below.

Study the **syntax** of the sentence. Beginning the sentence with "*To Luciana and the boys . . .* " is unusual. Consider the effect of this syntax. Rewrite the sentence beginning with "She gave . . . " How does the revision change the effect of the sentence?

Writing Prompt: Reread the final paragraphs of "The Stolen Party," when Señora Ines tries to hand Rosaura money instead of a gift like all the other children. This is a powerful moment as all three characters appear to be frozen in time and space. Think about how point of view has created the surprise and disappointment in both the reader and the main character.

Using the story starter that follows, write a continuation of the narrative that shows Rosaura's realizations, starting with Senora Ines's final words. Use dialogue, point of view, and imagery, as well as deliberate sentence structure, to emulate the author's style. You may want to devise an alternative resolution. Be sure to:

- Use dialogue to convey the experiences and attitudes of the characters.
- Provide a conclusion (resolution) that follows from the events of the story.
- Include precise language, details, and imagery to engage the reader.
- Maintain the limited point of view to show Rosaura's new perspective.

Rosaura glanced at the caged monkey as she and her mother turned from Señora Ines and walked out of the room. She gripped her money and, turning to her mother, said, "_____ . . . "

My Notes

INDEPENDENT READING LINK
Using a short story you have read independently, think about a scene that is not in the story (an "unseen scene"). Plot the events for this scene by outlining the sequence of events with a plot diagram, a list of events, or a visualization of the events in a storyboard. Also think about how you will establish point of view.

Introducing a Story of Revenge

LEARNING STRATEGIES:
Drafting, Graphic Organizer,
Sharing and Responding

Learning Targets
• Interpret meaning by identifying how writers use imagery to create style.
• Identify and cite textual evidence to support understanding of meaning.

Interpreting Meaning
1. Read and interpret the following quotations by writing the meaning of each in your own words.

Quotation	Interpretation of Quotation	Agree/ Disagree	Reason for Agreement/or Disagreement
"An eye for an eye only ends up making the whole world blind." —Mahatma Gandhi			
"Don't get mad, get even." —Robert F. Kennedy			
"She got even in a way that was almost cruel. She forgave them." —Ralph McGill (about Eleanor Roosevelt)			
"Success is the sweetest revenge." —Vanessa Williams			
"Revenge is often like biting a dog because the dog bit you." —Austin O'Malley			

Check Your Understanding
After reading and interpreting the quotations about revenge, note which have striking imagery, and consider how the imagery helps you understand the meaning of the quote. Next, choose your favorite quote from above and explain how you might use it as the basis for the conflict of a story between two characters.

In the next activity, you will read "The Cask of Amontillado," which takes place in an unnamed Italian city. As you will see when you read the informational text that follows, Poe had a specific reason to set his story in Italy at Carnival time.

Practice with Diffusing Unfamiliar Vocabulary

In the informational text that follows, notice how context provides clues to the meaning of unfamiliar words. Circle all the words in italics; then diffuse the meaning by underlining the words and phrases that suggest meanings. Use a dictionary to find the meanings of any words you do not know after diffusing the text.

Informational Text

Catacombs and Carnival

Centuries ago, in Italy, the early Christians buried their dead in *catacombs*, which are long, winding underground tunnels. Later, wealthy families built private catacombs beneath their *palazzos*, or palatial homes. *Nitre*, a crystalized salt growth, lined the dark, cool underground chambers, or *vaults*. In order to find their way in their underground tunnels, the owners would light torches or *flambeaux*.

These *crypts* were suitable not only for burial but also for storage of fine vintage wines such as *Amontillado, DeGrave,* and *Medoc.* A wine expert, or *connoisseur,* would store wine carefully in these underground vaults. Wine was stored in casks or *puncheons,* which held 72 to 100 gallons, or in *pipes,* which contained 126 gallons (also known as two hogsheads).

Edgar Allan Poe's story "The Cask of Amontillado" takes place in the catacombs during *Carnival,* a celebration that still takes place in many countries. The day before Ash Wednesday is celebrated as a holiday with carnivals, masquerade balls, and parades of costumed merrymakers. During Carnival, people celebrate by disguising themselves as fools, wearing *parti-striped dress or motley,* and capes, known as *roquelaires.* Women would celebrate wearing *conical caps.* Carnival is also called Mardi Gras, or Fat Tuesday, because of the feasting that takes place the day before Ash Wednesday. Starting on Ash Wednesday, which is the beginning of Lent, some Christians fast and do penance for their sins.

Check Your Understanding

Based on the information in this text, predict three elements that will probably be part of the setting of "The Cask of Amontillado."

Writing Prompt: Imagine that you are setting a story in a catacomb. Write a story starter describing the setting and introduce a character. Be sure to:

* Use figurative language and imagery to create a mood of suspense, fear, or terror.
* Use sentence structures effectively to create the mood you want.
* Use specific details to describe the setting and the character.

My Notes

KEY IDEAS AND DETAILS
Why might casks and catacombs exist in the same underground vault?

WORD CONNECTIONS

Foreign Words

Mardi Gras is a French term meaning "fat Tuesday." Mardi Gras is celebrated in many countries, including the United States, and it is a day of fun and eating before fasting for Lent.

Irony in the Vaults

My Notes

Learning Targets

- Identify how irony is conveyed through the words, actions, and situations in a story.
- Acquire an understanding of challenging vocabulary by diffusing unknown words.
- Demonstrate effective syntax by using parallel structure in writing.

Before Reading

1. Think about the **situational irony** in the two short stories by O. Henry and Heker. This situational irony leads to an understanding of the theme or major idea of each story. What was ironic about the situation in each of the stories?

2. You have seen how writers such as O. Henry and Heker use situational irony. Writers also use other types of irony to create an effect. Predict why they might use these types of irony.

   - Writers use **verbal irony** by having a speaker or narrator say one thing while meaning another.
   - Writers use **dramatic irony** when the reader knows more about what is to happen than the main characters know.

During Reading

3. As you read "The Cask of Amontillado," highlight areas of the text where Poe uses irony. Also, use the My Notes space to respond to the questions in "Key Ideas and Details."

ABOUT THE AUTHOR

Born in Boston, Edgar Allan Poe (1809–1849) was orphaned as a young child and taken in by the Allan family of Richmond, Virginia. Poe and the Allans eventually had a falling out because of Poe's irresponsible behavior. This situation was characteristic of Poe's short and tragic life. Despite his personal difficulties and an unstable temperament, Poe was a literary genius, writing short stories, poetry, and literary criticism, for which he became internationally famous. His dark imagination produced stories that are known for their atmosphere of horror.

Short Story

The Cask of Amontillado

by Edgar Allan Poe

WORD CONNECTIONS

Roots and Affixes

The word *impunity* has a Latin root (from *poena*) that means "penalty" or "punishment." The prefix *in-* (spelled *im-* here) means "not." To do something with impunity is to do it without fear of punishment or consequences.

1 The thousand injuries of Fortunato I had borne as I best could, but when he ventured upon insult, I vowed revenge. You, who so well know the nature of my soul, will not suppose, however, that I gave utterance to a *threat*. At *length* I would be avenged; this was a point definitively settled—but the very definitiveness with which it was resolved precluded the idea of risk. I must not only punish, but punish with impunity.[1] A wrong is unredressed[2] when retribution[3] overtakes its redresser. It is equally unredressed when the avenger fails to make himself felt as such to him who has done the wrong.

It must be understood that neither by word nor deed had I given Fortunato cause to doubt my good will. I continued as was my wont, to smile in his face, and he did not perceive that my smile *now* was at the thought of his immolation.[4]

He had a weak point—this Fortunato—although in other regards he was a man to be respected and even feared. He prided himself on his connoisseurship in wine. Few Italians have the true virtuoso spirit. For the most part their enthusiasm is adopted to suit the time and opportunity to practice imposture upon the British and Austrian millionaires. In painting and gemmary, Fortunato, like his countrymen, was a quack, but in the matter of old wines he was sincere. In this respect I did not differ from him materially; I was skillful in the Italian vintages myself, and bought largely whenever I could.

Chunk 1

It was about dusk, one evening during the supreme madness of the carnival season, that I encountered my friend. He accosted me with excessive warmth, for he had been drinking much. The man wore motley. He had on a tight-fitting parti-striped dress and his head was surmounted by the conical cap and bells. I was so pleased to see him that I thought I should never have done wringing his hand.

5 I said to him, "My dear Fortunato, you are luckily met. How remarkably well you are looking today! But I have received a pipe of what passes for Amontillado, and I have my doubts."

"How?" said he, "Amontillado? A pipe? Impossible! And in the middle of the carnival?"

"I have my doubts," I replied; "and I was silly enough to pay the full Amontillado price without consulting you in the matter. You were not to be found, and I was fearful of losing a bargain."

KEY IDEAS AND DETAILS

In Activity 2.8, you paraphrased or interpreted quotations about revenge. What is the narrator's opinion of revenge stated in the last two sentences of Paragraph 1? What does his explanation reveal about his character?

KEY IDEAS AND DETAILS

From the beginning, the narrator lets us, the readers, know he has plans. Based on the title and the first three paragraphs, predict what the narrator plans to do.

My Notes

---

[1] **impunity:** without consequences
[2] **unredressed:** not corrected or set right
[3] **retribution:** punishment, revenge
[4] **immolation:** destroying or killing, often by fire

Irony in the Vaults

WORD CONNECTIONS

Multiple Meaning Words
The word *match* has several meanings. Among its meanings are a sports competition, a device to light a fire, and compatibility or similarity. Use context clues to decide its meaning in this sentence: "And yet some fools will have it that his taste is a match for your own."

KEY IDEAS AND DETAILS
The narrator's ironic point of view is clear from his comment about his "attendants" or servants. How is the situation he speaks of ironic?

KEY IDEAS AND DETAILS
For Chunk 2, write two Level 1 and Level 2 questions for which you may not know the answer but think the answer may be important to understanding the story. Turn to a partner, share your questions, and answer each other's questions.

My Notes

"Amontillado!"

"I have my doubts."

10 "Amontillado!"

"And I must satisfy them."

"Amontillado!"

"As you are engaged, I am on my way to Luchesi. If anyone has a critical turn, it is he. He will tell me— "

"Luchesi cannot tell Amontillado from sherry."

15 "And yet some fools will have it that his taste is a match for your own."

"Come, let us go."

"Whither?"

"To your vaults."

"My friend, no; I will not impose upon your good nature. I perceive you have an engagement. Luchesi— "

20 "I have no engagement; come."

"My friend, no. It is not the engagement, but the severe cold with which I perceive you are afflicted. The vaults are insufferably damp. They are encrusted with nitre."

"Let us go, nevertheless. The cold is merely nothing. Amontillado! You have been imposed upon; and as for Luchesi, he cannot distinguish sherry from Amontillado."

Thus speaking, Fortunato possessed himself of my arm. Putting on a mask of black silk and drawing a *roquelaire* closely about my person, I suffered him to hurry me to my palazzo.

Chunk 2

There were no attendants at home; they had absconded to make merry in honour of the time. I had told them that I should not return until the morning and had given them explicit orders not to stir from the house. These orders were sufficient, I well knew, to insure their immediate disappearance, one and all, as soon as my back was turned.

25 I took from their sconces two flambeaux, and giving one to Fortunato, bowed him through several suites of rooms to the archway that led into the vaults. I passed down a long and winding staircase, requesting him to be cautious as he followed. We came at length to the foot of the descent, and stood together on the damp ground of the catacombs of the Montresors.

The gait of my friend was unsteady, and the bells upon his cap jingled as he strode.

"The pipe," said he.

"It is farther on," said I; "but observe the white webwork which gleams from these cavern walls."

He turned towards me and looked into my eyes with two filmy orbs that distilled the rheum of intoxication.

30 "Nitre?" he asked, at length.

"Nitre," I replied. "How long have you had that cough?"

"Ugh! ugh! ugh!—ugh! ugh! ugh!—ugh! ugh! ugh!—ugh! ugh! ugh!"

My poor friend found it impossible to reply for many minutes.

"It is nothing," he said, at last.

35 "Come," I said, with decision, "we will go back; your health is precious. You are rich, respected, admired, beloved; you are happy as once I was. You are a man to be missed. For me it is no matter. We will go back; you will be ill, and I cannot be responsible. Besides, there is Luchesi—"

"Enough," he said; "the cough is a mere nothing; it will not kill me. I shall not die of a cough."

"True—true," I replied; "and, indeed, I had no intention of alarming you unnecessarily—but you should use all proper caution. A draught of this Medoc will defend us from the damps." Here I knocked off the neck of a bottle which I drew from a long row of its fellows that lay upon the mould.

"Drink," I said, presenting him the wine.

He raised it to his lips with a leer. He paused and nodded to me familiarly, while his bells jingled.

40 "I drink," he said, "to the buried that repose around us."

"And I to your long life."

Chunk 3

He again took my arm and we proceeded.

"These vaults," he said, "are extensive."

"The Montresors," I replied, "were a great and numerous family."

45 "I forget your arms."

"A huge human foot d'or, in a field azure; the foot crushes a serpent rampant whose fangs are imbedded in the heel."

"And the motto?"

"*Nemo me impune lacessit.*"[5]

"Good!" he said.

50 The wine sparkled in his eyes and the bells jingled. My own fancy grew warm with the Medoc. We had passed through walls of piled bones, with casks and puncheons intermingling, into the inmost recesses of the catacombs. I paused again, and this time I made bold to seize Fortunato by an arm above the elbow.

"The nitre!" I said: "see, it increases. It hangs like moss upon the vaults. We are below the river's bed. The drops of moisture trickle among the bones. Come, we will go back ere it is too late. Your cough—"

"It is nothing," he said; "let us go on. But first, another draught of the Medoc."

My Notes

KEY IDEAS AND DETAILS
An important image in this section is Montresor's coat of arms. Visualize this by drawing it and including the motto. Consider how it symbolizes the idea of revenge.

---

[5] No one insults me with impunity.

Irony in the Vaults

GRAMMAR & USAGE
Syntax

Consider the word order of this sentence: "Its termination the feeble light did not enable us to see." What are the subject and verb? What effect does the inverted word order create? Why has Poe chosen to order the sentence in this manner?

My Notes

KEY IDEAS AND DETAILS
Chunk 4 is the climax of the story, when Montresor's intentions become clear. What is one thing he does that makes you understand what he intends to do?

KEY IDEAS AND DETAILS
What is the one clear example of verbal irony in this chunk? Explain how Montresor is being ironic.

I broke and reached him a flagon of De Grave. He emptied it at a breath. His eyes flashed with a fierce light. He laughed and threw the bottle upwards with a gesticulation I did not understand.

I looked at him in surprise. He repeated the movement—a grotesque one.

55 "You do not comprehend?" he said.

"Not I," I replied.

"Then you are not of the brotherhood."

"How?"

"You are not of the Masons."

60 "Yes, yes;· I said, "yes! Yes."

"You? Impossible! A Mason?"

"A mason." I replied.

"A sign," he said.

"It is this," I answered, producing from beneath the folds of my *roquelaire* a trowel.

65 "You jest," he exclaimed, recoiling a few paces. "But let us proceed to the Amontillado."

"Be it so," I said, replacing the tool beneath the cloak, and again offering him my arm. He leaned upon it heavily. We continued our route in search of the Amontillado. We passed through a range of low arches, descended, passed on, and descending again, arrived at a deep crypt, in which the foulness of the air caused our flambeaux rather to glow than flame.

Chunk 4

At the most remote end of the crypt there appeared another less spacious. Its walls had been lined with human remains piled to the vault overhead, in the fashion of the great catacombs of Paris. Three sides of this interior crypt were still ornamented in this manner. From the fourth the bones had been thrown down, and lay promiscuously upon the earth, forming at one point a mound of some size. Within the wall thus exposed by the displacing of the bones, we perceived a still interior recess, in depth about four feet, in width three, in height six or seven. It seemed to have been constructed for no special use in itself, but formed merely the interval between two of the colossal supports of the roof of the catacombs, and was backed by one of their circumscribing walls of solid granite.

It was in vain that Fortunato, uplifting his dull torch, endeavoured to pry into the depths of the recess. Its termination the feeble light did not enable us to see.

"Proceed," I said; "herein is the Amontillado. As for Luchesi—"

70 "He is an ignoramus," interrupted my friend, as he stepped unsteadily forward, while I followed immediately at his heels. In an instant he had reached the extremity of the niche, and finding his progress arrested by the rock, stood stupidly bewildered. A moment more and I had fettered him to the granite. In its surface were two iron staples, distant from each other about two feet, horizontally. From one of these depended a short chain, from the other a padlock. Throwing the links about his waist, it was but the work of a few seconds to secure it. He was too much astounded to resist. Withdrawing the key I stepped back from the recess.

"Pass your hand," I said, "over the wall; you cannot help feeling the nitre. Indeed it is *very* damp. Once more let me *implore* you to return. No? Then I must positively leave you. But I must first render you all the little attentions in my power."

"The Amontillado!" ejaculated my friend, not yet recovered from his astonishment.

"True," I replied; "the Amontillado."

Chunk 5

As I said these words I busied myself among the pile of bones of which I have before spoken. Throwing them aside, I soon uncovered a quantity of building stone and mortar. With these materials and with the aid of my trowel, I began vigorously to wall up the entrance of the niche.

75 I had scarcely laid the first tier of my masonry when I discovered that the intoxication of Fortunato had in a great measure worn off. The earliest indication I had of this was a low moaning cry from the depth of the recess. It was *not* the cry of a drunken man. There was then a long and obstinate silence. I laid the second tier, and the third, and the fourth; and then I heard the furious vibrations of the chain. The noise lasted for several minutes, during which, that I might hearken to it with the more satisfaction, I ceased my labours and sat down upon the bones. When at last the clanking subsided, I resumed the trowel, and finished without interruption the fifth, the sixth, and the seventh tier. The wall was now nearly upon a level with my breast. I again paused, and holding the flambeaux over the mason work, threw a few feeble rays upon the figure within.

A succession of loud and shrill screams, bursting suddenly from the throat of the chained form, seemed to thrust me violently back. For a brief moment I hesitated—I trembled. Unsheathing my rapier, I began to grope with it about the recess; but the thought of an instant reassured me. I placed my hand upon the solid fabric of the catacombs, and felt satisfaction. I reapproached the wall; I replied to the yells of him who clamored. I reechoed—I aided—I surpassed them in volume and in strength. I did this, and the clamorer grew still.

Chunk 6

It was now midnight, and my task was drawing to a close. I had completed the eighth, the ninth, and the tenth tier. I had finished a portion of the last and the eleventh; there remained but a single stone to be fitted and plastered in. I struggled with its weight; I placed it partially in its destined position. But now there came from out the niche a low laugh that erected the hairs upon my head. It was succeeded by a sad voice, which I had difficulty in recognizing as that of the noble Fortunato. The voice said—

"Ha! ha! ha!—he! he!—a very good joke indeed—an excellent jest. We will have many a rich laugh about it at the palazzo—he! he! he!—over our wine—he! he! he!"

"The Amontillado!" I said.

80 "He! he! he!—he! he! he!—yes, the Amontillado. But is it not getting late? Will not they be awaiting us at the palazzo, the Lady of Fortunato and the rest? Let us be gone."

"Yes," I said, "let us be gone!"

GRAMMAR & USAGE
Parallel Structure
Writers create parallel structure by presenting ideas, descriptions, or actions of equal importance in the same grammatical forms. Use of parallel structure helps writers emphasize important ideas or create a rhythmic feel to text.
When joining words or phrases of equal importance, be sure to use the same grammatical form.
Incorrect: He often enjoyed **walking and to eat**.
Correct: He often enjoyed **walking and eating**.
How does Poe effectively use parallel structure as he describes the building of the wall? What is the effect on the reader?

KEY IDEAS AND DETAILS
What do you learn about the narrator in Chunk 5? Cite textual details to support your understanding.

KEY IDEAS AND DETAILS
What textual evidence helps you determine whether Poe tells this story from a limited or omniscient point of view? Why might Poe have chosen to write in this point of view?

Irony in the Vaults

pa...

WORD CONNECTIONS

Foreign Phrases

Writers sometimes use words or phrases from another language for effect. The words "In pace requiescat" are Latin and mean "Rest in peace."

GRAMMAR & USAGE
Verbals

A **verbal** is form of a verb that is used as some other part of speech—a noun, an adjective, or an adverb.

A **participle** is a verbal that functions as an adjective.
> Example: **Throwing** them aside, I soon uncovered a quantity of stone and mortar. [*throwing modifies I*]

A **gerund** is a verbal that ends in -*ing* and functions as a noun.
> Example: When at last the **clanking** subsided, I resumed....

An **infinitive** is a verb form that can be used as a noun, an adjective, or an adverb. The word *to* usually appears in front of the verb form.
> Example: Unsheathing my rapier, I began **to grope** with it about the recess.

INDEPENDENT READING LINK

With a partner, share a plot summary of one of the stories that you have read independently. Explain to your partner the most prominent literary element in that story. Is it point of view? Imagery? Figurative language? Symbolism? Irony? Dialogue? Why does this element catch your attention and help to make "a good story"?

"For the love of God, Montresor!"

"Yes," I said, "for the love of God!"

But to these words I hearkened in vain for a reply. I grew impatient. I called aloud—

85 "Fortunato!"

No answer. I called again—

"Fortunato!"

No answer still. I thrust a torch through the remaining aperture and let it fall within. There came forth in return only a jingling of the bells. My heart grew sick—on account of the dampness of the catacombs. I hastened to make an end of my labor. I forced the last stone into its position; I plastered it up. Against the new masonry I reerected the old rampart of bones. For the half of a century no mortal has disturbed them.

In pace requiescat!

After Reading

4. Scan "The Cask of Amontillado" and highlight examples of each type of irony Poe uses. Try to find at least three examples of each type. Record your examples in the graphic organizer on the next page. Then respond to the following writing prompt.

Writing Prompt: In a well-supported paragraph, explain how Poe uses verbal irony in "The Cask of Amontillado" to emphasize the evil intentions of Montresor. Be sure to:

- Create a topic sentence that introduces your topic.
- Cite textual examples of verbal irony.
- Include commentary sentences that explain the importance or the effect of the irony.
- Use appropriate parallel structure of multiple ideas within a sentence.

Check Your Understanding

Look back at the various attempts you have made at creating a story. Discuss with your writing group how irony creates mystery and surprise in your reading audience. Why would you as a writer want to include irony in your story? How might you incorporate **situational, dramatic,** and/or **verbal irony** into your story?

Verbal Irony in "The Cask of Amontillado"

1. Verbal irony occurs when a speaker or narrator says one thing while meaning the opposite. For example, when Fortunato proposes a toast to the dead buried in the crypts around them, Montresor adds: "And I to your long life." Montresor is using verbal irony here, as he intends to end Fortunato's life very soon.

What is stated . . .	What it means . . .

Situational Irony in "The Cask of Amontillado"

2. Situational irony occurs when an event contradicts the expectations of the characters or the reader. For example, Fortunato expects to enjoy the rare Amontillado; however, he is killed.

What is expected . . .	What happens . . .

Dramatic Irony in "The Cask of Amontillado"

3. Dramatic irony occurs when the reader or audience knows more about circumstances or future events in the story than the characters within it. For example, from the beginning of "The Cask of Amontillado," the reader knows that Montresor will kill Fortunato, Fortunato does not know this.

What the reader knows . . .	What the character knows . . .

My Notes

Connecting Symbolism to Meaning

ABOUT THE AUTHOR
William Blake (1757–1827)
was an artist as well as a
poet. Born in London, he was
apprenticed to an engraver
when he was young. Blake
claimed to have mystical
visions, which he expressed
in his poems and engravings.
He engraved both the texts
and illustrations for his
poems. "A Poison Tree" is
from his collection called
Songs of Experience, which
reflect his complex view of
a world that includes good
and evil, innocence and
experience.

My Notes

Learning Targets
- Analyze how a poet explores the idea of revenge.
- Compare thematic elements and ideas across different texts and genres.

Before Reading
1. Think about the title "The Poison Tree." What image comes to mind? Predict what this poem will be about.

During Reading
2. First, read the poem and think about how its ideas are similar to or different from those in "The Cask of Amontillado." Then, reread the poem and use the strategy of diffusing to identify the words you do not know and substitute synonyms above them. For instance, above "wrath" you could write "anger."

Poetry

A Poison Tree

by William Blake

I was angry with my friend:
I told my wrath[1], my wrath did end.
I was angry with my foe:
I told it not, my wrath did grow.

5   And I watered it in fears,
Night and morning with my tears;
And I sunned it with smiles,
And with soft deceitful wiles[2].

And it grew both day and night,
10 Till it bore an apple bright.
And my foe beheld it shine.
And he knew that it was mine,

And into my garden stole
When the night had veiled the pole;
15 In the morning glad I see
My foe outstretched beneath the tree.

---

[1] **wrath:** Fierce anger; vengeance caused by anger
[2] **wiles:** tricky or clever behavior

After Reading

3. You have learned and practiced important strategies to improve your reading and writing skills:

- Diffusing
- SIFT
- Levels of Questions

Using either SIFT or Levels of Questions, reread and analyze "A Poison Tree." Create a graphic organizer that includes an area for you to respond to or interpret the poem, based on your questions or your evidence. Your goal is to write a thematic statement about this poem.

Be sure to identify literary elements such as diction, imagery, and symbols to help you decide on a thematic statement. Then, write your thematic statement below.

Check Your Understanding

"The Cask of Amontillado" and "A Poison Tree" feature the topic of revenge. In your discussion groups, compare and contrast how the authors develop this topic. In both the short story and the poem, analyze and identify the following points. Be sure to cite specific textual details and give an explanation of your understanding of these details in your Reader/Writer Notebook.

- How does the speaker use point of view?
- How does the speaker use imagery?
- Does the speaker use irony?
- What is the theme of the text? (Share the thematic statement that you wrote earlier.)

After you have answered these questions, share your responses to compare the two works. Then, write a thematic statement that unites the two works.

My Notes

INDEPENDENT READING LINK
Select one of the short stories you have read independently. Write a thematic statement for this story and identify literary elements that contribute to the development of its theme.

Writing a Short Story

Assignment

Your assignment is to write an original narrative from real or imagined experiences or events. Your story must include a variety of narrative techniques—such as foreshadowing, point of view, figurative language, imagery, symbolism, and/or irony—as well as effective details and a well-structured sequence of events.

Planning and Prewriting: Plan for your narrative.

- Review the unit activities and your Reader/Writer Notebook for ideas. What activities have you completed that will help you as you create a short story with the required narrative techniques?
- What events or experiences do you want to write about? What prewriting strategies can you use to help you create ideas?

Drafting: Determine the structure and how to incorporate the elements of a short story.

- What setting will you use? Point of view? Characters?
- Which additional narrative techniques will you use? Have you thought about including irony to create a sense of mystery, surprise, and tension?
- How does the story structure you created develop the events, characters, and plot of your story so that it engages your readers?

Technology TIP:

Storyboards are commonly used to sequence a story and to visualize events. If you want to use a storyboard, search for online storyboarding tools you might use to help you plan and write your story.

Evaluating and Revising: Create opportunities to review and revise to produce the best work.

- When and how will you share and respond with others to get feedback on all elements of your narrative?
- What words and phrases, details, and sensory language have you used to create for the reader a vivid picture of the setting, events/experiences, and characters?
- Is your story developing as you want it to? Are you willing to change your story if you must? Once you get suggestions, are you creating a plan to include revision ideas in your draft?
- Does your conclusion reflect on experiences in the narrative and provide an effective resolution?
- Have you used the Scoring Guide to help you evaluate how well your draft includes the required elements of the assignment?

Checking and Editing for Publication: Confirm that the final draft is ready for publication.

- How will you check for grammatical and technical accuracy? Cohesion?

Reflection

After completing this Embedded Assessment, think about how you set out and accomplished the tasks for this assignment. Write a reflection explaining how identifying and collecting information helped you create a short story. What did you do to review and revise your narrative, and how was the information you collected useful?

SCORING GUIDE

Scoring Criteria	Exemplary	Proficient	Emerging	Incomplete
Ideas	The narrative • sustains focus on setting, character, events, and/or ideas to strengthen the unity of the story • presents thought-provoking details, conflict, and resolution to heighten reader interest • develops engaging and authentic characters that grow in complexity throughout the story.	The narrative • generally focuses on setting, character, events, and/or ideas to maintain the unity of the story • includes well-developed conflict and resolution with appropriate details to sustain reader interest • develops believable characters that grow in depth throughout the story.	The narrative • does not sustain a focus on setting, character, events, and/or ideas, limiting the unity of the story • contains unfocused conflict and resolution • contains characters that are not developed or are not believable.	The narrative • does not contain essential details to establish setting, character(s), events, and/or ideas • does not contain believable characters • does not provide a conflict or resolution.
Structure	The narrative • follows the structure of the genre • engages the reader and uses a variety of techniques to sequence events and create a coherent whole • provides an insightful conclusion with a clear and reasonable resolution.	The narrative • follows the structure of the genre • orients the reader and includes a sequence of events that create a coherent whole • provides a conclusion and clear resolution.	The narrative • may follow only parts of the structure of the genre • presents disconnected events with limited coherence • contains an underdeveloped conclusion with little or no resolution.	The narrative • does not follow the structure of the genre • includes few if any events and no coherence • does not contain a conclusion or does not provide a resolution.
Use of Language	The narrative • purposefully uses precise language, telling details, and sensory language to enhance mood or tone • effectively uses a range of narrative techniques and literary devices to enhance the plot • demonstrates technical command of spelling and standard English conventions.	The narrative • uses precise language and sensory details to define the mood or tone • uses a range of narrative techniques and literary devices to establish the plot • demonstrates general command of conventions and spelling; minor errors do not interfere with meaning.	The narrative • uses limited sensory details resulting in an unfocused or vague mood or tone • contains few or no narrative techniques and devices • demonstrates limited command of conventions and spelling; errors interfere with meaning.	The narrative • uses no sensory details to create mood or tone • contains few or no narrative techniques and devices • contains numerous errors in grammar and conventions that interfere with meaning.

Previewing Embedded Assessment 2: Thinking About Style

Learning Targets

- Identify the knowledge and skills that I will need to complete Embedded Assessment 2 successfully and reflect on prior learning that supports the knowledge and skills needed.
- Expand my understanding of the elements that contribute to a writer's style.

Making Connections

In the first part of this unit, you have read short stories and studied elements that help create a writer's style. By writing story starters and a short story, you also started developing your own writing style. In this last part of the unit, you will continue looking at style, but this time through the lens of film. By viewing a specific director's films, you will make connections between the choices that writer's make with words and the choices that directors make with film techniques.

Essential Questions

Now that you have analyzed several short stories, how would you change your answer to the first essential question: What makes a good story?

My Notes

Developing Vocabulary

Look at your Reader/Writer Notebook and review the academic vocabulary, literary terms, and language and writer's craft terms you have studied so far in this unit. Which terms can you now move to a new category on a QHT chart? Which could you now teach to others that you were unfamiliar with at the beginnig of the unit?

Unpacking Embedded Assessment 2

Read the assignment for Embedded Assessment 2: Writing a Style Analysis Essay.

> Think about the Tim Burton films that you have viewed and analyzed. Choose three or four stylistic devices (cinematic techniques) that are common to these films. Write an essay analyzing the cinematic style of director Tim Burton. Your essay should focus on the ways in which the director uses stylistic techniques across films to achieve a desired effect.

In your own words, summarize what you will need to know to complete this assessment successfully. With your class, create a graphic organizer to represent the skills and knowledge you will need to complete the tasks identified in the embedded assessment.

INDEPENDENT READING LINK
Make a plan for reading additional stories and viewing film versions of those stories. You might also consider reading biographies or articles about filmmakers, as well as articles about Tim Burton. Viewing other Tim Burton films would also help you with the style analysis you will do in this unit.

Style Analysis

In the first half of the unit, you learned about writing style. You learned that the choices a writer makes in subject matter, diction, syntax, imagery, point of view, and tone all help to characterize a writer's style. With a partner, review the definition of style and think about aspects of your style that you discovered as you wrote your own original short story.

1. Using these elements, how would you describe your writing style?

2. The following text analyzes elements of Edgar Allan Poe's writing style. Use the My Notes space to list each element of style listed above, leaving space below each to add details from the essay. As you read the essay, mark key details that describe Poe's style. Be prepared to summarize and discuss the major points of the analysis of Poe's style.

Sample Style Analysis Essay

Although Poe wrote in many different genres, he is best remembered now as a writer of horror stories. Poe's style is characterized by an ability to create a mood of terror and ghastliness in his writing. His stories allow his reader to get lost in the mystery, the horror of the moment, and perhaps the fall into madness. Poe was more concerned about the effect he wanted to create in the reader than any kind of "moral lesson." "The Cask of Amontillado" exhibits Poe's concept that a story should be devoid of social, political, or moral teaching. In place of a moral, Poe creates a mood—terror, in this case— through his language. In this and many other of Poe's fictional and poetic pieces, the first-person narration compels the reader to identify with the narrator, in this case, Montresor, a revengeful murderer who, in his last act of revenge, insanely echoes his victim's screams for help.

The imagery of the story is mysterious and creates a perfect setting for a macabre act of revenge. The vaults or catacombs, populated with the bones of the dead, and whose damp walls are covered with the webbed whiteness of the nitre, create an ominous and forbidding setting characteristic of Poe's works. Poe's ornate prose also sets the tone by allowing the narrator to wield his ironic voice without much chance of the object of his revenge understanding. So when Montresor elegantly refers to the status of his victim, Fortunato, by saying, "You are rich, respected, admired, beloved; you are happy as once I was. You are a man to be missed. For me it is no matter," the irony of his carefully worded praise is lost on Fortunato and reminds the reader of the depth of Montresor's jealousy and hatred. Poe's ability to capture the imagination of his reader by creating a specific effect is his lasting legacy to the art of storytelling.

My Notes

Previewing Embedded Assessment 2: Thinking About Style

After Reading

3. Based on the text above and your summary of the content, what do you think are the stylistic characteristics of the work of Edgar Allan Poe?

4. Explain how the structure of Poe's language (syntax) contributes to his style.

Check Your Understanding

Expository Writing Prompt: Write a brief summary of the literary and syntactical elements that contribute to a writer's style. Be sure to:

• Create a topic sentence that clearly introduces the topic.

• Explain and orgaize the basic elements of style.

• Use at least one example of a style or syntactical element to illustrate your topic.

Working with Cinematic Techniques

Learning Targets
- Identify cinematic techniques and explain the effects of these techniques in visual text.
- Compare key stylistic elements in written and filmed texts and make connections between style in a writer's and a film director's texts.

LEARNING STRATEGIES:
Marking the Text, Visualizing, Note-taking, Drafting, Graphic Organizer, Discussion Groups

Analyzing Film

Film can be analyzed by understanding both literary elements and **cinematic techniques** that create effects for the audience. To learn to "read" a film, you must understand how film and written text are similar and different. Style in film has to do with how the visual images of the story are presented to create a certain effect. There are explicit connections between an author's choices of literary techniques and a director's choices of cinematic techniques.

1. In your Reader/Writer Notebook, draw a large Venn diagram with Film in one circle and Text in the other circle. At the top, label the middle overlapping section "Similarities." Above the "Text" circle write "Literary Techniques," and above the "Film" circle write "Cinematic Techniques."

2. With a partner, using the middle section, brainstorm elements shared by short stories, novels, and filmed stories.

3. Next, in the Text circle write all the terms you know that relate to stylistic elements in written literary texts.

Literary Terms
Cinematic techniques are the methods a director uses to communicate meaning and to evoke particular emotional responses from viewers.

WORD CONNECTIONS

Analogy

The relationship in an analogy may show an object and its description; for example, film: visual images. Complete the following analogy.
film : visual images :: _____ : words on a page.

Cinematic Techniques

The chart below provides an overview of cinematic elements used in creating film texts. Use the chart to review these elements by brainstorming terms you and your classmates may already know that refer to techniques used in the creation of film.

Shots and Framing	Camera Angles	Camera Movements	Lighting	Editing	Music/Sound
Shot	Eye level	Pan	High key	Cut	Diegetic
Establishing shot	High angle	Tilt	Low key	Fade	Non-diegetic
Long shot	Low angle	Zoom	Bottom or side lighting	Dissolve/Wipe	
Medium shot		Dolly/tracking	Front or back lighting	Flashback	
Close-up		Boom/crane		Shot-reverse-shot	
Extreme close-up				Cross cutting	
Two shot				Eye-Line Match	

Working with Cinematic Techniques

4. You will now view a television commercial or film clip. Choose one of the cinematic techniques listed on the previous page, and take notes on how the clip uses that technique to create an effect. After viewing the film clip, form an expert group with others who chose techniques from the same category (e.g., lighting), and together write a paragraph that explains the effects created in the clip by the techniques in your category. Each group member will write one sentence to develop the explanation. Continue around the table until your group has written a well-supported paragraph.

Your paragraph organization might follow this outline:

Topic sentence that introduces the category of techniques
1. Detail
   a. Explanation of the importance of this detail
2. Another Detail
   a. Explanation of the improtance of this detail
3. Another detail
   a. Explanation of the importance of this detail
Concluding sentence

5. After writing, select a spokesperson for your group to read your paragraph to the class. As you listen to other groups present their explanation, take notes to help you understand how all cinematic techniques work together to create an effect.

Check Your Understanding

Writing Prompt: From your notes, choose what you consider the three most significant and/or effective cinematic techniques used in the commercial or film clip you watched, and write a paragraph that explains the effect of the cinematic techniques in the film text. Be sure to:

• Include a well-stated topic sentence.
• Cite the best details from the film text to prove your opinion.

Film in Context: An Authorial Study

Learning Targets
- Identify the subject and important details in a main-idea statement.
- Write main-idea statements.

Before Reading

You will next read an essay about film director Tim Burton whose unique style you are about to explore. With an understanding of what has influenced his life and his work, you can begin to understand how the directorial choices he has made have defined his style.

A statement of a **main idea** is not the same as a text's subject or the **theme** of a literary work. For instance, the biographical essay below has a specific subject: Tim Burton's style as a film maker. The main-idea statement summarizes the important points of a text, usually informational in nature. Identifying the main idea of a text should begin with identifying the key points, or subjects, within the text. After you read the following information, you will be responsible for identifying the main idea of the text by summarizing its key points.

> **LEARNING STRATEGIES:**
> Close Reading, Marking the Text, Note-taking, Summarizing, Graphic Organizer, Oral Reading

> **Literary Terms**
> A **main idea** is a statement (often one sentence) that summarizes the key details of a text.
> A **theme** is the central message of a literary work.

Biographical Essay

Tim Burton: Wickedly Funny, Grotesquely Humorous

"There's a naughtiness in Tim that's similar to Roald Dahl. A little bit of wickedness, a little bit of teasing, a subversiveness. Both of them never lost the gift of knowing what it's like to be a child—a very rare gift . . ."—Felicity 'Liccy' Dahl[1]

1 Stories written for children haven't always been as tame as the stories created by Walt Disney. Grimm's fairy tales are notoriously violent and grisly, especially considering the sheer number of abandoned and mistreated children that populate the lore of fairy tales. Roald Dahl, who wrote the classic children's book, *James and the Giant Peach*, is as famous for his cruelly ironic adult short stories as he is for his popular and dark stories like *Charlie and the Chocolate Factory*, written for and about children. These are just two of the direct sources and inspirations for Tim Burton's films that have influenced his imagination and cinematic style.

2 Tim Burton's style is clearly influenced by his fascination with fairy tales and children's stories. Whether bringing to life his own literary creations such as *Frankenweenie* (2012) *or The Nightmare Before Christmas* (1993), or adapting popular works such as *Charlie and the Chocolate Factory* (2005) *or Alice in Wonderland* (2010), Burton offers a dark and delightful revisioning of childhood stories. Like fairy tales, Burton's stories encourage escapism into worlds of fantasy and the supernatural while often reminding his audience of traditional morals and lessons. Some of Burton's most important and recurring inspirations have come from children's books.

> **Literary Terms**
> A **biography** is a description or account of someone else's life or significant events from that person's life. In contrast, an **autobiography** is an account written by a person about his or her own life.

> **KEY IDEAS AND DETAILS**
> Summarize the writer's topic and opinion as presented in the first two paragraphs. Underline the thesis.

> **My Notes**
> _____
> _____
> _____
> _____
> _____
> _____

---

[1] Liccy Dahl was the executive producer of *Charlie and the Chocolate Factory* (2005) and is the widow of author Roald Dahl. This quote is from Leah Gallo, *The Art of Tim Burton*, Los Angeles: Steeles Publishing, 2009.

WORD CONNECTIONS

Roots and Affixes

The word *subversive* contains the prefix *sub-*, which means "under, beneath, or below." In the sense used in this essay, *subversive* means "to undermine established patterns."

KEY IDEAS AND DETAILS

In Paragraph 4, Burton's style is contrasted with the style of films produced by the Walt Disney Studios. How are they different?

My Notes

_____

_____

_____

_____

_____

_____

_____

_____

_____

_____

_____

_____

_____

_____

_____

_____

_____

_____

_____

_____

_____

_____

_____

_____

_____

3 Burton grew up loving Dr. Seuss. He thought Dr. Seuss's books were a perfect blend of subversive storytelling with a playful, innocent use of rhythm and rhyme. It is easy to see the influence of Seuss's imagination in Burton's *The Nightmare Before Christmas*. Based upon Burton's original three-page poem and drawings as well as inspired by the well-known poem *The Night Before Christmas* (1823), the film is a gentle horror story.

4 Burton worked for many years at Walt Disney Studios, whose approach to adapting fairy tales tends to understate the more sinister elements. Burton, however, embraces the dark elements. His first project as an apprentice was a six-minute film called, *Vincent* (1982), a tribute to actor Vincent Price and author Edgar Allan Poe, two significant childhood influences. Burton says he related deeply to these two icons of horror fiction and film. The film features a seven-year-old boy, Vincent Malloy, who fantasizes about acting out Poe's gothic horror stories and dreams of being an anguished character like Price. In many ways this first short film anticipates many of the common themes and influences that Burton has continued to explore throughout his cinematic career.

5 In his 2005 adaptation of *Charlie and the Chocolate Factory*, Burton brings to life Roald Dahl's subversive vision of childhood innocence. All of the children in the story, save Charlie, are undeserving wretches. Burton delights in including Dahl's graphic rhyming songs celebrating the fates of the repulsive and ungrateful children of the story.

> We very much regret that we
> Shall simply have to wait and see
> If we can get him back his height.
> But if we can't—it serves him right.

6 Just as classic children's literature can be enjoyed by adults with new appreciation, so too can Tim Burton's films be enjoyed and appreciated after multiple revisits. By examining and understanding the influence of writers such as E.A. Poe and Roald Dahl, as well as Dr. Seuss and classic fairy tales, the sources of Burton's cinematic style become clear. Characterized by a childlike innocence and playfulness coupled with a dark and somewhat grotesque sensibility, Burton's films have already become classics.

After Reading

Now that you have identified the subjects or key points of this text, summarize these into one main-idea sentence. You might use this sentence frame to guide your writing:

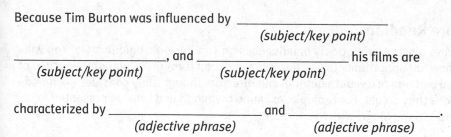

Because Tim Burton was influenced by _____
                                    (subject/key point)

_____, and _____ his films are
(subject/key point)   *(subject/key point)*

characterized by _____ and _____.
            (adjective phrase)   *(adjective phrase)*

Check Your Understanding

Writing Prompt: Once you have written and shared your main-idea statement, use your notes to write a paragraph that supports your topic sentence. Be sure to:

• Revise your main-idea statement if needed.

• Choose details about Tim Burton and his style that support your topic sentence.

• Organize the sentences in your paragraph and use correct grammar.

My Notes

Setting the Mood and Understanding Tone: Wonka Two Ways

Literary Terms
Mood is the atmosphere or predominant emotion in a literary work, the effect of the words on the audience.

My Notes

Learning Targets
- Compare written and film texts and identify how mood and tone are created in each.
- Cite textual evidence from written and film texts to support an interpretation.

Before Reading
You have discovered a variety of influences on Tim Burton's unique style. You will now have an opportunity to see that style in action through a comparative study of written and film texts. Both authors and directors thoughtfully consider the **mood** and tone they create. For example, examine the mood and tone as presented in "The Gift of the Magi" with this excerpt:

> There was clearly nothing to do but flop down on the shabby little couch and howl. So Della did it. Which instigates the moral reflection that life is made up of sobs, sniffles, and smiles, with sniffles predominating.
>
> While the mistress of the home is gradually subsiding from the first stage to the second, take a look at the home. A furnished flat at $8 per week. It did not exactly beggar description, but it certainly had that word on the lookout for the mendicancy squad.
>
> In the vestibule below was a letter-box into which no letter would go, and an electric button from which no mortal finger could coax a ring. Also appertaining thereunto was a card bearing the name "Mr. James Dillingham Young."

1. What details does the narrator include to create a mood of hopelessness and despair?

However, in this excerpt, the narrator's tone, or attitude, toward Della, shows a *superiority* and *amusement* at her predicament:

- The diction and picture created of Della as she "flop [s]" and "howl [s]" is more comic than tragic.
- The elevated language of referring to Della as the "mistress of the home" and the formality of the name "Mr. James Dillingham Young" shows a fondness for this young couple's efforts at respectability.

Writers make choices about diction, imagery, and details so that their audiences will experience a certain mood and, in turn, a certain tone in a piece. Similarly, a director can make choices to create a mood and tone by making specific directorial choices about cinematic techniques.

During Reading

2. To practice identifying mood and tone and the way they are created, you will now compare written text with film text. Give each a close reading by focusing on the details that the narrator or director chooses to share with the audience.

3. In Passage 1 from *Charlie and the Chocolate Factory*, you will examine the mood. Highlight diction, imagery, and details that help you to identify the atmosphere or predominant emotion in the text. You are highlighting textual evidence that will lead you to identify the mood of the passage.

ABOUT THE AUTHOR

Roald Dahl (1916–1990) was born in Wales to Norwegian parents. The stories he heard as a child greatly influenced his love of stories and books. Dahl wrote stories for adults and children. Many of his children's stories came about from the bedtime stories he made up for his daughters. *James and the Giant Peach* was his first book, followed by *Charlie and the Chocolate Factory*, both of which enjoyed huge success in the United Kingdom and the United States.

Novel Excerpt

from **Charlie** and the *Chocolate Factory*

by Roald Dahl

PASSAGE 1

1 The whole of this family—the six grownups (count them) and little Charlie Bucket—live together in a small wooden house on the edge of a great town.

2 The house wasn't nearly large enough for so many people, and life was extremely uncomfortable for them all. There were only two rooms in the place altogether, and there was only one bed. The bed was given to the four old grandparents because they were so old and tired. They were so tired, they never got out of it.

3 Grandpa Joe and Grandma Josephine on this side, Grandpa George and Grandma Georgina on this side.

4 Mr. and Mrs. Bucket and little Charlie Bucket slept in the other room, upon mattresses on the floor.

5 In the summertime, this wasn't too bad, but in the winter, freezing cold drafts blew across the floor all night long, and it was awful.

My Notes

KEY IDEAS AND DETAILS
What is the mood established in Paragraphs 1–5? Try to identify five details that help create this mood.

Setting the Mood and Understanding Tone: Wonka Two Ways

6 There wasn't any question of them being able to buy a better house—or even one more bed to sleep in. They were far too poor for that.

7 Mr. Bucket was the only person in the family with a job. He worked in a toothpaste factory, where he sat all day long at a bench and screwed the little caps onto the tops of the tubes of toothpaste after the tubes had been filled. But a toothpaste cap-screwer is never paid very much money, and poor Mr. Bucket, however hard he worked, and however fast he screwed on the caps, was never able to make enough to buy one-half of the things that so large a family needed. There wasn't even enough money to buy proper food for them all. The only meals they could afford were bread and margarine for breakfast, boiled potatoes and cabbage for lunch, and cabbage soup for supper. Sundays were a bit better. They all looked forward to Sundays because then, although they had exactly the same, everyone was allowed a second helping.

8 The Buckets, of course, didn't starve, but every one of them—the two old grandfathers, the two old grandmothers, Charlie's father, Charlie's mother, and especially little Charlie himself—went about from morning till night with a horrible empty feeling in their tummies.

9 Charlie felt it worst of all. And although his father and mother often went without their own share of lunch or supper so that they could give it to him, it still wasn't nearly enough for a growing boy. He desperately wanted something more filling and satisfying than cabbage and cabbage soup. The one thing he longed for more than anything else was . . . CHOCOLATE.

KEY IDEAS AND DETAILS
Evaluate the family's relationship as described in Passage 1. Using one word, describe the Buckets' relationships. Find three details in the text that led you to make this inference.

Diction, Imagery, Details/ Textual Evidence	Adjectives Describing Mood

In Passage 2, you will consider **tone**. Highlight words that help to identify the author's attitude toward the children he describes. List those words in the graphic organizer. Then, come up with one or two words that describe the tone of the passage.

My Notes

Novel Excerpt

from
Charlie and the
Chocolate Factory

by Roald Dahl

PASSAGE 2

1 The very next day, the first Golden Ticket was found. The finder was a boy called Augustus Gloop, and Mr. Bucket's evening newspaper carried a large picture of him on the front page. The picture showed a nine-year-old boy who was so enormously fat he looked as though he had been blown up with a powerful pump. Great flabby folds of fat bulged out from every part of his body, and his face was like a monstrous ball of dough with two small greedy curranty eyes peering out upon the world. The town in which Augustus Gloop lived, the newspaper said, had gone wild with excitement over their hero. Flags were flying from all the windows, children had been given a holiday from school, and a parade was being organized in honor of the famous youth.

2 "I just *knew* Augustus would find a Golden Ticket," his mother had told the newspapermen. "He eats so *many* candy bars a day that it was almost *impossible* for him *not* to find one. Eating is his hobby, you know. That's *all* he's interested in. But still, that's better than being a *hooligan* and shooting off *zip guns* and things like that in his spare time, isn't it? And what I always say is, he wouldn't go on eating like he does unless he *needed* nourishment, would he? It's all *vitamins*, anyway. What a *thrill* it will be for him to visit Mr. Wonka's marvelous factory! We're just as *proud* as can be!"

3 "What a revolting woman," said Grandma Josephine.

4 "And what a repulsive boy," said Grandma Georgina.

5 . . . Suddenly, on the day before Charlie Bucket's birthday, the newspapers announced that the second Golden Ticket had been found. The lucky person was a small girl called Veruca Salt who lived with her rich parents in a great city far away. Once again, Mr. Bucket's evening newspaper carried a big picture of the finder. She was sitting between her beaming father and mother in the living room of their house, waving the Golden Ticket above her head, and grinning from ear to ear.

KEY IDEAS AND DETAILS
Read closely the interview with Mrs. Gloop. What do her words tell the readers about her as a parent?

Setting the Mood and Understanding Tone: Wonka Two Ways

6   Veruca's father, Mr. Salt, had eagerly explained to the newspapermen exactly how the ticket was found. "You see, fellers," he had said, "as soon as my little girl told me that she simply *had* to have one of those Golden Tickets, I want out into the town and started buying up all the Wonka candy bars I could lay my hands on. *Thousands* of them, I must have bought. *Hundreds* of thousands! Then I had them loaded onto trucks and sent directly to my *own* factory. I'm in the peanut business, you see, and I've got about a hundred women working for me over at my joint, shelling peanuts for roasting and salting. That's what they do all day long, those women, they sit there shelling peanuts. So I says to them, 'Okay, girls,' I says, 'from now on, you can stop shelling peanuts and start shelling the wrappers off these crazy candy bars instead!' And they did. I had every worker in the place yanking the paper off those bars of chocolate full speed ahead from morning till night.

7   "But three days went by, and we had no luck. Oh, it was terrible! My little Veruca got more and more upset each day, and every time I went home she would scream at me, *"Where's my Golden Ticket! I want my Golden Ticket!"* And she would lie for hours on the floor, kicking and yelling in the most disturbing way. Well, sir, I just hated to see my little girl feeling unhappy like that, so I vowed I would keep up the search until I'd got her what she wanted. Then suddenly . . . on the evening of the fourth day, one of my women workers yelled, 'I've got it! A Golden Ticket!' And I said, 'Give it to me, quick!' and she did, and I rushed it home and gave it to my darling Veruca, and now she's all smiles, and we have a happy home once again."

8   "That's even worse than the fat boy," said Grandma Josephine.

9   "She needs a real good spanking," said Grandma Georgina.

KEY IDEAS AND DETAILS
Read the interview with Mr. Salt. What does the interview tell readers about him as a parent?

Words/Phrases/Textual Evidence	Adjectives for Tone

The Language of Style Analysis

There are common literary elements to consider when examining an author's **style** in a text: **tone, diction, imagery, syntax, structure,** and **point of view**. These elements can also be expressed through cinematic techniques. For the literary elements listed on the left side of the graphic organizer below, fill in the right side of the chart with cinematic techniques a director can use for the same purpose.

The Language of Style Analysis

Literary Element	Cinematic Technique
Tone: The writer's or speaker's attitude toward a subject, character, or audience; it is conveyed through the author's choice of words and detail. **Mood:** The atmosphere or predominant emotion in a literary work	
Diction: Word choice intended to convey a certain effect	
Imagery: Words or phrases appealing to the senses, which a writer uses to represent persons, objects, actions, feelings, and ideas	
Organization: The narrative structure of a piece—how a text begins and ends, is sequenced, paced, or arranged	
Syntax: The arrangement of words and the order of grammatical elements in a sentence	
Point of View: The perspective from which a narrative is told	

My Notes

Setting the Mood and Understanding Tone: Wonka Two Ways

Comparing Texts

Just as you did a close reading of passages from *Charlie and the Chocolate Factory*, now you will do a close "reading" of the beginning of Tim Burton's film version of that text. While viewing, pay special attention to the ways in which a director creates mood and tone through cinematic techniques such as lighting, sound, angles, framing and shots, editing, and camera movement.

As you watch this first segment, you might jigsaw this task with members of your viewing group so that each of you focuses on one technique and watches closely to understand Burton's manipulation of this technique.

Consider these questions as you watch the film:

1. How does Burton create mood and tone? What does a director have at his disposal that an author does not?
2. In terms of mood and tone, how is the film version similar to and different from the written version? What specific elements contribute to the mood/tone?

Film Notes on Burton's Style

Cinematic Technique	Textual Evidence	Mood/Tone
Framing or Camera Angles		
Setting		
Sound		
Other		

After Reading

If you have jigsawed this activity with your group, take time to share around your group what each of you noticed. As you listen to the discoveries of group members, add details to your graphic organizer. The more details you can cite, the more information you will have to prove your claim as you complete the writing prompt below.

Language and Writer's Craft: Combining Sentences

Sentence combining is the process of joining two simple sentences into one. For example, look at the first sentence in Paragraph 7 from Passage 2 of *Charlie and the Chocolate Factory*. Dahl's sentence is a *compound* sentence with two independent clauses. Had Roald Dahl written the following two simple sentences, the effect would have been choppy, hesitant writing.

> "Three days went by. We had no luck."

Dahl uses a coordinating conjunction to join the two (he also starts the sentence with a coordinating conjunction). You could also use a semicolon:

> "Three days went by; we had no luck."

You could join two short sentences to make a *complex* sentence by making one part an independent clause and one a dependent clause. For example,

> "Although three days went by, we had no luck."

As you complete the following writing prompt, review your work and combine short sentences into compound or complex sentences.

Check Your Understanding

Writing Prompt: Return to the questions you considered as you watched the film, and select either Question 1 or Question 2. Think about what you have analyzed in the novel excerpt and the film. Now write to explain your answer to the question you have chosen. Be sure to:

- Answer the question in the topic sentence.
- Cite textual evidence from both the written text and the film.
- Include a clear explanation of how the textual details support your topic sentence.

My Notes

Revisiting Wonka: Thinking About Effect

LEARNING STRATEGIES:
Close Reading, Drafting, Graphic
Organizer, Quickwrite, Role
Playing

My Notes

Learning Targets

- Apply cinematic techniques to design a scene that creates an intended effect.
- Interpret the effect of a director's cinematic choices.

You have seen examples of how Burton translated Roald Dahl's writing style into his own unique cinematic style by making cinematic choices in what and how he filmed the story. In this activity, you will study two more scenes from *Charlie and the Chocolate Factory* and take notes.

Viewing the Film Clips

As you watch these scenes, identify as many film techniques as you can. Using the information from the chart in Activity 2.12, your group may want to divide up the cinematic techniques in order to take better notes.

1. **Quickwrite:** After viewing the film clips, draft responses to the following questions:

   a. What effect do you think Burton wants to create in the scene at home and in the scene in front of the factory?

   b. What choices does Burton make to create these effects?

2. Now you will consolidate your understanding of cinematic techniques by taking on the role of director. With your group, you will create a scene and then apply five cinematic techniques to that scene. Describe the scene you and your group plan to demonstrate using the cinematic techniques either assigned to you or chosen by you.

   Present this scene to your class and explain your directorial choices.

   a. In your scene, what effect did you want to have on your audience?

   b. What choices did you make in your direction to achieve your desired effect?

Check Your Understanding

To elaborate on the concept of cinematic techniques, create a graphic organizer in your Reader/Writer Notebook. In one section, identify film technques; in another, describe the intended and actual effect of each technique. Discuss with your classmates and refer to your notes as you describe each effect.

More About Stylistic Effect

Learning Targets
- Create meaningful interpretive questions about stylistic elements.
- Make interpretive inferences about the effect of cinematic techniques

LEARNING STRATEGIES:
Close Reading, Graphic
Organizer, Levels of
Questions, Think-Pair-Share

Analyzing Style in Film

You will first view a segment of *Charlie and the Chocolate Factory* for its visual effects without hearing the sound track. In this first viewing, pay close attention to the following shots and lighting:

- **long shots** to establish the setting
- **medium shots** to display the body language of the characters
- **close-up shots** to display facial expressions of the characters
- **shot-reverse-shot** to show a conversation between characters and to build tension
- **lighting** to establish mood

1. As you view the film clip without sound, take notes in second column ("Observations") of the graphic organizer on next page. Then, share your observations with your class. If another class member identifies a detail that you missed, add it to your notes.

2. Next, you will view the film for its visual effects combined with the sound track. As you view the film this time, pay close attention to any shots or lighting that you might have missed. Also, listen closely to the sound track and distinguish between the following:

- **diegetic sound**, which could logically be heard by the characters (including dialogue and background noises)
- **non-diegetic sound**, which only the audience can hear (includes the film's musical track)

Note also the use of this visual plot device:

- **flashbacks**—A shift in a narrative to an earlier event that interrupts the normal chronological development of the story

My Notes

More About Stylistic Effect

Charlie and the Chocolate Factory	Observations: Note what you observe in this scene—camera movement, angles, shots, sound, lighting, setting, characters, etc.	Interpretation: What can you infer about the intended effect from your observations?
First viewing, without sound Scenes 14–16 40:24–49:40		
Second viewing, with sound		
Final viewing (optional)		

Levels of Questions

Questioning the text is an active reading strategy that keeps you alert and connected with the text as you read. Below is a review of the three levels of questions and examples of each level that you could ask about *Charlie and the Chocolate Factory*:

- **Literal**—recall questions for which you can find answers in the text

  Example: Who are the people living with Charlie Bucket?

- **Interpretive**—questions that require you to use text information to make inferences, draw conclusions, compare or contrast details, or consider the author's purpose

  Example: Why does Burton use a close-up shot of the Golden Ticket?

- **Universal**—questions that are text-related but go beyond the text by making text-to-world or text-to-self connections

  Example: Have you ever wished hard for something, and your wish came true?

3. Using your observations from the graphic organizer, pose questions that relate to Burton's film style. (Write your questions in the My Notes space.)

   - First, generate three Level 2 questions that would help you understand why certain film techniques were used.

   - With a partner, share your questions during a pair-share, and answer the questions by making inferences based on your observations.

   - Take turns asking and answering your questions with your partner until you have each shared all three of your questions.

Remember: A well-supported response includes proving your answer with textual details.

4. After you have discussed your questions and answers, complete the third column of the graphic organizer, "Interpretation." Work in your discussion groups to share details and understandings of what you saw. If someone mentions a detail that you have not noted, add this information to your chart.

Check Your Understanding

Using the notes from your graphic organizer, write short responses to each of these questions. Be sure to cite textual evidence to support your responses.

- How does Burton manipulate camera angles and lighting to create his intended effects?
- How does he use sound (diegetic and non-diegetic) to enhance this scene?
- Why does he use a flashback scene? What does he accomplish in doing so?

My Notes

Interpreting Style: Tim Burton's *Edward Scissorhands*

Learning Targets

- Identify the tone, mood, and imagery created by cinematic techniques in a film.
- Make inferences or predictions based on observations and context.

Segment One—Opening Credits

As you learned when watching *Charlie and the Chocolate Factory*, Burton creates a "fantastical world" by manipulating cinematic features. You will now begin a study of another film directed by Tim Burton, *Edward Scissorhands*. As the first segment begins, look at the opening credits. Viewers often overlook the opening credits and title sequence of a film. However, Burton presents a great deal of information in this part of the segment.

1. Study the opening sequence closely and note what you see in the "Observations" column of the graphic organizer below.

2. Apply your critical thinking skills to (a) make predictions, (b) identify the mood (effect on audience), and (c) identify the tone (attitude of director). Write your responses in the "Interpretations" column.

Segment of Film	Observations: What is happening in this scene?	Interpretations: What can you infer or predict based on your observations?
The Opening Credits	Images and Shapes	Predictions
		Mood
		Tone
	Music	

My Notes

Segment Two: Frame Story—Grandmother and Granddaughter

3. The story of Edward Scissorhands is introduced in the "frame story" of the movie; an old woman prepares to narrate the story of Edward to her granddaughter. Read this section closely, being especially observant of the camera movements—such as tilting, panning, dollying—and the kinds of shots such as long shots, close-ups, and boom/crane shots. Watch the frame story closely, and note in the "Observations" column below what you see.

4. After reading this frame story segment, apply your critical thinking skills to interpret (a) musical changes, (b) camera movements, and (c) frame story and to make predictions. Write your responses in the "Interpretations" column.

Segment of Film	Observations: What is happening in this scene?	Interpretations: What can you infer or predict based on your observations?
The Frame Story: Grandmother with Granddaughter		

Check Your Understanding

Respond to the following:

• In the opening sequence, the images, music, and lighting all create a mood of _____, which makes me think this will be a _____ movie.

• In the frame story sequence, the images, music, and lighting suggest the story is a bedtime story. How does this suggestion shift the mood?

My Notes

Analyzing Burton's Style: Supporting with Textual Evidence

My Notes

Learning Targets

- Determine a director's purpose for his choice of cinematic techniques.
- Write an analytical statement that includes textual evidence for a claim.

First Viewing—Cinematic and Story Elements

You will now view the first chunk of *Edward Scissorhands*, Scenes 3–5. Give this segment a close reading and focus on the camera angles, dialogue, and lighting to understand character development and plot. To study this segment, you will work in discussion groups. The first group will be your "home base" and the second group the "expert" group.

1. Study this segment closely for character, setting, and plot development, as well as cinematic techniques. Then, respond to the questions that follow.

Discussion Questions for the Home Base Group

2. In your home base group, conduct a discussion of the five questions below. Be sure to cite textual details to support your responses. As group members share responses, decide what is relevant and accurate support and record information in your Reader/Writer Notebook.

   a. How does Burton use color and costuming to create character?

   b. What do you know about Peg from this segment?

   c. How is Edward developed as a character? What conflict is being set up?

   d. How has the director established a connection between Edward and Kim?

   e. How is the neighborhood portrayed? How is the audience supposed to feel about it?

Second Viewing

You will now form expert groups to analyze cinematic techniques. You will become an expert on one of the five techniques listed as column heads in the graphic organizer below.

As you watch the key sequence in this segment, closely read the text and record your observations on the graphic organizer so you can be prepared for discussion. Pay attention to the changing music and the use of specific kinds of shots in the castle.

Notes for Jigsaw Discussion of Key Sequence

3. In the graphic organizer below, note particularly interesting or effective examples of your assigned cinematic technique. You may need to put additional notes on a separate sheet of paper.

Framing/Angles	Lighting	Camera Movement	Music/Sound	Editing

Analyzing Burton's Style: Supporting with Textual Evidence

4. After you have completed your individual notes for this segment, share your thoughts with your group. As part of a collaborative discussion, all members should participate by presenting examples of their observations about cinematic techniques and the inferences they made. As a group, consider the accuracy and insights as everyone shares, and record notes when the group has agreed on what to record. Add any new details or ideas to your own list; these will help you with writing an analytical statement.

Writing an Analytical Statement with Textual Support

You will now practice the first step in writing a style analysis paper by writing an analytical statement. Writing an analytical statement requires you to understand and identify style and effect, so review these terms with your group members. As you develop your analytical statement, keep the following in mind:

Author's Purpose: The use of a device (literary, rhetorical, or cinematic) to create an intended effect or suggest an intended meaning

Effect: The result or influence of using a specific device

5. In the space below, describe the specific cinematic technique you studied, its effect, and an example from the film.

Cinematic technique:

Example(s) of this cinematic technique:

Effect(s) of this cinematic choice:

6. One way to pull your observations together for an analytical statement is to follow the model below. Complete these sentences using your cinematic technique and example.

Tim Burton, in *Edward Scissorhands*, uses _____

(cinematic element)

to _____. For example,

(achieve what purpose)

_____

(evidence from the text to support the topic sentence)

_____.

7. Using the preceding sentence frame, each member of your group will now write an analytical statement using different examples of the assigned cinematic technique. Remember to focus on the effect. After completing your statements, rotate around your group, taking turns reading each sentence. Respond to your peers by answering the following questions for each sentence. Groups should decide how they will incorporate peer responses into any revisions of the analytical statements.

- Does the statement identify the cinematic technique assigned to your group?
- Does the statement clearly present an accurate effect?
- Does the evidence accurately support the statement of effect?

8. Now, return to your home base group to share your expertise and analytical statements, with textual support, from your expert group. As each group member presents, respond thoughtfully to the multiple perspectives presented. Make notes to help you get a full picture of all the cinematic techniques presented in this segment.

Check Your Understanding

Write about a cinematic technique that you think Burton used best to create a dramatic effect in these opening scenes. Give examples, describe the effect, and cite evidence to support your opinion.

My Notes

Analyzing Burton's Style: Explaining with Commentary

LEARNING STRATEGIES:
Close Reading, Discussion Groups, Graphic Organizer, Predicting

My Notes

Learning Targets
- Demonstrate understanding of the effect of specific cinematic techniques in film.
- Write an analytical statement, including reflective commentary explaining the supporting textual evidence

First Viewing
You will now view the second chunk of *Edward Scissorhands*, Scenes 5–13. Give this segment a close reading and focus on the camera angles, dialogue, and lighting to understand character development and plot. For a study of this segment, you will continue to work in groups.

1. Study this segment closely for character and plot development and cinematic techniques. Make notes as needed.

Discussion Questions for the Home Base Group

2. In your home base group, conduct a discussion of the five questions below. Be sure to come to the discussion prepared to cite textual details to support your response. As group members share their responses, record answers in your Reader/Writer Notebook.

   a. Why does the neighborhood welcome Edward into their lives so quickly?

   b. How does the neighborhood seem to change after Edward's arrival?

   c. Kim's reaction to Edward is played for humor, but in what way is hers the most natural or realistic response?

   d. What hints in this segment indicate that all will not work out well?

   e. What did you notice in the plot sequence that was a purposeful editing decision by Burton?

Second Viewing

After forming expert groups, choose a new cinematic technique to watch for.

3. Using a graphic organizer like the one in Activity 2.18, note particularly interesting or effective examples of your chosen or assigned cinematic element. Keep in mind that you must have a clear understanding of all of the cinematic techniques, so take good notes during the jigsaw discussion that will follow this viewing.

4. After you have completed your notes for this segment, share your discoveries with your group. Each person in the group should read one example that he or she has found. As you discuss, work with your peers to clarify examples and connect the techniques to their effects. Continue around your group until everyone has shared lists. Add any new details or ideas to your list. Your detailed list will help you write an analytical statement.

Writing an Analytical Statement with Textual Support and Reflective Commentary

5. In this writing exercise, you will add reflective commentary to your analytical statement. The reflective commentary comes after the example. The job of the commentary is to show your understanding of the relationship between your example and your original claim. You can make a comment, explain the connection, illustrate the point you made, or perhaps prompt a realization in the mind of the reader. In other words, if your example is the "what," then the reflective commentary is the "so what."

To make your analysis, complete this statement for your assigned cinematic technique. Each member of your group will write an individual statement. Remember to use details from the film to describe the purpose and effect of the technique.

Tim Burton, in *Edward Scissorhands*, uses _____

(cinematic element)

to _____. For example,

(achieve what purpose)

_____

_____

(evidence from the text to support the topic sentence)

_____

_____

(reflective commentary)

Analyzing Burton's Style: Explaining with Commentary

6. Rotate around your group, reading each sentence. Respond to your peers by answering these questions for each statement:

    a. Does the statement identify the cinematic technique assigned to your group?

    b. Does the statement clearly present an accurate effect?

    c. Does the evidence accurately support the statement of effect?

    d. Does the statement include a reflective commentary that logically extends the explanation of the effect?

7. Now, return to your home base group to share your expertise and analytical statements, with textual support, from your expert group. As each group member presents, make notes so that you get a full picture of all of the cinematic techniques present in this segment.

Check Your Understanding

Write an explanation of how Burton used a specific cinematic technique effectively. Cite examples and evidence to support your opinion.

Analyzing Burton's Style: Bringing to Closure

Learning Targets

- Analyze cinematic techniques for character and plot development.
- Create a complete analytical statement with textual evidence, commentary, and closure that demonstrates an understanding of cinematic techniques in film.

First Viewing

You will now view and study the third chunk of *Edward Scissorhands*, Scenes 13–19. Give this segment a close reading and focus on the camera angles, dialogue, and lighting to understand character development and plot. For a study of this segment, you will continue to work in groups. In your home base group, review what you have learned about cinematic techniques from the first two viewings of *Edward Scissorhands*.

1. Study this segment closely for character and plot development and cinematic techniques. Make notes to help you remember specific techniques, examples, and effects.

Discussion Questions for the Home Base Group

2. After viewing this segment, with your home base group, conduct a discussion of the five questions below. Be sure to cite textual details to support your responses. As group members share responses, record answers in your Reader/Writer Notebook.

- How would you describe Edward's personality and attitude toward others?
- What is different about the neighborhood's treatment of Edward?
- What is the effect of the scene with Kim dancing in the ice crystals? How have her feelings about Edward changed? Why?
- How has Edward tried to fit in? Why has he failed?
- What does the "ethics lesson" reveal about Edward?

Second Viewing

3. In your expert groups, choose a different cinematic technique to watch for. Read this segment closely and record your observations using a note-taking graphic organizer like the one in Activity 2.18. Listen closely to the music and watch the framing of each scene. Note particularly interesting or effective uses of your assigned cinematic technique. Again, keep in mind that you must have a clear understanding of all of the cinematic techniques, so take good notes during the jigsaw discussion.

4. After you have completed your notes for this segment, share your discoveries with your group. Each person in the group should read one example that he or she has found. Continue around your group until everyone has shared lists. Add any new details or ideas to your list.

My Notes

Analyzing Burton's Style: Bringing to Closure

GRAMMAR &USAGE
Parallel Structure

Parallel Structure When you write, it is important to use **parallel structure**, that is, to express similar ideas in the same grammatical form. In the following examples, the parallel structures are in boldface type.

The speaker **cajoled, remonstrated,** and **threatened,** but the audience remained unmoved.

Lincoln stressed " . . . a government **of the people, by the people, and for the people** shall not perish from the earth." Gettysburg Address

"I came, I saw, I conquered," said Julius Caesar.

Analytical Statement with Textual Support, Reflective Commentary, and Closure

5. In this writing exercise, you will add a sentence of closure to your analytical statement. The closure sentence is the last part of a well-organized analytical statement. The job of the closure is to make clear the relationship between your example and your original claim. You can summarize, highlight key examples in your statement, or remind readers of your claim. The important point is not to repeat the claim sentence that begins your analytical statement. Use the sentence frame below to write an analytical statement that includes all of these parts:

- claim statement that includes cinematic element and explanation of purpose
- evidence from the text
- reflective commentary
- statement of closure that summarizes the key idea without repeating the claim sentence

Tim Burton, in *Edward Scissorhands*, uses _____

_____ *(cinematic element)*

to _____. For example,

(achieve what purpose)

_____

(Provide evidence from the text to support the topic sentence)

_____

_____

(reflective commentary)

_____

sentence of closure

_____

Language and Writer's Craft: Transitions

Look back at the preceding sentence frame, and review the phrases "For example" and "Unlike the long shots." Both of these phrases are transitional devices, linking ideas; however, they serve different purposes. "For example" introduces the textual evidence from the film. "Unlike the long shots" sets up a contrast between two film shots.

As you prepare your analytical writings, be sure to link ideas with appropriate transitional devices that signal movement of thought.

6. Using the sentence frame, each member of your group will write an analytical statement. Remember to focus on your chosen or assigned cinematic technique. Rotate around your group, reading each sentence. Respond to your peers by answering these questions for each analytical statement:

   • Does the claim statement identify the assigned cinematic technique?
   • Does the statement accurately present a specific effect?
   • Does the evidence accurately support the statement of effect?
   • Does the statement include a reflective commentary that logically extends the explanation of the effect?
   • Does the last sentence provide appropriate closure without repeating the first sentence?

   Your analytical statement:

7. Now, return to your home base group to share your expertise and analytical statements, with textual support, from your expert group. As each group member presents, make notes so that you get a full picture of all of the cinematic techniques present in this segment.

Check Your Understanding

What three cinematic techniques are most apparent in Burton's *Edward Scissorhands*, and what effects does he create with his manipulation of these techniques?

My Notes

Analyzing Burton's Style: Writing the Analytical Paragraph

LEARNING STRATEGIES:
Close Reading, Discussion
Groups, Graphic Organizer,
Note-taking, Sharing and
Responding

My Notes

Learning Targets
- Understand the director's purpose for cinematic choices in order to interpret visual text.
- Write an extended paragraph of analysis.

First Reading

You will now view the last chunk of *Edward Scissorhands*, Scenes 19–24. Give this segment a close reading and focus on the camera angles, dialogue, and lighting to understand character development and plot. For a study of this segment, you will continue to work in groups.

1. In your home base group, review what you have learned about cinematic techniques from the first three viewings of *Edward Scissorhands*.

2. Read this segment closely for character and plot development and cinematic techniques. Make notes as needed to support your group discussions.

Discussion Questions for Home Base Group

3. After viewing this segment, with your home base group conduct a discussion of the five questions that follow. Be sure to cite textual details to support your response. As group members share their responses, record answers in your Reader/Writer Notebook.

   - Does Edward's action seem justified?
   - How does Edward appear to feel about Jim's death?
   - How does Kim appear to feel?
   - Why do you think Edward cuts his clothes off?
   - Most fairy tales have a lesson or a moral to teach. What do you think Kim wants her granddaughter to learn from her story?

Second Reading

4. In your expert groups, choose a different cinematic technique to watch for. By this time you should have taken expert notes on three other cinematic techniques used in the film. Listen closely to the music and watch the framing of each scene. Closely read and record your observations using a graphic organizer. Note the scenes in which you see particularly interesting or effective uses of your chosen cinematic element. Again, keep in mind that you must have a clear understanding of all of the cinematic techniques, so take good notes during the jigsaw discussion.

5. After you have completed your notes for this segment, share your discoveries with your group. Continue around your group until each member has shared one example. Add any new details or ideas to your list. Your detailed list wil help as you write an extended analytical statement about the purpose and effect of Burton's use of specific cinematic techniques.

The analytical statements that you have completed in previous activities are a mini-outline for a well-supported, well-organized paragraph. Notice how each piece of an analytical statement reflects the organizational parts of a paragraph. The paragraph should repeat the support and elaboration sections to explore more than one example or more than one piece of textual evidence. Link these examples, details, and commentaries with transitional devices.

Analytical Statement	Paragraph
Sentence that makes a claim about a cinematic technique	Topic sentence that introduces the main idea of the paragraph
Textual Evidence	Support by example or textual evidence
Reflective commentary	Elaboration, discussion, or explanation of the significance of the support
Closure statement	Closure, clincher, or summarizing sentence that draws the paragraph to an end

6. Before you return to your home base group, as a group, participate in the writing of an extended paragraph that analyzes your groups's assigned cinematic technique. Because this is a group effort, it is especially important that all members share information, determine what evidence is best, and agree on appropriate commentary about the significant effects. This is an opportunity to exchange ideas and actively challenge each other's thinking.

Writing Prompt: Write a well-developed paragraph analyzing Burton's use of one specific cinematic element in *Edward Scissorhands*. Be sure to include all the features that you have practiced, including:

- analytical claim and textual support
- reflective commentary and closure
- at least two examples of the use and effect of the cinematic technique

7. Now, return to your home base group to share your expertise and analytical statements, with textual support and closure, from your expert group. As each group member presents, make notes so you get a full picture of all of the cinematic techniques present in this segment.

My Notes

Independent Viewing

My Notes

Learning Targets

- Discover connections between cinematic techniques and their effects in multiple texts by the same director.
- Explain the effects of cinematic techniques on the audience.

You have viewed two Tim Burton movies and analyzed them for their overall effect on the audience. You will now view another Tim Burton film and work individually to identify film techniques and their effects, in order to:

- ensure that you can recognize film techniques and their effects
- ensure that you understand how these techniques influence the audience
- prepare you for success by ensuring that you have knowledge of three films by Burton to complete Embedded Assessment 2

Use the following double-entry journal or create your own for your individual notes, identifying film techniques and their effects in the next Tim Burton film. You will use these examples in your final writing assessment, so identify as many examples as you can. Use notebook paper if you need additional space.

Film Technique and Example (Framing/Angles, Lighting, Camera Movement, Music/Sound, and Editing)	Effect
1. In *Big Fish*, a dolly/tracking shot allows viewers to see the movement of the fish through its own eyes rather than those of an omniscient (all-seeing) observer.	1. Establishes a first-person point of view and helps the viewer to understand the perspective of the animal as a character rather than an object
2. In *Edward Scissorhands*, a tracking shot follows movement out the window with a boom/crane shot over the neighborhood to the mansion on the hill.	

Film Technique and Example (Framing/Angles, Lighting, Camera Movement, Music/Sound, and Editing)	Effect

Check Your Understanding

After viewing the film(s), what similarities or differences in style and/or theme did you notice in relation to the other Tim Burton films you have watched? Record your ideas on separate paper or in your Reader/Writer Notebook. Write a piece in which you identify the films and compare or contrast details from each.

Planning a Draft

LEARNING STRATEGIES:
Graphic Organizer,
Prewriting

Learning Targets
- Draft a thesis statement.
- Plan a well-organized style analysis essay by completing a content frame for comparison of text.

1. Consider all of the films you have viewed in class. Fill in the content frame below with details that help you understand how each element is used in each film. You will use this content frame organizer to synthesize similarities and differences among the films that you have studied. You can refer to your notes from Activities 2.14–2.22 to help you cite details.

Cinematic Technique	Charlie and the Chocolate Factory	Edward Scissorhands	Independent Film Title:
Framing			
Lighting			
Camera Movements			
Music/Sound			
Editing			

2. How does Tim Burton use cinematic techniques to achieve a particular effect? Cite examples from at least two films. Review Activities 2.14 through 2.22 to help you formulate your thesis statement.

3. Return to the comparison of the analytical statement and the paragraph. Just as the analytical statement is a "mini" paragraph in organization, so is the paragraph a "mini" essay in organizational pattern. Study the chart below to identify the differences and the similar components among the three types of organization.

Analytical Statement	Analytical Paragraph	Analytical Essay
Sentence that makes a claim about a cinematic technique	Topic sentence that introduces the main idea of the paragraph	Thesis sentence that summarizes the main idea of the essay; the thesis sentence is usually in the essay's first paragraph.
Textual Evidence	Support by example or textual evidence (often introduced by transitional devices)	Body paragraphs in which each idea is organized in the manner described in the "Paragraph" column. These paragraphs are linked with effective transitional devices.
Reflective commentary	Elaboration, discussion, or explanation of the significance of the support (often connected by transitional devices)	
Closure statement	Closure, clincher, or summarizing sentence that draws the paragraph to an end	Conclusion that summarizes the main idea and often answers these three questions: What did you say? (Literal) What does it mean? (Interpretive) Why does it matter? (Universal)

Check Your Understanding

Draft an analytical thesis statement that makes a claim about Tim Burton's style as represented by the effective use of specific cinematic techniques. From your completed content frame graphic organizer, select three or four of the cinematic techniques for which you have clear, relevant, and effective examples.

Thesis Statement:

Planning a Draft

Use the following topic outline to guide you as you craft your plan for a multiple-paragraph analytical essay. Use the space in the outline for your notes.

Body Paragraph: Topic Outline

Focus on one cinematic technique for each paragraph, and outline its effect in multiple films. For the topic sentence, think about the transition you could use to focus the reader's attention. You do not need to write complete sentences for your planning; include idea statements only.

Topic sentence:

    Evidence:

    Commentary:

    Evidence:

    Commentary:

    Evidence:

    Commentary:

Statement of closure:

For each body paragraph, develop your ideas following this organizational pattern. You should plan to write as many paragraphs as you need to prove the claim in your thesis statement.

Writing a Style Analysis Essay

Assignment

Think about the Tim Burton films that you have viewed and analyzed. Choose three or four stylistic devices (cinematic techniques) that are common to these films. Write an essay analyzing the cinematic style of director Tim Burton. Your essay should focus on the ways in which the director uses stylistic techniques across films to achieve a desired effect.

Planning and Prewriting: Take time to gather and organize your ideas.

- What films, graphic organizers, and notes will you need In order to write an analysis of Tim Burton's cinematic style?
- How can you use your Writing Group to help you craft an effective thesis statement and refine your thinking about the examples you will include for each stylistic element?

Drafting: Determine the structure of your essay.

- How will you be sure all the components of an expository essay—the thesis, introduction, body paragraphs, and conclusion—are coherently and clearly connected?
- What is the most effective textual evidence you can use to develop your topic and create a powerful commentary?
- How can you use your practice writing from *Edward Scissorhands* as a model for developing your body paragraphs?

Evaluating and Revising the Draft: Create opportunities to review and revise in order to make your work the best it can be.

- What questions and discussion starters can you use to guide sharing your draft with your Writing Group?
- How can you use the Scoring Guide criteria to guide responses and suggestions for revision?

Checking and Editing for Publication: Confirm that your final draft is ready for publication.

- How will you use available resources (e.g., spell check, digital dictionaries, Writer's Checklist) to edit for correctness of grammar and conventions and prepare your essay for publication?
- Your focus for editing should be on the skills that you have studied in this unit, including: sentence variety, syntax, sentence combining, parallel structure, punctuation of quotations, colon, semicolon, and conjunctive adverb with comma.

Reflection

Consider how your understanding of organizing and structuring your writing has guided your use of detail and commentary in writing an essay of analysis.

- How has the close analysis of film techniques in this unit changed the way you view non-print texts outside of class?
- How could your understanding of how directors use cinematic techniques for effect help you analyze author's purpose in a literary text?

My Notes

Writing a Style Analysis Essay

SCORING GUIDE

Scoring Criteria	Exemplary	Proficient	Emerging	Incomplete
Ideas	The essay • clearly identifies and analyzes Burton's style, uses evidence from multiple films, and provides insightful commentary • displays in-depth understanding of cinematic techniques and how they create specific effects.	The essay • clearly identifies and describes the director's style, using support from more than one film • displays a clear understanding of the effect of the director's cinematic choices.	The essay • shows limited understanding of the director's style; support is insufficient or inaccurate • confuses how the director achieves an intended effect and/or may include a plot summary rather than an analysis.	The essay • summarizes the plot with little attention to elements of style • does not show an understanding of the director's cinematic choices and their intended effect.
Structure	The essay • is logically organized • introduces the topic clearly and develops a strong thesis; body paragraphs develop the topic with examples and details leading to a perceptive conclusion • uses transitions effectively to clarify ideas and create cohesion.	The essay • is well-organized • introduces a clear thesis, uses detailed body paragraphs, and provides a conclusion that supports the explanation • uses transitions to create clarity and cohesion.	The essay • is not well-organzied • may have an unfocused thesis, undeveloped body paragraphs, and/or inadequate conclusion • uses few, if any, transitions to create clarity or cohesion.	The essay • is confusing and/or missing key parts • omits the thesis or does not develop it • uses no transitions to create clarity or cohesion.
Use of Language	The essay • uses a formal style and demonstrates a precise and sophisticated use of terminology to knowledgeably discuss cinematic style • has few or no errors in standard English usage.	The essay • maintains a formal style and demonstrates correct use of film and literary vocabulary to discuss style • is generally error free.	The essay • uses informal or inappropriate diction and demonstrates limited use of film vocabulary to discuss style • contains errors that distract from meaning.	The essay • shows little use of the vocabulary of literary and style analysis • contains multiple errors in language and conventions that interfere with meaning.

Coming of Age in Changing Times

Visual Prompt: What do you think is the context for this photograph? When and where was it taken? What clues help you make inferences about the setting? Why is the time and place important to understanding the significance of the imagery?

Unit Overview

Of Harper Lee's *To Kill a Mockingbird*, Oprah Winfrey said, "I think it is our national novel." The book's narrator, Scout Finch, reflects on her coming-of-age experiences as a young girl confronting prejudice in her own community and learning how to live in a less-than-perfect world. In this unit, you will examine how social, cultural, geographical, and historical context can affect both the writer's construction of a text and readers' responses to it. You will conduct and present research to understand both the setting of the novel *To Kill a Mockingbird* and the civil rights struggles that surrounded its controversial publication. While reading the novel, you will analyze literary elements in selected passages in order to discover how an author develops the overall themes of the work. Every part of To *Kill a Mockingbird* contributes to the whole—from a little girl rolling down the street inside a tire to a black man standing trial for his life.

Coming of Age in Changing Times

GOALS:

- To gather and integrate relevant information from multiple sources to answer research questions
- To present findings clearly, concisely, and logically, making strategic use of digital media
- To analyze how literary elements contribute to the development of a novel's themes
- To write a literary analysis, citing textual evidence to support ideas and inferences

ACADEMIC VOCABULARY
context
primary source
secondary source
plagiarize
parenthetical citations
valid
rhetoric
bibliography
annotated bibliography
evaluate
censor
censorship

Literary Terms
expository writing
flashback
motif
plot
subplot
symbol
flat/static character
round/dynamic character

Contents

Activities

Texts not included in these materials

Previewing the Unit

My Notes

Learning Targets
- Explore preliminary thinking by writing responses to the Essential Questions.
- Identify the skills and knowledge required to complete Embedded Assessment 1 successfully.

Making Connections
In this unit, you will study the novel *To Kill a Mockingbird* in depth. As part of this study, you will examine the historical and cultural context of the novel and analyze literary elements that develop the themes of the novel. You will also apply your knowledge of film techniques as you examine clips from the film *To Kill a Mockingbird*, analyze the director's choices, and make comparisons between film and literary elements in the novel.

Essential Questions
Based on your current knowledge, write your answers to these questions.

1. What impact does context have on a novel and on the reactions of readers to it?

2. How does a key scene from a novel contribute to the work as a whole?

Developing Vocabulary
Review the terms listed on the Contents page for Academic Vocabulary and Literary Terms. Use a QHT or other strategy to analyze and evaluate your knowledge of those words. Use your Reader/Writer Notebook to make notes about meanings you know already. Add to your notes as you study this unit and gain greater understanding of each of these words.

Unpacking Embedded Assessment 1
Read the assignment for Embedded Assessment 1: Historical Investigation and Presentation.

> Your assignment is to research the historical, cultural, social, and/or geographical context of the novel *To Kill a Mockingbird* and investigate how individuals, organizations, and events contributed to change in the United States during the Civil Rights Movement. You will work collaboratively to create an oral presentation of your findings with multimedia support and guiding questions for your audience.

In your own words, summarize what you will need to know to complete this assessment successfully. With your class, create a graphic organizer to represent the skills and knowledge you will need to complete the tasks identified in the Embedded Assessment.

INDEPENDENT READING LINK
For independent reading in this unit, you might choose another novel or you might read informational texts about the United States during the 1930s—the time period in which *To Kill a Mockingbird* is set.

Picturing the Past

Learning Targets

- Identify the historical, cultural, social, and geographical contexts of the setting, writing, and publication of the novel *To Kill a Mockingbird*.
- Summarize observations about context from visual images.

Developing Context

1. With a partner, brainstorm what you already know about the idea of **context**. Create a web graphic organizer below.

   Once you have investigated the idea of context, add branches for historical, cultural, social, and geographical aspects. In your discussion, be sure you understand what each term describes in relation to context.

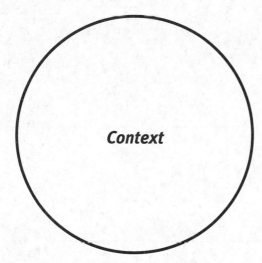

Context

2. To develop an understanding of the context for the novel *To Kill a Mockingbird*, view the photographs your teacher has provided. Keep in mind that the novel is set in the 1930s, but it was written years later and first published in 1960.

   Note your observations and questions about the images on the graphic organizer on the next page.

> **LEARNING STRATEGIES:**
> Graphic Organizer, Word Maps, Drafting, Discussion Groups

> **ACADEMIC VOCABULARY**
> When reading a text, you may find words that you do not know. You can use the **context**—the words around the text—to infer meaning. In the same way, the context of a novel or a situation refers to the circumstances or conditions in which the thing exists or takes place. Knowing context helps you understand the novel or situation better.

My Notes

Picturing the Past

Photo #	Observation: Note the details of the image in the photograph.	Reflection: What is your response to the images in the photograph?	Questions: What questions come to mind that might lead to further exploration or research?
Unit Opener photo			

3. **Discussion Groups:** After viewing the photographs, meet with your group to discuss the questions you have created. You may want to use these questions to prompt your research for the Embedded Assessment. Share and respond to others' questions, and add new questions to your own list.

Writing Prompt: Summarize what you learned from the photographs about the context of the setting, writing, and publication of the novel *To Kill a Mockingbird*. Be sure to:

- Begin with a topic sentence summarizing your understanding of the context provided by the photographs.
- Include specific relevant details about images that stood out or informed your understanding.
- Provide commentary about what you saw and learned.

INDEPENDENT READING LINK

As you begin your independent reading, think about the historical, cultural, and social contexts reflected in the setting; for example, in the ways that characters behave. If you are reading a novel, consider the ways that the contexts, together with literary elements, contribute to the general effect of the novel and its theme.

My Notes

Setting the Context

LEARNING STRATEGIES:
Marking the Text, Metacognitive
Markers, Previewing

Learning Target

- Analyze a secondary and a primary source to understand the cultural, social, and legal contexts of the novel *To Kill a Mockingbird*.

Before Reading

1. Consider the following quotations by American presidents. What do they tell you about the progress toward equal rights for all races during this period of time in our country?

"Every segment of our population, and every individual, has a right to expect from his government a fair deal." —*Harry S. Truman, 1945*

"The final battle against intolerance is to be fought—not in the chambers of any legislature—but in the hearts of men." —*Dwight D. Eisenhower, 1956*

"There are no 'white' or 'colored' signs on the foxholes or graveyards of battle." —*John Fitzgerald Kennedy, 1963*

"The vote is the most powerful instrument ever devised by man for breaking down injustice and destroying the terrible walls which imprison men because they are different from other men." —*Lyndon B. Johnson, 1965*

During Reading

2. **Focus Question:** What were Jim Crow laws? As you read the following article, mark the text to identify the words and phrases that help you to define the meaning of the term *Jim Crow* and understand its importance in American history.

My Notes

Informational Text

Jim Crow:
Shorthand for **Separation**

by Rick Edmonds

"Jim Crow" the term, like Jim Crow the practice, settled in over a long period of time. By the 1950s, Jim Crow was the colloquialism whites and blacks routinely used for the complex system of laws and customs separating the races in the South. Hardly anyone felt a particular need to define it or explore its origins.

The term appears to date back at least to the eighteenth century, though there is no evidence that it refers to an individual. Rather it was mildly derogatory slang for a black everyman (Crow, as in black like a crow). A popular American minstrel song of the 1820s made sport of a stereotypic Jim Crows. "Jump Jim Crow" was a sort of jig. By the mid-1800s, a segregated rail car might be called the "Jim Crow." As segregation laws were put into place—first in Tinnessee, then throughout the South—after Reconstruction, such diverse things as separate public facilities and laws restricting voting rights became known collectively as Jim Crow.

A bit like "political correctness" in recent years, the term was particularly popular with opponents of the practice. It was a staple of NAACP conversations of the '30s and '40s. Ralph Bunche once said he would turn down an appointment as ambassador to Liberia because he "wouldn't take a Jim Crow job." A skit at Morehouse College during Martin Luther King's student days portrayed a dramatic "burial" of Jim Crow. And . . . at the eventful Republican National Convention in 1964 in San Francisco, picketers outside the hall chanted, "Jim Crow (clap, clap) must go." . . .

From material in *American Heritage Dictionary*, *Safire's Political Dictionary*, and *From Slavery to Freedom*.

After Reading

3. Work with your class to create a working definition of Jim Crow laws, and write the definition below.

GRAMMAR &USAGE
Prepositional Phrases
The second sentence in this essay begins with a prepositional phrase, "By the 1950s." A prepositional phrase consists of a preposition, its object, and any modifiers of the object.

Common prepositions include *about, across, in, by, after, on, for, until, at*, and *up*. A preposition shows the relationship or connection between its object and some other word. In the sentence identified above, for example, *by* shows the relationship between "1950s" and the term "Jim Crow."

My Notes

My Notes

_____
_____
_____
_____
_____
_____
_____
_____
_____
_____
_____
_____
_____
_____
_____
_____
_____

KEY IDEAS AND DETAILS
What is the significance of the references to gender as well as race in some of these laws?

_____
_____
_____
_____
_____
_____
_____
_____
_____
_____
_____
_____
_____
_____
_____
_____

Before Reading

4. Scan the Jim Crow laws on the next few pages. Using the bold type as a guide, work with other members of your group to create a list of possible categories into which you might sort the laws.

During Reading

5. **Focus Question:** How did Jim Crow laws deprive American citizens of their rights? As you read, use metacognitive markers to respond to the text as follows:

- Put a ? next to lines that are confusing or bring up questions.
- Put a * next to lines that are interesting or reinforce what you already know.
- Put a ! next to lines that are surprising or help you make predictions.

Informational Text

Jim Crow Laws
Martin Luther King Jr. National Historic Site

Compiled by the National Park Service, US Department of the Interior

1 Nurses No person or corporation shall require any white female nurse to nurse in wards or rooms in hospitals, either public or private, in which negro men are placed. *Alabama*

2 Buses All passenger stations in this state operated by any motor transportation company shall have separate waiting rooms or space and separate ticket windows for the white and colored races. *Alabama*

3 Restaurants It shall be unlawful to conduct a restaurant or other place for the serving of food in the city, at which white and colored people are served in the same room, unless such white and colored persons are effectually separated by a solid partition extending from the floor upward to a distance of seven feet or higher, and unless a separate entrance from the street is provided for each compartment. *Alabama*

4 Pool and Billiard Rooms It shall be unlawful for a negro and white person to play together or in company with each other at any game of pool or billiards. *Alabama*

5 Intermarriage The marriage of a person of Caucasian blood with a Negro, Mongolian, Malay, or Hindu shall be null and void. *Arizona*

6 Intermarriage All marriages between a white person and a negro, or between a white person and a person of negro descent to the fourth generation inclusive, are hereby forever prohibited. *Florida*

7 Education The schools for white children and the schools for negro children shall be conducted separately. *Florida*

8 Mental Hospitals The Board of Control shall see that proper and distinct apartments are arranged for said patients, so that in no case shall Negroes and white persons be together. *Georgia*

9 Barbers No colored barber shall serve as a barber [to] white women or girls. *Georgia*

10 Burial The officer in charge shall not bury, or allow to be buried, any colored persons upon ground set apart or used for the burial of white persons. *Georgia*

11 Restaurants All persons licensed to conduct a restaurant shall serve either white people exclusively or colored people exclusively and shall not sell to the two races within the same room or serve the two races anywhere under the same license. *Georgia*

12 Amateur Baseball It shall be unlawful for any amateur white baseball team to play baseball on any vacant lot or baseball diamond within two blocks of a playground devoted to the Negro race, and it shall be unlawful for any amateur colored baseball team to play baseball in any vacant lot or baseball diamond within two blocks of any playground devoted to the white race. *Georgia*

13 Parks It shall be unlawful for colored people to frequent any park owned or maintained by the city for the benefit, use and enjoyment of white persons . . . and unlawful for any white person to frequent any park owned or maintained by the city for the use and benefit of colored persons. *Georgia*

14 Reform Schools The children of white and colored races committed to the houses of reform shall be kept entirely separate from each other. *Kentucky*

15 Circus Tickets All circuses, shows, and tent exhibitions, to which the attendance of . . . more than one race is invited or expected to attend shall provide for the convenience of its patrons not less than two ticket offices with individual ticket sellers, and not less than two entrances to the said performance, with individual ticket takers and receivers, and in the case of outside or tent performances, the said ticket offices shall not be less than twenty-five (25) feet apart. *Louisiana*

16 The Blind The board of trustees shall . . . maintain a separate building . . . on separate ground for the admission, care, instruction, and support of all blind persons of the colored or black race. *Louisiana*

17 Railroads All railroad companies and corporations, and all persons running or operating cars or coaches by steam on any railroad line or track in the State of Maryland, for the transportation of passengers, are hereby required to provide separate cars or coaches for the travel and transportation of the white and colored passengers. *Maryland*

WORD CONNECTIONS

Foreign Words
Legal documents use many foreign words and phrases, primarily Latin. *Quid pro quo* means "to give something of value to get something else of value in return." *Ipso facto* means "by the fact itself." It may be used to describe factual evidence.

KEY IDEAS AND DETAILS
Why is the Jim Crow law about care of the blind particularly ironic?

My Notes

Setting the Context

KEY IDEAS AND DETAILS
How might the law about hospital entrances be dangerous to people who could not use the main entrance?

My Notes

_____
_____
_____
_____
_____
_____
_____

18 **Promotion of Equality** Any person . . . who shall be guilty of printing, publishing or circulating printed, typewritten or written matter urging or presenting for public acceptance or general information, arguments or suggestions in favor of social equality or of intermarriage between whites and negroes, shall be guilty of a misdemeanor and subject to fine not exceeding five hundred (500.00) dollars or imprisonment not exceeding six (6) months or both. *Mississippi*

19 **Intermarriage** The marriage of a white person with a negro or mulatto or person who shall have one-eighth or more of negro blood, shall be unlawful and void. *Mississippi*

20 **Hospital Entrances** There shall be maintained by the governing authorities of every hospital maintained by the state for treatment of white and colored patients separate entrances for white and colored patients and visitors, and such entrances shall be used by the race only for which they are prepared. *Mississippi*

21 **Prisons** The warden shall see that the white convicts shall have separate apartments for both eating and sleeping from the negro convicts. *Mississippi*

22 **Education** Separate free schools shall be established for the education of children of African descent; and it shall be unlawful for any colored child to attend any white school, or any white child to attend a colored school. *Missouri*

23 **Intermarriage** All marriages between . . . white persons and negroes or white persons and Mongolians . . . are prohibited and declared absolutely void . . . . No person having one-eighth part or more of negro blood shall be permitted to marry any white person, nor shall any white person be permitted to marry any negro or person having one-eighth part or more of negro blood. *Missouri*

24 **Education** Separate rooms [shall] be provided for the teaching of pupils of African descent, and [when] said rooms are so provided, such pupils may not be admitted to the school rooms occupied and used by pupils of Caucasian or other descent. *New Mexico*

25 **Textbooks** Books shall not be interchangeable between the white and colored schools, but shall continue to be used by the race first using them. *North Carolina*

26 **Libraries** The state librarian is directed to fit up and maintain a separate place for the use of the colored people who may come to the library for the purpose of reading books or periodicals. *North Carolina*

27 **Transportation** The . . . Utilities Commission . . . is empowered and directed to require the establishment of separate waiting rooms at all stations for the white and colored races. *North Carolina*

28 **Teaching** Any instructor who shall teach in any school, college or institution where members of the white and colored race are received and enrolled as pupils for instruction shall be deemed guilty of a misdemeanor, and upon conviction thereof, shall be fined in any sum not less than ten dollars ($10.00) nor more than fifty dollars ($50.00) for each offense. *Oklahoma*

29 Fishing, Boating, and Bathing The [Conservation] Commission shall have the right to make segregation of the white and colored races as to the exercise of rights of fishing, boating and bathing. *Oklahoma*

30 Telephone Booths The Corporation Commission is hereby vested with power and authority to require telephone companies . . . to maintain separate booths for white and colored patrons when there is a demand for such separate booths. That the Corporation Commission shall determine the necessity for said separate booths only upon complaint of the people in the town and vicinity to be served after due hearing as now provided by law in other complaints filed with the Corporation Commission. *Oklahoma*

31 Lunch Counters No persons, firms, or corporations, who or which furnish meals to passengers at station restaurants or station eating houses, in times limited by common carriers of said passengers, shall furnish said meals to white and colored passengers in the same room, or at the same table, or at the same counter. *South Carolina*

32 Libraries Any white person of such county may use the county free library under the rules and regulations prescribed by the commissioners court and may be entitled to all the privileges thereof. Said court shall make proper provision for the negroes of said county to be served through a separate branch or branches of the county free library, which shall be administered by [a] custodian of the negro race under the supervision of the county librarian. *Texas*

33 Education [The County Board of Education] shall provide schools of two kinds; those for white children and those for colored children. *Texas*

34 Railroads The conductors or managers on all such railroads shall have power, and are hereby required, to assign to each white or colored passenger his or her respective car, coach or compartment. If the passenger fails to disclose his race, the conductor and managers, acting in good faith, shall be the sole judges of his race. *Virginia*

35 Theaters Every person . . . operating . . . any public hall, theatre, opera house, motion picture show or any place of public entertainment or public assemblage which is attended by both white and colored persons, shall separate the white race and the colored race and shall set apart and designate . . . certain seats therein to be occupied by white persons and a portion thereof, or certain seats therein, to be occupied by colored persons. *Virginia*

36 Intermarriage All marriages of white persons with Negroes, Mulattos, Mongolians, or Malayans hereafter contracted in the State of Wyoming are and shall be illegal and void. *Wyoming*

WORD CONNECTIONS

Multiple Meaning Words

The word *provision* has several meanings. It may mean to supply or fit out, as in to provision a campsite. As a noun, it may mean something provided (or supplies in the plural). It may also mean a stipulation or qualification, such as a clause in a document or agreement. Use context clues to determine the meaning of *provision* as it is used in paragraph 32.

KEY IDEAS AND DETAILS

What do the names of the states tell you about the scope of Jim Crow laws?

My Notes

_____

_____

_____

_____

_____

_____

_____

_____

_____

_____

_____

_____

_____

_____

_____

_____

Setting the Context

ACTIVITY 3.3
continued

ACADEMIC VOCABULARY

A **primary source** is an original document containing firsthand information about a subject.
A **secondary source** is a discussion about or commentary on a primary source; the key feature of a secondary source is that it offers an interpretation of information gathered from primary sources.

WORD CONNECTIONS

Analogies

An analogy may use both words and phrases. For example, Jim Crow laws : segregation as negligence : accident. This analogy shows a cause-effect relationship. Write two additional cause-effect analogies, either on your own or as part of a class activity. Use both phrases and words.

My Notes

_____
_____
_____
_____
_____
_____
_____
_____
_____
_____
_____
_____
_____
_____
_____
_____

After Reading

5. Revisit your list of categories of Jim Crow laws, revising it if needed. Work with your group to create a poster that represents 3–4 categories and includes brief summaries of several laws that fall into each category.

6. Which of the sources in this activity is a **primary source**?

7. What are the benefits of a primary source?

8. Which is a **secondary source**?

9. What are the benefits of a secondary source?

10. Which source was more helpful to you in answering the research questions about Jim Crow laws, and why?

Researching and Presenting Information

Learning Targets

- Conduct research by exploring a website and gathering information for a presentation on the rise and fall of Jim Crow laws.
- Organize information into a coherent piece and make an oral presentation.

LEARNING STRATEGIES:
KWHL, Note-taking, Graphic Organizer

Organizing Information

1. Based on the photographs and sources you examined in the previous activities, fill out the first two columns of the KWHL chart below KWHL. A KWHL chart is an effective tool to help focus and refine research activity by determining which topics need further research and where to find the needed information.

K: What do I know about Jim Crow?	W: What more do I want to know about Jim Crow?	H: How will I find information?	L: What have I learned about Jim Crow?

Researching and Presenting Information

ACADEMIC VOCABULARY
Plagiarism is using another person's ideas without giving credit. Researchers must always give credit by citing sources. **Parenthetical citations** are used for citing sources directly in an essay. In contrast, some writers place citations in footnotes or endnotes.

My Notes

2. Choose at least three questions that you will use to guide your investigation of the PBS website "The Rise and Fall of Jim Crow": www.pbs.org/wnet/jimcrow. As you explore the website, complete the graphic organizer as follows:

- In the "H" column, record the URLs of the page or pages where you find information to answer your questions so that you can easily find them again.
- In the "L" column, take notes to summarize the answers to your questions.
- Add new questions generated by your research to the "W" column.

3. Select one question that you were able to answer in your investigation of the website. Copy the following onto an index card:

- The research question and webpage URL
- A brief summary of the information you learned
- At least one new question generated by the answers

4. Present your findings to at least two of your peers. Display the appropriate webpage as a visual for your audience, but use your index cards so that you can maintain eye contact instead of reading information from the computer screen. Be prepared to answer any questions your audience may have about the information you are presenting.

5. As you listen to your peers' presentations, evaluate how well each presenter summarizes the information on the webpage in a clear and concise manner, faces the audience, and uses eye contact. Take notes in the graphic organizer on the next page. After each presentation, be sure to ask questions to clarify your understanding of the information presented.

Language and Writer's Craft: Citing Sources

When you quote a source verbatim or include information that is not common knowledge, you must cite the source to avoid **plagiarism**. Several different style guides provide information on how to cite sources, such as the *Chicago Manual of Style*, the APA (American Psychological Association), and MLA (Modern Language Association). This book uses MLA; you should be consistent and use only one style in a document.

To use a **parenthetical citation**, write the author's last name (and a page number if available) in parentheses at the end of the sentence. If no author is given, use the first words of the title. Examples:

. . . became known collectively as Jim Crow (Edmonds 7).

. . . entirely separate from each other ("Jim Crow Laws").

. . . was actually supported by Plessy v. Ferguson ("The Rise and Fall of Jim Crow").

Presenter Name and Research Question	Information Learned from the Investigation	My Thoughts and Questions	Evaluation of Presenting Skills

Notice that the writing prompt below is labeled **"Expository."** You have used this method of writing whenever you have explained something or have written directions. Expository writing answers the questions of *who, what, where, when, why,* and *how.* Expository writing should do the following:

- Focus on a main topic.
- Provide details, explanations, and examples presented in a logical order.
- Present clear, precise ideas connected with smooth transitions to create coherence.

Expository Writing Prompt: Explain how Jim Crow laws and practices deprived American citizens of their civil rights. Use information from the website you researched as well as from the two informational texts in Activity 3.3. Avoid plagiarism by using precise citations. Be sure to:

- Define the term "Jim Crow" in your topic sentence.
- Include well-chosen textual evidence with parenthetical citations from at least two sources.
- Provide commentary on the specific civil rights violations: educational rights, social freedoms, voting rights.

Literary Terms

Expository writing is a form of writing whose purpose is to explain, describe, or give information about a topic in order to inform a reader.

My Notes

_____
_____
_____
_____
_____
_____
_____
_____
_____
_____
_____
_____

A Time for Change

LEARNING STRATEGIES:
SOAPSTone, Marking the Text,
Drafting

My Notes

Learning Targets
• Analyze a historical document for its purpose, audience, claims, and evidence.

Before Reading

1. In 1962, Bob Dylan's song "Blowin' in the Wind" asked "How many roads must a man walk down / Before you call him a man?" Sam Cooke was so disturbed and inspired by the lyrics, as well as the fact that they came from a white man, that he wrote "A Change is Gonna Come" in response: "It's been a long, a long time coming / But I know a change gonna come, oh yes it will."

   Discuss: Why would these musicians choose to write about social injustice in their songs? Do you think music can inspire change?

2. Work with your class to complete the first column of the SOAPSTone graphic organizer on page 191 by reviewing and defining each of the terms.

During Reading

3. As you read "Letter from Birmingham Jail," underline words or phrases that will help you complete the SOAPSTone analysis that follows the text.

ABOUT THE AUTHOR
Martin Luther King, Jr. (January 15, 1929–April 4, 1968) was an American clergyman, activist, and leader in the African American Civil Rights Movement. In 1964, King became the youngest person to receive the Nobel Peace Prize for his work to end racial segregation and racial discrimination through civil disobedience and other nonviolent means.

King's letter is a response to a statement made by eight white Alabama clergymen on April 12, 1963, titled "A Call for Unity." The clergymen agreed that social injustices existed but argued that the battle against racial segregation should be fought solely in the courts, not in the streets.

Letter

from
"Letter from Birmingham Jail"
by *Martin Luther King, Jr.*

16 April 1963

My Dear Fellow Clergymen:

While confined here in the Birmingham city jail, I came across your recent statement calling my present activities "unwise and untimely." Seldom do I pause to answer criticism of my work and ideas. If I sought to answer all the criticisms that cross my desk, my secretaries would have little time for anything other than such correspondence in the course of the day, and I would have no time for constructive work. But since I feel that you are men of genuine good will and that your criticisms are sincerely set forth, I want to try to answer your statement in what I hope will be patient and reasonable terms.

I think I should indicate why I am here in Birmingham, since you have been influenced by the view which argues against "outsiders coming in." I have the honor of serving as president of the Southern Christian Leadership Conference, an organization operating in every southern state, with headquarters in Atlanta, Georgia. We have some eighty five affiliated organizations across the South, and one of them is the Alabama Christian Movement for Human Rights. Frequently we share staff, educational and financial resources with our affiliates. Several months ago the affiliate here in Birmingham asked us to be on call to engage in a nonviolent direct action program if such were deemed necessary. We readily consented, and when the hour came we lived up to our promise. So I, along with several members of my staff, am here because I was invited here. I am here because I have organizational ties here.

But more basically, I am in Birmingham because injustice is here. Just as the prophets of the eighth century B.C. left their villages and carried their "thus saith the Lord" far beyond the boundaries of their home towns, and just as the Apostle Paul left his village of Tarsus and carried the gospel of Jesus Christ to the far corners of the Greco Roman world, so am I compelled to carry the gospel of freedom beyond my own home town. Like Paul, I must constantly respond to the Macedonian call for aid.

Moreover, I am cognizant of the interrelatedness of all communities and states. I cannot sit idly by in Atlanta and not be concerned about what happens in Birmingham. Injustice anywhere is a threat to justice everywhere. We are caught in an inescapable network of mutuality, tied in a single garment of destiny. Whatever affects one directly, affects all indirectly. Never again can we afford to live with the narrow, provincial "outside agitator" idea. Anyone who lives inside the United States can never be considered an outsider anywhere within its bounds.

You deplore the demonstrations taking place in Birmingham. But your statement, I am sorry to say, fails to express a similar concern for the conditions that brought about the demonstrations. I am sure that none of you would want to rest content with the superficial kind of social analysis that deals merely with effects and does not grapple

My Notes

KEY IDEAS AND DETAILS
What examples of diction and rhetoric seem particular to Martin Luther King, Jr.'s role as a clergyman?

KEY IDEAS AND DETAILS
What evidence does King present to support his claim that he had a right to be in Birmingham? What is the most compelling evidence?

A Time for Change

KEY IDEAS AND DETAILS
King claims that justice has been denied to the Negro community. Evaluate whether the evidence King gives is relevant and sufficient to make his point.

with underlying causes. It is unfortunate that demonstrations are taking place in Birmingham, but it is even more unfortunate that the city's white power structure left the Negro community with no alternative . . .

We know through painful experience that freedom is never voluntarily given by the oppressor; it must be demanded by the oppressed. Frankly, I have yet to engage in a direct action campaign that was "well timed" in the view of those who have not suffered unduly from the disease of segregation. For years now I have heard the word "Wait!" It rings in the ear of every Negro with piercing familiarity. This "Wait" has almost always meant "Never." We must come to see, with one of our distinguished jurists, that "justice too long delayed is justice denied."

We have waited for more than 340 years for our constitutional and God given rights. The nations of Asia and Africa are moving with jetlike speed toward gaining political independence, but we still creep at horse and buggy pace toward gaining a cup of coffee at a lunch counter. Perhaps it is easy for those who have never felt the stinging darts of segregation to say, "Wait." But when you have seen vicious mobs lynch your mothers and fathers at will and drown your sisters and brothers at whim; when you have seen hate filled policemen curse, kick and even kill your black brothers and sisters; when you see the vast majority of your twenty million Negro brothers smothering in an airtight cage of poverty in the midst of an affluent society; when you suddenly find your tongue twisted and your speech stammering as you seek to explain to your six year old daughter why she can't go to the public amusement park that has just been advertised on television, and see tears welling up in her eyes when she is told that Funtown is closed to colored children, and see ominous clouds of inferiority beginning to form in her little mental sky, and see her beginning to distort her personality by developing an unconscious bitterness toward white people; when you have to concoct an answer for a five year old son who is asking: "Daddy, why do white people treat colored people so mean?"; when you take a cross country drive and find it necessary to sleep night after night in the uncomfortable corners of your automobile because no motel will accept you; when you are humiliated day in and day out by nagging signs reading "white" and "colored"; when your first name becomes "nigger," your middle name becomes "boy" (however old you are) and your last name becomes "John," and your wife and mother are never given the respected title "Mrs."; when you are harried by day and haunted by night by the fact that you are a Negro, living constantly at tiptoe stance, never quite knowing what to expect next, and are plagued with inner fears and outer resentments; when you are forever fighting a degenerating sense of "nobodiness"—then you will understand why we find it difficult to wait. There comes a time when the cup of endurance runs over, and men are no longer willing to be plunged into the abyss of despair. I hope, sirs, you can understand our legitimate and unavoidable impatience. You express a great deal of anxiety over our willingness to break laws. This is certainly a legitimate concern. Since we so diligently urge people to obey the Supreme Court's decision of 1954 outlawing segregation in the public schools, at first glance it may seem rather paradoxical for us consciously to break laws. One may well ask: "How can you advocate breaking some laws and obeying others?" The answer lies in the fact that there are two types of laws: just and unjust. I would be the first to advocate obeying just laws. One has not only a legal but a moral responsibility to obey just laws. Conversely, one has a moral responsibility to disobey unjust laws. I would agree with St. Augustine that "an unjust law is no law at all."

. . . I wish you had commended the Negro sit inners and demonstrators of Birmingham for their sublime courage, their willingness to suffer and their amazing discipline in the midst of great provocation. One day the South will recognize its real heroes. They will be the James Merediths, with the noble sense of purpose that enables them to face jeering and hostile mobs, and with the agonizing loneliness that characterizes the life of the pioneer. They will be old, oppressed, battered Negro women, symbolized in a seventy two year old woman in Montgomery, Alabama, who rose up with a sense of dignity and with her people decided not to ride segregated buses, and who responded with ungrammatical profundity to one who inquired about her weariness: "My feets is tired, but my soul is at rest." They will be the young high school and college students, the young ministers of the gospel and a host of their elders, courageously and nonviolently sitting in at lunch counters and willingly going to jail for conscience' sake. One day the South will know that when these disinherited children of God sat down at lunch counters, they were in reality standing up for what is best in the American dream and for the most sacred values in our Judaeo Christian heritage, thereby bringing our nation back to those great wells of democracy which were dug deep by the founding fathers in their formulation of the Constitution and the Declaration of Independence.

Never before have I written so long a letter. I'm afraid it is much too long to take your precious time. I can assure you that it would have been much shorter if I had been writing from a comfortable desk, but what else can one do when he is alone in a narrow jail cell, other than write long letters, think long thoughts and pray long prayers?

. . . Let us all hope that the dark clouds of racial prejudice will soon pass away and the deep fog of misunderstanding will be lifted from our fear drenched communities, and in some not too distant tomorrow the radiant stars of love and brotherhood will shine over our great nation with all their scintillating beauty.

Yours for the cause of Peace and Brotherhood,

Martin Luther King, Jr.

ACADEMIC VOCABULARY
"Letter from Birmingham Jail" is a blend of exposition, narrative, and argument. An analysis of King's writing must determine whether he makes valid points. In this sense, **valid** refers to reasoning, examples, and facts that support a main point.

My Notes

KEY IDEAS AND DETAILS
How is it valid to say that demonstrators who sat down at lunch counters were true American heroes?

KEY IDEAS AND DETAILS
What metaphor does King use to end the letter, and why is it appropriate?

A Time for Change

ACADEMIC VOCABULARY
Using rhetorical appeals is part
of the art of **rhetoric,** or using
words to persuade in writing
or speaking.

My Notes

After Reading

4. Complete a SOAPSTone analysis using the graphic organizer on the next page.
Then, go back to the text and highlight words, phrases, clauses, or sentences
that stand out as being important, profound, and/or moving. Look for the
following:

- Examples of powerful diction, particularly words with strong connotations
- Imagery, sensory detail, and figurative language
- Rhetorical appeals to emotion, ethics, or logic

5. Revisit the photographs from Activity 3.2. Use your analysis of the photos
to decide how quotations from Martin Luther King, Jr.'s letter could serve as
captions for those photographs.

What other words would you need to add to the caption in order to link the
quotation to the image?

6. **Think ahead to the Embedded Assessment:** How could you use famous quotes
or song lyrics to enhance a presentation?

7. **Group Discussion:** With the members of your group, discuss responses to the
following questions:

- What is King's purpose in writing this letter?
- How does King use rhetoric to achieve his purpose? Give specific examples of
his rhetorical appeals to logic, emotion, and ethos.
- How does he appeal to a specific audience with his language and details?
- How can you use rhetoric and an awareness of your audience to enhance
your oral presentation?

SOAPSTone	Analysis	Textual Evidence
Speaker:		
Occasion:		
Audience:		
Purpose:		
Subject:		
Tone:		

Voices of Change

LEARNING STRATEGIES:
Skimming/Scanning, Marking
the Text, Drafting, Discussion
Groups

KEY IDEAS AND DETAILS
What can you infer from this
timeline about the context
for the publication of *To Kill a
Mockingbird*?

My Notes

Learning Targets

- Analyze a timeline to understand how social change occurred during the Civil Rights Movement.
- Respond to a cause-and-effect writing prompt.

Analyzing Chronological Text

1. Skim the following list of events that contributed to social change before and during the American Civil Rights Movement. Mark the text by highlighting the names of significant individuals, organizations, groups, events, places, and laws. In the margin, list questions you may want to research further.

Civil Rights Timeline

1863 President Lincoln issues the Emancipation Proclamation.

1868 The 14th Amendment, which requires equal protection under the law to all persons, is ratified.

1870 The 15th Amendment, which bans racial discrimination in voting, is ratified.

1948 President Truman issues Executive Order 9981 outlawing segregation in the U.S. military.

1954 The Supreme Court declares school segregation unconstitutional in *Brown v. Board of Education of Topeka, Kansas*.

1955 Rosa Parks refuses to give up her seat on a Montgomery bus. Bus boycott begins and lasts for more than a year. Buses desegregated in 1956.

1957 The National Guard is called in to block "The Little Rock Nine" from integrating Little Rock High School. President Eisenhower sends in federal troops to allow the black students to enter the school.

1960 Four black college students begin sit-ins at the lunch counter of a Greensboro, North Carolina, restaurant where black patrons are not served.

To Kill a Mockingbird **is published on July 11**.

1961 CORE (Congress of Racial Equality) and SNCC (Student Nonviolent Coordinating Committee) sponsor "Freedom Rides," which bus student volunteers into Southern states to test new laws prohibiting segregation.

To Kill a Mockingbird **wins the Pulitzer Prize for literature**.

1962 James Meredith becomes the first black student to enroll at the University of Mississippi. The Supreme Court rules that segregation is unconstitutional in all transportation facilities.

Gregory Peck wins an Academy Award for best actor in the film *To Kill a Mockingbird*.

1964 Congress passes the Civil Rights Act, declaring discrimination based on race illegal.

1965 A march from Selma to Montgomery, Alabama, leads to the signing of a new Voting Rights Act.

1967 Thurgood Marshall becomes the first black Supreme Court justice. In *Loving v. Virginia*, the Supreme Court rules that prohibiting interracial marriage is unconstitutional.

1968 President Lyndon B. Johnson signs the Civil Rights Act of 1968, which prohibits discrimination in the sale, rental, and financing of housing.

Expository Writing Prompt: Explain the role of **cause and effect** in the excerpt from Martin Luther King, Jr.'s "Letter from Birmingham Jail." Be sure to:

- Begin with a topic sentence stating the purpose of King's words.
- Include textual evidence of the cause (or context) that inspired the writer.
- Provide commentary about the intended effect (or desired social change).

INDEPENDENT READING LINK

In a novel that you are reading independently, identify a cause-and-effect relationship between two significant events or situations. Write a sentence or two of commentary explaining the cause and effect.

My Notes

Historical Research and Citation

p.ic

ACADEMIC VOCABULARY
A **bibliography** is a list of the sources used for research. This list may also be called a Works Cited list.
An **annotated bibliography** includes comments about or summaries of each of the sources and the information found there.

My Notes

Learning Targets
- Write research questions, conduct research to choose a focus for a historical investigation, and begin to gather evidence by taking notes.
- Create an annotated bibliography that conforms to the guidelines of a style manual.

Writing Research Questions

1. Review the first sentence of the assignment for Embedded Assessment 1: Historical Investigation and Presentation.

   Your assignment is to research the historical, cultural, social, or geographical context of the novel To Kill a Mockingbird and investigate how individuals, organizations, and events contributed to change in the United States during the Civil Rights Movement.

   Rewrite the sentence as a question (or questions) that could guide your research.

Citing Sources

2. An annotated bibliography is a tool for tracking and giving credit to sources used for your research. Entries typically consist of two parts: a *citation* which follows the guidelines of a style manual—such as MLA—for the source, and an annotation (a brief summary of and commentary about the source). Examine the model entry below. Then, mark the text to identify the key elements of an annotated bibliography entry: information and details, evaluation of usefulness, and source description.

   Edmonds, Rick. "Jim Crow: Shorthand for Separation." FORUM Magazine. Summer 1999: 7.

   Edmonds reviews the origins of the term "Jim Crow" and the significance of Jim Crow laws and customs as a social factor in the South. He also traces how awareness of the term's meaning has changed over time as our society has become more politically correct. This source is useful for understanding how racial attitudes led to the creation of the "separate but equal" laws that existed in the South before the Civil Rights Movement. This magazine article is a secondary source that draws from other reliable sources, such as the American Heritage Dictionary.

3. Complete the bibliography that follows by annotating each of the sources listed. Explain how each of the texts you have analyzed in this unit so far could help you address the research question(s) that you just wrote.

Under the citation, write a summary that includes the following:

- Specific information learned from the source, including key details
- An evaluation of the source's usefulness in answering the research question(s)
- A description of the type of source, including its relevance and authority

"Jim Crow Laws," Martin Luther King Jr. National Historic Site. National Park Service. 21 July 2012. Web. 06 Aug. 2012. <http://www.nps.gov/malu/forteachers/jim_crow_laws.htm/index.htm>

Annotation:

King, Martin Luther, Jr. "Letter from Birmingham Jail." The Norton Anthology of African-American Literature. Eds. Henry Louis Gates, Jr. and Nellie Y. McKay. New York: Norton, 1997.

Annotation:

My Notes

Historical Research and Citation

My Notes

4. Work with your class to brainstorm some of the people, organizations, and events that contributed to positive social change in the United States during the Civil Rights Movement. Write your notes on the graphic organizer below.

5. Explore a website or timeline about the Civil Rights Movement to identify more subjects and add them to your research list.

People	Organizations	Events

6. With a partner or group of three, choose a subject as the focus of your historical investigation and presentation. Generate at least three research questions to guide your investigation. (You can revise these later if needed.) Include at least one of each of the following:

- A question that explores a **cause** by setting the context; for example, *What factors influenced what life was like for African Americans in Birmingham, Alabama, before the Civil Rights Movement?*

- A question that explores your **subject**; for example, *What were "sit-ins," and where did they take place?*

- A question that explores an **effect** by evaluating the change; for example, *How did the "Freedom Riders" help enforce anti segregation laws?*

7. Write a research proposal that includes the following:
   - Your group members' names
   - The subject of your investigation
   - At least three research questions

8. After your proposal is approved, assign a different research question to each group member. As you conduct research, think about the following questions:
   - Is the research question too broad or too narrow? Revise if needed.
   - Do the sources provide useful information to answer your question?
   - Are you using both print and digital sources for research? Are they reliable?
   - Does the initial information lead you to advanced research beyond your preliminary information?

9. **Evaluate** how well each source answers your questions. Then, complete a note card for each different source you use in your research, noting each site's usefulness in answering the research questions. You will use these note cards to create your annotated bibliography.

Creating Research Note Cards

On one side of an index card, include the citation for each source, according to the MLA guidelines provided by your teacher or an appropriate guide such as the Purdue OWL (Online Writing Lab) website or the *MLA Handbook for Writers of Research Papers*.

On the other side of the index card, include the following:
- Quotes, paraphrases, and summaries of the information from the source
- A description of the type of source and an evaluation of its usefulness
- Ideas for how to use the source in a presentation, including specific notes about integrating images and multimedia

My Notes

ACADEMIC VOCABULARY
When you **evaluate** something, you are making a judgment—one that most likely results from some degree of analysis about the value or worth of the information, idea, or object.

Historical Research and Citation

10. Before creating your own note cards, work with your class to create a sample note card for the website "The Rise and Fall of Jim Crow" based on the notes you took during Activity 3.4.

Example

Front:

Back:

Reaching an Audience

Learning Targets

- Analyze photo essays, videos, and multimedia presentations in order to plan effective ways to reach an audience of my peers in a presentation.

LEARNING STRATEGIES:
Graphic Organizer,
Questioning the Text,
Sharing and Responding

Elements of Effective Presentations

1. As you view at least three different types of presentations, take notes in the graphic organizer below to evaluate the effectiveness of each.

Subject and Type of Presentation: (Photo Essay, Video, Multimedia, etc.)	Facts and Information: What claim was being made by the presenter? Was the reasoning convincing and the evidence relevant to the claim?	Audio and Visual Components: How did the kind of media used determine which details were emphasized?	Effectiveness of the Presentation: How engaging was the presentation? Did it grab and hold my attention? Did it feel relevant and important?

2. **Discuss:** Which of the presentations were effective, and why?

Reaching an Audience

3. Based on your class discussion on the effectiveness of the presentations, work with your group to analyze an audience of your peers. Include answers to the following questions:
   - What does my audience already know about my subject, and how is my presentation going to expand that knowledge?
   - What audio and visual components appeal to my audience, and how will I use these in my presentation?
   - What connections can I make between my subject and my target audience to make my presentation relevant to their lives?

4. Meet with another group to share and respond to each other's analysis of the audience. Make and consider suggestions for improvement.

5. Create **guiding questions** for your audience's note-taking during your presentation. You will either incorporate these questions into the media you choose (for example, as titles of PowerPoint slides), write them clearly on a poster to display during your presentation, or make copies for the class.

Levels of Questions

6. Work with your group to write questions that will guide both the organization and the audience's note-taking on your presentation.

Start with your research questions and generate at least two more questions for each, using a variety of levels.

Level 1 Questions: Literal (Questions of Fact)

Example: *In what ways did Jim Crow laws affect schools?*

For my subject:

Level 2 Questions: Interpretive (Questions of Meaning)

Example: *Why was Brown v. Board of Education such an important landmark case?*

For my subject:

Level 3 Questions: Universal (Questions of Relevance)

Example: *Does everyone in the United States today receive the same quality education? In the world? What still needs to change to make that happen?*

For my subject:

Historical Investigation and Presentation

Assignment

Your assignment is to research the historical, cultural, social, or geographical context of the novel *To Kill a Mockingbird* and investigate how individuals, organizations, and events contributed to change in the United States during the Civil Rights Movement. You will work collaboratively to create an oral presentation of your findings with multimedia support and guiding questions for your audience.

Planning: Take time to plan, conduct, and record your research.

- What individual, organization, or event will your group investigate?

- What research questions will help you explore the subject and investigate your subject's contribution to change (cause and effect)?

- How will you record citations, information, and source evaluations as you gather answers and evidence?

- How will you record sources to create an alphabetized annotated bibliography?

Creating and Rehearsing: Collaborate with your group to create and prepare a multimedia oral presentation.

- How will you select the most relevant facts and sufficient details to develop your presentation for your audience?

- How will you organize your presentation to emphasize the cause-and-effect relationship between the 1930's context of the novel *To Kill a Mockingbird* and the Civil Rights Movement?

- How will you divide the speaking responsibilities and make smooth transitions between speakers?

- How will you collaborate to create an audience analysis and plan how to present your findings to your peers?

- How will you select and incorporate audio and visual components into your presentation? What is your plan for rehearsing your presentation delivery and getting feedback from your peers to revise and improve your presentation?

Presenting and Listening: Use effective speaking and listening as a presenter and audience member.

- How will you use notes for your talking points so that you can maintan eye contact with your audience?

- During your peers' presentations, how will you use the guiding questions to organize your notes on the subject of each presentation?

Reflection

As you read and study *To Kill a Mockingbird*, take notes on how your topic (or another that interests you more) surfaces in the novel. Record both textual evidence and personal commentary. After you have finished the novel, reflect on the following questions: How did the class presentations enhance your understanding and appreciation of the novel?

My Notes

Technology TIP:

Consider using presentation media such as PowerPoint, Prezi, or PhotoStory.

Historical Investigation and Presentation

SCORING GUIDE

Scoring Criteria	Exemplary	Proficient	Emerging	Incomplete
Ideas	The presentation • is thoughtful and well-organized • demonstrates a comprehensive understanding of significant aspects of the topic and its relevance to the novel.	The presentation • is organized and displays a solid understanding of the topic • clearly connects the topic and the novel for the audience.	The presentation • is somewhat organized • contains information that shows a limited understanding of the topic or how it connects to the novel.	The presentation • is not well organized and/or does not contain relevant content • provides few or no clear facts and details to help the audience connect the topic and the novel.
Structure	The presentation • skillfully uses a variety of audio/visual resources to keep the audience engaged • includes media resources that are used creatively to enhance understanding of the topic • includes a well-organized audience guide with thoughtful questions to focus information for the audience and adequate space for recording responses.	The presentation • uses audio/visual resources to engage the audience • uses media effectively to support information about the topic and ideas connecting it to the novel.	The presentation • uses some audio/visual resources that do not engage the audience • uses media choices that are distracting and do not serve the group's purpose.	The presentation • does not use audio/visual resources.
Use of Language	The presentation • demonstrates accomplished oral communication skills and rehearsal to create a well-planned delivery • includes participation by all group members.	The presentation • demonstrates adequate oral communication skills and rehearsal to plan the delivery • includes participation by all group members, although some may present more than others.	The presentation • demonstrates inadequate oral communication skills and shows little evidence of rehearsal • is delivered by only some of the group members.	The presentation • shows inadequate oral communication skills and no evidence of rehearsal • is not delivered by all group members.

Previewing Embedded Assessment 2: A Story of the Times

Learning Targets

- Identify and analyze the knowledge and skills needed to complete Embedded Assessment 2 successfully.
- Revise, refine, and reflect on my understanding of vocabulary words and the essential questions.

LEARNING STRATEGIES:
QHT, Graphic Organizer, Summarizing, Marking the Text, Note-taking, Discussion Groups

Making Connections

To Kill a Mockingbird is set in the 1930s before the major changes brought about by the Civil Rights Movement. At that time, Jim Crow laws governed the civil rights of minorities, and segregation was the law of the land. In this last part of the unit, you will begin reading the novel and exploring the historical, social, and cultural contexts of its setting.

Developing Vocabulary

Return to the Table of Contents and note the Academic Vocabulary and Literary Terms you have studied so far in this unit. Which words/terms can you now move to a new category on a QHT chart? Which could you now teach to others that you were unfamiliar with at the beginning of the unit?

Essential Questions

How would you answer each of these questions now?

1. What impact does context have on a novel and on the reactions of readers to it?

2. How does a key scene from a novel contribute to the work as a whole?

Unpacking Embedded Assessment 2

Read the assignment for Embedded Assessment 2: Writing a Passage Analysis.

Your assignment is to write a passage analysis of a key coming-of-age scene from *To Kill a Mockingbird*. After annotating the text to analyze Harper Lee's use of literary elements in your selected passage, write an essay explaining how the literary elements in this passage help develop a theme of the novel.

In your own words, summarize what you will need to know to complete this assessment successfully. With your class, create a graphic organizer to represent the skills and knowledge you will need to complete the tasks identified in the Embedded Assessment.

My Notes

Previewing Embedded Assessment 2: A Story of the Times

Before Reading

1. In the first half of the unit, you began to explore the idea of context and how different aspects of context (historical, cultural, geographical, and social) can affect a reader's response to a novel. With a partner, review the aspects of context that you explored in Activity 3.2 and read a brief preview of the novel *To Kill a Mockingbird* (either on the book's back cover or provided by your teacher). Discuss the following:

   • How might your response to the novel differ from someone who read the book in the 1960's?

   • What other aspects of context might impact your response to the novel?

During Reading

2. The following excerpts are from a variety of readers responding to the novel *To Kill a Mockingbird*. As you read one, mark the text by highlighting words or phrases that identify the reader's tone or attitude toward the novel and aspects of his or her personal context that shaped the response.

Reflective Texts

from *Scout, Atticus & Boo:*
A Celebration of To Kill a Mockingbird

by Mary McDonagh Murphy

Reverend Thomas Lane Butts, pastor, born in Alabama in 1930:

I was in Mobile as a pastor of the Michigan Avenue Methodist Church. I had gone through an encounter with the Ku Klux Klan. They were after me because I'd signed a petition to integrate the buses there. This was in 1960 when *To Kill a Mockingbird* came out, and it was a great comfort to those of us who had taken some stand on this particular issue.

The book was written in a way that it could not be refuted. It was a soft opposition to people who were against civil rights. It was just a great comfort to those of us who had been involved in the civil rights movement that somebody from the Deep South had given us a book that gave some comfort to us in what we had done.

I understood the context in which the book was written, because that's how I grew up. It was a rural, poverty-stricken situation during the Depression, where people did not have much. It was hardscrabble for most people to make a living. It was a time in which black people were treated terribly and people took in racism with their mother's milk. Here in this novel, you have a person bucking the tradition in order to advocate the rights of a person without regard to color.

James Patterson, author of over 50 novels including the *Maximum Ride* series, born in New York in 1947:

I read *To Kill a Mockingbird* in high school, and it was one of the few books I really liked. Part of my problem with going to this particular high school is they just didn't give us many books that would turn us on. I was a good student, but I just didn't get turned on to reading. What I remember most about *To Kill a Mockingbird* was—and I think this probably is more of an American trait than in other places—I think we are particularly attuned to injustice. The stories that deal with injustice are really powerful here. I think we have more of a sense of that than they do in some places where injustice is more a fact of life. I loved the narration, how it went from a pleasant story to a quite horrifying one.

Sometimes people will criticize *To Kill a Mockingbird* because of certain language, but it expresses views of how certain people thought in the 1930s. Similarly people will write books about us now, and I am sure [in the future] people will be scandalized by the way we eat and the fact we're still having all these ridiculous wars and whatever. But I think it's useful to kids, and it was useful to me to look back on an earlier time and see how different things were.

My connection was more to Jem, because he was a boy. I found the drama just kept building and building and building. In the beginning, you are suspecting something about Boo, which should tell you something about yourself, that you suspect him for no reason.

Oprah Winfrey, talk-show host, TV/film producer, actress, philanthropist, born in Mississippi in 1954:

At the time that I read *To Kill a Mockingbird*, I was living with my mother in Milwaukee. I would not have had any money to buy it, so I would undoubtedly have chosen it from the library . . . I remember starting it and just devouring it, not being able to get enough of it, because I fell in love with Scout. I wanted to be Scout. I thought I was Scout. I always took on or wanted to take on the characteristics of whoever I was reading about, so I wanted to be Scout and I wanted a father like Atticus.

I remember watching the movie with my father many years after I read the book. The impact of the movie on my father caused me to see the book differently and experience the book differently. I am right after the cusp of the civil rights movement. I wasn't a child of the civil rights movement. I am one of those people who has been one of the greatest beneficiaries of the civil rights movement. I don't know what it is like to be told to go to the back door.

I did not live a Jim Crow segregated life, because I was one of the fortunate ones who were able to escape Mississippi. And I do mean escape—1960, when this book was published, was about the time I was leaving Mississippi.

My Notes

Previewing Embedded Assessment 2:
A Story of the Times

My Notes

I left for Milwaukee and left my grandmother when I was six years old, so I never experienced the segregation of the South. I moved to an integrated school and was the smartest kid in the class, and when you are the smartest kid in the class, you always get a lot of attention. I never felt any of the oppressiveness of racism. I always recognize that life would have been so different for me had I been raised in a segregated environment, if I had to experience even secondhand what was happening in that environment.

After Reading

3. Write a brief, objective summary of your passage. Meet with a partner or small group of students who read different passages. Introduce each passage by reading your summary and sharing textual evidence related to the questions below:

- How did each reader's personal experiences impact his or her reaction to the novel?

- How were the responses similar? How were they different?

- What predictions can you make about the novel based on these passages?

A Scouting Party

Learning Target

- Analyze the first chapter of a novel to identify details that establish point of view, character, and setting.

Before Reading

1. View the opening clip of *To Kill a Mockingbird,* noting your observations on the graphic organizer.

LEARNING STRATEGIES:
Graphic Organizer,
Marking the Text,
Visualizing, Sketching,
Discussion Groups

Viewing the Opening Credits of *To Kill a Mockingbird*

What do you observe? What images did you see on screen?	What do you notice about the lighting?	What do you notice about the sound?	What predictions can you make?

2. **Collaborative Discussion:** Refer to and add to your notes as you discuss the following with your classmates:

- Usually the opening credits of a film set a mood and provide clues about conflicts or themes. What predictions can you make based on the opening credits of this film?

- From the sounds and images, what can you infer about the perspective or point of view from which this story will be told?

- When this film was made, color film technology was available. Why do you think the director chose to shoot this film in black and white?

Literary Terms

A **flashback** is an interruption in the sequence of events to relate events that occurred in the past.

During Reading

3. As you read the opening paragraphs of *To Kill a Mockingbird*, mark the text as follows:

- Highlight words and phrases that give you clues about the narrator's personality and establish her voice.

- Circle the names of characters who are related to the narrator as well as the words that tell you how they are related.

- Put an asterisk next to the phrase that indicates that the rest of the novel is a **flashback**.

A Scouting Party

KEY IDEAS AND DETAILS
What clues does the narrator provide about the other characters and the setting of the novel in these first few paragraphs?

_____
_____
_____
_____
_____
_____
_____
_____
_____
_____
_____
_____

ABOUT THE AUTHOR
American writer Nelle Harper Lee (b. 1926) was born and grew up in Alabama. As an adult, she moved to New York City, where she wrote and published several short stories. She then took a year off from work to write *To Kill a Mockingbird*, using her father as a model for Atticus Finch. *To Kill a Mockingbird* won much acclaim when it was published and a Pulitzer Prize in 1961. Harper Lee has never written another novel.

Novel

from *To Kill a Mockingbird*

by Harper Lee

When he was nearly thirteen, my brother Jem got his arm badly broken at the elbow. When it healed, and Jem's fears of never being able to play football were assuaged, he was seldom self-conscious about his injury. His left arm was somewhat shorter than his right; when he stood or walked, the back of his hand was at right angles to his body, his thumb parallel to his thigh. He couldn't have cared less, so long as he could pass and punt.

When enough years had gone by to enable us to look back on them, we sometimes discussed the events leading to his accident. I maintain that the Ewells started it all, but Jem, who was four years my senior, said it started long before that. He said it began the summer Dill came to us, when Dill first gave us the idea of making Boo Radley come out.

I said if he wanted to take a broad view of the thing, it really began with Andrew Jackson. If General Jackson hadn't run the Creeks up the creek, Simon Finch would never have paddled up the Alabama, and where would we be if he hadn't? We were far too old to settle an argument with a fist-fight, so we consulted Atticus. Our father said we were both right.

After Reading

4. From what point of view is the novel told? How is it both similar to and different from the point of view established in the opening credits of the film? Why is each point of view appropriate for its medium—film or literature?

Introducing the Characters

5. Form groups of three. Each group member should choose one of the following characters:

- Scout (the narrator): a five year-old girl
- Jem: her nine-year-old brother
- Dill: a strange new kid on the block

6. As you read the following excerpt from Chapter 1, highlight details of characterization. Look for textual evidence that reveals your character's appearance, thoughts, actions, or words.

from *To Kill a Mockingbird* (Chapter 1, Pages 6–8)

by Harper Lee

Early one morning as we were beginning our day's play in the back yard, Jem and I heard something next door in Miss Rachel Haverford's collard patch. We went to the wire fence to see if there was a puppy—Miss Rachel's rat terrier was expecting— instead we found someone sitting looking at us. Sitting down, he wasn't much higher than the collards. We stared at him until he spoke:

"Hey."

"Hey yourself," said Jem pleasantly.

"I'm Charles Baker Harris," he said. "I can read."

"So what?" I said.

"I just thought you'd like to know I can read. You got anything needs readin' I can do it . . . ."

"How old are you," asked Jem, "four-and-a-half?"

"Goin' on seven."

"Shoot no wonder, then," said Jem, jerking his thumb at me. "Scout yonder's been readin' ever since she was born, and she ain't even started to school yet. You look right puny for goin' on seven."

"I'm little but I'm old," he said.

Jem brushed his hair back to get a better look. "Why don't you come over, Charles Baker Harris?" he said. "Lord, what a name."

"'s not any funnier'n yours. Aunt Rachel says your name's Jeremy Atticus Finch."

Jem scowled. "I'm big enough to fit mine," he said. "Your name's longer'n you are. Bet it's a foot longer."

"Folks call me Dill," said Dill, struggling under the fence.

"Do better if you go over it instead of under it," I said. "Where'd you come from?"

Dill was from Meridian, Mississippi, was spending the summer with his aunt, Miss Rachel, and would be spending every summer in Maycomb from now on. His family was from Maycomb County originally, his mother worked for a photographer in Meridian, had entered his picture in a Beautiful Child contest and won five dollars. She gave the money to Dill, who went to the picture show twenty times on it.

My Notes

KEY IDEAS AND DETAILS
What do the characters have in common? What are some of the key differences between them?

A Scouting Party

Why does Jem tell Scout to hush, and what does this action reveal about the difference in their maturity and understanding?

My Notes

"Don't have any picture shows here, except Jesus ones in the courthouse sometimes," said Jem. "Ever see anything good?"

Dill had seen *Dracula*, a revelation that moved Jem to eye him with the beginning of respect. "Tell it to us," he said.

Dill was a curiosity. He wore blue linen shorts that buttoned to his shirt, his hair was snow white and stuck to his head like duck-fluff; he was a year my senior but I towered over him. As he told us the old tale his blue eyes would lighten and darken; his laugh was sudden and happy; he habitually pulled at a cowlick in the center of his forehead.

When Dill reduced Dracula to dust, and Jem said the show sounded better than the book, I asked Dill where his father was: "You ain't said anything about him."

"I haven't got one."

"Is he dead?"

"No..."

"Then if he's not dead you've got one, haven't you?"

Dill blushed and Jem told me to hush, a sure sign that Dill had been studied and found acceptable. Thereafter the summer passed in routine contentment.

After Reading

7. As a group, sketch the characters and the scene you just read, indicating the relationships among the children in your drawing. Annotate the sketch with textual evidence to support your analysis of the scene. Include details about how your character looks, acts, speaks, and thinks as well as other characters' reactions.

8. **Independent Practice:** As you read the rest of Chapter 1, choose a passage that describes a setting, such as the town of Maycomb or the Radley house. Visualize and sketch the setting, and then annotate your sketch with textual evidence. In addition to details about the setting's appearance, include examples of the diction and imagery that help to create the author's attitude or tone.

Clauses

Relative clauses can be **restrictive** (essential) or **nonrestrictive** (nonessential). Notice the use and punctuation of the adjective clauses in the following examples:

Nonrestrictive: She gave the money to Dill, **who went to the picture show twenty times on it.**

Restrictive: He wore blue linen shorts **that buttoned to his shirt** . . .

In your writing, use commas to set off nonrestrictive adjective clauses in complex sentences.

Conflict with Miss Caroline

Learning Targets

- Analyze fictional text and make connections to characters and plot events.
- Demonstrate understanding of conflict in writing.

Before Reading

1. Think about the different kinds of **conflicts** you have studied. **Internal conflict** occurs when a character struggles between opposing needs, desires, or emotions within his or her own mind. **External conflict** occurs when a character struggles against an outside force, such as another character, society, or nature. Using the graphic organizer below, brainstorm examples of conflicts from your life, the world, books, television, or films.

Internal Conflict: Man vs. Self Struggles against one's own opposing needs, desires, emotions	External Conflict: Man vs. Man Struggles against another person	External Conflict: Man vs. Society Struggles against laws or expectations	External Conflict: Man vs. Nature Struggles against the physical world

During Reading

2. As you read Chapter 2, work with a partner or small group to locate textual evidence of the conflict between Scout and Miss Caroline. Write quotes below with commentary to explain why these two are "starting off on the wrong foot in every way."

Scout's Side	Caroline's Side

Conflict with Miss Caroline

After Reading

3. Fill in the circles below, making connections to Scout's first-day-of-school experiences. As you read Chapter 3, fill in the circles with more connections.

- text-to-self: when the text makes you think of your own life
- text-to-text: when the text makes you think of another text
- text-to-world: when the text makes you think of world events

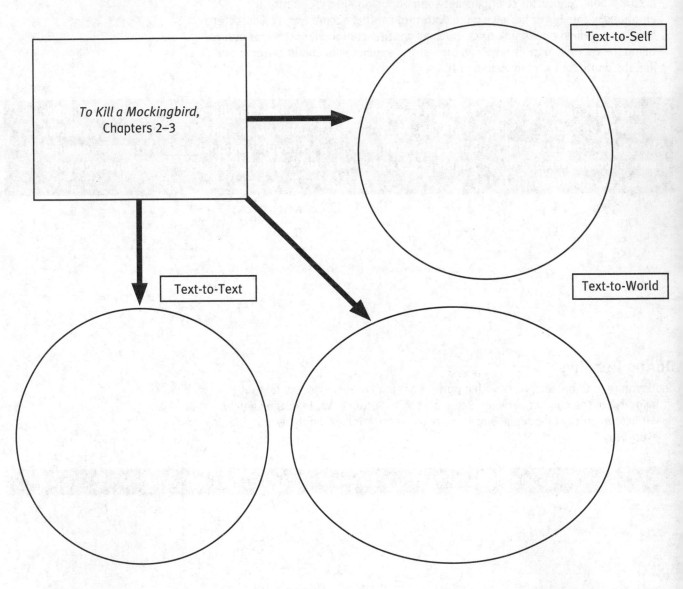

To Kill a Mockingbird,
Chapters 2–3

Text-to-Self

Text-to-Text

Text-to-World

Expository Writing Prompt: Write an introduction to an essay analyzing the conflict between Scout and Miss Caroline in Chapter 2 of *To Kill a Mockingbird*. Be sure to:

- Begin with a QQAS (question, quote, anecdote, or statement of intrigue) that introduces a connection to Scout's experiences.
- Provide a brief summary of the chapter.
- End with a statement about the conflict and what Scout learns from it.

Analyzing Boo

Learning Targets

- Analyze subplot and motif in a text to determine how characters develop through coming-of-age experiences.
- Make predictions, form inferences, draw conclusions, and find evidence to support an analysis of a literary text.

LEARNING STRATEGIES:
Graphic Organizer, Marking the Text, Discussion Groups

Before Reading

1. Go back to the pages in Chapter 1 that introduce the story of Boo Radley. Complete the graphic organizer below to separate fact from rumor, and provide textual evidence of each. Add your own questions about Boo's story and your opinion or personal commentary.

Boo Radley's Story	Textual Evidence	Questions/Commentary
Facts		
Rumors		

My Notes

During Reading

2. In Chapters 4–6, the children are beginning to come of age as they question their assumptions about Boo and the Radley place. As you read the following excerpt, mark the text for significant details. Annotate your evidence with the following:

- **Questions and/or commentary** about details related to Boo or the Radley Place
- **Predictions** about how details will be developed later in the text
- **Inferences and conclusions** that you draw from "reading between the lines" of suggestive details.

Novel

from

To Kill a Mockingbird

(Chapter 4)

by Harper Lee

As the year passed, released from school thirty minutes before Jem, who had to stay until three o'clock, I ran by the Radley Place as fast as I could, not stopping until I reached the safety of our front porch. One afternoon as I raced by, something caught my eye and caught it in such a way that I took a deep breath, a long look around, and went back.

Two live oaks stood at the edge of the Radley lot; their roots reached out into the side-road and made it bumpy. Something about one of the trees attracted my attention.

Some tinfoil was sticking in a knot-hole just above my eye level, winking at me in the afternoon sun. I stood on tiptoe, hastily looked around once more, reached into the hole, and withdrew two pieces of chewing gum minus their outer wrappers.

My first impulse was to get it into my mouth as quickly as possible, but I remembered where I was. I ran home, and on our front porch I examined my loot. The gum looked fresh. I sniffed it and it smelled all right. I licked it and waited for a while. When I did not die I crammed it into my mouth: Wrigley's Double-Mint.

When Jem came home he asked me where I got such a wad. I told him I found it.

"Don't eat things you find, Scout."

"This wasn't on the ground, it was in a tree."

Jem growled.

"Well it was," I said. "It was sticking in that tree yonder, the one comin' from school."

"Spit it out right now!"

I spat it out. The tang was fading, anyway. "I've been chewin' it all afternoon and I ain't dead yet, not even sick."

Jem stamped his foot. "Don't you know you're not supposed to even touch the trees over there? You'll get killed if you do!"

"You touched the house once!"

"That was different! You go gargle—right now, you hear me?"

"Ain't neither, it'll take the taste outa my mouth."

"You don't 'n' I'll tell Calpurnia on you!" Rather than risk a tangle with Calpurnia, I did as Jem told me. For some reason, my first year of school had wrought a great change in our relationship: Calpurnia's tyranny, unfairness, and meddling in my business had faded to gentle grumblings of general disapproval. On my part, I went to much trouble, sometimes, not to provoke her.

Summer was on the way; Jem and I awaited it with impatience. Summer was our best season: it was sleeping on the back screened porch in cots, or trying to sleep in the treehouse; summer was everything good to eat; it was a thousand colors in a parched landscape; but most of all, summer was Dill.

The authorities released us early the last day of school, and Jem and I walked home together. "Reckon old Dill'll be coming home tomorrow," I said.

"Probably day after," said Jem. "Mis'sippi turns 'em loose a day later."

As we came to the live oaks at the Radley Place I raised my finger to point for the hundredth time to the knot-hole where I had found the chewing gum, trying to make Jem believe I had found it there, and found myself pointing at another piece of tinfoil.

"I see it, Scout! I see it—"

Jem looked around, reached up, and gingerly pocketed a tiny shiny package. We ran home, and on the front porch we looked at a small box patchworked with bits of tinfoil collected from chewing-gum wrappers. It was the kind of box wedding rings came in, purple velvet with a minute catch. Jem flicked open the tiny catch. Inside were two scrubbed and polished pennies, one on top of the other. Jem examined them.

"Indian-heads," he said. "Nineteen-six and Scout, one of 'em's nineteen-hundred. These are real old."

"Nineteen-hundred," I echoed. "Say—"

"Hush a minute, I'm thinkin'."

"Jem, you reckon that's somebody's hidin' place?"

"Naw, don't anybody much but us pass by there, unless it's some grown person's—"

"Grown folks don't have hidin' places. You reckon we ought to keep 'em, Jem?"

"I don't know what we could do, Scout. Who'd we give 'em back to? I know for a fact don't anybody go by there—Cecil goes by the back street an' all the way around by town to get home."

My Notes

KEY IDEAS AND DETAILS
How has Jem's attitude shifted now that he is with Scout when she finds something in the knot-hole?

Analyzing Boo

KEY IDEAS AND DETAILS
What do you think Jem is
thinking? With the difference
in their ages, what might
he understand that Scout
doesn't?

My Notes

Cecil Jacobs, who lived at the far end of our street next door to the post office, walked a total of one mile per school day to avoid the Radley Place and old Mrs. Henry Lafayette Dubose. Mrs. Dubose lived two doors up the street from us; neighborhood opinion was unanimous that Mrs. Dubose was the meanest old woman who ever lived. Jem wouldn't go by her place without Atticus beside him.

"What you reckon we oughta do, Jem?"

Finders were keepers unless title was proven. Plucking an occasional camellia, getting a squirt of hot milk from Miss Maudie Atkinson's cow on a summer day, helping ourselves to someone's scuppernongs was part of our ethical culture, but money was different.

"Tell you what," said Jem. "We'll keep 'em till school starts, then go around and ask everybody if they're theirs. They're some bus child's, maybe—he was too taken up with gettin' outa school today an' forgot 'em. These are somebody's, I know that. See how they've been slicked up? They've been saved."

"Yeah, but why should somebody wanta put away chewing gum like that? You know it doesn't last."

"I don't know, Scout. But these are important to somebody . . . . "

"How's that, Jem . . . . ?"

"Well, Indian-heads—well, they come from the Indians. They're real strong magic, they make you have good luck. Not like fried chicken when you're not lookin' for it, but things like long life 'n' good health, 'n' passin' six-weeks tests . . . these are real valuable to somebody. I'm gonna put 'em in my trunk."

Before Jem went to his room, he looked for a long time at the Radley Place. He seemed to be thinking again.

After Reading

3. Form a discussion group to share your annotations and textual evidence. Work together to construct an interpretive statement about how the experience of finding gifts in the knot-hole of the Radley live-oak tree has helped Jem and Scout come of age.

4. The character of Boo Radley is a motif in *To Kill a Mockingbird*, and the incidents involving the children's fascination with him form one of the major subplots of the novel. In your discussion group, divide up the following passages that explore this motif and subplot in further depth.

Passage 1: Chapter 4 (from "Let's roll in the tire . . . " to the end of Chapter 4)

Passage 2: Chapter 5 (from "Next morning when I . . . " to the end of Chapter 5)

Passage 3: Chapter 6 (from "What are you gonna do?" to "Settle it yourselves.")

Form an expert group with other students who have selected the same passage. Conduct a close reading of your passage, using sticky notes to mark textual evidence and record your questions, commentary, predictions, inferences, and conclusions.

Work together to complete the appropriate row of the graphic organizer on the next page.

5. Go back to your discussion group and share your expert group's observations, interpretations, and evidence. Take notes in the appropriate row as you listen to the other group members analyze their passage.

6. **Independent Practice:** As you read the rest of Chapters 4–6, revisit this graphic organizer to add additional details, commentary, and evidence, and to evaluate whether or not you agree with the "expert" analysis.

Literary Terms

A **motif** is a recurring image, symbol, theme, character type, subject, or narrative detail that becomes a unifying element in an artistic work.

The **plot**, or sequence of events that make up a story, is often accompanied by a **subplot,** or secondary or side story, that develops from and supports the main plot and usually involves minor characters.

My Notes

Analyzing Boo

Objective Summary of the Passage	Statement About How This Is a Coming-of-Age Experience	Key Textual Evidence to Support Your Interpretation
Passage 1:		
Passage 2:		
Passage 3:		

Questions and Conclusions

Learning Targets

- Use Levels of Questions to identify themes in Chapters 7–9.
- Write a conclusion to an essay.

Before Reading

1. In Activity 3.11, you made text-to-text, text-to-self, and text-to-world connections in relation to Scout's first-day-of-school experiences. Make these same types of connections to the chapters in Activity 3.12 involving the children's fascination with Boo Radley:

   Text-to-self:

   Text-to-text:

   Text-to-world:

2. **Themes** in literature usually revolve around ideas that apply to multiple situations. Using Levels of Questions can help you identify those universal themes in a text.

   Sample: What does Harper Lee have to say about prejudice through Boo Radley's character?

During Reading

3. Read and analyze the first chunk of Chapter 7 with your class, generating questions at all three levels. Share your responses to the questions in a class discussion.

Chunk 1: From the start of Chapter 7 to "I'd have the facts."

Level 1 Question: Literal Questions ("What does the text say?")

Level 2 Question: Interpretive Questions ("What does the text mean?")

Level 3 Question: Universal Questions ("Why does it matter?")

---

4. Read and analyze the second and third chunks with a small group, and generate three Levels of Questions for each chunk. Share your responses to the questions in a group discussion.

My Notes

Questions and Conclusions

Chunk 2: From "There are no clearly defined seasons . . ." to "Huh?"

Level 1 Question: Literal Questions ("What does the text say?")

Level 2 Question: Interpretive Questions ("What does the text mean?")

Level 3 Question: Universal Questions ("Why does it matter?)

Chunk 3: From "You reckon we oughta write a letter . . ." to the end of the chapter.

Level 1 Question: Literal Questions ("What does the text say?")

Level 2 Question: Interpretive Questions ("What does the text mean?")

Level 3 Question: Universal Questions ("Why does it matter?)

After Reading

5. Work with your discussion group to identify several topics and thematic statements that can be made by examining the character of Boo Radley and how the children interact with him. What coming-of-age lessons have the children learned from these experiences?

6. Read the following sample conclusion from a passage analysis. Mark the text as follows:
   - Highlight the thesis statement.
   - Put an "L" in the margin next to literal statements.
   - Put an "I" in the margin next to interpretive statements.
   - Put a "U" in the margin next to universal statements.

Sample Conclusion

In this passage, Harper Lee uses the motif of Boo Radley to convey the theme that sometimes sterotypes limit our expectations. When Jem goes back to the Radley Place to retrieve his lost pants, his pants are folded across the fence, waiting for him. The way that they are sewn—all crooked—shows that someone inexperienced with sewing is trying to help him stay out of trouble: the same someone who has been watching the children, leaving them gifts, and laughing when a tire rolls into his yard carrying a dizzy and frightened little girl. Jem and Scout had come to expect only evil from Boo Radley, so Boo's friendliness and helpfulness are unexpected. The message we might all take away from this passage is that peoples' actions are more important than what others say about them.

7. **Independent Practice:** As you read Chapters 8 and 9, chunk each chapter into at least three sections and use sticky notes to generate Levels of Questions for each chunk.

8. Return to your discussion group to share and respond to one another's questions. Work together with your class to identify topics introduced in these chapters, and write thematic statements that show Harper Lee's opinion.

Expository Writing Prompt: Choose one of the topics that is introduced in a passage from Chapters 7–9 and write a conclusion to an essay analyzing how motif (Boo), subplot (the fire), conflict (Scout vs. Francis), setting (Finch's Landing), or character (Uncle Jack) contributes to that theme. Be sure to:

- Begin with a statement that reflects the thesis of the essay as in the model above.
- Include factual, interpretive, and universal statements.
- Use the present tense, literary vocabulary, and formal style consistently.

GRAMMAR & USAGE
Present Tense

In a literary analysis essay, always use present tense to discuss the action of the plot: "When Jem *goes* back to the Radley place, his pants *are* folded . . ."

My Notes

Two Views of "One Shot"

LEARNING STRATEGIES:
Chunking the Text, Questioning
the Text, Discussion Groups

Literary Terms

A **symbol** is anything (object, animal, event, person, or place) that represents itself but also stands for something else on a figurative level.

My Notes

Learning Targets

- Analyze how an author uses multiple literary elements in one passage to develop a theme.
- Compare a key scene in text and film to identify how literary elements are portrayed in each medium.

Before Reading

1. **Quickwrite:** How much do you think you know about your parents' "coming of age" experiences? Do you think it's possible that there are things about their past that you don't know? How would you feel if you found out one of your parents had a secret talent?

During Reading

2. Conduct a close reading of the passage below from Chapter 10. As you read, highlight references to the title. In the margin, predict what you think the mockingbird might symbolize.

> **Novel**
>
> from
> # To Kill a Mockingbird
> (Chapter 10)

When he gave us our air rifles Atticus wouldn't teach us to shoot. Uncle Jack instructed us in the rudiments thereof; he said Atticus wasn't interested in guns. Atticus said to Jem one day, "I'd rather you shot at tin cans in the back yard, but I know you'll go after birds. Shoot all the bluejays you want, if you can hit 'em, but remember it's a sin to kill a mockingbird."

That was the only time I ever heard Atticus say it was a sin to do something, and I asked Miss Maudie about it.

"Your father's right," she said. "Mockingbirds don't do one thing but make music for us to enjoy. They don't eat up people's gardens, don't nest in corncribs, they don't do one thing but sing their hearts out for us. That's why it's a sin to kill a mockingbird."

Collaborative Discussion

- Based on your understanding of Atticus's character, why do you think he isn't interested in guns?
- How does Miss Maudie's information about mockingbirds add to Atticus's comment that "it's a sin to kill a mockingbird"?
- Based on this passage, what might a mockingbird symbolize?

3. Work with a small group to conduct a close reading of Chapter 10. Choose one of the following literary elements to focus on: character, conflict, or setting. Use sticky notes to mark the text for evidence of the importance of your chosen literary element.

After Reading

4. After you discuss each of the literary elements and textual evidence with your group, you will view a film clip of the scene. Take notes below on how each of the elements is portrayed similarly or differently in the film.

Setting	Conflict	Character

5. Compare the two versions of the scene. Why is each appropriate for the medium of film or literature?

6. If the mad dog symbolizes the madness of racism, what is a possible theme introduced in this chapter?

7. Consider the following thesis statement: *In Chapter 10, Harper Lee uses the killing of the mad dog as a symbolic act to develop the theme that racism is a dangerous threat to any peaceful community.*

   Write your own thesis statement about how the literary element that you analyzed from Chapter 10 contributes to a theme.

My Notes

Pin the Quote on Atticus

LEARNING STRATEGIES:
Skimming/Scanning, Diffusing,
Marking the Text, Drafting,
Discussion Groups

GRAMMAR & USAGE
Clauses

An **independent clause** is a group of words that contains a subject and a verb and can stand alone as a sentence. A sentence having more than one independent clause is a **compound sentence**. One way to combine two such clauses is to use a coordinating conjunction: and, or, but. Unless the clauses are both short and simple, you need to place a comma before the coordinating conjunction between the two independent clauses.

Example: I did not remember our mother, but Jem did . . . .

My Notes

_____

_____

_____

_____

_____

_____

_____

_____

_____

_____

_____

_____

_____

_____

Learning Targets
- Write an interpretive statement about the significance of literary elements.
- Gather textual evidence to generate theme statements.
- Respond to an analytical writing prompt.

Before Reading
1. Work with a small group to skim the passage below and highlight unfamiliar vocabulary. Diffuse the text by looking up the highlighted words in a dictionary or thesaurus and replacing your highlighted vocabulary with definitions or synonyms.

During Reading
2. Read the passage below and mark the text further by annotating in the margins with questions, inferences, predictions, and connections.

> **Novel**

from
To Kill a Mockingbird
(Chapter 11)

When we were small, Jem and I confined our activities to the southern neighborhood, but when I was well into the second grade at school and tormenting Boo Radley became passé, the business section of Maycomb drew us frequently up the street past the real property of Mrs. Henry Lafayette Dubose. It was impossible to go to town without passing her house unless we wished to walk a mile out of the way. Previous minor encounters with her left me with no desire for more, but Jem said I had to grow up some time.

Mrs. Dubose lived alone except for a Negro girl in constant attendance, two doors up the street from us in a house with steep front steps and a dog-trot hall. She was very old; she spent most of each day in bed and the rest of it in a wheelchair. It was rumored that she kept a CSA pistol concealed among her numerous shawls and wraps.

Jem and I hated her. If she was on the porch when we passed, we would be raked by her wrathful gaze, subjected to ruthless interrogations regarding our behavior, and given a melancholy prediction on what we would amount to when we grew up, which was always nothing. We had long ago given up the idea of walking past her house on the opposite side of the street; that only made her raise her voice and let the whole neighborhood in on it.

We could do nothing to please her. If I said as sunnily as I could, "Hey, Mrs. Dubose," I would receive for an answer, "Don't you say hey to me, you ugly girl! You say good afternoon, Mrs. Dubose!"

She was vicious. Once she heard Jem refer to our father as "Atticus" and her reaction was apoplectic. Besides being the sassiest, most disrespectful mutts who ever passed her way, we were told that it was quite a pity our father had not remarried after our mother's death. A lovelier lady than our mother never lived, she said, and it was heartbreaking the way Atticus Finch let her children run wild. I did not remember our mother, but Jem did—he would tell me about her sometimes—and he went livid when Mrs. Dubose shot us this message.

After Reading

3. Consider the significance of character, conflict, and setting in the passage you just read and annotated. Ask yourself: Why is this literary element important? How does it connect to the larger issues in the novel?

   Use the following sentence stems to generate an interpretive statement about each of these elements.

   • The character of Mrs. Dubose represents . . .

   • The conflict between the children and Mrs. Dubose is similar to . . .

   • The setting of Mrs. Dubose's house, halfway between the Finch home and the town, is significant because . . .

4. In the following quotation, Atticus gives Jem advice on how to deal with Mrs. Dubose. Consider how this advice might foreshadow the way Atticus wants the children to act during the trial.

   "You just hold your head high and be a gentleman. Whatever she says to you, it's your job not to let her make you mad."

   Rewrite Atticus's advice as a statement or "life lesson."

5. **Independent Practice:** As you read the rest of Chapter 11, use sticky notes to record textual evidence of Atticus's advice to Jem and Scout concerning Mrs. Dubose.

My Notes

Pin the Quote on Atticus

6. Work with your class to gather evidence of Atticus's "life lessons" from other chapters. Create and illustrate a poster with the quotes and life lessons.

7. Use the quotes to identify themes based on the lessons Atticus wants his children to learn as they come of age. Create a web of these and other themes Harper Lee explores in Part One of *To Kill a Mockingbird*.

When identifying themes, keep in mind the following:

- A theme is a message, not just a topic, and it cannot be just a word, such as *prejudice*. A theme from *To Kill a Mockingbird* would be "Prejudice is based on fear."
- Avoid clichés such as "Blood is thicker than water."
- Don't state a theme as an order: "People must not be racist."
- Themes should be universal, not limited to the characters in a novel. "Scout is a tomboy" is not a theme.

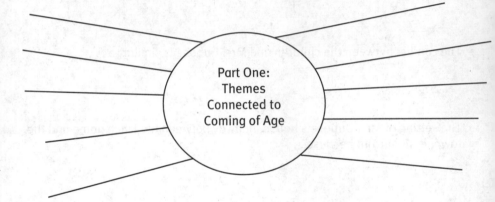

Part One:
Themes
Connected to
Coming of Age

Analytical Writing Prompt: Analyze how character, conflict, or setting contribute to a "coming of age" theme in Chapter 11. Be sure to:

- Begin with a topic sentence that connects your chosen literary element to a theme.
- Include textual evidence in the form of direct quotations from Chapter 11.
- Provide commentary explaining how your quotes support your analysis

Language and Writer's Craft: Incorporating Quotations

The smooth and careful use of quotations is important in successful analytical writing.

Use the **TLQC** (Transition, Lead-in, Quote, Commentary) method to integrate your quotes, with commentary, in a literary analysis essay.

Example:

As he reads to Mrs. Dubose, Jem never loses his calm. Scout observes that "Through the weeks he had cultivated an expression of polite and detached interest, which he would present to her in answer to her most blood-curdling inventions." Jem is taking his father's advice and growing into the kind of man who will not get dragged down by other people's anger.

8. Revise your analysis of a literary element by using the TLQC method of quoting.

My Notes

Shifting Perspectives

My Notes

Learning Target

- Create an outline for an analytical essay about how literary elements contribute to a theme.

Before Reading

1. **Discuss:** Before you begin Part 2 of the novel, review your notes from the first half of this unit in which you researched and presented the context of the novel's setting and publication.

   - How did the experience of researching and presenting context enhance your understanding of the novel?

   - How has it informed your understanding of how readers would have responded to the text in 1960?

   - What specific topics from the presentations are relevant to the issues raised so far in the novel?

2. Part of "coming of age" is understanding that your perspective of the world is not the only one—that other perspectives based on different cultures, nationalities, religions, political beliefs, customs, languages, and values are just as real and valid as your own. Brainstorm experiences that you have had that have exposed you to different perspectives:

During Reading

3. You will conduct a close reading of a passage from Chapter 12, marking the text for evidence of how setting, character, and conflict contribute to following theme:

   "Coming of age" involves recognizing different perspectives.

After Reading

4. Work with your class to complete the outline that follows for an essay about how literary elements in this passage contribute to the theme "Coming of age involves recognizing different perspectives."

Outline for a Passage-Analysis Essay

I. **Introduction:**

    Hook: Anecdote, Quote, Question, or Statement of Intrigue

    Thesis:

II. **Body (Support Paragraph)**

    Topic Sentence:

    Textual Evidence:

III. **Body (Support Paragraph):**

    Topic Sentence:

    Textual Evidence:

IV. **Body (Support Paragraph):**

    Topic Sentence:

    Textual Evidence:

V. **Conclusion:**

    Restate Thesis:

    Literal/Interpretive/Universal Statements:

My Notes

5. As you read the rest of Chapter 12, look for more textual evidence to support the topic sentences in your outline.

6. **Independent Practice:** After you read Chapters 13–14, choose a passage to reread and mark for at least two different literary elements. Use the outline above as a model of an outline for your passage analysis.

A Solitary Light

My Notes

Learning Target

- Compare and contrast how a theme is developed in a key scene in film and text.

Before Reading

1. **Quickwrite:** Your teacher will show you a photo (or photos) of Atticus and Scout as a visual prompt for exploring how character, setting, and conflict are conveyed in a film text. What can you infer from the image about each of these literary elements?

During Reading

2. Conduct a close reading of the passage in Chapter 15 that begins with a description of the Maycomb jail and continues until the end of the chapter. Work with a small group to record textual evidence of significant literary elements in the graphic organizer below.

Setting	Conflict	Character	Other: (plot, symbol, motif)

After Reading

3. Work together to identify a theme. Ask yourself what Scout, Dill, or Jem could learn from this experience, even if they may not recognize it yet.

4. Write at least two interpretive statements about how different literary elements contributed to the theme.

5. As you view a film version of this scene, use the graphic organizer below to take notes on the cinematic techniques. Review cinematic techniques in Unit 2 if necessary.

Angles/Framing	Lighting	Sound	Other
High/low angles, eye level, close-up, two shot, long shot	Bottom/side/front/back, high/low key	Diegetic (including dialogue), non-diegetic	Camera movements, editing techniques

6. **Discuss:** What are some of the differences between the film and text version? What changes in dialogue were made? Why might changes have been made in the transformation from text to film?

Writing Prompt: Compare and contrast the text and film versions of this scene. How do different literary and cinematic elements contribute to a theme? Which do you think is more effective? Be sure to:

- Begin with a topic sentence or thesis that clearly states a theme.
- Include textual evidence from the text and the film.
- Provide commentary comparing and contrasting the use of literary elements and cinematic techniques.

7. **Independent Practice:** Choose a key scene from Chapter 16 to visualize and sketch. Annotate your scene with textual evidence and commentary to explain the choices you made in details, angles, framing, and background.

My Notes

Characters' Voices

My Notes

Learning Target

- Explain how diction, imagery, and syntax create tone and voice, and support explanations with textual evidence.

Identifying Voice

1. Try to identify the speaker of each of the following quotes.

   - "Now you tell your father not to teach you any more. It's best to begin reading with a fresh mind."

   - "You ain't sendin' me home, missus. I was on the verge of leavin' –I done done my time for this year."

   - "No, putting his life history on display for the edification of the neighborhood . . . You stop this nonsense right now."

   - "Scout, I'm tellin' you for the last time, shut your trap or go home—I declare to the Lord you're gettin' more like a girl every day!"

   - " Why, I'll build me a little house and take me a couple of roomers and— gracious, I'll have the finest yard in Alabama."

   - "Grandma says that all men should learn to cook, that men oughta be careful with their wives and wait on 'em when they don't feel good."

   - "Don't you contradict me! And you—what are you doing in those overalls? You should be in a dress and camisole, young lady!"

   - "He's gonna want to be off to himself a lot now, doin' whatever boys do, so you just come right on in the kitchen when you feel lonesome."

   - "Atticus, it's all right to be soft-hearted, you're an easy man, but you have a daughter to think of. A daughter who's growing up."

   - "They ain't mean. They buy me anything I want, but it's now-you've-got-it-go-play-with-it. You've got a roomful of things."

   - "Maybe he told you about me, I beat him up one time but he was real nice about it. Tell him hey for me, won't you?"

2. Choose five of the quotes, and write them on a graphic organizer. Then, answer the following questions for each quote:

   a. What do you notice about each speaker's voice as presented by his or her diction, imagery, and syntax?

   b. How would you describe the tone of each quote? Can you remember the context of each quote?

   c. What was happening in the plot when the quoted words were said?

Analyzing Atticus's Closing Argument

Learning Targets

- Recognize the rhetorical appeals used in a speech.
- In a written paragraph, compare and contrast the use of rhetorical appeals in a key scene in two mediums.

Before Reading

1. Review the testimony presented in Chapters 17–19. Which rhetorical appeals do the lawyers and witnesses use? Find textual evidence of each of the following:

   Logos: an appeal to logic or reason

   Ethos: an appeal to ethics or the character of the speaker

   Pathos: an appeal to senses or emotions

   Discuss:
   - Which speakers rely primarily on pathos?
   - Which speakers would have had difficulty appealing to ethos?
   - What evidence comes to light through appeals to logos?

During Reading

2. Mark the text of Atticus's closing argument by highlighting rhetorical appeals (pathos, ethos, and logos) and taking notes in the margins on the elements of an argument (hook, claim, reasons, evidence, counterclaim(s), and concluding statement/call to action).

LEARNING STRATEGIES:
Rereading, Marking the Text, SMELL, Graphic Organizer, Drafting

My Notes

_____

_____

_____

_____

_____

_____

_____

_____

_____

_____

_____

_____

_____

_____

_____

_____

KEY IDEAS AND DETAILS
How is Atticus's use of language significant in his statement that the case is "as simple as black and white"?

_____

_____

_____

_____

_____

_____

Novel

from

To Kill a Mockingbird

(Chapter 20)

"Gentlemen," he was saying, "I shall be brief, but I would like to use my remaining time with you to remind you that this case is not a difficult one, it requires no minute sifting of complicated facts, but it does require you to be sure beyond all reasonable doubt as to the guilt of the defendant. To begin with, this case should never have come to trial. This case is as simple as black and white.

"The state has not produced one iota of medical evidence to the effect that the crime Tom Robinson is charged with ever took place. It has relied instead upon the testimony of two witnesses whose evidence has not only been called into serious question on cross-examination, but has been flatly contradicted by the defendant. The defendant is not guilty, but somebody in this courtroom is.

"I have nothing but pity in my heart for the chief witness for the state, but my pity does not extend so far as to her putting a man's life at stake, which she has done in an effort to get rid of her own guilt.

Analyzing Atticus's Closing Argument

WORD CONNECTIONS

Roots and Affixes

Circumstantial is an adjective
meaning "having to do with
certain facts or conditions."
The prefix *circum-* derives from
the Latin word *circum*, meaning
"around." English has many
words beginning with *circum-*.
They include *circumference,
circumnavigate*, and *circumvent*.

GRAMMAR & USAGE
Parallel Structure

Parallel structure is the use
of the same grammatical
structures—words, phrases,
or clauses—to balance
related ideas. Writers perform
this balancing act because
it makes their writing more
effective. Readers can see
the commonalities and
relationships clearly when the
structures are parallel.

Example: . . . the
assumption . . . *that all
Negroes lie, that all Negroes
are basically immoral beings,
that all Negro men are not
to be trusted around our
women.* . . . (parallel adjective
clauses)

"I say guilt, gentlemen, because it was guilt that motivated her. She has committed no crime, she has merely broken a rigid and time-honored code of our society, a code so severe that whoever breaks it is hounded from our midst as unfit to live with. She is the victim of cruel poverty and ignorance, but I cannot pity her: she is white. She knew full well the enormity of her offense, but because her desires were stronger than the code she was breaking, she persisted in breaking it. She persisted, and her subsequent reaction is something that all of us have known at one time or another. She did something every child has done—she tried to put the evidence of her offense away from her. But in this case she was no child hiding stolen contraband: she struck out at her victim—of necessity she must put him away from her—he must be removed from her presence, from this world. She must destroy the evidence of her offense.

"What was the evidence of her offense? Tom Robinson, a human being. She must put Tom Robinson away from her. Tom Robinson was her daily reminder of what she did. What did she do? She tempted a Negro.

"She was white, and she tempted a Negro. She did something that in our society is unspeakable: she kissed a black man. Not an old Uncle, but a strong young Negro man. No code mattered to her before she broke it, but it came crashing down on her afterwards.

"Her father saw it, and the defendant has testified as to his remarks. What did her father do? We don't know, but there is circumstantial evidence to indicate that Mayella Ewell was beaten savagely by someone who led almost exclusively with his left. We do know in part what Mr. Ewell did: he did what any God-fearing, persevering, respectable white man would do under the circumstances—he swore out a warrant, no doubt signing it with his left hand, and Tom Robinson now sits before you, having taken the oath with the only good hand he possesses—his right hand.

"And so a quiet, respectable, humble Negro who had the unmitigated temerity to 'feel sorry' for a white woman has had to put his word against two white people's. I need not remind you of their appearance and conduct on the stand—you saw them for yourselves. The witnesses for the state, with the exception of the sheriff of Maycomb County, have presented themselves to you gentlemen, to this court, in the cynical confidence that their testimony would not be doubted, confident that you gentlemen would go along with them on the assumption—the evil assumption—that *all* Negroes lie, that *all* Negroes are basically immoral beings, that *all* Negro men are not to be trusted around our women, an assumption one associates with minds of their caliber.

"Which, gentlemen, we know is in itself a lie as black as Tom Robinson's skin, a lie I do not have to point out to you. You know the truth, and the truth is this: some Negroes lie, some Negroes are immoral, some Negro men are not to be trusted around women— black or white. But this is a truth that applies to the human race and to no particular race of men. There is not a person in this courtroom who has never told a lie, who has never done an immoral thing, and there is no man living who has never looked upon a woman without desire."

Atticus paused and took out his handkerchief. Then he took off his glasses and wiped them, and we saw another "first": we had never seen him sweat—he was one of those men whose faces never perspired, but now it was shining tan.

"One more thing, gentlemen, before I quit. Thomas Jefferson once said that all men are created equal, a phrase that the Yankees and the distaff side of the Executive branch in Washington are fond of hurling at us. There is a tendency in this year of grace, 1935, for certain people to use this phrase out of context, to satisfy all conditions. The most ridiculous example I can think of is that the people who run public education promote the stupid and idle along with the industrious—because all men are created equal, educators will gravely tell you, the children left behind suffer terrible feelings of inferiority. We know all men are not created equal in the sense some people would have us believe—some people are smarter than others, some people have more opportunity because they're born with it, some men make more money than others, some ladies make better cakes than others—some people are born gifted beyond the normal scope of most men.

"But there is one way in this country in which all men are created equal—there is one human institution that makes a pauper the equal of a Rockefeller, the stupid man the equal of an Einstein, and the ignorant man the equal of any college president. That institution, gentlemen, is a court. It can be the Supreme Court of the United States or the humblest J.P. court in the land, or this honorable court which you serve. Our courts have their faults, as does any human institution, but in this country our courts are the great levelers, and in our courts all men are created equal.

"I'm no idealist to believe firmly in the integrity of our courts and in the jury system—that is no ideal to me, it is a living, working reality. Gentlemen, a court is no better than each man of you sitting before me on this jury. A court is only as sound as its jury, and a jury is only as sound as the men who make it up. I am confident that you gentlemen will review without passion the evidence you have heard, come to a decision, and restore this defendant to his family. In the name of God, do your duty."

Atticus's voice had dropped, and as he turned away from the jury he said something I did not catch. He said it more to himself than to the court. I punched Jem. "What'd he say?"

"'In the name of God, believe him,' I think that's what he said."

After Reading

3. Perform a close reading of Atticus's closing statement. Use the SMELL strategy to complete your analysis.

My Notes

_____

_____

_____

_____

_____

_____

KEY IDEAS AND DETAILS
Who are some of the famous people Atticus mentions in his speech? Why do you think he does this?

_____

_____

_____

_____

_____

_____

WORD CONNECTIONS

Foreign Words

Legal arguments often use a persuasive technique of *ad hominem*, which is Latin for "argument against the person." An *ad hominem* appeal points out that a person may be disposed to take a particular position. Find an example of *ad hominem* in the excerpt from Chapter 20 of *To Kill a Mockingbird*.

Analyzing Atticus's Closing Argument

S = Sender-Receiver relationship. Atticus is the sender. The jury and the audience are the receivers. What is the relationship among Atticus, the jury, and the audience? Whom does Atticus mean to influence with his statement? What attitudes and assumptions does his target audience hold toward his subject? Toward Atticus himself?

M = Message. What is Atticus's message? Summarize the statements made in his closing argument.

E = Emotional strategies. Does Atticus use any statements that are meant to get an emotional reaction from his audience? Explain. If so, what is the desired effect?

L = Logical strategies. Does Atticus use any statements or appeals that are logical? Explain. How does the logic (or its absence) affect the message?

L = Language. Look for specific words and phrases used by Atticus, and consider how the language affects his message.

4. As you watch the film version of the courtroom scene, fill out the chart below with specific details from the scene.

What images does the director present to the audience?	What images does the director consciously choose NOT to present to the audience?	What do you notice about the relationship between the speech and the images?	What changes or deletions do you notice in the text of Atticus's speech?

Writing Prompt: Write a paragraph analyzing the use of appeals in the text and film versions of Atticus's closing argument. Which version of the argument do you think is more convincing? Be sure to:

- State your opinion in a topic sentence.
- Provide textual evidence from the film and the text.
- Integrate quotes from the text using the TLQC method (transition, lead-in, quote, and commentary).

5. **Independent Practice:** As you read Chapters 21–23, take notes on the different characters' reactions to the verdict.

My Notes

Aftermath and Reflection

LEARNING STRATEGIES:
Socratic Seminar, Graphic
Organizer, Revising

Learning Targets
- Analyze the significance of literary elements in a passage in relation to a theme of the novel.
- Write a thesis statement and topic sentences for an essay that explains how literary elements contribute to a theme of the novel.

Before Reading

1. **Socratic Seminar:** Your teacher will place you in a group to discuss a question or questions regarding the verdict. Write the question(s) and your initial response below.

2. After your discussion, work with your group to co-construct a statement synthesizing your response to the question(s):

3. Work with your class to co-construct a statement about how the trial was a "coming of age" experience for Jem:

4. Revisit the web that you created in Activity 3.15, and consider the lessons Scout and Jem learn in Part 2 as they interact with the world outside their neighborhood. Add more thematic statements related to "coming of age" to your web.

My Notes

During Reading

5. As you read Chapter 24, consider the significance of the chapter to the meaning of the novel as a whole. Complete the graphic organizer below by analyzing how different literary elements contribute to a recurring theme of the novel.

Analysis of a Literary Element in Chapter 24	Textual Evidence (Quote from Text)	Theme of the Novel as a Whole	Evidence of This Theme in Another Chapter
Character: Grace Merriweather's character represents the irony of someone who claims to be religious but is actually a hypocrite.		Racism is a disease that infects a person's mind and soul.	
Setting: The setting of the missionary tea in the Finches' livingroom			
Conflict:			
Plot Event:			

After Reading

6. **Discuss:** How does Scout's perspective on what it means to be a lady evolve during this scene? How are the events in this chapter a "coming of age" experience for her?

7. Work with your discussion group to write a thesis statement and topic sentences for an essay about how the literary elements in Chapter 24 contribute to a theme of the work as a whole.

Thesis:

Topic Sentence:

Topic Sentence:

Topic Sentence:

Language and Writer's Craft: Three-fold Transitions

Three-fold transitions help you make logical connections between your points in an essay. A three-fold transition sentence does the following:

- Refers subtly to the idea discussed in the previous paragraph
- Refers briefly to the overall thesis idea
- Refers more specifically to new ideas to be discussed in the next paragraph

8. Work with your group to revise at least one of your topic sentences using three-fold transitions. Sample: After recognizing the irony in her society, Scout matures even further as she recognizes the strength of Miss Maudie's quiet, calm responses to her conflict with Grace Merriweather.

9. **Independent Practice:** As you read Chapters 25–27, consider passages that you could analyze to show how literary elements contribute to a theme of the novel as a whole.

Standing in Borrowed Shoes

Learning Targets

- Identify character traits and create a character profile poster collaboratively.
- Evaluate how primary and secondary characters and their interactions contribute to the development of a novel's themes.

Analyzing Characters

1. **Quickwrite:** Consider the following quote from the novel:

   "Atticus was right. One time he said you never really know a man until you stand in his shoes and walk around in them." —*Scout*

   When have Scout, Jem, or Dill had to look at the world from other people's perspectives? What have they learned from other residents of Maycomb?

2. Work in a small group to list the *primary* (major) and *secondary* (minor) characters you can identify from the novel. When you have finished, make notes on the thematic subjects that secondary characters might represent in the novel.

Primary Characters	Secondary Characters and Thematic Topics They Represent

LEARNING STRATEGIES:
Quickwrite, Graphic Organizer, Marking the Text

Literary Terms

A **flat** or **static character** is uncomplicated, staying the same without changing or growing during the story. A **round** or **dynamic character** evolves and grows in the story and has a complex personality.

WORD CONNECTIONS

Roots and Affixes

The word **dynamic** comes from the Greek word meaning "powerful." The root *dyna-* appears in *dynamo, dynamite,* and *dynasty.*
Static also comes from a Greek word, *statikos,* referring to something firm or fixed. Other English words with the root *-stat-* include *status, station, statistics,* and *statue.*

My Notes

_____

_____

_____

_____

_____

_____

_____

_____

_____

Standing in Borrowed Shoes

3. Working with a partner, create a character profile poster. Your poster should include the following elements:

- A picture or graphic representation of the character
- A physical description from the novel
- A list of several adjectives describing the character's personality, values, and/or motives
- A description of the plot events in which this character is involved
- A quotation about him or her from another character
- A quotation by the character that reveals his or her values

4. As you view the posters your class creates, take notes in the graphic organizer below on at least two characters other than your own.

Character and Description	Events Involving the Character	Textual Evidence	Theme Related to This Character

5. **Reflect:** Work with a partner to review the Events column of your graphic organizer. Choose an event that you think is important, and locate the most significant passage describing that event. Use a passage that is no more than two pages long and annotate it in detail.

6. **Independent Practice:** As you read Chapter 28, annotate each page with sticky notes. Pay close attention to the literary elements, and note how the tone shifts with different plot events.

Controversy in Context

Learning Targets

- Analyze a nonfiction text about various controversies surrounding the novel *To Kill a Mockingbird*.
- Evaluate the techniques and effectiveness of an argument.
- Use the RAFT strategy to compose an argument in writing.

Before Reading

1. **Quickwrite:** Chapter 27 ended with the line "Thus began our longest journey together." What are the literal and figurative meanings of the word "journey"? How is reading a novel similar to and different from taking a journey?

2. **Discuss:** Revisit your notes from **Embedded Assessment 1: Historical Investigation and Presentation**.

   Now that you have read most of *To Kill a Mockingbird*, consider what you have learned about the early 1960s and make inferences about how readers would respond to this novel at the time of its publication:

   - How would the experience of reading the book then be different from the experience of reading it now?

   - How could the novel itself have contributed to the Civil Rights Movement?

During Reading

3. Mark the first paragraph of the text, noting textual evidence of the reader response to the novel.

4. Chunk the remaining paragraphs into two sections of two paragraphs each. As you read each chunk, mark the text and take notes to identify the following:
   - What were the arguments against the novel?
   - What groups of people opposed the novel?
   - What reasons does the author give in defense of the novel?

5. After each chunk, evaluate the validity of the arguments for and against *To Kill a Mockingbird*.

My Notes

KEY IDEAS AND DETAILS
What is the claim this author
makes about the career of the
novel *To Kill a Mockingbird*?

My Notes

ABOUT THE AUTHOR
Nicholas Karolides is an author and editor of books for young adults. He has
often written about the topics of the politics of suppression and censorship
of literary works.

Essay

from "In Defense of *To Kill a Mockingbird*"

by Nicholas J. Karolides, et al.

The critical career of *To Kill a Mockingbird* is a late twentieth- century case study
of censorship. When Harper Lee's novel about a small southern town and its prejudices
was published in 1960, the book received favorable reviews in professional journals
and the popular press. Typical of that opinion, Booklist's reviewer called the book
"melodramatic" and noted "traces of sermonizing," but the book was recommended for
library purchase, commending its "rare blend of wit and compassion." Reviewers did
not suggest that the book was young-adult literature, or that it belonged in adolescent
collections; perhaps that is why no one mentioned the book's language or violence.
In any event, reviewers seemed inclined to agree that *To Kill a Mockingbird* was a
worthwhile interpretation of the South's existing social structures during the 1930s. In
1961 the book won the Pulitzer Prize Award, the Alabama Library Association Book
Award, and the Brotherhood Award of the National Conference of Christians and
Jews. It seemed that Harper Lee's blend of family history, local custom, and restrained
sermonizing was important reading, and with a young girl between the ages of six
and nine as the main character, *To Kill a Mockingbird* moved rapidly into junior and
senior high school libraries and curriculum. The book was not destined to be studied
by college students. Southern literature's critics rarely mentioned it; few university
professors found it noteworthy enough to "teach" as an exemplary southern novel.

By the mid-sixties *To Kill a Mockingbird* had a solid place in junior and senior high
American literature studies. Once discovered by southern parents, the book's solid place
became shaky indeed. Sporadic lawsuits arose. In most cases the complaint against the
book was by conservatives who disliked the portrayal of whites. Typically, the Hanover
County School Board in Virginia first ruled the book "immoral," then withdrew their
criticism and declared the ruckus "was all a mistake" (Newsletter [on Intellectual
Freedom] 1966). By 1968 the National Education Association listed the book among
those which drew the most criticism from private groups. Ironically it was rated directly
behind *Little Black Sambo* (*Newsletter* 1968). And the seventies arrived.

Things had changed in the South during the sixties. Two national leaders who had supported integration and had espoused the ideals of racial equality were assassinated in southern regions. When John F. Kennedy was killed in Texas on November 27, 1963, many southerners were shocked. Populist attitudes of racism were declining, and in the aftermath of the tragedy southern politics began to change. Lyndon Johnson gained the presidency: blacks began to seek and win political offices. Black leader Martin Luther King had stressed the importance of racial equality, always using Mahatma Gandhi's strategy of nonviolent action and civil disobedience. A brilliant orator, King grew up in the South; the leader of the [Southern Christian Leadership Conference], he lived in Atlanta, Georgia. In 1968, while working on a garbage strike in Memphis, King was killed. The death of the 1965 Nobel Peace Prize winner was further embarrassment for white southerners. Whites began to look at public values anew, and gradually southern blacks found experiences in the South more tolerable. In 1971 one Atlanta businessman observed [in *Ebony*], "The liberation thinking is here. Blacks are more together. With the doors opening wider, this area is the mecca...." Southern arguments against *To Kill a Mockingbird* subsided. *The Newsletter on Intellectual Freedom* contained no record of southern court cases during the seventies or eighties. The book had sustained itself during the first period of sharp criticism; it had survived regional protests from the area it depicted.

The second onslaught of attack came from new groups of censors, and it came during the late seventies and early eighties. Private sectors in the Midwest and suburban East began to demand the book's removal from school libraries. Groups, such as the Eden Valley School Committee in Minnesota, claimed that the book was too laden with profanity (*Newsletter* 1978). In Vernon, New York, Reverend Carl Hadley threatened to establish a private Christian school because public school libraries contained such "filthy, trashy sex novels" as *A Separate Peace* and *To Kill a Mockingbird* (*Newsletter* 1980). And finally, blacks began to censor the book. In Warren, Indiana, three blacks resigned from the township Human Relations Advisory Council when the Warren County school administration refused to remove the book from Warren junior high school classes. They contended that the book "does psychological damage to the positive integration process and represents institutionalized racism" (*Newsletter* 1982). Thus, censorship of *To Kill a Mockingbird* swung from the conservative right to the liberal left. Factions representing racists, religious sects, concerned parents, and minority groups vocally demanded the book's removal from public schools. . . .

The censors' reactions to *To Kill a Mockingbird* were reactions to issues of race and justice. Their moves to ban the book derive from their own perspectives of the book's theme. Their "reader response" criticism, usually based on one reading of the book, was personal and political. They needed to ban the book because it told them something about American society that they did not want to hear. That is precisely the problem facing any author of realistic fiction. Once the story becomes real, it can become grim. An author will use first-person flashback in a story in order to let the reader lie in another time, another place. Usually the storyteller is returning for a second view of the scene. The teller has experienced the events before and the story is being retold because the scene has left the storyteller uneasy. As the storyteller recalls the past, both the listener and the teller see events in a new light. Both are working through troubled times in search of meaning. In the case of *To Kill a Mockingbird* the first-person retelling is not pleasant, but the underlying significance is with the narrative. The youthful personalities who are recalled are hopeful. Scout tells us of a time past when white people would lynch or convict a man because of the color of his skin. She also shows us three children who refuse to believe that the system is right, and she leaves us with the thought that most people will be nice if seen for what they are: humans with frailties. When discussing literary criticism, Theo D'Haen suggested [in *Text to Reader*] that

KEY IDEAS AND DETAILS
What evidence is presented to support the author's claim about the importance of *To Kill a Mockingbird* during the 20th century?

WORD CONNECTIONS

Roots and Affixes

The word *psychological* (adj.) means "mental" or "of the mind." The prefix *psycho-* comes from the Greek word *psychē*, meaning "soul" or "spirit." Other words with the prefix *psycho-* include *psychoanalysis*, *psychobabble*, and *psychodrama*.

My Notes

Controversy in Context

KEY IDEAS AND DETAILS
What does it mean that a literary work should have "a life within the world," and how does *To Kill a Mockingbird* still remain "a part of the ongoing activities" of our world?

the good literary work should have a life within the world and be "part of the ongoing activities of that world." *To Kill a Mockingbird* continues to have life within the world; its ongoing activities in the realm of censorship show that it is a book which deals with regional moralism. The children in the story seem very human; they worry about their own identification, they defy parental rules, and they cry over injustices. They mature in Harper Lee's novel, and they lose their innocence. So does the reader. If the readers are young, they may believe Scout when she says, "nothin's real scary except in books." If the readers are older they will have learned that life is scary, and they will be prepared to meet some of its realities.

After Reading

6. Use the RAFT strategy to compose an argument defending or challenging the use of the novel *To Kill a Mockingbird* in the ninth-grade curriculum of your high school.

   Role: Student

   Audience: Parent, teacher, censor, administrator, school board member

   Format: Letter, speech, or e-mail

   Topic: Whether or not the novel *To Kill a Mockingbird* should be part of the ninth-grade curriculum

   As you write your argument, be sure to:

   - Start with a claim defending or challenging the use of *To Kill a Mockingbird* in the ninth-grade curriculum.
   - Use textual evidence from your research, your reading of the novel, and/or the Karolides article.
   - Raise at least one counterargument and rebut it.

GRAMMAR & USAGE
Parallel Structure

Verbs have **active** and **passive** voice in all six tenses. When the subject of the verb does the acting, the verb is in the active voice. When the subject of the verb receives the action, the verb is in the passive voice. A passive-voice verb always contains a form of *be* along with the past participle of the verb:

- Active voice (past perfect): Things **had changed** in the South. . . .
- Passive voice (past perfect): Things **had been changed**. . . .

Note the following examples of passive-voice verbs in the essay:

- Two national leaders. . . were assassinated. . . .
- John F. Kennedy was killed. . .

These examples demonstrate one reason to use passive voice: when you want to emphasize the receiver of the action.

My Notes

_____

_____

_____

_____

Learning Targets

- Analyze and annotate a literary passage.
- Write an essay about how literary elements contribute to a theme.

Before Reading

1. **Discuss:** Part of coming of age is accepting that the world is imperfect and does not always make sense. In Chapter 23, Jem says to Scout:

   "If there's just one kind of folks, why can't they get along with each other? If they're alike, why do they go out of their way to despise each other? Scout, I think I'm beginning to understand something. I think I'm beginning to understand why Boo Radley's stayed shut up in the house all this time . . . it's because he *wants* to stay inside."

   How else do the events involving Boo Radley foreshadow the events and themes of Part 2 of the novel?

2. Before reading Chapters 29 and 30, complete the first row of the graphic organizer below, which asks about Scout's mental picture of Boo Radley from the early chapters of the book.

During Reading

3. As you read Chapters 29–31, complete the rest of the graphic organizer. In the Textual Evidence column, first write the inference you are making from the topic of the commentary, and then provide the textual evidence to support that inference.

Commentary	Textual Evidence
Scout's mental picture of Boo before Chapter 29	
The reality of Boo	
Scout's understanding of Boo after she meets him	

> **LEARNING STRATEGIES:**
> Chunking the Text, Levels of Questions, Graphic Organizer, Discussion Groups

> **My Notes**

"Hey, Boo"

After Reading

4. With a small group, brainstorm a list of the literary elements you have studied in this unit and take turns explaining their meaning so that you can use them in your writing and also for Embedded Assessment 2.

5. Conduct a close reading of the passage in Chapter 31 that begins "I led him to the front porch" and ends with "Just standing on the Radley porch was enough." Use sticky notes to annotate the text with your interpretation and analysis.

6. Work together with your group to write an essay about how the literary elements in the passage you have just annotated help develop a theme of the novel. If you have computers, try using something like Google docs or a wiki to compose the analysis and your essay together. Be sure to:

- Include an introduction with a hook that connects to a thesis.
- Provide multiple support paragraphs with topic sentences, textual evidence, and commentary.
- End with a conclusion that makes connections between the literal, interpretive, and universal.

Writing a Literary Analysis Essay

Assignment

Your assignment is to write a passage analysis of a key coming-of-age scene from *To Kill a Mockingbird*. After annotating the text to analyze Harper Lee's use of literary elements in your selected passage, write an essay explaining how the literary elements in this passage help develop a theme of the novel.

Planning and Prewriting: Take time to select and annotate a passage.

- Which passage from the novel will you choose to illustrate a significant coming-of-age moment?

- How will you be sure you understand all the literary elements that you have studied in this unit? (See the list you created in Activity 3.23.)

- How can you be sure readers know what passage you have chosen to mark and annotate to analyze literary elements?

- How will you use your annotations to generate a working thesis that shows the significance of the passage to a theme of the book?

Drafting: Determine the structure of your essay and how to incorporate necessary elements.

- How will you organize your essay? What tools will you use to help you organize?

- What is your thesis? Do your topic sentences support your thesis?

- What textual evidence do you need to support your thesis and topic sentences?

- What elements do you need to include in your introduction and conclusion?

Evaluating and Revising: Create opportunities to review and gain feedback for revisions.

- How will you ask for feedback on your draft? Whom will you ask?

- How will you revise your draft for seamless integration of quotations using the TLQC method (transition, lead in, quote, and commentary)?

Editing for Publication: Confirm that the final draft is ready for publication.

- How will you proofread and edit your draft to demonstrate command of the conventions of standard English (capitalization, punctuation, spelling, grammar, and usage)?

- How will you use the Scoring Guide to be sure you have met all of the criteria for this assignment?

Reflection

After completing this Embedded Assessment, think about how you went about accomplishing this task, and respond to the following question: What have you learned about the significance of individual passages to a novel as a whole?

My Notes

Writing a Literary Analysis Essay

SCORING GUIDE

Scoring Criteria	Exemplary	Proficient	Emerging	Incomplete
Ideas	The essay • includes a well-chosen passage that reveals the complex relationship between the literary elements and the major ideas and concepts of the entire work • provides supporting details to enhance understanding of the writer's position • relates commentary directly to the thesis.	The essay • reflects a careful choice of passage to show the relationship between a scene and the major ideas and concepts of the novel • provides relevant details to explain the writer's position • uses appropriate commentary.	The essay • attempts to link a passage to a major theme of the novel • presents supporting details that may be fully developed or provide an understanding of the writer's position • has commentary that may not relate directly to the thesis or may be a plot summary.	The essay • has a passage that does not represent a major theme of the novel • is missing supporting details or presents undeveloped ideas • is missing commentary or includes commentary that does not relate directly to the thesis.
Structure	The essay • has multiple paragraphs and a clear and precise thesis that directs the organization of the body • uses transitions to clarify and connect ideas • provides relevant and insightful commentary; the conclusion follows from the ideas presented.	The essay • has multiple paragraphs and is organized with an introduction, detailed body paragraphs, and a conclusion • uses transitions to establish connections between ideas.	The essay • attempts to organize ideas but key pieces are lacking • may be missing an introduction, detailed body paragraphs, and/or a conclusion • uses few or no transitions to connect ideas.	The essay • does not have a focus with a clear organization of introduction, body paragraphs, and conclusion • does not use transitions to connect paragraphs and/or ideas.
Use of Language	The essay • uses a formal style • seamlessly incorporates literary analysis vocabulary • is mostly error-free, with proper punctuation and capitalization to embed quotations into the text.	The essay • uses diction that is appropriate for an academic topic • incorporates some literary analysis vocabulary • has few errors.	The essay • uses simple language that is not appropriate for an academic topic • includes little literary analysis vocabulary • has errors that interfere with meaning.	The essay • uses slang or informal words that are not appropriate for an academic topic • includes little or no literary analysis vocabulary • has numerous errors that interfere with meaning.

Coming of Age on Stage

Visual Prompt: The balcony scene is one of the most famous in *The Tragedy of Romeo and Juliet*. How do you visualize this scene?

Unit Overview

The Tragedy of Romeo and Juliet, a coming-of-age drama about two young star-crossed lovers, was one of William Shakespeare's most popular plays in his lifetime. To this day, it is one of his most widely performed plays, and it has inspired countless artists, musicians, and filmmakers to bring to life their own visions of this timeless tragedy. In this unit, you will join their ranks by planning and performing your own collaborative interpretation of a scene. After reflecting on this experience, you will conduct research to support an argument about the relevance of Shakespeare in today's world.

Coming of Age on Stage

GOALS:

- To cite textual evidence to support analysis of a dramatic text
- To analyze the representation of key scenes in text, film, and other mediums
- To collaborate with peers on an interpretive performance
- To conduct research to answer questions and gather evidence
- To analyze how an author uses rhetoric to advance a purpose
- To write an argument to support a claim

ACADEMIC VOCABULARY

vocal delivery
visual delivery
argument
claim
evidence
synthesis
counterclaim
concession
refutation
hook
concluding statement
call to action

Literary Terms

monologue
drama
tragedy
sonnet
theatrical elements
blocking
dramaturge
foil
soliloquy
subtext

Contents

Activities

*Texts not included in these materials

Language and Writer's Craft
- Rhetorical Questions, Citing Sources (5.16)
- Transitions (Compare/Contrast) (5.17)
- Transitions (5.18)

Previewing the Unit

LEARNING STRATEGIES:
QHT, Marking the Text,
Skimming/Scanning

My Notes

Learning Targets

- Preview the big ideas and vocabulary for the unit.
- Identify the skills and knowledge required to complete Embedded Assessment 1 successfully.

Making Connections

In this unit, you will focus on drama. You will learn the elements of drama and of staging a play, and you will engage in a debate about the relevance of William Shakespeare. As you work through the activities, you will apply your skills of analysis, interpretation, research, writing, and collaboration.

Essential Questions

To get started thinking about drama and theater, answer the essential questions. Based on your current knowledge, write your answers to these questions.

1. How do actors and directors use theatrical elements to create a dramatic interpretation?

2. Why do we study Shakespeare?

Developing Vocabulary

Look at the vocabulary terms on the Contents page. Use a QHT strategy to analyze your knowledge of each term and your ability to explain and use each term correctly.

Unpacking Embedded Assessment 1

Read the assignment for Embedded Assessment 1: Presenting a Dramatic Interpretation.

> Your assignment is to work collaboratively with your acting company to interpret, rehearse, and perform a scene from William Shakespeare's *Romeo and Juliet*. In preparation, each member of the acting company will create a staging notebook providing textual evidence and commentary on the planned interpretation. Finally, you will write a reflection evaluating your final performance.

In your own words, summarize what you will need to know to complete this assessment successfully. With your class, create a graphic organizer to represent the skills and knowledge you will need to complete the tasks identified in the Embedded Assessment.

INDEPENDENT READING LINK

Your study of drama in this unit will focus on *The Tragedy of Romeo and Juliet*. To further your knowledge of drama and dramatists, choose another play to read on your own. Your teacher can guide you in choosing a play or playwright.

Shakespeare's Age

ACTIVITY
5.2

Learning Targets

- Analyze a poem and make connections to the themes in the unit.
- Research Shakespeare to develop a context for the play.

Before Reading

1. **Discuss:** What do you know about William Shakespeare, his work, and the times he lived in? How and when have you learned about Shakespeare previously?

During Reading

2. The **monologue** on the next page is delivered by the character Jaques. It is often referred to as "Seven Ages of Man" speech. As you read the monologue on the following page, mark the text as follows:

   - Put an asterisk (*) next to each line that introduces a new "age of man."
   - Next to each asterisk, put an age range that you think Shakespeare is describing (for example, 0–2 years).
   - Put a box around the section or sections that you think refer to the period in life described as "coming of age."

3. Work with a small group to diffuse the text by highlighting and defining unfamiliar words, using a dictionary when needed.

4. Plan and rehearse a choral reading by assigning different sections of the monologue to individuals or pairs within your group. Use appropriate tone of voice and gestures to enhance your performance.

ABOUT THE AUTHOR
William Shakespeare (1564–1616) is considered one of the most gifted and perceptive writers in the English language. He left his home in Stratford-upon-Avon for London, where he pursued a career as an actor. He was more successful as a playwright and poet, however, producing more than three dozen plays, which are still performed centuries after his death.

LEARNING STRATEGIES:
Think-Pair-Share, Marking the Text, Diffusing, Quickwrite, Choral Reading

WORD CONNECTIONS
Roots and Affixes

The root *-logue* comes from the Latin *-logus* and means "to speak." Words that use this root and communicate different forms of speaking include *monologue*, *prologue*, *dialogue*, and *epilogue*.

Literary Terms
A **monologue** is a dramatic speech delivered by a single character in a play.

My Notes

Shakespeare's Age

Drama

Monologue from *As You Like It*

by William Shakespeare

KEY IDEAS AND DETAILS
Which "age" do you think
the main characters of *Romeo
and Juliet* will fit into? Does
this "age" match the text
you marked as coming-of-
age years?

All the world's a stage,
And all the men and women merely players:
They have their exits and their entrances;
And one man in his time plays many parts,
5 His acts being seven ages. At first, the infant,
Mewling and puking in the nurse's arms.
And then the whining school-boy, with his satchel
And shining morning face, creeping like snail
Unwillingly to school. And then the lover,
10 Sighing like furnace, with a woeful ballad
Made to his mistress' eyebrow. Then a soldier,
Full of strange oaths and bearded like the pard,
Jealous in honour, sudden and quick in quarrel,
Seeking the bubble reputation
15 Even in the cannon's mouth. And then the justice,
In fair round belly with good capon lined,
With eyes severe and beard of formal cut,
Full of wise saws and modern instances;
And so he plays his part. The sixth age shifts
20 Into the lean and slipper'd pantaloon,
With spectacles on nose and pouch on side,
His youthful hose, well saved, a world too wide
For his shrunk shank; and his big manly voice,
Turning again toward childish treble, pipes
25 And whistles in his sound. Last scene of all,
That ends this strange eventful history,
Is second childishness and mere oblivion,
Sans teeth, sans eyes, sans taste, sans everything.

After Reading

5. Reread the first four lines of the monologue. What metaphor is Shakespeare using to describe human life? How and why is this an appropriate comparison?

6. In your group, assign a different research topic from the list below to each member. Visit the Folger Shakespeare Library website (www.folger.edu) to conduct research on your assigned topic by exploring the "Discover Shakespeare" link. Summarize the key points you learned on an index card. Copy the website addess onto the back side of your notecard.

   • **Shakespeare's Life:** Stratford Beginnings, Success in London, Final Years, An Expansive Age, Shakespeare's Story, Questioning Shakespeare's Authorship

   • **Shakespeare's Work:** The Plays, The Poems, Publication, First Folio

   • **Shakespeare's Theatre:** London Playhouses, Inside the Theaters, Staging and Performance, Business Arrangements

7. Present your findings to your group. Access and include visual or audio media in your presentation. Work together to generate a list of questions you still have about Shakespeare and his times.

My Notes

A Sonnet Sets the Stage

LEARNING STRATEGIES:
Marking the Text, Diffusing, Metacognitive Markers, Visualizing, Previewing

My Notes

Literary Terms

A **drama** is a play written for stage, radio, film, or television, usually about a serious topic or situation.

A **tragedy** is a dramatic play that tells the story of a character, usually of a noble class, who meets an untimely and unhappy death or downfall, often because of a specific character flaw or twist of fate.

Literary Terms

A **sonnet** is a fourteen-line lyric poem, usually written in iambic pentameter and following a strict pattern of rhyme.

Learning Targets

- Analyze the prologue to *Romeo and Juliet* to preview and make predictions about the play.
- Define *drama* and *tragedy* in context of the play.
- Create a collaborative tableau to preview the characters and their relationships.

Before Reading

1. The story of *Romeo and Juliet* was well known to those who attended the play in Shakespeare's day. The audience knew that the end result would be a **tragedy**. Brainstorm a list of modern films that have endings known to the audience. How do these films keep the audience interested?

2. The Prologue serves as an introductory speech in which an actor, in this case probably just one man called the "Chorus," provides the audience with a brief outline of the plot.

   In this play, the Prologue is a 14-line poem with a defined structure that is called an English or Shakespearean **sonnet**. Note that this sonnet, like all Shakespeare's sonnets, uses iambic pentameter to create a distinct rhythm. The most noticeable feature of this rhythmic pattern is the use of pentameter, which means that each line includes 10 syllables or 5 feet (pairs of syllables). Try counting the number of syllables for each line. Work with your class to label the lines of the Prologue on the following page to show its rhyme and rhyme scheme.

3. Work with your class to diffuse the text by highlighting and defining unfamiliar vocabulary with the aid of a dictionary or thesaurus. Write a synonym for each unfamiliar word.

During Reading

4. Listen to the Prologue as it is read aloud. Use metacognitive markers to mark the text as follows:
   - Put a question mark (?) next to lines that are confusing or bring up questions.
   - Put an asterisk (*) next to lines that are interesting or reinforce what you already know.
   - Put an exclamation mark (!) next to lines that are surprising or help you make predictions.

from The Tragedy of *Romeo* and *Juliet*

by William Shakespeare

WORD CONNECTIONS

Roots and Affixes

Prologue contains the root *-log-*, from the Greek word *logos*, meaning *word*. This root also appears in *dialogue*, *catalogue*, and *eulogy*. The prefix *pro-* means "before."

PROLOGUE

Enter Chorus

Two households, both alike in dignity,

In fair Verona, where we lay our scene,

From ancient grudge break to new mutiny,

Where civil blood makes civil hands unclean.

5 From forth the fatal loins of these two foes

A pair of star-crossed lovers take their life,

Whose misadventured piteous overthrows

Doth with their death bury their parents' strife.

The fearful passage of their death-marked love,

10 And the continuance of their parents' rage,

Which, but their children's end, naught could remove,

Is now the two hours' traffic of our stage;

The which if you with patient ears attend,

What here shall miss, our toil shall strive to mend.

My Notes

After Reading

5. Examine the masks, which are a common graphic representation of drama. What do the two masks represent?

6. List words that you associate with the term tragedy. Add a few key words from the prologue.

A Sonnet Sets the Stage

7. A *tableau* is a purposeful arrangement of characters frozen as if in a painting or a photograph. After you are assigned a character name, work with your class to create a tableau based on the information provided in the prologue and in the cast of characters in your copy of *Romeo and Juliet*. Think about the following as you prepare to assume your role in the class tableau:

- Body positions (who you stand next to, distance)
- Postures and poses
- Facial expressions and gestures

To help you keep track of the characters, create a bookmark to use while you are reading *Romeo and Juliet*. Fold a sheet of paper in half lengthwise, and write the Capulets on one side, the Montagues on the other side, and unaffiliated characters inside. Identify the characters using both images and text to describe what you know about them.

Conflict Up Close

Learning Targets
- Analyze the opening scene of *Romeo and Juliet* to understand Shakespeare's language.
- Annotate the text for vocal and visual delivery to communicate meaning in a performance.

LEARNING STRATEGIES:
Skimming/Scanning, Quickwrite, Close Reading, Visualizing, Diffusing, Paraphrasing

Before Reading

1. **Discussion:** In this scene a fight breaks out over an apparently minor or trivial thing. Is this true to life?

2. Working with a partner, skim and scan the text of the excerpt from Scene 1 and diffuse some of Shakespeare's unfamiliar language using the translation table below. What resources could you use to help diffuse Shakespeare's language?

My Notes

Shakespeare	Translation	Shakespeare	Translation
Thee/Thou	You	Ay	Yes
Thy/Thine	Your	Would	Wish
Hath	Has	Alas	Unfortunately
Art	Are	'Tis	It is
Wilt/Wouldst	Will/Would	Marry	Really
An	If	Canst/Didst/Hadst/Dost	Can/Did/Had/Does

During Reading

3. In your groups, assume the roles of the characters. As you work with your class to make meaning of the first chunk of text, take notes in the margins to paraphrase what your character is saying in each line.

4. Once you have made meaning of the chunk, prepare to read it through aloud by annotating the text with tone cues to indicate the appropriate **vocal delivery** (angry, confused, bragging, laughing).

   Use punctuation as cues for vocal delivery. Pause briefly after commas, semicolons, colons, and periods. Adjust your pitch to indicate a question, and emphasize lines that end in an exclamation mark.

5. As you read the chunk, visualize how this scene would look onstage. When, where, and how would the actors use movement and gestures to communicate meaning to the audience? Add annotations to the text to indicate appropriate **visual delivery** for each character.

6. Form groups of six to read the following section of Scene 1 at least twice as you paraphrase and annotate the text for vocal and visual delivery. Assign the roles of Samson, Gregory, Abraham, Benvolio, Tybalt, and Balthasar (who has no lines but should still have gestures and movement).

ACADEMIC VOCABULARY
Vocal delivery refers to the way a performer on stage expresses the meaning of a text through volume, pitch, rate or speed of speech, pauses, pronunciation, and articulation.
Visual delivery refers to the way a performer on stage interprets plot, character, and conflict through movement, gestures, and facial expressions.

Conflict Up Close

My Notes

_____
_____
_____
_____
_____
_____
_____

KEY IDEAS AND DETAILS
What physical gesture sets off the conflict in this scene? How will your visual delivery emphasize the importance of this gesture?

KEY IDEAS AND DETAILS
How and why does Benvolio's attitude shift at the end of this scene?

_____
_____
_____
_____
_____
_____
_____
_____
_____
_____
_____
_____
_____

from **Act 1, Scene1**

SAMPSON: My naked weapon is out: quarrel, I will back thee.

GREGORY: How! turn thy back and run?

SAMPSON: Fear me not.

GREGORY: No, marry; I fear thee!

SAMPSON: Let us take the law of our sides; let them begin.

GREGORY: I will frown as I pass by, and let them take it as they list.

SAMPSON: Nay, as they dare. I will bite my thumb at them, which is a disgrace to
    them, if they bear it.
             Enter ABRAHAM and BALTHASAR

ABRAHAM: Do you bite your thumb at us, sir?

SAMPSON: I do bite my thumb, sir.

ABRAHAM: Do you bite your thumb at us, sir?

SAMPSON: [*Aside to GREGORY*] Is the law of our side, if I say ay?

GREGORY: No.

SAMPSON: No, sir, I do not bite my thumb at you, sir, but I bite my thumb, sir.

GREGORY: Do you quarrel, sir?

ABRAHAM: Quarrel sir! No, sir.

SAMPSON: If you do, sir, I am for you: I serve as good a man as you.

ABRAHAM: No better.

SAMPSON: Well, sir.

GREGORY: Say 'better:' here comes one of my master's kinsmen.

SAMPSON: Yes, better, sir.

ABRAHAM: You lie.

SAMPSON: Draw, if you be men. Gregory, remember thy swashing blow.
    They fight. Enter BENVOLIO

BENVOLIO: Part, fools!

Put up your swords; you know not what you do. [*Beats down their swords.*]
    Enter TYBALT

TYBALT: What, art thou drawn among these heartless hinds?

Turn thee, Benvolio, look upon thy death.

BENVOLIO: I do but keep the peace: put up thy sword,

Or manage it to part these men with me.

TYBALT: What, drawn, and talk of peace! I hate the word,

As I hate hell, all Montagues, and thee:

Have at thee, coward!
    They fight.

After Reading

7. Work with your group to rehearse a performance in which you use vocal and visual delivery to communicate meaning. Present to another group.

8. **Reflect:** Rate your comfort level with reading and performing Shakespeare on a scale of 1 (lowest) to 10 (highest). Explain your rating. What are your strengths and challenges?

   Reading Shakespeare: _____ Performing Shakespeare: _____

9. Continue reading Act 1 in a small group as follows:
   * Chunk the text into manageable sections and assign roles.
   * Preview your lines before reading each chunk, using sticky notes to paraphrase and annotate for vocal delivery.
   * After each chunk, discuss and rehearse visual delivery.

My Notes

Talking by Myself

LEARNING STRATEGIES:
Skimming/Scanning, SIFT, Graphic Organizer, Drafting, Discussion Groups

My Notes

Learning Targets
- Make inferences about characters from textual evidence.
- Explore symbols, imagery, and figurative language.
- Cite textual evidence to support a theme.

Before Reading

1. **Discuss:** In real life, can you think of times when people give long, rambling speeches without interruption? What are the circumstances?

2. Review the literary term *monologue*. Then, skim and scan Act 1 of *Romeo and Juliet* looking for examples of monologues.

3. Choose one of the monologues and describe a modern-day situation in which someone might give a similarly long speech.

During Reading

4. In Act 1, Scene 3, Lady Capulet has a monologue in which she uses figurative language to describe Paris in a way that she thinks will appeal to Juliet. Reread the monologue and make inferences about why Lady Capulet favors the match.

Textual Evidence	Inferences

5. **Reflect:** If you were planning a performance of Lady Capulet's monologue, how would you use vocal and visual delivery to express her character?

6. Choose another monologue from Act 1. Work in small groups to define each element of the SIFT strategy (using your glossary if needed) and complete the graphic organizer by citing textual evidence and making inferences.

Literary Element	Textual Evidence	Inference
Symbol:		
Imagery:		
Figurative Language:		
Tone and Theme:		

After Reading

7. Rehearse and present your interpretation of a monologue from Act 1 to students in another group, each of whom has analyzed a different monologue from Act 1.

Writing Prompt: Explain how you would use visual and vocal delivery in your monologue to communicate character, tone, and/or theme to the audience. Be sure to:

- Use a topic sentence that adresses the prompt.
- Provide a brief summary of the monologue.
- Cite textual evidence with commentary to support your analysis.

Party Blocking

LEARNING STRATEGIES:
Graphic Organizer, Note-taking,
Group Discussion, Sketching

My Notes

Learning Targets

- Compare and contrast two interpretations of a scene.
- Visualize a stage performance of a text and make a plan for blocking a scene.

Comparing Film and Theater

1. How is a live performance different from a film? Thinking like an actor, use the graphic organizer below to compare/contrast and explore the benefits and challenges of each medium.

Film   **Live Performance**

2. **Discuss:** For the play to work, the audience has to believe in Romeo and Juliet's love. What are some of the challenges an actor or director faces in convincing the audience that the love between Romeo and Juliet is real? How could actors and directors overcome these challenges?

3. As you view the same scene from different film versions of *Romeo and Juliet*, take notes in the graphic organizer below to explore how the directors use **theatrical elements** to interpret the scene. These elements include costumes, makeup, props, set (the place where the action takes place, as suggested by objects, such as furniture, placed on a stage), and acting choices (gestures, movements, staging, and actors' vocal techniques to convey their characters and tell a story).

<table>
<tr><td colspan="2">**Literary Terms**</td></tr>
</table>

Literary Terms
Theatrical elements are elements used by dramatists and directors to tell a story and create an interpretation on stage (or in a filmed version of a staged play).

Act I, Scene 5: The Capulet Party—first meeting between Romeo and Juliet

Director	Actors' Appearance: Costumes & Makeup	Actors' Choices: Vocal & Visual Delivery	Objects: Set Design & Props
Zeffirelli 1968	Lady Capulet has a large ornamental headpiece. Tybalt is wearing a turban. Lord Capulet has a fur collar. Most of the partygoers have formal, ornate dress. Romeo wears a silver mask with a cat-like design. Juliet has on a red dress with a gold headband and a simple braid with a ribbon.	Lord Capulet is loud and cheery, possibly drunk. Tybalt sounds morose and angry and keeps looking at Romeo. Romeo whispers and sighs when he first notices Juliet, then hides behind his mask when Tybalt notices him. Juliet acts dizzy from dancing just before meeting Romeo.	Columns and curtains are used to hide behind. Chandelier torches and candles light the scene. Lady Capulet and others use bells as part of a dance. The other actors stand in a circle around a singer while Romeo and Juliet seek each other.

Party Blocking

My Notes

4. Choose three different theatrical elements observed in the film clips, and explain why you think the director chose each one. What effect was the director trying to convey?

Director	Theatrical Element	Intended Effect

Check Your Understanding

Which version is more successful in capturing the essence of Romeo and Juliet's first meeting and convincing the audience that their love is real? Use textual evidence of specific theatrical elements and their effect to support your opinion.

Literary Terms
Blocking is the way actors position themselves on stage in relation to one another, the audience, and the objects on the stage.

5. Because there are no cameras for close-ups, one of the challenges faced in a live performance is **blocking** the scene so that the audience will focus on the speakers even when there are a number of people onstage (as in a party scene.)

On a separate page, work with a partner to make a "playbook" sketch showing an aerial view of how you would block the Capulets' party on stage. Use an X for Juliet, an O for Romeo, and initials for the other key characters in the scene (Lord Capulet, Tybalt, the Nurse). Leave a one-inch margin at the bottom of the page and write the word "audience" inside the margin to remind you where the actors should be facing.

Acting Companies

Learning Targets
- Discuss and evaluate possible scenes for performance.
- Preview the requirements for the Staging Notebooks.

Choosing a Scene to Perform

1. With your acting company, preview and discuss the scenes in the chart that follows, and put an asterisk next to scenes that you agree to consider for your interpretation. **Note:** Some scenes have characters with very small roles; these can be assigned to a group member who wants to work primarily as the Director or Dramaturge, combined with another role, or cut from the scene. Other scenes have long monologues that can be shortened with your teacher's direction and approval.

Performance Scenes

Act and Scene	Description	Characters	Research Suggestions
Act I, Scene 1, lines 153–232: **80 lines** From "Good morrow, cousin" to "die in debt."	Benvolio tries to cheer up Romeo, who pines for Rosaline.	Benvolio Romeo	Family relationships, courtship, convents
Act I, Scene 2, entire scene: **103 lines**	Paris asks Lord Capulet for Juliet's hand in marriage. Benvolio and Romeo find out about the Capulets' party from Peter, a servant.	Lord Capulet Paris Peter Benvolio Romeo	Servants, marriage customs, patriarchy
Act I, Scene 3, entire scene: **107 lines**	Lady Capulet and the Nurse are discussing Paris with Juliet before the party.	Juliet Lady Capulet Nurse Peter	Marriage customs, nobility, nursemaids
Act I, Scene 4, lines 1–116: **116 lines** From "What, shall this speech" to "Strike, drum."	Romeo is worried about going to the party because he had a bad dream and Mercutio is teasing him.	Romeo Mercutio Benvolio	Superstitions, festivities
Act I, Scene 5, lines 41–141: **101 lines** From "Oh, she doth teach" to "all are gone."	Romeo and Juliet meet and fall in love; meanwhile Tybalt complains to Lord Capulet about Romeo crashing the party.	Romeo Juliet Tybalt Capulet Nurse	Festivities, courtship, dancing
Act II, Scene 2, lines 33–137: **105 lines**	Romeo visits Juliet after the party and overhears her declaring her love on the balcony.	Romeo Juliet	Courtship, architecture

Acting Companies

Act and Scene	Description	Characters	Research Suggestions
Act II, Scene 3, entire scene: **94 lines**	Romeo visits the Friar to tell him about his love for Juliet and ask him to perform the wedding.	Romeo Friar Lawrence	Friars, herbal medicine
Act II, Scene 4, lines 1–85: **85 lines**	Mercutio and Benvolio discuss Tybalt's challenge and give Romeo a hard time.	Mercutio Benvolio Romeo	Dueling
Act II, Scene 5, entire scene: **77 lines**	Juliet is trying to get the Nurse to tell her Romeo's message about their wedding plans.	Juliet Nurse	Nursemaids, marriage customs
Act III, Scene 1, lines 34–132: **99 lines** From "Follow me close" to "I am fortune's fool!"	Mercutio, Tybalt, and Romeo engage in a street fight that has tragic consequences.	Mercutio Tybalt Romeo Benvolio	Fencing, banishment laws
Act III, Scene 2, lines 37–143: **107 lines** From "Ay me" to "last farewell."	The Nurse delivers news of Romeo's banishment to Juliet.	Nurse Juliet	Nursemaids, banishment laws
Act III, Scene 3, lines 1–108: **108 lines** From "Romeo, come," to "desperate hand."	Romeo receives word of his banishment, and the Friar is trying to calm him when the Nurse arrives.	Romeo Friar Nurse	Friars, banishment laws
Act III, Scene 5, lines 112–205: **94 lines** From "Marry, my child" to "how shall this be prevented?"	Juliet, her parents, and the Nurse argue about her proposed marriage to Paris.	Lady Capulet Juliet Capulet Nurse	Courtship customs, female rights
Act IV, Scene 1, lines 1–122: **122 lines** From "On Thursday, sir?" to "tell me not of fear!"	Juliet meets Paris on the way to church. The Friar gives her a potion to fake her death and avoid marriage.	Paris Friar Lawrence Juliet	Burial vaults, herbal potions

Act and Scene	Description	Characters	Research Suggestions
Act IV, Scene 5, lines 1–95: **95 lines** From "Mistress" to "crossing their high will."	The Nurse thinks Juliet is dead, and she informs the household.	Nurse Capulet Lady Capulet Friar Paris	Funeral customs, astrology
Act V, Scene 1, entire scene: **88 lines**	Balthasar tells Romeo of Juliet's "death." Romeo buys poison to kill himself.	Romeo Balthasar Apothecary	Apothecary, poisons
Act V, Scene 3, lines 84–170: **87 lines** From "For here lies Juliet" to "let me die."	Romeo and Juliet commit suicide. Note: The exchange between Friar Lawrence and Balthasar may be deleted from this scene.	Romeo Juliet Friar Lawrence Balthasar	Burial customs

2. After you have selected your scene, brainstorm possible interpretations. Film adaptations of *Romeo and Juliet* have explored a variety of interpretations by casting rival gangs in *West Side Story*, garden gnomes in *Gnomeo and Juliet*, and kung fu cops and mobsters in *Romeo Must Die*. Consider the time, place, and characters that would enhance your scene.

3. In Shakespeare's day, acting companies named themselves just as bands do today. Shakespeare belonged first to the Lord Chamberlain's Men and later to the King's Men. Your acting company should think of a name that reflects the characteristics of your group.

Create a contract like the one below, and sketch a rough draft of a poster design advertising your performance. Include a performance date, cast (character and student name), director, and dramaturge, as well as words and images that reflect your interpretation.

We, the _____ (name of acting company), pledge to plan, rehearse, and perform _____ (act and scene) from William Shakespeare's *The Tragedy of Romeo and Juliet*.

My Notes

_____
_____
_____
_____
_____
_____
_____
_____
_____
_____
_____
_____
_____
_____
_____
_____
_____
_____
_____

Acting Companies

My Notes

4. Every member of the Acting Company will complete a Staging Notebook to prepare for the performance. Based on your primary role in the performance, prepare an Actor's Notebook, Director's Notebook, or a Dramaturge Notebook. Read the description of your notebook, highlighting key elements. Create a "To Do" list that you can refer to as you work with your acting company.

Director's Notebook:

Interpretation: Write a paragraph describing the interpretation you have chosen for your scene. Provide textual evidence to explain the reasoning and plan for the theatrical elements that will create your interpretation.

Visuals: Decide whether you will use visuals for your scene (posters, large photographs, etc.), and create them.

Text: Print a copy of your scene and annotate it with suggestions for your actors' vocal and visual delivery. Be sure to describe interactions and reactions. (See Activity 5.9)

Set Diagram: Sketch the scene from the audience's perspective as well as an aerial view. Use the "playbook" approach to block your scene for character placement and movement. (See Activity 5.6)

Lighting, Sound, and Props: Create a plan for lighting and sound (effects or music) that will enhance your acting company's performance. Include an explanation of your intended effect. Make a list of the props for your scene and where you will get them.

Introduction: Write an introduction that provides context (what happened prior to your scene) and previews the content of your scene. Memorize and present the introduction before your performance. Like the Prologue, it could be in sonnet form. (See Activity 5.3)

Meeting Log: After every meeting, you will be responsible for writing a dated log that records how the meeting went. Some questions you might answer in your log include the following:

- What did the group accomplish?
- What obstacles were identified?
- Which problems have been resolved? How?
- What needs to be done before and at the next meeting?

Director's "To Do" List: This will be the first entry in your Director's Staging Notebook.

Actor's Notebook:

Interpretation: Write a paragraph describing the interpretation you have chosen for your character. Provide textual evidence to explain the reasoning and plan for the theatrical elements that will create your interpretation.

Text: Print out or make a copy of your scene and highlight your lines. Paraphrase each of your lines and annotate them with your plan for vocal and visual delivery. Annotate the other characters' lines with notes on your nonverbal reactions.

Costume: Decide on an appropriate costume for your character. Sketch, photograph, cut out of a magazine, or print out an online image of both your ideal costume and your real costume. (See Activity 5.10)

Character Analysis: Create a visual representation of your character's thoughts, desires, actions, and obstacles. Focus on your scene, but you can include evidence from other parts of the play. (See Activity 5.9)

Actor's "To Do" List: This will be your first entry in your Actor's Staging Notebook.

Dramaturge's Notebook:

Research Questions: Generate research questions related to the scene. In addition to the suggestions in this activity, consider the following:

- The history and context of the play
- Unfamiliar references or vocabulary in your scene
- Theater and performance in Shakespeare's time

Note cards: Conduct research to answer questions and take careful notes.

Annotated Bibliography: Create a bibliography of the works you consulted in your research. Include annotations that summarize what you learned, and provide commentary on how this information enhances your understanding of Shakespeare, *Romeo and Juliet*, and/or your scene.

Suggestions: Based on your research findings, prepare a list of suggestions for the director and the actors. Present them to the group and be prepared to explain your reasons for the suggestions.

Interpretation: Write an explanation of how your research helped the acting company interpret its scene. Cite specific sources and quotes from your research. Memorize this explanation and present it after the performance.

Dramaturge's "To Do" List: This will be the first entry in the Dramaturge's Staging Notebook.

My Notes

Literary Terms
A **dramaturge** is a member of an acting company who helps the director and actors make informed decisions about the performance by researching information relevant to the play and its context.

What's in a Setting?

LEARNING STRATEGIES:
Graphic Organizer, Drafting

Learning Targets

- Analyze set designs, blocking, and other theatrical elements to compare and contrast two interpretations of a scene.
- Evaluate the effectiveness of a director's choices.

Viewing Film Versions

1. The famous balcony scene is where Romeo and Juliet declare their love for one another. How do Romeo and Juliet interact with each other and with the balcony itself in these images? What do you think is the significance of the balcony?

2. As you view the scene from two different film versions of *Romeo and Juliet*, take notes in the chart below to explore how the director uses set design, blocking, and other theatrical elements to convey the emotional impact that Shakespeare intended for this scene.

Act II, Scene 2: The Balcony Scene—Romeo and Juliet declare their love

Director	Set Design: everything you see in the scene including structures, nature, props	Blocking: how the actors move and interact with the set and each other	Other Theatrical Elements: sound effects, lighting, music, costumes
Zeffirelli 1968			

3. Describe one choice that each director made in set design or blocking, and reflect on its effect on you as an audience member. Does the director's choice effectively convey an emotional impact?

Director	Director's Choice	Effective? Why or why not?
Luhrman 1996		
Zeffirelli 1968		

GRAMMAR & USAGE
Transitions

Using effective transitions helps create coherence in writing.

Transitions for Comparison: *also, in the same way, likewise, similarly, in addition, moreover, another*

Transitions for contrast: *but, however, in contrast, instead, yet, although, nevertheless, on the other hand*

Writing Prompt: Write a review stating a preference for one director's interpretation of the balcony scene over another. Compare and contrast how the set design, blocking, and/or other theatrical elements contribute to an emotional impact. Be sure to:

• Clearly state your preference in a topic sentence or thesis.

• Include evidence in the form of details comparing both films.

• Provide commentary on the effectiveness of the directors' choices.

• Include appropriate transition words.

Shakespeare's Influence on Modern Works

One of the best-known modern works that draws on Shakespeare's *Romeo and Juliet* is the musical *West Side Story*. The story of feuding families in *Romeo and Juliet* becomes the story of warring street gangs in 1950s New York City. The Montagues and Capulets of Shakespeare's play become the Jets and Sharks of the West Side neighborhood. The Jets are white teenagers of European descent while the Sharks are teens of Puerto Rican ancestry. Each group is determined to protect its side of the neighborhood.

During Reading

4. As you read the following scene, mark the text to identify similarities to and differences from *Romeo and Juliet*.

My Notes

What's in a Setting?

My Notes

_____
_____
_____
_____
_____
_____

KEY IDEAS AND DETAILS
Which characters from Romeo and Juliet are represented in this scene? What are their names in this story?

_____
_____
_____
_____
_____
_____
_____
_____
_____
_____
_____
_____
_____
_____
_____

ABOUT THE AUTHOR
Arthur Laurents (1918–2011) was considered one of American theater's greatest writers for musical theater. Among the well-known plays he wrote are *West Side Story* (1957), *Gypsy* (1959), *The Way We Were* (1973), and *The Turning Point* (1977). Laurents grew up in Brooklyn, New York, and began his career by writing scripts for radio programs. After a stint in the Army during World War II, where he wrote training films, he began writing musicals for Broadway.

Script

from

SCENE FIVE. *Maria and Tony have just met at a high school dance. They danced and kissed and now Tony is looking for Maria.*

11:00 P.M. A back alley. A suggestion of buildings; a fire escape climbing to the rear window of an unseen flat. As Tony sings, he looks for where Maria lives, wishing for her. And she does appear, at the window above him, which opens onto the fire escape. Music stays beneath most of the scene.

TONY [*sings:*] Maria, Maria . . .

MARIA: Ssh!

TONY: Maria!

MARIA: Quiet!

TONY: Come down.

MARIA: No.

TONY: Maria . . .

MARIA: Please. If Bernardo–

TONY: He's at the dance. Come down.

MARIA: He will soon bring Anita home.

TONY: Just for a minute.

MARIA [*smiles*]: A minute is not enough.

TONY [*smiles*]: For an hour then.

MARIA: I cannot.

TONY: Forever!

MARIA: Ssh!

TONY: Then I'm coming up.

WOMAN'S VOICE [*from the offstage apartment*]: Maria!

MARIA: Momentito, Mama . . .

TONY [*climbing up*]: Maria, Maria–

MARIA: Cállate! [*Reaching her hand out to stop him.*] Ssh!

TONY [*grabbing her hand*]: Ssh!

MARIA: It is dangerous.

TONY: I'm not "one of them."

MARIA: You are; but to me, you are not. Just as I am one of them—[*she gestures toward the apartment.*]

TONY: To me, you are all the—[*She covers his mouth with her hand.*]

MAN'S VOICE [*from the unseen apartment*]: Maruca!

MARIA: Sí, ya vengo, Papa.

TONY: Maruca?

MARIA: His pet name for me.

TONY: I like him. He will like me.

MARIA: No. He is like Bernardo: afraid. [*Suddenly laughing.*] Imagine being afraid of you!

TONY: You see?

MARIA [*touching his face*]: I see you.

TONY: See only me.

MARIA [*sings:*]

Only you, you're the only thing I'll see forever.

In my eyes, in my words and in everything I do,

Nothing else but you

Ever!

TONY

And there's nothing for me but Maria,

Every sight that I see is Maria

MARIA: Tony, Tony . . .

TONY

Always you , every thought I'll ever know,

Everywhere I go, you'll be.

MARIA [*And now the buildings, the world fade away, leaving them suspended in space.*]

All the world is only you and me!

Tonight, tonight,

It all began tonight,

My Notes

KEY IDEAS AND DETAILS
How and why does the script change the setting from the original?

What's in a Setting?

My Notes

I saw you and the world went away.

Tonight, tonight,

There's only you tonight,

What you are, what you do, what you say.

TONY

Today, all day I had the feeling

A miracle would happen—

I know now I was right.

For here you are

And what was just a world is a star

Tonight!

BOTH

Tonight, tonight,

The world is full of light,

With suns and moons all over the place.

Tonight, tonight,

The world is wild and bright,

Going mad, shooting stars into space.

Today the world was just an address,

A place for me to live in,

No better than all right,

But here you are

And what was just a world is a star

Tonight!

MAN'S VOICE [*offstage*]: Maruca!

MARIA: Wait for me! [*She goes inside as the buildings begin to come back into place.*]

TONY [*sings*]

Tonight, tonight,

It all began tonight,

I saw you and the world went away.

MARIA [*returning*]: I cannot stay. Go quickly!

TONY: I'm not afraid.

MARIA: They are strict with me. Please.

TONY [*kissing her*]: Good night.

MARIA: Buenos noches.

TONY: I love you.

KEY IDEAS AND DETAILS
What is the significance of the setting where Tony and Maria agree to meet next? Why do you think the director chose this setting?

MARIA: Yes, yes. Hurry. [*He climbs down.*] Wait! When will I see you? [*He starts back up.*] No!

TONY: Tomorrow.

MARIA: I work at the bridal shop. Come there.

TONY: At sundown.

MARIA: Yes. Good night.

TONY: Good night. [*He starts off.*]

MARIA: Tony!

TONY: Ssh!

MARIA: Come to the back door.

TONY: Si. [*Again he starts out.*]

MARIA: Tony! [*He stops. A pause.*] What does Tony stand for?

TONY: Anton.

MARIA: Te adoro, Anton.

TONY: Te adoro, Maria.

[*Both sing as music starts again:*]

Good night, good night,

Sleep well and when you dream,

Dream of me

Tonight.

[*She goes inside; he ducks out into the shadows just as Bernardo and Anita enter.*]

After Reading

5. Compare this scene with the balcony scene in *Romeo and Juliet*. How do the authors use Shakespeare's play as the inspiration for this scene?

Friends and Foils

My Notes

Learning Targets
- Analyze the relationships between the protagonists and their foils, and emphasize interactions in vocal and visual delivery.
- Create a visual representation of a character's motivation: thoughts, desires, actions, and obstacles.

Before Reading

1. Work with your acting company to take turns role-playing at least two of the following scenarios:

   a. A student shows up in his teacher's room one morning asking for help. He is madly in love and wants to get married in secret. The teacher is doubtful because this same student was in love with a different girl the day before.

   b. Two friends are talking about a third friend who ditched them mysteriously the previous night. The third friend shows up and they start teasing him about what he was doing the night before.

   c. A girl sent her best friend on a mission to find out if the boy she likes will go out with her. The best friend returns but will not answer the girl's questions. Instead, she just wants to talk about herself.

2. **Discuss:** How did you use vocal and visual delivery to express the relationships between the characters?

During Reading

3. Each of the scenarios above describes a situation similar to a scene from Act II in which one of the protagonists interacts with a **foil**. With your Acting Company, choose one of the following scenes:
   (Note: Do not choose the scene that you are performing for Embedded Assessment 1.)

   a. Act II, Scene 3: Romeo and Friar Lawrence

   b. Act II, Scene 4: Mercutio, Benvolio, Romeo (until the Nurse enters)

   c. Act II, Scene 5: Juliet and the Nurse

Work with your group to conduct an oral reading of the scene. Chunk the text into sections by stopping about every 30–50 lines to paraphrase.

4. Use sticky notes to annotate the text for the following:
   - Vocal and visual delivery
   - Physical interactions between the characters (for example, one character shoves another)
   - Facial reactions of one character to the words or action of another character (for example, eye-rolling to express boredom or frustration)

5. Rehearse the scene with an emphasis on the interactions between the protagonist and the **foil** and their reactions to each other. Perform your scene for at least one other group.

Literary Terms
A **foil** is a character whose actions or thoughts are juxtaposed against those of a major character in order to highlight key attributes of the major character.

After Reading

6. Choose one of the characters in your scene. On separate paper, create a visual representation of your character's motivation. See the example below for Tybalt. Sketch an outline and annotate it with your analysis on the corresponding body parts as follows:

- Head: your character's thoughts
- Heart: your character's desires
- Arms: your character's actions
- Legs: your character's obstacles

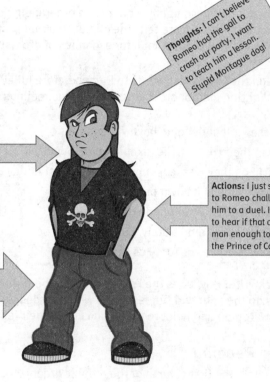

Thoughts: I can't believe Romeo had the gall to crash our party. I want to teach him a lesson. Stupid Montague dog!

Desires: I love my family and I would do anything to protect the Capulet honor. Risk my life? Get in trouble with the law? Bring it on!

Actions: I just sent a letter to Romeo challenging him to a duel. I'm waiting to hear if that coward is man enough to face the Prince of Cats.

Obstacles: My uncle told me to ignore Romeo and leave him alone. Also, the last time I started a fight the Prince threw a bit of a fit . . . something about "on pain of death" and my uncle's life. I wasn't really listening—it was a pretty long speech.

My Notes

A Wedding and a Brawl

LEARNING STRATEGIES:
Oral Reading, Rereading,
Marking the Text, Visualizing,
Sketching, Graphic Organizer,
Chunking the Text

Learning Targets
- Analyze a scene for dramatic irony.
- Compare and contrast the representation of a scene in two different media.
- Analyze characters' interactions and evaluate how their conflicting motives advance the plot.

Identifying Irony

Literary Terms

Dramatic irony is a form of irony in which the reader or audience knows more about the circumstances or future events than the characters within the scene.

1. Act II, Scene 6 ends just as Romeo and Juliet are heading to church to be married. Why do you think Shakespeare has the wedding take place off stage?

2. With your acting company, conduct an oral reading of Act II, Scene 6. Keeping in mind that Shakespeare tells the audience about Romeo's and Juliet's untimely deaths in the Prologue, look for examples of **dramatic irony** in this scene.

3. Reread the Friar's last words to Romeo before Juliet's arrival. Mark the text by highlighting metaphors that reveal his true feelings about the wedding.

My Notes

"These violent delights have violent ends

And in their triumph die, like fire and powder,

Which, as they kiss, consume. The sweetest honey

Is loathsome in its own deliciousness

And in the taste confounds the appetite.

Therefore love moderately. Long love doth so.

Too swift arrives as tardy as too slow."

4. **Quickwrite:** How does the Friar really feel about Romeo and Juliet's wedding? Why do the Friar and Nurse, adults who care deeply about the young lovers, allow Romeo and Juliet to act so quickly on their feelings?

Before Reading

5. Complete the first column of the graphic organizer on the next page in a small group in which each group member takes a different character.

Character: What are the main thoughts, desires, actions, and obstacles motivating him at the end of Act II?	Textual Evidence: What are the lines that reveal his thoughts, desires, actions and obstacles in Act III, Scene 1?	Commentary: What do these lines tell you about conflicts or shifts in the character's motivation?
Romeo:		
Mercutio:		
Tybalt:		
Benvolio:		

During Reading

6. With your group, take the roles of characters and conduct an oral reading of Act III, Scene 1. Chunk the text by stopping after every 30–50 lines to discuss each character's motivation. Work together with your group to add textual evidence and commentary to the graphic organizer.

My Notes

_____

_____

_____

_____

_____

_____

_____

_____

KEY IDEAS AND DETAILS
How does Mercutio continue
the metaphor comparing
Tybalt to a cat?

7. Using the information embedded in the text as the basis for your interpretation, annotate the chunk below for your character's vocal and visual delivery. With "Benvolio" acting as director, rehearse the scene several times.

ROMEO:

I do protest, I never injured thee,
But love thee better than thou canst devise,
Till thou shalt know the reason of my love:
And so, good Capulet,—which name I tender
As dearly as my own,—be satisfied.

MERCUTIO:

O calm, dishonourable, vile submission!
Alla stoccata carries it away   *Draws*
Tybalt, you rat-catcher, will you walk?

TYBALT:

What wouldst thou have with me?

MERCUTIO:

Good king of cats, nothing but one of your nine
lives; that I mean to make bold withal, and as you
shall use me hereafter, drybeat the rest of the
eight. Will you pluck your sword out of his pitcher
by the ears? Make haste, lest mine be about your
ears ere it be out.

TYBALT:

I am for you.   *Drawing*

ROMEO:

Gentle Mercutio, put thy rapier up.

MERCUTIO:

Come, sir, your passado.   *They fight*

ROMEO:

Draw, Benvolio; beat down their weapons.
Gentlemen, for shame, forbear this outrage!
Tybalt, Mercutio, the Prince expressly hath
Forbidden bandying in Verona streets:
Hold, Tybalt! good Mercutio!

TYBALT under ROMEO's arm stabs MERCUTIO, and flies with his followers

MERCUTIO:

I am hurt.
A plague o' both your houses! I am sped.
Is he gone, and hath nothing?

After Reading

8. Revisit the textual evidence column of your graphic organizer, and choose one key line for each character. Copy these lines into the first column of the organizer below. Be sure to choose lines from different chunks of Act III, Scene 1, so that you are not trying to evaluate several lines in quick succession.

9. As you view a film interpretation of Act III, Scene 1, take notes on how the actor's delivery and blocking communicate a character's motivation.

Act III, Scene 1 — Director: _____

Character: Key Line	Vocal Delivery: Describe the tone, volume, pitch, rate, and/or pauses used.	Visual Delivery: Describe the actor's movements, gestures, and facial expressions.	Blocking: How and where is the actor positioned when delivering the line?
Romeo:			
Mercutio:			
Tybalt:			
Benvolio:			

A Wedding and a Brawl

WORD
CONNECTIONS

Roots and Affixes

Motive, motivate, and
motivation all have the Latin
root *mōtīvus,* which means
"serving to move," so "motive"
is literally whatever moves
someone to action.

My Notes

Collaborative Discussion in your Acting Groups

- How do the actors emphasize key lines, and how is their interpretation different from yours?
- How does the director use other theatrical elements, such as set design, sound, music, and lighting, to indicate a shift in the mood of the scene?
- What is added to or absent from the scene in this interpretation?
- How do the conflicting motives of the characters in this scene advance the plot of the drama?

Writing Prompt: How effectively does the film performance convey the character **motivation** of Shakespeare's text through the actors' vocal delivery, visual delivery, and/or blocking? Be sure to:

- State your opinion clearly in a topic sentence or thesis.
- Provide evidence along with your commentary.
- Use appropriate transitions.

Emotional Roller Coaster

Learning Targets

- Analyze the development of a theme over the course of the play through an illustrated timeline.
- Make connections between plot events and their effect on character's emotions.

Before Reading

1. **Quickwrite:** How is *Romeo and Juliet* a coming-of-age drama? What does it have in common with other coming-of-age texts that you have studied this year? Which issues do Romeo and Juliet face that teenagers still deal with today?

2. Coming-of-age stories involve characters who are learning how to deal with the intense emotions of young adulthood. Use the graphics below to brainstorm some of the events that have caused the "ups" and "downs" of Juliet's emotions.

My Notes

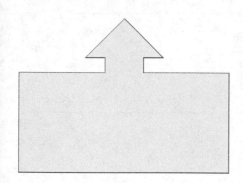
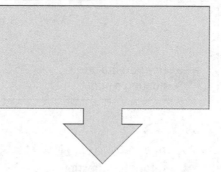

3. Do the same below for events that have had an impact on Romeo's emotions.

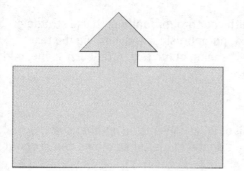
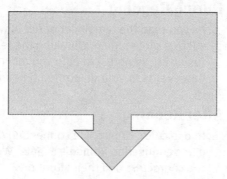

Emotional Roller Coaster

4. Work with a partner or small group to create an illustrated timeline on poster paper that graphs the emotional roller coaster of the protagonists' emotions so far in the play. Follow these guidelines:

- Use two different colors (or symbols) to distinguish Juliet's emotional responses from Romeo's (in the example, a sun is used for Juliet, a moon for Romeo).
- Put positive emotions above the line (the stronger the emotion, the closer to the top of the page).
- Put negative emotions below the line (the stronger the emotion, the closer to the bottom of the page).
- Place events in chronological order (Act I on the far left).
- Add images to illustrate each event (practice by sketching images for the two events in the example).
- Leave room for events in the remainder of the play.

Her parents are hosting a party.

Rosaline does not return his affection.

During Reading

5. As you read the remainder of Act III with your group, continue to use strategies such as oral reading, chunking the text, paraphrasing, and marking the text (using sticky notes) to help you make meaning of the text. After each scene, add new events to your illustrated timeline.

After Reading

6. In one color, draw a line connecting all of Juliet's events. In another color, draw a line connecting Romeo's events. What do the ranges of emotions reveal about the characters and their situations?

Check Your Understanding

Work with your group to construct a thesis statement that answers the following question: What is Shakespeare's theme relating to coming of age in *Romeo and Juliet?*

TWISTing Their Words

Learning Targets
- Analyze soliloquies for performance cues.
- Examine how complex characters develop a theme.

Before Reading

2. Review the literary term *monologue* in your Reader/Writer Notebook or in Activity 5.5. In your own words, explain the difference between a **soliloquy** and a monologue.

2. Work with a small group to skim and scan Acts II and III to find examples of soliloquies and monologues; add them to the graphic organizer below. Identify them by act, scene, speaker, and first line as in the examples. Try to find two more of each.

Monologues in Acts II and III	Soliloquies in Acts II and III
Act III, Scene 2, Juliet: "Shall I speak ill of him that is my husband?"	Act II, Scene 3, Friar Lawrence: "The grey-eyed morn smiles on the frowning night"

3. With your acting company, choose a soliloquy that is not part of the scene you are performing in Embedded Assessment 1.

4. Work together to review and define each element of the TWIST strategy, using your glossary if needed. Note that you already defined some of these terms in Activity 5.5.

LEARNING STRATEGIES:
Skimming/Scanning, Graphic Organizer, Chunking the Text, Rereading, TWIST

Literary Terms
A **soliloquy** is a long speech delivered by an actor alone on the stage, usually representing his or her internal thoughts.

My Notes

TWISTing Their Words

5. Complete the TWIST graphic organizer, citing textual evidence and making inferences about how Shakespeare intended the lines to be performed. Consider vocal and visual delivery.

Literary Element	Textual Evidence	Inferences
Tone:		
Word Choice (Diction):		
Imagery:		
Symbol:		
Theme:		

6. Select a key segment of the soliloquy to deliver from memory. Try some of these strategies to help you memorize lines:

   a. Visualize the lines by creating word pictures in your head in response to the imagery and diction.

   b. Chunk the text into phrases and lines. Learn them one chunk at a time, building on what you have memorized.

   c. Say the lines out loud using the vocal and visual delivery that you would use in performance.

   d. Write down the lines several different times during the process of committing them to memory.

7. After you have rehearsed, perform your lines for your acting company. With your group, develop a rubric for effective performance, including vocal delivery, visual delivery, and other theatrical elements (including blocking). Use this rubric to evaluate your own and your peers' performance rehearsals. Refer to the performance section of the Scoring Guide for Embedded Assessment 1 for ideas.

8. **Quickwrite:** Choose at least one of the following prompts to respond to in writing.

   • What performance clues does Shakespeare provide within the language of his soliloquy?

   • What other purposes does a soliloquy serve? Why does Shakespeare include them?

   • What does the audience learn from watching characters struggle aloud with conflicting motives (thoughts, desires, actions, obstacles)?

9. Work with your class to identify several themes that Shakespeare develops in the soliloquies in Acts II and III.

WORD CONNECTIONS

Roots and Affixes

Soliloquy contains the root -*sol*- from the Latin word *soli*, meaning "one," "alone," or "lonely." This root also appears in *solo*, *solitary*, and *solitude*.

My Notes

A Desperate Plan

Learning Targets

- Analyze the subtext of a passage to determine the true meaning and impact of a character's words.
- Plan, rehearse, and perform exaggerated visual delivery to communicate meaning to an audience.

Before Reading

1. Part of the process of coming of age is learning and accepting that sometimes parents and other trusted adults make mistakes. Complete the graphic organizer below to identify how the adults in Juliet's life are making mistakes that contribute to her frustration by the end of Act III.

Adult Decision or Advice

Juliet's father threatens to disown her if she refuses to marry Paris.

Juliet's mother. . .

The Nurse. . .

Effect on Juliet

She has the impossible choice of breaking her wedding vows or losing her family and starving on the streets.

Literary Terms

Subtext is the underlying or implied meaning in dialogue or the implied relationship between characters in a book, movie, play, or film. The subtext of a work is not explicitly stated.

2. As Juliet becomes more alienated from her family and friends, she relies more frequently on the audience understanding the **subtext**. Revisit the passage in Act III, Scene 5, in which Lady Capulet visits Juliet's bedroom immediately after Romeo has left.

Summarize her statements to her mother about Romeo.

Summarize the subtext of her statements (what she really means).

During Reading

3. At the start of Act IV, Juliet goes to seek advice from Friar Lawrence on how she can avoid marrying Paris. When she arrives at church, Paris is there. Mark the text of the passage by putting Juliet's subtext in parentheses next to each line (Juliet's first line is done for you).

PARIS:

Happily met, my lady and my wife!

JULIET:

That may be, sir, when I may be a wife. *(Which is never, because I'm already married.)*

PARIS:

That may be must be, love, on Thursday next.

JULIET:

What must be shall be.

FRIAR LAWRENCE:

That's a certain text.

PARIS:

Come you to make confession to this father?

JULIET:

To answer that, I should confess to you.

PARIS:

Do not deny to him that you love me.

JULIET:

I will confess to you that I love him.

PARIS:

So will ye, I am sure, that you love me.

JULIET:

If I do so, it will be of more price,

Being spoke behind your back, than to your face.

PARIS:

Poor soul, thy face is much abused with tears.

JULIET:

The tears have got small victory by that;

For it was bad enough before their spite.

PARIS:

Thou wrong'st it, more than tears, with that report.

JULIET:

That is no slander, sir, which is a truth;

And what I spake, I spake it to my face.

PARIS:

Thy face is mine, and thou hast slander'd it.

JULIET:

It may be so, for it is not mine own.

My Notes

KEY IDEAS AND DETAILS
Why does Juliet refuse to give Paris a straight answer to any of his questions?

A Desperate Plan

After Reading

4. In a small group, conduct an oral reading of the passage. In addition to Paris, Juliet, and Friar Lawrence, assign one group member the role of Juliet's subtext. After every time Juliet speaks, that group member will read aloud Juliet's true thoughts.

5. In an actual performance, subtext has to be expressed through visual delivery. Use the graphic organizer below to make a plan for visual delivery as you read the rest of Act IV, Scene 1.

What Juliet Would Rather Do Than Marry Paris: Textual Evidence	Plan for Visual Delivery (movements, expressions, gestures)

The Friar's Plan for Juliet: Textual Evidence	Plan for Visual Delivery (movements, expressions, gestures)

6. Choose a section of lines (either Juliet's or the Friar's) to rehearse and perform with exaggerated visual delivery.

7. As you continue to read Act IV, look for other examples of subtext.

Check Your Understanding

Collaborative Discussion: Discuss your responses to these questions:

- Why is it important to keep the subtext in mind when you are performing a scene?

- Why do stage actors usually use more exaggerated visual delivery than film actors, particularly when performing Shakespeare?

The Fault in Their Stars

Learning Targets
- Plan an interpretation that emphasizes the emotional impact and dramatic irony of Act V.
- Compare my plan to a film director's interpretation and evaluate the effectiveness of each.

LEARNING STRATEGIES:
Skimming/Scanning, Graphic Organizer, Chunking the Text, Rereading

Before Reading

1. In the Prologue to Act I, Shakespeare called Romeo and Juliet "star-crossed lovers." In Act V, when Romeo thinks Juliet is dead, he declares, "Then I defy you stars!" What accidental and unfortunate events in the play support the theme that Romeo and Juliet are the victims of fate, or "the stars"?

My Notes

During Reading

2. As you read Act V, Scenes 1 and 2, gather more evidence that Romeo and Juliet are victims of fate. What key events, without which there could be no tragic ending, happen in these scenes?

3. Before you read Scene 3, review the definition of dramatic irony (introduced in Activity 5.10). What key information does the audience have that Romeo is lacking?

4. As you read Scene 3, think like a director and take notes in the graphic organizer below on how you would use vocal and visual delivery as well as other theatrical elements to intensify the emotional impact and emphasize the dramatic irony.

The Fault in Their Stars

Theatrical Element/ My Choices as Director	How My Choices Would Intensify the Emotional Impact	How My Choices Would Emphasize the Dramatic Irony
Vocal Delivery:		
Visual Delivery:		
Other Theatrical Elements:		

After Reading

5. Work with a partner to visualize the scene. On separate paper, one of you should sketch the scene from the audience's perspective while the other sketches an aerial view. Use the "playbook" approach to block your scene for character placement and movement.

6. Observe how a film director interprets the scene. Take notes on choices the director makes concerning vocal delivery, visual delivery, and other theatrical elements. In the last column, make inferences about the effect you think the director intended to create.

Theatrical Element	Director's Choices	Intended Effect
Vocal Delivery		
Visual Delivery		
Other Theatrical Elements		

Check Your Understanding

Discuss the following with your group:

- How effective are the director's choices in intensifying the emotional impact and emphasizing dramatic irony?
- What other effects do you think the director intended?
- After seeing another interpretation, would you change anything about your performance plan?

Reflect on the Essential Question: How do actors and directors use theatrical elements to create a dramatic interpretation? Go back to Activity 5.1 and consider how your response to this question has grown, changed, or developed through your work in this unit.

My Notes

Presenting a Dramatic Interpretation

Assignment

Your assignment is to work collaboratively with your acting company to interpret, rehearse, and perform a scene from William Shakespeare's *Romeo and Juliet*. In preparation, each member of the acting company will create a staging notebook providing textual evidence and commentary on the planned interpretation. Finally, you will write a reflection evaluating your final performance.

Planning: Take time to make a performance plan.

- How will you prepare a staging notebook that reflects your primary role in the production? (See Activity 5.7 for guidelines.)

- How will your acting company effectively integrate theatrical elements such as vocal and visual delivery, blocking, props, costumes, lighting, music, sound, and set design into your final performance?

- As an actor, how will you learn your lines and prepare vocal and visual delivery?

- As a director, how will you guide the acting company and prepare theatrical elements?

- As a dramaturge, how will you research to provide background information?

Rehearsing: Collaborate with your acting company to polish your performance.

- When and where will you meet to rehearse your scene several times?

- How can the director's feedback and the dramaturge's research enhance the acting company's performance?

- How could you use a video recording of one of your rehearsals to help you improve the quality of the performance?

- How can another acting company help you rehearse by providing feedback on your performance?

Performing: Perform your scene for an audience of your peers.

- How will the director introduce the scene?

- Who will prompt actors who need assistance with their lines?

- After the performance, how will the dramaturge explain how the performance reflects his or her research?

Evaluating: Write an evaluation of your group's final performance.

- What were the strengths of your performance? What challenges did you face?

- How can you use the Scoring Guide to ensure your understanding of the criteria for this piece?

Reflection

After completing this Embedded Assessment, think about how you went about accomplishing this task, and respond to the following:

- How did different acting companies use theatrical elements to enhance their performance in memorable ways?

- How did performing a scene help you understand or appreciate the play?

Technology TIP:

As you collaborate on this project, find ways to create collaborative documents using wikis or Google Docs as a way of creating a rehearsal schedule, establishing a common document format, and sharing performance ideas with other members of your acting company.

SCORING GUIDE

Scoring Criteria	Exemplary	Proficient	Emerging	Incomplete
Ideas	The performance • represents an insightful interpretation of the scene and clearly communicates the intended effect to the audience • includes a reflection that represents the creative thinking of the entire acting company, with insightful commentary on the challenges and the final performance.	The performance • represents a clear interpretation of the scene and communicates it effectively to the audience • includes a reflection on the process of preparing for and performing the scene, including commentary on challenges faced and an evaluation of the final performance.	The performance • shows an attempt to interpret the scene • may not clearly communicate the scene to the audience • includes a reflection that summarizes the process rather than the thinking behind the interpretation and the performance.	The performance • is not coherent and does not clearly communicate the scene to the audience • includes a reflection that is minimal and simply lists the steps in the process; it does not reflect the thinking of the group or the effect of the performance.
Structure	• The staging notebook is detailed and shows evidence of a high degree of collaboration • The interpretive performance shows a high degree of planning for visual and vocal delivery.	• The staging notebook contains all required entries in a clearly organized format • An effective performance communicates planning for visual elements and rehearsal for vocal delivery.	• The staging notebook does not contain all required entries and may be poorly organized • The performance shows some planning for visual elements and rehearsal for vocal delivery.	• The staging notebook contains few if any of the required entries • The performance shows a lack of planning for visual elements and rehearsal for vocal delivery.
Use of Language	The performance • demonstrates a creative use of diction to communicate the scene • includes a thorough script (in staging notebook) with annotations for effective delivery of lines.	The performance • includes appropriate and effective vocal and visual delivery of dialogue • includes a script (in staging notebook) annotated for appropriate delivery of lines.	The performance • attempts the use of appropriate dialogue to communicate the scene • includes some elements of a script (in staging notebook) annotated for delivery of lines.	The performance • includes little evidence of an attempt to craft appropriate dialogue for the scene • may not include a script (in staging notebook) or annotations for delivery of lines.

Previewing Embedded Assessment 2: Is Shakespeare Relevant?

LEARNING STRATEGIES:
Debate, Note-taking, Fishbowl, Graphic Organizer

My Notes

_____

_____

_____

_____

_____

_____

_____

_____

_____

ACADEMIC VOCABULARY

You have encountered the concept of **argument** in previous grades and know that it is a form of writing that presents a particular opinion or idea and supports it with **evidence** (examples, facts, details). Other forms of the word are **argumentative**, which refers to the idea that an argument often addresses a controversial issue, and **argumentation**, which refers to the structure of the writing of an argument.

INDEPENDENT READING LINK

With help from your teacher, librarian, and peers, find another play by William Shakespeare or a novel that was inspired by his work such as *The Wednesday Wars* by Gary Schmidt or *Romeo's Ex: Rosaline's Story* by Lisa Fiedler.

Learning Targets

- Analyze the skills and knowledge needed to complete Embedded Assessment 2 successfully.
- Analyze and evaluate reasons and evidence in an online debate.
- Identify and apply rhetorical appeals in a debate.

Making Connections

Describe one of the activities in the first half of the unit that helped prepare you to do well on Embedded Assessment 1. What did you do and learn in the activity, and how did it prepare you for success?

Essential Questions

How would you answer the questions now?

1. How do actors and directors use theatrical elements to create a dramatic interpretation?

2. Why do we study Shakespeare?

Developing Vocabulary

Return to the Table of Contents and note the Academic Vocabulary and Literary Terms you have studied so far in this unit. Which words/terms can you now move to a new category on a QHT chart? Which could you now teach to others that you were unfamiliar with at the beginning of the unit?

Unpacking Embedded Assessment 2

Read the assignment for Embedded Assessment 2: Writing a Synthesis Argument.

> Your assignment is to compose an argument for or against the inclusion of William Shakespeare's *Romeo and Juliet* in the ninth-grade curriculum. You will evaluate research and gather evidence from a variety of sources about Shakespeare's relevance and influence in today's world. Finally, you will synthesize and cite your evidence in an argumentative essay that maintains a formal style and tone appropriate to your audience and purpose, uses rhetorical appeals including logical reasoning, and includes all the organizational elements of an argumentative essay.

In your own words, summarize what you will need to know to complete this assessment successfully. With your class, create a graphic organizer to represent the skills and knowledge you will need to complete the tasks identified in Embedded Assessment 2.

Choosing Sides

3. For each sentence below, circle your response, from 1 (Strongly Agree) to 5 (Strongly Disagree). If you are neutral or have no opinion, circle 3.

1 2 3 4 5: I believe in love at first sight.

1 2 3 4 5: Reading classical literature is important.

1 2 3 4 5: I like to perform onstage.

1 2 3 4 5: Teenagers often lie to their parents.

1 2 3 4 5: Friends are more important than boyfriends and girlfriends.

1 2 3 4 5: My parents know what's best for me.

1 2 3 4 5: The government should support theater and the arts.

1 2 3 4 5: Teenagers can experience true love.

1 2 3 4 5: *Romeo and Juliet* is too violent.

1 2 3 4 5: You should forgive your enemies.

1 2 3 4 5: Murderers do not deserve to be citizens of society.

1 2 3 4 5: I would risk my life for someone I loved.

1 2 3 4 5: I doubt that Shakespeare wrote all his plays himself.

1 2 3 4 5: I would try to get revenge if someone killed my friend.

1 2 3 4 5: Music is important to me.

1 2 3 4 5: Getting married very young is a mistake.

1 2 3 4 5: I believe in fate.

1 2 3 4 5: I like to argue.

4. Choose one of the statements that you strongly agree or disagree with. List three reasons to support your opinion.

5. Review the definitions of the rhetorical appeals that you studied previously in Unit 1. Consider the reasons you listed to support your opinion; label each with the type of rhetorical appeal your reason emphasized: pathos, logos, or ethos. Revise your support to include only valid or logical reasons.

My Notes

Previewing Embedded Assessment 2: Is Shakespeare Relevant?

My Notes

6. Together with a group of your peers, you will explore an online debate website to gather reasons and evidence for one side of an issue related to Shakespeare and/or *Romeo and Juliet*. Write down your issue and the website address and take notes in the column for either PRO (in favor of) or CON (against) in the following graphic organizer.

Evaluate the validity of the arguments in the debate with the following questions:

- Is the reasoning valid? That is, is the reasoning sound and supported by evidence?
- Is the evidence relevant and sufficient?
- Are any of the statements false or illogical?

Choose the reasons that best support your assigned side. Try to emphasize reasons that are logical first, then reasons that appeal to ethos. Avoid support that depends on pathos.

Issue:_____

Website:_____

PRO	CON

7. Use your notes to stage an informal debate with the group that researched the opposing viewpoint. While you are listening to their side, take notes in the appropriate column so that you can respond to their points during rebuttal.

8. As you listen to your classmates debate another issue related to Shakespeare, take notes in the graphic organizer below to record the different rhetorical appeals used in the debate.

Issue:_____

Rhetorical Appeals	PRO	CON
Logos		
Ethos		
Pathos		

Check Your Understanding

What was the most convincing evidence that you heard or used today? What kind of appeals were used?

Argumentative Writing Prompt: Take a position on the topic for Embedded Assessment 2: Should all ninth graders study William Shakespeare's *Romeo and Juliet*? (You can change your mind later if you choose.) Be sure to:

• List several valid reasons to support your position.

• Emphasize logos and ethos. Avoid support that involves pathos.

• Carefully avoid illogical or false reasoning.

My Notes

Shakespeare in the Modern Age

Learning Targets

- Analyze two texts to evaluate whether the author's tone is appropriate to the audience and purpose.
- Identify reasons and gather evidence to support a claim.
- Write and revise a support paragraph for an argument.

Before Reading

1. **Quickwrite:** Helen Mirren is an English actor who has worked with the Royal Shakespeare Company and won an Academy Award for Best Actress for her role in *The Queen*. Speaking out against compulsory (required) Shakespeare study in the United Kingdom, she said the following:

   "I think children's very first experience of Shakespeare should always be in performance, in the theatre, or on film—mostly in theatre, but it should be a performance because that makes it alive and real."

   Do you agree with her statement? Why or why not?

2. Work with your class to complete the first column of the graphic organizer on the next page by defining each of the terms.

During Reading

3. As you read the article "On the Bard's birthday, is Shakespeare still relevant?" with your class, underline words or phrases that will help you complete the SOAPSTone analysis.

4. After you have completed the SOAPSTone analysis, go back with two different colored highlighters and mark the text for evidence that could help you support or challenge the inclusion of *Romeo and Juliet* in the ninth-grade curriculum.

   Note: As you examine the different texts in this unit, continue to use the same color coding (for example, yellow for PRO, pink for CON) so that you will be able to identify your evidence easily when you start writing your **synthesis** argument.

5. With a partner or small group, complete a SOAPSTone analysis of an additional print or non-print text about Shakespeare's relevance to today's society.

My Notes

Define each term before reading the article:	"On the Bard's birthday, is Shakespeare still relevant?"	Title:_____
Speaker:		
Occasion:		
Audience:		
Purpose:		
Subject:		
Tone:		

On the **Bard's birthday,** is Shakespeare still relevant?

by Alexandra Petri

Whenever I want to depress myself, I make a list of Shakespeare plays and cross out all the ones whose plots would be ruined if any of the characters had a smartphone. It's a depressingly short list.

Soon, if we want to do a modern staging of his work, we'll have to stipulate that "In fair Verona, where we lay our scene/The cell reception was spotty/From ancient grudge that brake the AT&T." Well, not that. Something better.

"Romeo and Juliet would obviously text each other about the poison," audiences would point out. "Why doesn't Hermia use her GPS?" "If he was so worried about the Ides, Caesar should have just telecommuted."

My Notes

_____
_____
_____
_____
_____

KEY IDEAS AND DETAILS
Can you think of other ways that modern technology would interfere with the plot of *Romeo and Juliet*?

_____
_____
_____

Shakespeare in the Modern Age

My Notes

_____

_____

_____

_____

_____

_____

_____

_____

Misunderstandings and missed communications now come in entirely different flavors. We are all in touch all the time, and the confusions that blossom from that are not quite the ones the Bard guessed at. Autocorrect replaces malapropism. You don't leave your fiancée asleep in the woods unless you want to wind up on a "Dateline" special. When your coworker implies that Desdemona is cheating on you with Cassio, you don't go ballistic demanding handkerchiefs. You just log her keystrokes.

And the words. ("Words! Words! Words!" as Hamlet says.) What are we supposed to do with them?

To make it through his works, high school students are forced to consult books like "No Fear Shakespeare," which drains all the poetry out in the hopes of making him moderately comprehensible.

Insert Hamlet's most famous soliloquy into the grinder of that book:

KEY IDEAS AND DETAILS
What is lost in translation between the original Shakespeare text and the "No Fear" version?

> "To be, or not to be? That is the question—
>
> Whether 'tis nobler in the mind to suffer
>
> The slings and arrows of outrageous fortune,
>
> Or to take arms against a sea of troubles,
>
> And, by opposing, end them? To die, to sleep—
>
> No more—and by a sleep to say we end
>
> The heartache and the thousand natural shocks
>
> That flesh is heir to—'tis a consummation
>
> Devoutly to be wished! To die, to sleep.
>
> To sleep, perchance to dream—ay, there's the rub"

and you get: "The question is: is it better to be alive or dead? Is it nobler to put up with all the nasty things that luck throws your way, or to fight against all those troubles by simply putting an end to them once and for all? Dying, sleeping—that's all dying is—a sleep that ends all the heartache and shocks that life on earth gives us—that's an achievement to wish for. To die, to sleep—to sleep, maybe to dream. Ah, but there's the catch!"

"But Shakespeare is beautiful! Shakespeare is life glimpsed through the cut glass of poetry!"

Ah, but there's the catch! What's the point, if the language is so far away that we have to do that to it?

Maybe Shakespeare has nothing to say to us. Nobody else from the early 1600s still sees himself so regularly adapted. When was the last time you watched a BBC version of Marlowe's "Tamburlaine"?

Bardolatry[1] seems infinitely old, but it is of comparatively recent vintage. First, Bowdler had his way with the works, removing all the naughty bits and notably tacking on a happy ending to "King Lear." The apotheosis[2] was not instant. The sonnets weren't in vogue for years. Shakespeare has only gradually clawed his way up to the pinnacle of English letters, shoving Chaucer and Tennyson and Melville and Dickens down whenever they got grabby and even elbowing Jane Austen from time to time.

---

[1] **Bardolatry:** unquestioning admiration for Shakespeare (the Bard)
[2] **apotheosis:** the elevation of someone to the highest status

There's a certain level of celebrity occupied by people who are famous primarily because they are famous.

Is Shakespeare one of them? Do we only read him because we've seemingly always read him?

Why do we keep dragging class after class, kicking and screaming, through the wilds of "Romeo and Juliet"?

We don't even know who the guy was.

Perhaps Shakespeare was born today.

Possibly he died today.

He's an awfully hard man to nail down. As a historical figure, he is proverbially skittish. He might have been Francis Bacon, for Pete's sake. You wouldn't get in the car of a man who said he might be Francis Bacon but was not sure. Why read one?

Besides, the man was obviously a hack. Jonathan Franzen clearly takes his craft more seriously. Nobody is as prolific as Shakespeare who thinks he's producing Great Lasting Works Of Genius. He's more a P. G. Wodehouse or an Agatha Christie. Stephen King could learn a thing or two from Shakespeare when it comes to pleasing the groundlings.

Why give him this place of honor?

Look at his most famous play. "Hamlet"? A whiny college student, evidently overeducated and underemployed, comes home for break, sees a ghost and dithers.[3] Eventually some pirates show up, but wouldn't you know, they remain offstage. Shakespeare is one of the few writers in history who, given the option of including pirates in a play, thinks, "Nah, you know what? I'd rather have this dithering hipster talk about mortality some more."

Come to think of it, maybe he's never been more relevant.

People complain about their Millennials moving home. Try having Hamlet in your basement for a semester. "Tis not alone my inky cloak, good mother, nor customary suits of solemn black . . ." That would get old at breakfast, I imagine.

My Notes

_____

_____

_____

_____

_____

_____

_____

_____

KEY IDEAS AND DETAILS
How does Petri use Shakespeare's popularity and productivity to introduce the idea that he should not be taken seriously as a great writer?

KEY IDEAS AND DETAILS
What other basic truths do you think Shakespeare expresses in the play *Romeo and Juliet*?

_____

_____

_____

_____

_____

_____

_____

_____

_____

---

[3] **dithers:** is indecisive

Shakespeare in the Modern Age

My Notes

His plays still tell the truth, boiled down to their essences.

"King Lear": Your kids put you in a home? You should be so lucky!

"Titus Andronicus" (or, Guess Who's Coming As Dinner?): Cannibalism is never the answer.

"Romeo and Juliet": Check your messages before ingesting poison.

"The Tempest": Wizards pretty much get to do whatever they want.

And he's one of the few writers we still have in common. We're dragged through the thorns of his work so that we'll have something to talk about on the other side.

That is a definite part of his charm. He's a common vocabulary, a common set of heroes and villains and everyone in between.

These are not plays we read and see together as a generation or a country. They're works we enjoy as a species. Shakespeare offers a roadmap to the human. And he does it in verse—sometimes tightly knotted little ornate gardens of verse like "Midsummer Night's Dream," other times vast prosy expanses like "Hamlet." Before Sarah Palin was coining new words, the Bard was on it.

In their proper place, the bright lines that have since sunk into cliche⁴ still retain their power to dazzle.

Write what you know? Shakespeare adamantly didn't. But in the process, he wrote what we all know.

And he didn't need a smartphone to do it.

After Reading

6 Consider the tone, purpose, and intended audience of each text.

- Do you think that the writer or speaker uses an appropriate tone for the audience and purpose?
- How might the style change if the author were rewriting it for a different medium (book, newspaper, magazine, speech, email, Twitter post, letter . . .)?
- How might the style change if the author were rewriting it for a different audience (children, teenagers, lawmakers, college professors . . .)?

Language and Writer's Craft: Rhetorical Questions

In an argument, writers use rhetorical questions to appeal to an audience. A rhetorical question is one for which no answer is expected or required. For example, Petri asks the following rhetorical questions:

What's the point, if the language is so far away that we have to do that to it?

When was the last time you watched a BBC version of Marlowe's "Tamburlaine"?

What is the effect of these rhetorical questions on you as a reader?

---

⁴ **cliche:** trite or obvious

Language and Writer's Craft: Using and Citing Sources

When quoting from a source, put quotation marks around the material that you copy verbatim from the text. After the quotation, cite the source by putting the author's name in parentheses unless you incorporate the author's name within your writing (in-text citation). Both of the following are correct methods for citing a quotation from Alexandra Petri's article:

> According to Petri, "We don't even know who the guy was."

> We study Shakespeare even though "We don't even know who the guy was" (Petri).

Practice using two different methods to cite a different quotation from one of the texts in this activity.

Writing Prompt: Write a support paragraph for an argument for or against the inclusion of William Shakespeare's *Romeo and Juliet* in the ninth-grade curriculum. Be sure to:

- Use a topic sentence that states your claim and a reason that supports it.
- Cite evidence from at least one of the texts in this activity.
- Integrate the evidence with commentary that explains how the evidence supports your claim.
- Include a properly cited quotation from at least one of the texts in this activity.

Check Your Understanding

- Read several of your peers' paragraphs. For each one, suggest an additional quotation that the writer could use as evidence.
- Choose one of your peers' suggestions and revise your paragraph to include another properly cited quotation.

My Notes

Shakespeare's Globe

LEARNING STRATEGIES:
Mark the Text, Drafting, Adding,
Graphic Organizer

Learning Targets

- Gather and evaluate evidence from a variety of sources.
- Write a synthesis paragraph.
- Use transition words, phrases, and clauses to make my writing coherent.

Before Reading

1. Before becoming the first black president of South Africa, Nelson Mandela spent 27 years in prison for his struggles against his country's racist policies of apartheid. While in prison, he signed his name next to his favorite quotation from a copy of *The Complete Works of William Shakespeare*:

   "Cowards die many times before their deaths,
   The valiant never taste of death but once." — from *Julius Caesar*

   What does this quote mean to you? What significance might it have had for Nelson Mandela?

2. In the previous activity, you analyzed articles that explored Shakespeare's **modern relevance**. This activity examines his **global influence**. What is the difference between relevance and influence?

During Reading

3. Mark the text of the article "Britain puts on a Shakespeare marathon as world arrives for the Olympic Games" as follows:

   - Underline Shakespeare's name and titles and character names from his work.
   - Circle the words *globe, global, world,* and names of countries.
   - Put a box around paragraphs that emphasize the connection between Shakespeare and the world.

4. **Plan Ahead for Embedded Assessment 2:** As you read the texts in this activity, also look for evidence that relates to your argument for or against inclusion of *Romeo and Juliet* in the ninth-grade curriculum. Highlight evidence for both sides using the same color code you chose in the previous activity.

My Notes

Informational Text

Britain puts on a Shakespeare marathon as world arrives for the Olympic Games

The Washington Post/Associated Press

LONDON — As the world comes to Britain for the Olympics, Britain is celebrating arguably its greatest gift to the world—the plays of William Shakespeare.

Anyone who doubts that accolade for the playwright dead almost 400 years might want to go to the new "Shakespeare: Staging the World" exhibition at the British Museum, and look at the final exhibit, a well-worn, one-volume collection of Shakespeare's plays.

The book is the property of Sonny Venkatrathnam, a former South African anti-apartheid prisoner. He secretly kept it in the notorious Robben Island prison but shared it with other inmates, who underlined and autographed the passages that meant the most to them.

The book lies open at lines from "Julius Caesar"—"Cowards die many times before their deaths/The valiant never taste of death but once"—signed "N. R. D. Mandela."

"In a way, Nelson was the Caesar of the ANC," said Venkatrathnam, who spent several years in the prison with African National Congress leader Mandela in the 1970s. "I think it resonated with his philosophy."

Mandela—now the revered 94-year-old former president of post-apartheid South Africa—is one of more than 30 inmates whom Venkatrathnam asked to sign the volume. It became known as the "Robben Island Bible," because Venkatrathnam told prison warders—who had banned nonreligious books—that it was "the Bible by William Shakespeare." He plastered its cover with cards celebrating the Hindu festival of Diwali in a successful bid to disguise the contents from guards.

"They would come and say, 'What's that?' I'd say 'It's my Bible,'" said Venkatrathnam, a dapper 76-year-old who traveled to London for the opening of the exhibition. "For all the years on the island they wouldn't touch it."

British Museum director Neil MacGregor said the book is "a wonderful symbol of what Shakespeare means to all of us."

The exhibition, which opens Thursday, is part of an outpouring of Shakespearean activity in Britain that includes the opening ceremony of the July 27-Aug. 12 Olympic Games. Director Danny Boyle's ceremony, entitled "Isles of Wonder," is inspired by the strange and enchanted island of "The Tempest."

Other helpings of the Bard include a cycle of history plays, currently being shown on Saturday night prime-time BBC television, and the Royal Shakespeare Company's epic World Shakespeare Festival. Since April, the RSC, based in Shakespeare's home town of Stratford-upon-Avon, has been bringing companies from around the world to stage his plays in Britain.

My Notes

KEY IDEAS AND DETAILS
How did the Robben Island prison inmates get around the banning of nonreligious books?

Shakespeare's Globe

My Notes

KEY IDEAS AND DETAILS
The American director Peter Sellars implies that Shakespeare called his theater "The Globe" for a reason. What do you think that reason was?

The productions, in more than 40 languages, have ranged from an Iraqi "Romeo and Juliet" to a Russian "Midsummer Night's Dream" and a Brazilian circus "Richard III."

American director Peter Sellars, whose contribution to the festival is "Desdemona"—a reimagining of "Othello" by U.S. writer Toni Morrison and Malian singer Rokia Traore—said Shakespeare is truly a writer for the whole world.

"He was a guy who—and not for reasons of branding—called his theater 'The Globe,'" Sellars said.

The British Museum show, which runs through Nov. 25, combines artifacts from Shakespeare's time—including the only surviving manuscript in the playwright's handwriting—with recorded readings by actors to evoke an era that seems both familiar and alien.

In Shakespeare's day, London was just beginning to attract people from around the world, emerging as the center of a nascent empire.

"As the world comes to London in 2012, this Olympic summer, we are going to look at how the world came to London and how London saw the world 400 years ago," said Jonathan Bate, co-curator of the exhibition.

The exhibition roams through Shakespeare's influences, from the rural English landscapes of his youth to the country's dynastic power struggles, the discoveries emerging from the New World, the arrival of visitors from abroad and the creation of Britain as a country with the union of the crowns of England and Scotland under James I.

Some items suggest a cold, violent world a long way from our own. There's King Henry V's jousting helmet, a bear skull excavated from the site of an Elizabethan theater—where bear-baiting went on alongside drama—and an iron "witch's collar" and metal gag used to punish women accused of sorcery.

But the parallels with our own era of migration, globalization and political uncertainty are ever-present.

It is hard to nail down the secret of Shakespeare's genius. It rests on some combination of the exuberance of his language and the resonance of the human predicaments he depicts, from lovers battling family disapproval to kings struggling to live up to the burdens of power.

Shakespeare set plays in Venice and Verona, Denmark and Egypt—places he had read about but never visited. His plays in turn helped create the world view of his audience, and have been influencing audiences around the world ever since.

"He was genuinely a global figure—perhaps the greatest global export this country has ever produced," Bate said.

His ability to speak to audiences around the world is undimmed.

"The great thing about Shakespeare is that he speaks to everyone," Venkatrathnam said. "Regardless of your political or ideological position, you can find something that speaks directly to you. To me, he is the universal philosopher."

Check Your Understanding

Write a draft of a paragraph to support the claim that Shakespeare has a significant global influence. Be sure to:

- Use a topic sentence that states your claim.
- Use parenthetical or in-text citations for at least one quotation of support (Associated Press).
- Integrate the evidence with commentary that explains how the evidence supports your claim.

5. With a partner, read the following article, marking the text for evidence of Shakespeare's global influence. Record your evidence in the graphic organizer following the article.

Informational Text

On **love** and **war,**
Iraq learns from Shakespeare

by Shelina Zahra Janmohamed

Daily Star

As part of the 2012 Summer Olympics hosted in London, the Royal Shakespeare Company challenged theater groups around the world to create contemporary re-imaginings of 16th century playwright William Shakespeare's classics. Of the many unique and creative performances, "Romeo and Juliet in Baghdad," performed by the Iraqi Theatre Company, caught my eye. Could one of Europe's greatest romantic tragedies, written in the 16th century, tell us something about Iraq in the 21st century?

Adapted into colloquial Arabic and performed by an Iraqi cast with English subtitles above the stage, the story, while written in an Iraqi context, is a familiar one. It opens with two brothers, Montague and Capulet, who have feuded for nine years over who will steer their family's pearl-diving ship. This serves as an apropos metaphor for Iraq at the beginning of the war. Romeo and Juliet, who like all the play's characters retain their original Shakespearean names, have already met and fallen in love before the feud. They have been kept apart by the cycle of violence resulting from the feud between their fathers.

My Notes

KEY IDEAS AND DETAILS
Why does *Romeo and Juliet in Baghdad* focus less on the romance and more on war?

Shakespeare's Globe

My Notes

_____
_____
_____
_____
_____
_____
_____

KEY IDEAS AND DETAILS
What are some of the
universal truths and themes
that are emphasized in this
version of the play?

_____
_____
_____
_____
_____
_____
_____
_____
_____
_____
_____
_____
_____
_____
_____
_____
_____
_____
_____
_____
_____

The play focuses less on their romance and more on how families, communities and nations can easily and quickly be torn apart. The story prompts the audience to reflect on how pride, regret, a lack of mutual understanding and interference from the outside are obstacles to resolving conflicts peacefully. Once blood has been spilled, we are never sure if peace can be restored.

The play's director, Monadhil Daood, fled Iraq in his 20s after staging a play under Saddam Hussein about the Iran-Iraq war. In 2008, he founded the Iraqi Theatre Company to "bring a contemporary cultural voice of unity and inclusiveness into the civic discourse in Iraq." Monadhil says that "I think my [play] 'Romeo and Juliet in Baghdad' will be a mirror. The audience will see themselves on the stage."

In the buzzing auditorium, I saw his prediction come true. The emotional effect the play had on its audience was clear. During the performance, many had eyes filled with tears. At joyous moments, audience members tapped along to the wedding songs and laughed at the inclusion of an old Iraqi folk story about a beetle looking for love.

During the most emotional moment of all, I felt almost swept off my chair at the audience's roar of approval as the imposter, who was betrothed to Juliet against her will, and who had stoked the tension between the two families, was cast out by Juliet's father, Capulet. This character, a miserable hard-liner, represents the presence of Al-Qaeda in Iraq. Through Capulet's action, the betrothal is reversed and his presence is no longer accepted.

The real story of "Romeo and Juliet in Baghdad" is of the audience, who see their lives played out before their eyes. The drama was a chance to create enough distance from their own stories so that they could look at the effect of the last nine years on their homeland, with its immense loss, death and suffering. It was an opportunity to move on, make sense, find catharsis and even laugh.

The play at its heart is a universal story of the birth and development of conflict, stoked by fear, misunderstanding and pride. It shows how outside forces can stoke conflict and divide groups of people, and reflects on the need for unity.

In this case, a love story is a portal into a world that audiences might otherwise never be able to begin to understand. By connecting with the story of young lovers—a theme that transcends time and culture—we can learn about the nuances of today's Iraqi society. The play helps viewers understand tight-knit family structures and the once strong historic relationships between Sunni and Shiite Muslims that are now being broken down. In fact, people around the world might find a lot in common with the ordinary folk of Iraq and their aspirations to bring an end to violence and live better lives.

But more importantly, through such plays, we are confronted with universal truths: conflict persists across human societies and it must be addressed before it spirals out of control. But most of all, the aspiration to love and be loved is present in all times and places, whether in Baghdad or Verona, for lovers like Romeo and Juliet, or for brothers like Montague and Capulet.

After Reading

6. Meet with another pair of students. Summarize the key points and share your textual evidence and commentary to complete the graphic organizer.

Article	Textual Evidence of Shakespeare's Influence on the Community	Commentary on his Relevance to the Community
"On Love and War . . ." (Janmohamed) Community: Baghdad, Iraq		

Writing Prompt: To synthesize what you learned, revise the paragraph that you wrote about Shakespeare's global influence to include more support for your claim. Be sure to:

- Include evidence about Shakespeare's relevance to a community outside of London, England.
- Use transitions as you add new ideas and evidence.

Language and Writer's Craft: Transitions

Transitions link ideas, clarify relationships, and create cohesion in your writing. Review the transitions for comparing and contrasting that you used in Activity 5.8. Also consider the following transitions for addition and illustration:

   Addition: *also, another, furthermore, in addition, likewise*

   Illustration: *for example, in this case, for instance, specifically, such as*

Use appropriate transitions as you add new ideas and evidence to your paragraph.

Did Shakespeare Invent Teenagers?

ACADEMIC VOCABULARY
A **counterclaim** is an alternate or opposing claim with **concessions** that the opposing side has valid points and/or **refutations** explaining why the writer's position is more valid.

My Notes

Learning Targets
- Analyze how an author's point of view is developed and supported by evidence.
- Write an argumentative paragraph that distinguishes claims and counterclaims.

Before Reading
1. **Quickwrite:** Compare and contrast the teenagers in *Romeo and Juliet* with teenagers today. What do you and your peers have in common with Romeo, Juliet, Mercutio, Benvolio, and Tybalt? How are you different?

2. In the book excerpt that follows, Stephen Marche argues that Shakespeare practically invented teenagers as we know them today. Consider his claim, and then work with your class to develop a **counterclaim** that states an opposing viewpoint.

During Reading
3. After each chunk of the text, stop and summarize the purpose of the chunk in developing Marche's argument. After taking notes on the reasons and evidence the author provides, generate your own reasons and evidence to support a counterclaim. Use rhetorical appeals emphasizing logos and ethos. Examples:
   - **Logos:** *Most teenagers know more about technology than their parents.*
   - **Ethos:** *My friends and I are more level-headed than Romeo and Juliet.*
   - **Pathos:** *It is unkind and unfair to call teenagers ignorant.*

4. **Plan Ahead for Embedded Assessment 2:** Remember to look for evidence that relates to your argument for or against inclusion of *Romeo and Juliet* in the ninth-grade curriculum. Highlight evidence for both sides using a color code for support of both your claim and counterclaim(s).

ABOUT THE AUTHOR
Stephen Marche is a novelist who writes a monthly column about culture for *Esquire* magazine. Ten years ago he chose Shakespeare as the subject of his Ph.D. dissertation because he believed that Shakespeare would never bore him. He was correct. In the introduction to *How Shakespeare Changed Everything*, he writes: "I learned when I was a professor that teaching Shakespeare to undergraduates is one of the easiest gigs in the history of the world. If you can't make a room full of young people care about Shakespeare, then you probably shouldn't be around young people or Shakespeare."

Nonfiction

from How Shakespeare Changed Everything

by Stephen Marche

Chunk 1

Shakespeare described the terrifying beauty of the adolescent so early in its development, and so definitively and so thoroughly, that it is only a slight exaggeration to say that he invented teenagers as we know them today. *Romeo and Juliet*, his extended study of the humiliations and glories of adolescence, is the biggest hit of all time; everybody knows the story even if they haven't seen the play. Just one year after its first performance in 1596, the Quarto publication proclaimed that "it hath been often (with great applause) plaid publiquely." Unlike most of Shakespeare's plays, it has never slipped out of fashion. *Hamlet*—Shakespeare's other great play about adolescence—is the only piece performed more regularly onstage, and when you consider how often and how successfully *Romeo and Juliet* has been adapted into other media, into operas and ballads and musicals, its popularity is even more staggering. The most popular brand of Cuban cigars? *Romeo y Julietta*. People just love to watch a couple of dumb kids make out and die. And they are awfully young, these dumb Veronese kids who make out for us and then die. Shakespeare doesn't ever tell us Romeo's exact age, but we know about Juliet. In the first act, her nurse discusses her age at length, and it's creepy. In two weeks she will be fourteen.

Chunk 2

Romeo and Juliet has to be fudged. In the eighteenth century, David Garrick understood that his audiences wanted a pure and innocent Romeo and Juliet, and he gave them a sentimentalized version of the play, which was so much to their liking that his version survived intact for over a century. To make the young lovers totally heroic, he had to make them less complicated—the first thing to go was Romeo's love for Rosaline at the beginning of the play. Romeo's mooning over another girl is embarrassing to everybody; he seems unreliable, and it's a bit insulting to Juliet. Garrick's audience wanted Romeo and Juliet to be proper first lovers. He gave the audience what it wanted. He also fiddled with several lines, in order to remove, in his words, "the Jingle and Quibble which were always thought a great objection to performing it." He cut the dirty jokes…. And he also cut down on the rhyming—it made the lovers seem too silly and too unrealistic. The biggest change, however, was the death scene. Garrick let Juliet wake up before Romeo is properly dead—a flamboyant effect that is not in the original.

Garrick created teenagers who were icons of purity in a corrupt adult world. But Shakespeare, unlike Garrick, never spares his adolescents their ridiculousness. The first snatch of dialogue between Romeo and Juliet is beautiful and absurd. Notice that the dialogue follows the rhyme pattern of a Shakespearean sonnet.

Did Shakespeare Invent Teenagers?

ROMEO: If I profane with my unworthiest hand

This holy shrine, the gentle sin is this,

My lips, two blushing pilgrims, ready stand

To smooth that rough touch with a tender kiss.

JULIET: Good pilgrim, you do wrong your hand too much,

Which mannerly devotion shows in this,

For saints have hands that pilgrims' hands do touch,

And palm to palm is holy palmers' kiss.

ROMEO: Have not saints lips, and holy palmers too?

JULIET: Ay, pilgrim, lips that they must use in prayer.

ROMEO: O, then, dear saint, let lips do what hands do;

They pray, grant thou, lest faith turn to despair.

JULIET: Saints do not move, though grant for prayers' sake.

ROMEO: Then move not, while my prayer's effect I take.   *They kiss.*

Thus from my lips, by yours, my sin is purged.

JULIET: Then have my lips the sin that they have took.

ROMEO: Sin from thy lips? O trespass sweetly urged!

Give me my sin again.   *He kisses her.*

JULIET   You kiss by the book.

The vague but palpable effect of this sudden advent of ABAB CDCD EFEF GG rhyme is inexplicable beauty. Only the sharpest members of the audience could conceivably be sharp enough to notice that the lovers have dipped into sonnet form, but Shakespeare leaves us with an inarticulate impression that the young lovers are somehow strange and magical. Garrick took the sonnet out of the scene exactly because it made their love seem too ridiculous and artificial. But Shakespeare wants them ridiculous. That's how kids are. And the last line is perfect: "You kiss by the book." It sounds to me exactly like what a thirteen-year-old girl says after a first kiss, like she's been kissing forever, like she knows all about kissing, like she's read the book.

Chunk 3

Nothing could seem more natural to us than the rebellion of teenagers, which explains why *Romeo and Juliet* has fit easily into twentieth-century pop culture. Irving Berlin referred to the pair in a bunch of different songs, as have Bob Dylan, Bruce Springsteen, Madonna, Tom Waits, Dire Straits, Alanis Morissette, Aerosmith, Elvis Costello, and the Indigo Girls. Lou Reed's "Romeo Had Juliette" is a surprisingly conservative retelling of the story. On the street, the young crack dealers dream of automatic weapons, random murder, and the decline of Western civilization. Inside, Romeo clutches a cross and Juliet. The young in Lou Reed's song are the harbingers of apocalyptic social decay, and their only redemption is the love they preserve against the despair everywhere around them.

In *The Wild One*, a woman at a bar asks Marlon Brando what he's rebelling against. "Whaddaya got?" he slurs back. The teenage rebel cannot say: "I believe that the incidental tax rate is too high for local corporations," or "our agribusiness policies are short-sighted." No. That would not be nearly stupid or grand enough. The most important feature of adolescent rebellion is that it's doomed. It must come to an end. In this, as well, Shakespeare was right at the beginning. He defined what it means to be "star-cross'd." The opposition between the adolescent and the mature orders of the world can have only two possible endings. One is comic: The teenager grows up, develops a sense of humor, gets married, has kids, moves to the suburbs, gets fat, and becomes boring. That's what happens to most Romeos and Juliets. The other is tragic: The teenager blows up in a blaze of glory. We much prefer to live in the comedy. We much prefer to watch the tragedy.

Shakespeare loves his teenagers as he paints them in all their absurdity and nastiness. That basic honesty, neither idealizing nor afraid, has kept Romeo and Juliet fresh. Leonardo DiCaprio and Claire Danes became the dominant young actors of their generation through their performances in Baz Luhrman's *Romeo + Juliet*. Justin Bieber, with his swagger coach and overwhelming fame, comes appropriately from Stratford, the home of North America's biggest Shakespeare festival.

Shakespeare created this category of humanity, which now seems as organic to us as the spring. In place of nostalgia and loathing, Shakespeare would have us look at teenagers in a spirit of wonder, even the spotty ones and the awkward ones and the wild ones. They're us before we fall into categories: not children, not adults, not monsters, not saints. They're beautiful because they do not fit. They're too much themselves and not enough.

My Notes

KEY IDEAS AND DETAILS

What does the author mean when he says that we prefer to live in the comedy and watch the tragedy? Do you agree?

Did Shakespeare Invent Teenagers?

My Notes

_____
_____
_____
_____
_____
_____
_____
_____
_____
_____
_____
_____
_____
_____
_____
_____
_____
_____
_____
_____
_____
_____
_____
_____
_____
_____
_____
_____
_____
_____
_____
_____
_____
_____
_____
_____
_____
_____
_____
_____
_____

Claim: Shakespeare invented teenagers as we know them today.

Counterclaim:
Teenagers today are very different from the characters in Shakespeare's plays.

Objective Summary: Main idea of the text	Claim: Reasons and textual evidence the author uses to support his argument	Concessions and Refutations: Reasons and personal evidence why the argument is valid or not
Chunk 1:		
Chunk 2:		
Chunk 3:		

After Reading

4. Review your graphic organizer with a partner or small group and identify the strongest reasons and evidence in support of both the claim and counterclaim.

5. The paragraph that follows supports Marche's claim by acknowledging and responding to counterclaims. Mark the text as follows:

- Underline sentences or clauses that support Marche's claim.

- Put brackets around sentences or clauses that acknowledge counterclaims.

- Circle transition words that clarify the relationship between claims and counterclaims.

Shakespeare presents teenagers that seem true to life and realistic even though they were portrayed 500 years ago. Even though today's teen is more likely to be carrying an iPhone than a broadsword, they act exactly the same. As Stephen Marche observes, "The opening scene of *Romeo and Juliet* shows young men terrorizing the streets of Verona with instantly recognizable teenage nastiness" (Marche). The modern teenager did not invent the practice of bullying, although that doesn't make it any less of a problem. Teenagers today continue to make rash decisions and struggle with the consequences. They also endure parental meddling that is less than helpful just as in *Romeo and Juliet*. Teenage accessories and fashion may have changed since Shakespeare's day, but adolescence itself is still the same ordeal.

Writing Prompt: Write a paragraph arguing against Stephen Marche by stating your own claim and responding to his ideas with your own reasons and evidence. (The reasons and evidence in the counterclaim column of your graphic organizer will now become the reasons and evidence to support your claim.) Be sure to:

- Include a topic sentence that states your claim.

- Use transitions and properly cited textual evidence to introduce counterclaims.

- Respond to Marche's counterclaims, using transitions and rhetorical appeals of logos and ethos.

Language and Writer's Craft: Transitions

In addition to transition words of contrast to demonstrate differences between ideas or a change in argument direction, use transition words of exception to introduce an opposing idea.

Examples: *however, on the other hand, even though, nevertheless, on the contrary, but one could also say*

Trade papers with one of your peers and mark the text as you did with the sample paragraph above. Mark the rhetorical appeals used with L for logos and E for ethos.

My Notes

Shakespeare Behind Bars

LEARNING STRATEGIES:
Metacognitive Markers, Note-taking, Graphic Organizer, Discussion Groups

Learning Targets

- Evaluate evidence and make inferences.
- Use the elements of an argument in writing.

Before Reading

1. Consider the following quotations about prisons. What does each one mean? To what extent do you agree or disagree?

   "The degree of civilization in a society can be judged by entering its prisons." —Fyodor Dostoyevsky

   "All in all, punishment hardens and renders people more insensible; it concentrates; it increases the feeling of estrangement; it strengthens the power of resistance." —Friedrich Nietzsche

   "One is absolutely sickened, not by the crimes that the wicked have committed, but by the punishments that the good have inflicted; and a community is infinitely more brutalized by the habitual employment of punishment than it is by the occasional occurrence of crime." —Oscar Wilde

   "And where the offence is, let the great axe fall." —William Shakespeare

2. **Discuss:** Two of the primary purposes of our criminal justice system are punishment and rehabilitation. For prisoners, "rehabilitation" means to restore a person to a useful life, often through education. Which one do you think is more important? Why?

During Reading

3. Mark the text of the following news article with metacognitive markers as follows:

   ? = Questions about the text

   ! = Reactions related to the text

   *= Comments about the text

   Underline key ideas and details

   Take notes in the margin on the 5 Ws and an H (who what, when, where, why, and how).

4. **Plan Ahead for Embedded Assessment 2:** Remember to look for evidence that relates to your argument for or against inclusion of *Romeo and Juliet* in the ninth-grade curriculum. Highlight evidence for both sides using a color code for support of both your claim and counterclaim(s).

My Notes

News Article

Kentucky inmates turned actors explore selves through Shakespeare play

by Sean Rose, *Courier Journal*

Gene Vaughn waited nervously behind two swinging doors in the prison chapel of the Luther Luckett Correctional Complex.

On any other day this would be just a chapel and Vaughn would be just one of the 1,072 inmates locked in the medium security Oldham County prison.

But on a recent June night, Vaughn and 23 other inmates became characters in Shakespeare's *Merchant of Venice*, reviewing their lines in the final moments before the curtain drew back on opening night.

For some, the nine months they spent preparing marked their first foray into acting. For others, it was a journey into self-exploration, a chance to review past mistakes and analyze an uncertain future.

"I used to think that acting was acting, that it was something I'd be good at, that all of us convicts would be good at," said cast member Jerry Guenther, who is serving 45 years for murder. "We live a lie. But in here, our acting is not acting: it's telling the truth."

Each year the Shakespeare Behind Bars program at Luther Luckett takes on a new play. Their stage is converted from a chapel within the razor wire-ringed state prison near La Grange.

"Shakespeare understood the human condition like nobody else," said Matt Wallace, now in his third year directing the program of inmate performances. "The themes that are in these plays resonate so deeply in these guys. Through these plays they're digging up some of the most painful and horrific parts of their lives."

Since October, the cast and crew has gathered three times a week to prepare for performances that began June 2 and will wrap up Thursday—eight shows put on to entertain other inmates, the cast members' families and state correction officials.

The actors are a varied group, serving sentences from 4 years to life without parole for a host of crimes, including sex offenses, robbery and murder.

And those backgrounds help them identify with Shakespeare's characters in a way many outside prison walls can't.

At the heart of the play is Shylock, a Jewish money lender played by Vaughn, a convicted murderer serving a 40-year sentence. Ostracized because of his religion, Shylock tries to exact revenge upon a hateful rival who comes to him for a loan, demanding that he wager his life against the loan.

"It deals with race. It deals with discrimination. It deals with gambling, debt, cutting people. It deals with it all," Tim Jett, an inmate serving as assistant director, said in an interview during early rehearsal. "And we were all living that some way, somehow. We were all living it."

KEY IDEAS AND DETAILS
What elements of *The Merchant of Venice* can the inmates relate to?

Shakespeare Behind Bars

Every man must play a part

Putting on a full-length Shakespeare production in a prison setting brings a host of unique challenges.

Rehearsals rarely last more than two hours because of the prison's daily schedule. Some men quit, and others are forced to drop out if they're sent to solitary confinement or shipped to another institution.

Some finish their sentences and are released.

Jett, after five years behind bars for sexual abuse, served out his term in April. To the rest of the crew, he was the luckiest man in Shakespeare Behind Bars.

But Jett thought otherwise, and decided to write a letter asking Secretary of Justice and Public Safety J. Michael Brown to defer his release for 60 days so he could stay until the end of the show. He received no response and was released in March.

Unlike other prison programs, Shakespeare Behind Bars offers no "good time" or credits for early release.

"The only thing they get for being in this is the satisfaction of completing something," said Josh Lewis, a classification and treatment officer who is the program's sponsor.

Do we not bleed?

Early rehearsals were rough. The prison radios drowned out the actors' lines. And the Elizabethan speech taxed some of the play's eight new members.

But the cast and crew eventually formed a bond that turned the gatherings into a mix of theater work and group therapy. Although many of them have trusted few people in their lives, they increasingly confided in each other.

Before opening night, with all on edge, Wallace sought to refocus their attention on what's important. He asked everyone to go around and explain why they joined the program. Up went the hand of Guenther, a 13-year member and one of the elder statesmen of Shakespeare behind Bars.

"This is the safest place in the world," Guenther told the other inmates.

Guenther is one of the more experienced actors in the group, having played Hamlet in a previous performance, but took a minor role this season because of a parole hearing in February. He hoped to be released after 25 years of a 45-year sentence for killing an undercover Shively police officer during a botched drug deal.

Instead the parole board ruled that he wouldn't be eligible for release for another 10 years.

The news hit Guenther and his fellow Shakespeare cast hard.

At 6-feet-5 and 330 pounds, the former star high school offensive lineman brings an enthusiasm to the play that is contagious.

"The thing I always flash back to is how fast a bad decision can lead to complete catastrophe," Guenther told the group. "The only thing I can say is I was a kid and I didn't mean for it to happen. You can't fix what's already broken. And God knows I wish I could."

Vaughn, a close friend of Guenther, spoke up.

"Regardless of what you do, you're always going to be reminded of what you did," he said.

Those in the circle nodded silently in agreement.

Quality of mercy is not strain'd

Within each man's sentence is a separate punishment, one that many of them see as inescapable even after leaving prison. For the rest of their lives they will be convicted felons.

It's a burden they recognize as unavoidable, as much a part of their lives as prison meals and daily dorm counts.

Months into rehearsal, the members are quick to connect with Shylock's status as a second-class citizen amid his Christian neighbors. When Shylock lashes out, a small debate stirs among the men as to whether he is victim or villain.

Judging a character outright is damaging, Wallace said. And the same applies to the Shakespeare Behind Bars members, he said.

"Society has already judged them," Wallace said. "It's going to do no good if I come in here and judge them for what they've done."

Reading over *The Merchant of Venice*, Vaughn said "it just reminds you of yourself, of the things you've done in your life."

As the season progressed, inmates dug deeper into their own lives through their characters, in some instances making peace with a past they'd rather forget.

That was the case for Vaughn, who saw his link to Shylock through abuse.

Vaughn said he was 6 years old when two neighbors sexually abused him. Until last year he never told anyone, though, and the burden of the secret bore on him.

Vaughn doesn't blame his situation in life on that, but he's sure he's acted more recklessly because of it. The recklessness reached critical mass on March 22, 1989, when Vaughn was involved in the death of a Louisville woman he met at a night club. He was sentenced to 40 years.

"I didn't care," Vaughn said of his life then. "I didn't care what people thought about me. I didn't care what happened to me. At that point you feel like nothing is going to change for you anyway. But that's where I was totally wrong."

In prison and through Shakespeare, Vaughn said he has had time to contemplate mercy, and how it offers something to aspire toward.

My Notes

KEY IDEAS AND DETAILS
What connections can you make between Guenther's words and the catastrophes in *Romeo and Juliet*?

KEY IDEAS AND DETAILS
How could a program like Shakespeare Behind Bars benefit not just the inmates but the rest of society as well?

Shakespeare Behind Bars

My Notes

_____
_____
_____
_____
_____
_____
_____
_____
_____
_____
_____
_____
_____
_____
_____

"When you have done something in your life so bad, you try to go about the right way to tell people that you're sorry," he said. "But there's certain people you're not going to be able to say you're sorry to, like my victim, my victim's family. So I can only hope that somewhere in their life they can say I forgive you to a certain extent. To me that's some type of mercy."

Outside to behold

About 50 inmates turned out for opening night, and after the final scene they gave the performance a standing ovation.

"For those two hours, those three hours, you don't even feel like you're in prison," said inmate Kevin Hesson, a new Shakespeare member. "You feel like you're in a theater outside of here. You don't feel the razor wire."

After congratulations, the men hurried to change out of their costumes and get back to their dorms, first spreading their arms and legs at the chapel entrance to be frisked.

There would be more performances, but for now they were back on the prison schedule—and the 9 P.M. head count was just 10 minutes away.

After Reading

4. Prepare to write a letter to a representative from the state or federal government either in support of or against funding for programs like Shakespeare Behind Bars by completing the graphic organizer below.

Hook:

Claim:

Reasons and evidence to support the claim:	Counterclaim:	
	Reasons and evidence to support counterclaim:	**Concessions and refutations:**

Concluding statement/call to action:

Argumentative Writing Prompt: Find a partner or small group that agrees with your claim and work together to write a letter of argument. Be sure to:

- Include an introduction that uses a hook and states your claim.
- Defend your claim and respond to the counterclaims with support that depends primarily on logic and ethos.
- Use transitions and properly cited textual evidence (Rose).

Check Your Understanding

Present your letter to another group. If possible, find a group that disagrees with your claim. As you listen to their letter, add new reasons and evidence to the graphic organizer or write notes in the My Notes space.

ACADEMIC VOCABULARY
In an argument, the **hook** is an opening that grabs the reader's attention and establishes a connection between the reader and the writer.
The **concluding statement** should follow from and support the argument. It may include a **call to action** or plea for the reader to do something about the issue.

My Notes

Arguments for Arts and Literature

LEARNING STRATEGIES:
Marking the Text, SMELL,
Discussion Groups

Learning Targets

- Evaluate the purpose and effectiveness of a spoken and a written argument.
- Analyze how diction and rhetorical appeals strengthen an argument.

Before Reading

My Notes

1. According to legend, sometime during World War II, Britain's finance minister recommended to Winston Churchill that they cut arts funding in order to better support the war effort. Churchill's reply was, "Then what are we fighting for?"

Do you think funding for the arts (theater, music, art, literature) should be a priority for the federal government? Why or why not?

During Reading

2. As you read the abridgment of Kevin Spacey's speech defending arts funding, mark the text as follows:

- Label rhetorical appeals: E for ethos, L for logos.
- Circle at least five words that have strong positive or negative connotations.
- Underline words or phrases that are repeated multiple times.

3. **Plan Ahead for Embedded Assessment 2:** Remember to look for evidence that relates to your argument for or against inclusion of *Romeo and Juliet* in the ninth-grade curriculum. Highlight evidence for both sides using a color code for support of both your claim and counterclaim(s).

ABOUT THE AUTHOR

Kevin Spacey has served as Artistic Director of the Old Vic Theatre Company in London since 2003. Mr. Spacey began his career as a stage actor and in 1991 won the Tony Award for Best Feature Actor in *Lost in Yonkers*. During the 1990s, he garnered critical acclaim for his work in film, culminating in his first Academy Award® for *The Usual Suspects* (Best Supporting Actor), followed by a Best Actor Academy Award® for *American Beauty* (1999).

Speech

Nancy Hanks Lecture on Arts and Public Policy

*Excerpts of the lecture delivered by Mr. Spacey on
April 4th 2011, in Washington, D.C. at the Kennedy Center*

by Kevin Spacey

Art and creativity is one of the most significant ways that humanity uses to fight back against, and to lift itself out of, the muck, and dirt, and the grime, and the horror, and the unfairness of political persecution, racist attacks, hatred, intolerance, and downright cruelty.

I'm going to quote President Kennedy, because we are in his hall, and I want you to listen to the words of this young President on this subject:

"There is a connection, hard to explain logically, but easy to feel, between achievement in public life and progress in the arts. The age of Lorenzo De'Medici was also the age of Leonardo da Vinci. The age of Elizabeth was also the age of Shakespeare. In America, artists quite often contribute not only to the size of our nation but to our spirit, not only to our political beliefs but to our esteem, not only to our self-esteem but to our self-comprehension.

And like the great poet, Robert Frost, who saw poetry as the means of saving power from itself when he said: "When power corrupts, poetry cleanses."

We must never forget: Art is not a form of propaganda; it is a form of truth. For art establishes the basic human truth which must serve as the touchstone of our judgment.

The highest duty of the writer, of the composer, the artist is to remain true to themselves, and let the chips fall where they may, and the nation that disdains the mission of art invites nothing to have to look backward with pride, and nothing to look forward with hope.

I look forward to America which will not be afraid of grace and beauty.

I look forward to America which will steadily raise the standard of artistic accomplishments and large cultural opportunities for all of our citizens.

I look forward to America which commands respect throughout the world, not only for its strength, but for its civilization.

I see little of more importance for this country, for its people, for our future and our civilization than the full recognition of the place of the artist."

And you can find some of those remarkable words of President Kennedy's just outside this building, inscribed on the marble walls on the terrace, just beyond the grand foyer, and the idea for this Cultural Center dates back to 1933 when First Lady Eleanor Roosevelt discussed ideas to create a cultural center, to employ artists who were unemployed during the Great Depression. But we weren't quite ready for it.

> **KEY IDEAS AND DETAILS**
> Was President Kennedy's argument about the value of the arts primarily an appeal to reason or to emotion? Cite evidence to prove your answer.

> **KEY IDEAS AND DETAILS**
> Spacey builds an ethical foundation for his argument with Kennedy's words, but then uses logos to indicate how valuable the arts are to the United States. What does he say?

Arguments for Arts and Literature

My Notes

It took until September 4th 1958, when a bill was finally passed in Congress and President Eisenhower signed into law the National Cultural Act.

It was the first time in United States history that the Federal Government financed a public structure. This structure dedicated to the performing arts. 1958. The year before I was born. And look at where we are now.

The creative industries are perhaps the most important export the United States shares around the world. I genuinely believe the United States's pre-eminence in the arts and its creative industries are one of the nation's most powerful natural resources.

But many arts institutions are suffering already, and the future of arts funding is uncertain to say the least—and whatever cuts are pursued in the government over these next several weeks and months, champions of the arts are having to make a very good case to hang on to what they have—while others are sure to feel the potentially devastating effect, which will make it difficult to operate and to make any real progress. The fact is, with or without any cuts, the effect of the economic downturn will be felt for the years to come.

But if we don't act now—to encourage the members of Congress and the Senate to continue the work of the National Endowment of the Arts, we risk our cultural life to be diminished.

. . . Why do I do this? To repay the debt I owe Jack Lemmon. Jack Lemmon had a phrase that he used all the time that I've now adopted as my own. If you've been successful in your chosen path, then "sending the elevator back down" is your obligation.

. . . Are artistic endeavors luxury items? No, they are a necessity. Culture provides the magic of our experience.

KEY IDEAS AND DETAILS
Can you provide evidence to support Spacey's claim that American art, music, film, and theater are relevant around the world?

After Reading

4. Discuss the following questions:

   • Does Spacey's speech rely primarily on pathos, ethos, or logos to make his argument? Support your opinion with textual evidence.

   • Which of his words do you think create the strongest emotional response from his audience? Does his diction have primarily positive or negative connotations?

   • What words or phrases does he repeat multiple times? Why do you think he does this?

5. Use the SMELL strategy to analyze Spacey's speech in the graphic organizer on the following page.

Essential Questions:	Kevin Spacey's Speech	Niall Ferguson's Article
Sender-receiver relationship: What is the sender-receiver relationship? Who are the images and language meant to attract? Describe the speaker of the text.		
Message: What is the message? Summarize the statement made in the text.		
Emotional Strategies: What is the desired effect?		
Logical Strategies: What is the desired effect?		
Language: What does the language of the text describe? How does it affect the meaning and effectiveness of the writing? Consider the language of the images as well as the words.		

My Notes

6. With a partner or small group, read the article "Texting Makes U Stupid" by Niall Ferguson. Then, complete the third column of the graphic organizer, applying the SMELL strategy to the text.

Article

Texting makes U Stupid

The U.S. is producing civilizational illiterates. How will they compete against America's global rivals?

by Niall Ferguson, *Newsweek*

The good news is that today's teenagers are avid readers and prolific writers. The bad news is that what they are reading and writing are text messages.

According to a survey carried out last year by Nielsen, Americans between the ages of 13 and 17 send and receive an average of 3,339 texts per month. Teenage girls send and receive more than 4,000.

It's an unmissable trend. Even if you don't have teenage kids, you'll see other people's offspring slouching around, eyes averted, tapping away, oblivious to their surroundings. Take a group of teenagers to see the seven wonders of the world. They'll be texting all the way. Show a teenager Botticelli's *Adoration of the Magi*. You might get a cursory glance before a buzz signals the arrival of the latest SMS. Seconds before the earth is hit by a gigantic asteroid or engulfed by a super tsunami, millions of lithe young fingers will be typing the human race's last inane words to itself:

C u later NOT: (

Now, before I am accused of throwing stones in a glass house, let me confess. I probably send about 50 emails a day, and I receive what seem like 200. But there's a difference. I also read books. It's a quaint old habit I picked up as a kid, in the days before cellphones began nesting, cuckoolike, in the palms of the young.

KEY IDEAS AND DETAILS
What counterclaim does Ferguson make to the importance of digital communication, and how does he refute it?

Half of today's teenagers don't read books—except when they're made to. According to the most recent survey by the National Endowment for the Arts, the proportion of Americans between the ages of 18 and 24 who read a book not required at school or at work is now 50.7 percent, the lowest for any adult age group younger than 75, and down from 59 percent 20 years ago.

Back in 2004, when the NEA last looked at younger readers' habits, it was already the case that fewer than one in three 13-year-olds read for pleasure every day. Especially terrifying to me as a professor is the fact that two thirds of college freshmen read for pleasure for less than an hour per week. A third of seniors don't read for pleasure at all. Why does this matter? For two reasons. First, we are falling behind more literate societies. According to the results of the Organization for Economic Cooperation and Development's most recent Program for International Student Assessment, the gap in reading ability between the 15-year-olds in the Shanghai district of China and those in the United States is now as big as the gap between the U.S. and Serbia or Chile.

But the more important reason is that children who don't read are cut off from the civilization of their ancestors.

So take a look at your bookshelves. Do you have all—better make that any—of the books on the Columbia University undergraduate core curriculum? It's not perfect, but it's as good a list of the canon of Western civilization as I know of. Let's take the 11 books on the syllabus for the spring 2012 semester: (1) Virgil's *Aeneid*; (2) Ovid's *Metamorphoses*; (3) Saint Augustine's *Confessions*; (4) Dante's *The Divine Comedy*; (5) Montaigne's *Essays*; (6) Shakespeare's *King Lear*; (7) Cervantes's *Don Quixote*; (8) Goethe's *Faust*; (9) Austen's *Pride and Prejudice*; (10) Dostoevsky's *Crime and Punishment*; (11) Woolf's *To the Lighthouse*.

Step one: Order the ones you haven't got today. (And get *War and Peace, Great Expectations*, and *Moby-Dick* while you're at it.)

Step two: When vacation time comes around, tell the teenagers in your life you are taking them to a party. Or to camp. They won't resist.

Step three: Drive to a remote rural location where there is no cell-phone reception whatsoever.

Step four: Reveal that this is in fact a reading party and that for the next two weeks reading is all you are proposing to do—apart from eating, sleeping, and talking about the books.

Welcome to Book Camp, kids.

After Reading

7. After reading and analyzing the text, go back and mark the text for the essential elements of an argument: hook, claim, reasons, evidence, counterclaim(s), and concluding statement/call to action.

8. **Quickwrite:** Which argument do you find more effective, Spacey's or Ferguson's? How do the speaker or writer's diction and rhetorical appeals strengthen the arguments?

My Notes

KEY IDEAS AND DETAILS
Why does Ferguson feel it is so important for children to feel connected to the "civilization of their ancestors"?

Give Up the Bard

LEARNING STRATEGIES:
Graphic Organizer, Note-taking,
Marking the Text, Discussion
Groups

My Notes

Learning Targets

- Identify the essential elements of an argument in a news article.
- Create a graphic organizer and a writer's checklist, in preparation for writing a synthesis argument.

Before Reading

1. Consider the essential elements of an argument. On a separate paper, create a graphic organizer that represents each of these elements and leaves sufficient room for notes as you plan a synthesis argument. (You may want to revisit the graphic organizer in Activity 5.19 for one idea of what this could look like, but feel free to create your own version.)

Essential Elements of an Argument

- **Hook:** an opening that grabs the reader's attention and establishes a connection between the reader and the writer.
- **Claim(s):** a clear and straightforward statement of the writer's belief and what is being argued.
- **Reasons and Evidence:** in support of a claim, reasons are developed through the use of evidence and rhetorical appeals (pathos, ethos, and logos).
- **Counterclaim(s):** alternative or opposing claims with concessions that the opposing side has valid points and/or refutations explaining why the writer's position is more valid.
- **Concluding Statement:** a summary or call to action that follows from and supports the argument.

During Reading

2. As you read Robshaw's argument in the article that follows, look for evidence that relates to your argument for or against inclusion of *Romeo and Juliet* in the ninth-grade curriculum. Highlight evidence for both sides using the same color code that you have used throughout the unit to represent support for your claim and counterclaim(s).

3. Take notes in each area of your graphic organizer to reflect the elements that you find in the text.

Article

Why it's time to give the **Bard** the heave-ho!

by Brandon Robshaw, *The Independent*

As a tribute to Shakespeare this St George's day, isn't it time we dropped him from the National Curriculum? The Bard is a national monument. Nor is there anything wrong with that. Along with a flag, an anthem and a football team, a national writer is part of the trappings of nationhood. The Italians have Dante, the Germans have Goethe, the French have a pantheon which includes Molière, Racine, Victor Hugo and Proust.

And Shakespeare is peculiarly well-suited to be ours, for both literary and non-literary reasons. The date of his death and the putative date of his birth neatly fall on our patron saint's day; he belongs to the golden age of Elizabethan expansionism; his history plays chronicle our kings and queens and contain quotable patriotic gobbets ("This precious stone set in the silver sea," "We few, we happy few," etc.). His output is staggeringly prolific—38 dramatic works in all the genres, several long poems and over 150 sonnets—and his plays work well enough dramatically to be constantly performed today. He had, as George Orwell put it, an amazing skill at putting one word beside another; as well as acute psychological insight, the largeness of mind to give great lines even to minor or unfavored characters, an unmatched ear for rhythm, and an uncanny ability to coin memorable phrases which, in many cases, have passed into general usage.

One might even say that appreciation of Shakespeare is the touchstone of an educated literary taste. If you don't like him, you don't get it. Voltaire and Tolstoy famously didn't, but then English wasn't their mother tongue.

The trouble is that most schoolchildren today don't like him and don't get it. And this isn't their fault. Shakespeare wrote over 400 years ago. Few people realize how much English has changed in just the last generation. Grammar and vocabulary have altered to the extent that teenagers tend to dismiss anything written before about 1960 as "Old English."

Besides, the large and increasing number of second-language speakers are in the same boat as Voltaire and Tolstoy from the start. We don't have anything like the unified national culture we had when I first studied Shakespeare in the 1970s. Then, most schoolchildren had at least some exposure to the King James Bible, the Book of Common Prayer and Hymns Ancient and Modern. We still didn't find Shakespeare easy, but at least we didn't need to have "thee" and "thou" explained to us.

Even the key selling point that many Shakespearisms have entered common usage is gradually losing its force as the years go by. I was recently taken aback to discover that virtually none of a class of London teenagers had encountered the expression "one fell swoop." Well, you might say, here's your chance to teach them, then. But that cannot be the justification for making Shakespeare compulsory—to teach outdated idioms that no one under the age of 40 uses.

KEY IDEAS AND DETAILS
What clues are there to the nationality of this writer?

Give Up the Bard

KEY IDEAS AND DETAILS
What does the author mean by comparing Shakespeare to a locked treasure chest?

My Notes

We need to think more clearly about the purpose of enshrining Shakespeare in this manner. If it's to preserve his national monument status, this is an unnecessary and counter-productive way of going about it. If it is to teach those things that literature is supposed to teach—aesthetic pleasure, understanding of character, moral sensitivity, liberal humanist values, an inkling of the techniques by which literary texts work their magic—then Shakespeare is simply not delivering. It's like handing pupils treasure in a locked chest. More contemporary texts may not offer quite such riches, but at least the kids could open the box.

Making today's school children read Shakespeare is about as sensible as compelling them to read Ulysses or Tristram Shandy. For all but a few—the brightest and best-read—it is a form of torture. Yet it's laid down in the National Curriculum that all British children of secondary school age must study not one but two Shakespeare plays. It is, as Will himself would say, a custom more honored in the breach than in the observance—and in practice, many teachers circumvent the difficulty by teaching a fragment of Romeo and Juliet and then showing the class West Side Story.

By the time students come to choose their AS-levels [preparation for college], those with a liking for literature should be ready to appreciate the riches Shakespeare has to offer. Let them wait until then. This isn't "dumbing down." Force-feeding children Shakespeare can only induce nausea and a lifelong aversion. If we want Shakespeare to be for all time as well of an age, we must let students come to him when they are willing and able to make the effort needed to enjoy him. Surely this is a tribute our national writer deserves?

After Reading

4. Use the notes you have taken on your graphic organizer to evaluate the effectiveness of Robshaw's argument. Consider any other criteria that you would use to evaluate an effective argument.

5. Using the Scoring Guide for Embedded Assessment 2, create a Writer's Checklist to evaluate a synthesis argument.

6. Work with a partner or small group to evaluate Robshaw's argument using your Writer's Checklist. What suggestions would you make to strengthen his writing through revision?

7. **Quickwrite:** How prepared do you feel to write a synthesis argument for or against the inclusion of William Shakespeare's Romeo and Juliet in the ninth-grade curriculum? Are there any questions that you still need to answer?

Writing a Synthesis Argument

Assignment

Your assignment is to compose an argument for or against the inclusion of William Shakespeare's *Romeo and Juliet* in the ninth-grade curriculum. You will evaluate research and gather evidence from a variety of sources about Shakespeare's relevance and influence in today's world. Finally, you will synthesize and cite your evidence in an argumentative essay that maintains a formal style and tone appropriate to your audience and purpose, uses rhetorical appeals including logical reasoning, and includes all the structual elements of an argument.

My Notes

Planning: Take time to make a plan for your essay.

- What is your position on the topic?

- How can you state your claim as a preliminary thesis statement?

- How can you use the print and nonprint texts in this unit as possible evidence for your claim?

- How will you evaluate evidence to be sure that the reasoning is valid and the evidence relevant as support for both your claim and the opposing viewpoint?

- How will you develop reasons for and against your claim and be sure that you are using a variety of rhetorical appeals (logos and ethos)?

- How can you use an outline or other graphic organizer to plan your essay and be sure that you include all the elements of an effective argument: a hook, claim, reasons, evidence, counterclaim(s), and a concluding statement or call to action?

Drafting and Revising: Compose your synthesis argument.

- How can you be sure you're not plagiarizing? How will you use parenthetical or in-text citation to credit the sources of your evidence and quotes?

- How will you develop and strengthen your draft through revision to produce clear and coherent writing?

- How will you check that you have maintained a formal style and tone appropriate to your audience and purpose?

- How can you use transitional words, phrases, and clauses to link ideas and clarify relationships?

Editing and Publishing: Prepare a final draft for publication.

- How will you proofread and edit your essay for proper conventions of standard English capitalization, punctuation, spelling, grammar, and usage?

- What tools are available for you to further polish and refine your work, such as a dictionary, thesaurus, spellcheck, or grammar check?

- How can the Scoring Guide help you evaluate how well you have met the requirements of the assignment?

Reflection

After completing this Embedded Assessment, think about how you went about accomplishing this task, and respond to the following question: Which articles from this unit did you select to support your argument, and why? What made a source useful for your purpose?

Writing a Synthesis Argument

SCORING GUIDE

Scoring Criteria	Exemplary	Proficient	Emerging	Incomplete
Ideas	The argument • skillfully presents a claim and provides appropriate background for the issue • synthesizes evidence from a variety of sources that strongly support the claim • summarizes and refutes counterclaims with relevant reasoning and clear evidence • concludes by clearly summarizing the main points and reinforcing the claim.	The argument • supports a claim that is clearly presented with appropriate background details • synthesizes evidence from multiple sources to support the claim • develops claims and counterclaims fairly and uses valid reasoning, relevant and sufficient evidence, and a variety of rhetorical appeals • concludes by revisiting the main points and reinforcing the claim.	The argument • states a thesis but does not adequately explain the issue or provide background details • attempts to synthesize evidence from several sources to support the claim • develops some counterclaims, but reasoning may not be completely relevant or sufficient for the evidence cited • concludes by listing the main points of the thesis.	The argument • states a vague or unclear thesis and does not explain the issue or provide background details • contains no synthesis of evidence from different sources to support the claim • may not develop counterclaims, and reasoning may not be relevant or sufficient for the evidence cited • concludes without restating the main points of the thesis.
Structure	The argument • follows a clear structure with a logical progression of ideas that connect the essential elements of hook, claim, evidence, counterclaims, and conclusion • links main points with effective transitions that establish coherence.	The argument • establishes clear relationships between the essential elements of hook, claim, evidence, counterclaims, and conclusion/call to action • uses transitions to link the major sections of the essay and create coherence.	The argument • demonstrates an awkward progression of ideas, but the reader can understand them • uses some elements of hook, claim, evidence, and conclusion • spends too much time on some irrelevant details and uses few transitions.	The argument • does not follow a logical organization • includes some details and elements of an argument, but the writing lacks clear direction and uses no transitions to help readers follow the line of thought.
Use of Language	The argument • uses a formal style and tone appropriate to audience and purpose • smoothly integrates and cites textual evidence from multiple sources • shows excellent command of standard English.	The argument • uses a formal style and tone appropriate to the audience and purpose • correctly cites textual evidence from at least three sources • follows conventions of standard English.	The argument • mixes informal and formal writing styles • cites some textual evidence but citations may be missing or inaccurate • includes some incorrect capitalization, punctuation, spelling, grammar, or usage.	The argument • uses mostly informal writing style • uses some textual evidence but does not include citations • includes incorrect capitalization, punctuation, spelling, grammar, or usage that interfere with meaning.

Grammar Handbook

Part 1: Grammar

Words, Word Groups, and Sentences

Words: Parts of Speech

Part of Speech	Function	Examples
Noun	names a person, place, thing, or idea	Taylor, mayor, ship, Missouri River, log, happiness
Pronoun	takes the place of a noun or other pronoun	I, you, she, us, they, himself, this, who, whom, that, which, each, none
Verb	expresses an action or state of being	go, be, startle, break, feel, do
Adjective	modifies a noun or pronoun	green, large, English, two
Adverb	modifies a verb, adjective, or other adverb	suddenly, awhile, yesterday, really
Preposition	relates one word to another word	in, on, to, above, before, with, between
Conjunction	joins words or word groups	and, or, but, so, either . . . or, because
Interjection	expresses emotion	ow, whew, uh-oh, hooray

Word Groups: Phrases

A **phrase** is a word group that functions as a specific part of speech and does NOT contain both a subject and its verb.

Kind of Phrase	Description	Examples
noun phrase	functions as a noun (names a person, place, thing, or idea)	**The cold dark woods** looked like **a forbidding place to be.**
verb phrase	functions as a verb (expresses an action or state of being)	We **were looking** for his house, where the old parrot cage **was stored**.
adjective phrase	functions as an adjective (modifies a noun or pronoun)	The book **on the left** is the one **to read** if you are working on the report **assigned in class.**
adverb phrase	functions as an adverb (modifies a verb, adjective, or other adverb)	He turned **to the left** when he was ready **to leave**.
participial phrase	begins with a past or present participle and functions as an adjective (modifies a noun or pronoun)	The book **sitting on the shelf** is the one **given by Uncle Dan**; you can use it for the report **assigned in class.**
infinitive phrase	begins with an infinitive verb form (to + base form) and functions as a noun, adjective, or adverb	He wants **to leave the theater** whenever you are ready **to go home.**
gerund phrase	begins with an –ing verb form and functions as a noun	**Leaving the theater early** and **going home** are our next steps.
prepositional phrase	introduced by a preposition and usually acts as an adjective or adverb	The book **on the left** is the one to read if you are working **on the report** assigned **in class.**

(Continued)

appositive phrase	renames or identifies another noun or pronoun	My best friends, **Meredith and Emily,** say that they are going to New Orleans, **my favorite city.**
absolute phrase	consists of a noun and its modifiers and functions as a modifier of a verb or whole clause.	**The sunset waning,** we decided to head back to camp. There, we found our friend Jackson, **his backpack leaning against the picnic table.**

Word Groups: Clauses

A **clause** is a word group that contains both a subject and its verb. An **independent clause** can stand alone as a sentence and expresses a complete thought. A **dependent clause,** or **subordinate clause,** does not express a complete thought and cannot stand alone as a sentence.

Independent Clause: **The pear tree grows.**
Dependent Clause: The pear tree **that Aunt Kim gave us** grows well.

Dependent clauses can function as nouns, adjectives, or adverbs.

Noun clause: Do you know **who planted the tree**?
Adjective clause: Do you see the birds **that are nesting**?
Adverb clause: We'll start the mosaic **after Eric arrives.**

A **noun clause** functions as a noun does—for example, as the subject of a sentence or as a direct or indirect object.

Whoever wants a copy should send me a message.

An **adjective clause,** or **relative clause,** modifies a noun or pronoun. Adjective clauses can be **restrictive** (essential to a sentence's meaning) or **nonrestrictive** (nonessential to the sentence's meaning). Nonrestrictive clauses are set off by commas.

Restrictive: The boys **who want a copy** have added their names to the list.
Nonrestrictive: The four broken containers, **which are stacked in the corner**, need to be returned.

Sentences

A **sentence** is a word group that has both a subject and a verb and that expresses a complete thought. Sentences are made of words, phrases, and clauses. A **phrase** is a word group that functions as a specific part of speech and does NOT contain both a subject and its verb. A **clause** is a word group that contains both a subject and its verb and that may act as a part of speech.

A **simple sentence** is made of one independent clause and no dependent clauses. It may contain any number of phrases.

The pear tree grows.
The pear tree given to us by Aunt Kim grows very well in that corner of the yard.

A **compound sentence** is made of two or more independent clauses and no dependent clauses. It may contain any number of phrases.

The sun shines, and the pear tree grows.
The pear tree given to us by Aunt Kim grows very well in that corner of the yard, and we may plant another one near it in the fall.

A **complex sentence** is made of one independent clause and at least one dependent clause. It may contain any number of phrases.

The pear tree that we planted last season grows well.
The pear tree that we planted last season and that Aunt Kim gave us grows well.

A **compound-complex sentence** is made of one independent clause and at least one dependent clause. It may contain any number of phrases.

The pear tree that we planted last season grows well, and so does the apple tree.
The pear tree that we planted last season and that Aunt Kim gave us grows well, and so does the apple tree.

Part 2: Usage

Subject-Verb Agreement

Compound Subjects
When the subject of a sentence is composed of two or more nouns or pronouns connected by *and*, use a plural verb.

Sara and **her sisters are** at the movie theater.

When two or more singular nouns or pronouns are connected by *or* or *nor*, use a singular verb.

Clive or **Penny is** in the yard.

When a compound subject contains both a singular and a plural noun or pronoun joined by *or* or *nor*, the verb should agree with the noun or pronoun that is nearer the verb.

George or **his teammates practice** daily.

Other Problems in Agreement
Doesn't is a contraction of *does not* and should be used with a singular subject. *Don't* is a contraction of *do not* and should be used with a plural subject. Exception: With the pronouns *I* and *you*, the contraction *don't* should be used.

He doesn't **like** it.
They don't **like** it.

Do not be misled by a phrase that comes between the subject and the verb. The verb agrees with the subject, not with a noun or pronoun in the interrupting phrase.

One of the stores **is** closed.
The people who love that band **are** many.
The captain of the team, as well as his rivals, **is** ready.
The movie, including all the trailers that come before, **is** very long.
A teenager with a skateboard and basketball **walks** past this bus stop each day.

The terms *each, each one, either, neither, everyone, everybody, anybody, anyone, nobody, somebody, someone,* and *no one* are singular and require a singular verb.

Each of these platters **is** full.
Everybody knows the answer.
Either is fine with me.

Some nouns that are plural in form, such as *civics*, *mathematics*, *measles*, and *news*, require singular verbs.

> **Measles is** a serious illness.

Some nouns, such as *scissors*, *tweezers*, *pants*, and *shears*, identify singular objects but name things that have two parts. These nouns take plural verbs.

> These **scissors are** sharp.
> Those **pants are** made of heavy fabric.

In sentences beginning with *there is* or *there are*, the subject follows the verb, but the verb must still agree with the subject.

> There **are** many **owls** in the woods.
> There **is** a **question**.

Collective nouns are words that can take a singular or plural verb, depending on if they refer to the group as a whole or to the group as a collection of different members or elements. Examples include *group*, *team*, *committee*, *class*, and *family*.

> The **family has** a long history.
> My **family have** never been able to agree.

Pronoun-Antecedent Agreement

When a pronoun takes the place of a singular noun, use a singular pronoun.

> **Incorrect:** If a student parks a car on campus, they have to buy a parking sticker.
> **Correct:** If a **student** parks a car on campus, **he or she** has to buy a parking sticker.

If using *he or she* sounds wordy, you can revise a sentence to use a plural form instead:

> **Students** who park on campus have to buy parking stickers for **their** cars.

The pronouns *each*, *each one*, *either*, *neither*, *everyone*, *everybody*, *anybody*, *anyone*, *nobody*, *somebody*, *someone*, and *no one* require a singular verb.

> **Everybody** ought to do **his or her** job.
> **Neither** of the girls brought **her** backpack.

Other Problems in Agreement

Agreement in Person

Pronouns should agree in person with their antecedents. Do not switch between first, second, and third person without reason.

> **Incorrect:** When a person comes to class, you should have your homework ready.
> **Correct:** A **person** arriving in class should have **his or her** homework ready.

Clear Reference

Pronouns should refer specifically and clearly to their antecedents. In some cases, you may need to reword or reorganize a sentence to make it clearer.

> **Ambiguous:** Although the car hit the building, it was not damaged. [Is *it* the car or the building?]
> **Revised:** Although it hit the building, the car was not damaged.
> **Ambiguous:** Stella told Kathryn that she ought to help build the set. [Does *she* refer to Stella or Kathryn?]
> **Revised:** According to Stella, Kathryn ought to help build the set.

Unclear: In the newspaper they say that the drought will last all summer. [Who are "they"?]
Revised: An article in the newspaper says that the drought will last all summer.
Unclear: Armand had a job as a ranger in a state forest last summer. This may be his life's work. [What word does this refer to?]
Revised: Armand had a job as a ranger in a state forest last summer. Protecting nature may be his life's work.

Pronoun Case

Pronouns have three cases.

- **Subjective (nominative) case:** pronouns used as subjects or predicate nominatives
- **Objective case:** pronouns used as objects of verbs or prepositions
- **Possessive case:** pronouns that express ownership

Subjective Case	Objective Case	Possessive Case
I	me	my (mine)
you	you	your (yours)
he, she, it	him, her, it	his, her (hers), it (its)
we	us	our (ours)
they	them	their (theirs)
who	whom	whose

Reflexive and Intensive Pronouns

	Singular	Plural
First person	myself	ourselves
Second person	yourself	yourselves
Third person	himself, herself, itself	themselves

A **reflexive pronoun** refers back to the subject of a clause or sentence. It functions as a complement or as the object of a preposition.

I told myself to be brave. [The reflexive pronoun is the indirect object of *told*.]

An **intensive pronoun** emphasizes the word it refers to.

I myself led the team to safety. [The reflexive pronoun emphasizes the subject.]

Compound Structures

In compound structures that include two pronouns or a noun and a pronoun, pay attention to pronoun case. Hint: If you're not sure which form to use, try each pronoun on its own in the sentence.

Incorrect: Dylan and me play soccer. [Would you say, "me play"?]
Correct: Dylan and I play soccer.

Incorrect: He gave the message to the faculty and I. [Would you say, "he gave the message to I"?]
Correct: He gave the message to the faculty and me.

Incorrect: Us musicians like the conductor. [Would you say, "us like the conductor"?]
Correct: We musicians like the conductor.

Comparisons

In comparisons, pay attention to pronoun case. Hint: You can "finish" the comparison, as shown below, to determine which case to use.

> Connor is more talented **than I** (am).
> This helps Eliot **as much as** (it helps) **me**.

Who and *Whom*

In formal writing, use *whom* and its related forms as an object of a verb or of a preposition.

> **Informal:** Who am I talking to?
> **Formal:** To **whom** am I talking?
> **Informal:** I will be sitting next to whoever Senator Gorm invites.
> **Formal:** I will be sitting next to **whomever** Senator Gorm invites.

Appositives

An **appositive** is a noun or pronoun that identifies or explains another noun or pronoun.

> Your friend **Bill** is in Dr. Levine's AP class.
> My sister's cat, **Chimmy**, doesn't like your dog.

An **appositive phrase** usually follows the word it explains or identifies, but it may also precede it.

> **A state known for its cold climate**, Alaska is closer to the North Pole than to Texas.

Some appositives are **restrictive,** or essential to a sentence's meaning. Restrictive appositives are not set off by punctuation.

> The civil rights leader **Martin Luther King, Jr.**, is often quoted. [Without the appositive, we would not know who is often quoted.]

If the appositive is **nonrestrictive,** or not essential to a sentence's meaning, it is set off with commas.

> Martin Luther King, Jr., **a famous civil rights leader**, is often quoted. [Without the appositive, we would still know who is often quoted.]

Verbals

Gerunds and Gerund Phrases

A **gerund** is a verbal that ends in *-ing* and functions as a noun. Since a gerund functions as a noun, it can be used as a subject, direct object, subject complement, or object of preposition.

> **Traveling** might satisfy your desire for new experiences.
> Are you excited about **arriving**?

Gerund phrases include a gerund and any modifiers or complements of the gerund. A gerund phrase functions as a noun.

> **Traveling to Asia** might satisfy your desire for new experiences.
> Are you excited about **arriving tomorrow**?

Participles and Participial Phrases

A **participle** is a verbal that is used as an adjective and most often ends in *–ing* or *–ed*. Participles modify nouns or pronouns. Present participles end in *–ing*. Past participles end in *–ed, –d, –en, –t,* or *–n*, as in the words *used, beaten, dealt,* and *seen*.

The **dangling** toy caught the kitten's attention.
The **broken** shutter banged in the wind.

A **participial phrase** includes the participle and any modifiers or complements of the participle. A participial phrase modifies a noun or pronoun.

The toy **dangling off the sofa** caught the kitten's attention.
The shutter **broken in the winter storm** banged in the wind.

A participial phrase should clearly modify a word in the sentence and should be placed near the word it modifies.

Incorrect: Carrying a stack of plates, his foot caught on a step. [His foot was not carrying plates. This participial phrase is a **dangling modifier**; it does not clearly modify any word in the sentence.]
Correct: Carrying a stack of plates, he caught his foot on a step.
Incorrect: Flying across the sky, Eugene saw a huge flock of gorgeous birds. [Eugene was not flying. This participial phrase is a **misplaced modifier**; it appears to modify *Eugene* rather than *flock.*]
Correct: Eugene saw a huge flock of gorgeous birds **flying across the sky.**

Punctuating Participial Phrases

When a participial phrase begins a sentence, a comma should be placed after the phrase.

Arriving at the park, Tara found that it had just closed.
Exercising regularly, Miguel found that his health and his attitude both improved.

When a participial phrase comes in the middle of a sentence, it should be set off with commas only if the information in the phrase is not essential to the meaning of the sentence.

Gricelda, **performing in the play**, found that she enjoyed being on stage. [not essential]
The teenager **performing in the play** was very talented. [essential]

When a participial phrase comes at the end of a sentence, a comma usually precedes the phrase if it modifies an earlier word in the sentence but not if the phrase directly follows the word it modifies.

The rangers watched the caribou **heading toward the stream**. [The phrase modifies *caribou.*]
The rangers watched the caribou, **admiring the animals' beauty and strength**. [The phrase modifies *rangers*, not *caribou.*]

Infinitives and Infinitive Phrases

An infinitive is a verbal consisting of the word *to* and the base form of a verb. It can function as a noun, adjective, or adverb. The infinitive may function as a subject, direct object, subject complement, adjective, or adverb in a sentence.

To stay seemed rude. [subject]
Jerome wanted **to go**. [direct object]
Her preference was **to delay**. [predicate nominative]
He lacked the willingness **to insist**. [adjective]
They finally were ready **to depart**. [adverb]

Don't confuse an infinitive—a verbal consisting of *to* plus a verb—with a prepositional phrase beginning with *to.*

Infinitives: to paint, to become, to exit, to sit, to throw
Prepositional Phrases: to Jason, to the field, to all of us, to the hour

An **infinitive phrase** includes an infinitive and its modifiers or complements.

> **To stay past 10:00 p.m**. seemed rude. [subject]
> Jerome wanted **to go right away**. [direct object]
> Her preference was **to delay till her aunt arrived**. [predicate nominative]
> He lacked the willingness **to insist that they say goodnight**. [adjective]
> They finally were ready **to depart around midnight**. [adverb]

Punctuating Infinitives and Infinitive Phrases

If an infinitive or infinitive phrase is used as an adverb and begins a sentence, it should be set off with a comma; otherwise, no punctuation is needed.

> **To convince me to read the book**, Jacob read me his favorite passages. [adverb]
> **To plant a garden** is my next goal. [noun]

Split infinitives

Split infinitives occur when words come between *to* and the verb in an infinitive. Although splitting infinitives is sometimes acceptable, it is often awkward, and some readers find split infinitives overly informal. You may wish to avoid splitting infinitives in formal writing.

> **Awkward:** He began **to**, all of a sudden, **talk** excitedly about his new job.
> **Revised:** He began, all of a sudden, **to talk** excitedly about his new job.

Prepositions

Preposition Use: Expressions of Time

On is used with days:

> I will see Tim on Wednesday.

At is used with *noon, night, midnight,* and with the time of day:

> The movie is **at** noon.

In is used with other parts of the day, with months, with years, with seasons:

> We will gather **in** the afternoon.
> **In** the spring, we can visit Kansas.

To express continuing action, English uses the following prepositions: *since, for, by, from . . . to, from . . . until, during, (with)in.*

> The visitors have been here **since** yesterday.
> I'm going to Atlanta **for** two weeks.
> Mike's cousins were in Austin **from** August **to** October.

Preposition Use: Expressions of Place

English uses the following prepositions:

- to talk about a specific point or place: *in*
  There is an egg **in** the nest.
- to express something contained: *inside*
  What is **inside** that blue box?
- to talk about the surface: *on*
  What is **on** the counter?
- to talk about a general vicinity: *at*
  We left him **at** Antietam.

Preposition Use: Objects of Verbs

English uses the following prepositions to introduce objects of the following verbs.

At: *glance, laugh, look, rejoice, smile, stare*

> I'm laughing **at** the puppets' antics.
> The toddler smiled **at** you.

Of: *approve, consist, smell*

> Aunt Irene approves **of** your career choice.
> That smells **of** mildew.

Of (or about): *dream, think*

> Zac dreams **of** starting anew.
> Zeb thinks **about** leaving for Seattle.

For: *call, hope, look, wait, watch, wish*

> Caroline hopes **for** success.
> The stranded sailor waits and watches **for** rescue.

Sentence Construction: Connecting Clauses

Coordinating conjunctions and **conjunctive adverbs** can be used to connect independent clauses.

Coordinating Conjunctions: The coordinating conjunctions used to join independent clauses are *and, but, or, for, nor, so,* and *yet.* When the second independent clause in a sentence begins with a coordinating conjunction, a comma is needed before the coordinating conjunction:

> Ben wanted to play soccer, **but** Miles wanted to run track.

Conjunctive Adverbs: Some common conjunctive adverbs are *also, consequently, furthermore, however, moreover, nevertheless,* and *therefore.* A conjunctive adverb can begin an independent clause or can be used to join independent clauses. When the second independent clause in a sentence has a conjunctive adverb, a semicolon is needed before it.

> Ben wanted to play soccer; **however**, Miles wanted to run track.

Subordinating conjunctions can connect dependent clauses to independent clauses. Common subordinating conjunctions include *after, although, as, as if, because, before, even if, even though, if, in order to, since, though, unless, until, when, whenever, whether,* and *while.*

> **Even if** she does prefer vanilla, I think she will enjoy the coconut cake.
> I will help you with the dishes **whenever** you are ready.
> The chicken likes to roost outside **unless** it is raining.

Common Sentence Construction Errors

Comma Splices: A comma splice is the use of a comma to join two independent clauses. You can usually fix the error in one of these ways:

- changing the comma to a period and turning the two clauses into separate sentences
- changing the comma to a semicolon
- making one clause dependent by inserting a subordinating conjunction
- adding a coordinating conjunction after the comma

Incorrect:
I love that movie, I have watched it ten times.
Correct:
I love that movie. I have watched it ten times.
I love that movie; I have watched it ten times.
Because I love that movie, I have watched it ten times.
I love that movie, and I have watched it ten times.

Fused Sentences: A fused sentence is two or more independent clauses run together with no punctuation. This error is also known as a run-on sentence. The error can sometimes be corrected by adding a period, semicolon, or colon between the clauses.

Incorrect: I love that movie I have watched it ten times.
Correct: I love that movie. I have watched it ten times.
Correct: I love that movie; I have watched it ten times.
Correct: I love that movie: I have watched it ten times.

Sentence Fragments: A sentence fragment is a word groups that does not express a complete thought and cannot stand alone as a sentence. You can usually fix a fragment by combining it with another sentence to make a complete thought or by removing a subordinating conjunction.

Incorrect: Because today I have band practice.
Correct: Because today I have band practice, I won't be riding the bus.
Correct: Today I have band practice.

Using Verbs Correctly

Verbs express different times through tenses. Do not change tenses unnecessarily. Use tenses consistently unless you are deliberately expressing differences in time or sequence.

Inconsistent: I **was talking** to Roseanne, and I **say**, "Will you be in Florida in June?"
Consistent: I **was talking** to Roseanne, and I **said**, "Will you be in Florida in June?"

Sequence of Tenses
Present Perfect: They have walked.
Present: They walk.
Past Perfect: They had walked.
Past: They walked.
Future Perfect: They will have walked.
Future: They will walk.

Problems in sequencing tenses usually occur with the perfect tenses, which are formed by adding an auxiliary or auxiliaries to the past participle.

Verb	Past form	Perfect tenses
ring	rang	has/have/had rung; will have rung
walk	walked	has/have/had walked; will have walked

The most common auxiliaries are *can, do, may, must, ought, shall, will, has, have, had,* and forms of *be.*

Present Perfect: The present perfect consists of a past participle preceded by has or have. It expresses action that began in the past and that continues into the present.

past: Ms. Gage **taught** for ten years. [She no longer teaches.]
present perfect: Ms. Gage **has taught** for ten years. [She is still teaching.]

Past Perfect: The past perfect tense expresses action in the past that is completed before another past action.

past: Mr. Geiser played in a band for years.
past perfect: Mr. Geiser had played in a band for years before he went solo.

Future Perfect: The future perfect tense expresses action that will have been completed at a specified time in the future.

future: Mr. Catalano will teach for seventeen years.
future perfect: Mr. Catalano will have taught for seventeen years this November.

Mood and Modal Forms

Mood refers to the form the verb takes to indicate the speaker's attitude. Avoid unnecessary shifts in mood.

Indicative mood expresses a fact or opinion. It is used in declarative sentences.

The Rogers family **raises** chickens.

Imperative mood expresses a command or request.

Bring me the eggs, please.

Subjunctive mood expresses a suggestion, necessity, condition contrary to fact, or a wish.

I recommend that you **be seated** now.
It is necessary that you **be seated**.
If I **were** you, I would be seated.
I wish I **were** seated already.

Interrogative sentences express a question.

Did you **go** to the farm?
Are they **raising** chickens?

Conditional verbs express actions or states of being that depend on other conditions.

If the sun had already set, we **would have gone** home.

Irregular Verbs

In English, verbs have a base form (the present), a past form, and a past participle. Regular verbs add –ed to the base form to make both the past form and past participle. Irregular verbs do not follow this pattern.

Present	Past	Past Participle
be	was, were	been
become	became	become
begin	began	begun
blow	blew	blown
break	broke	broken
bring	brought	brought
build	built	built

(Continued)

burst	burst	burst
buy	bought	bought
catch	caught	caught
choose	chose	chosen
come	came	come
cut	cut	cut
deal	dealt	dealt
do	did	done
drink	drank	drunk
drive	drove	driven
eat	ate	eaten
fall	fell	fallen
feed	fed	fed
feel	felt	felt
fight	fought	fought
find	found	found
fly	flew	flown
forbid	forbade	forbidden
forget	forgot	forgotten
forgive	forgave	forgiven
freeze	froze	frozen
get	got	gotten
give	gave	given
go	went	gone
grow	grew	grown
have	had	had
hear	heard	heard
hide	hid	hidden
hold	held	held
hurt	hurt	hurt
keep	kept	kept
know	knew	known
lay	laid	laid
lead	led	led
leave	left	left
let	let	let
lie	lay	lain
lose	lost	lost
make	made	made
meet	met	met
pay	paid	paid

quit	quit	quit
read	read	read
ride	rode	ridden
run	ran	run
say	said	said
see	saw	seen
seek	sought	sought
sell	sold	sold
send	sent	sent
shake	shook	shaken
shine	shone	shone
sing	sang	sung
sit	sat	sat
sleep	slept	slept
speak	spoke	spoken
spend	spent	spent
spring	sprang	sprung
stand	stood	stood
steal	stole	stolen
swim	swam	swum
swing	swung	swung
take	took	taken
teach	taught	taught
tear	tore	torn
tell	told	told
think	thought	thought
throw	threw	thrown
understand	understood	understood
wake	woke (waked)	woken (waked)
wear	wore	worn
win	won	won
write	wrote	written

Commonly Confused Verbs

Lie vs. Lay		
Present	Past	Past Participle
lie, lying (to tell a falsehood)	I lied to no one.	I have lied to no one.
lie, lying (to recline)	I lay in bed because I was tired.	He has lain in bed all morning.
lay, laying (to put, place)	I laid the doll in the cradle.	We have laid the doll in the cradle.

Sit vs. Set		
Present	**Past**	**Past Participle**
sit (to be seated or come to a resting position)	I sat on the curb to wait.	You have sat on the curb all afternoon.
set (to put or place)	I set my dish in the sink.	She has set her dishes in the sink.

Rise vs. Raise		
Present	**Past**	**Past Participle**
rise (steady or customary upward movement)	The helicopter rose into the air.	The helicopter has risen into the air.
raise (to cause to rise)	They raised their hands to give the answer.	I have raised my hands in class many times.

Part 3: Style

Parallel Structure

Parallel structure is the use of similar grammatical structures to show that two or more ideas are similar in importance or meaning or to provide emphasis. Words, phrases, and clauses can be parallel.

Words and Phrases

Not Parallel: Carla likes hik**ing**, swimm**ing**, and **to ride** a bicycle.
Parallel: Carla likes hik**ing**, swimm**ing**, and rid**ing** a bicycle.

Not Parallel: The manager wrote his report quick**ly**, accurate**ly**, and **in a detailed manner**.
Parallel: The manager wrote his report quick**ly**, accurate**ly**, and thorough**ly**.

Not Parallel: He wait**ed** until the last minute to study for the exam, completed his lab problems in a careless manner, and **his motivation was** low.
Parallel: He wait**ed** until the last minute to study for the exam, complet**ed** his lab problems in a careless manner, and lack**ed** motivation.

Clauses

Not Parallel: The teacher told the students **that they should get** a lot of sleep, **that they should not worry** too much, and **to go over their notes**.
Parallel: The teacher told the students **that they should get** a lot of sleep, **that they should not worry** too much, and **that they should go over their notes**.

Not Parallel: I asked **when the order would be ready, where the package should be delivered,** and **the name of the recipient**.
Parallel: I asked **when the order would be ready, where the package should be delivered,** and **who would receive the package**.

Lists

Be sure to keep the elements in a list parallel.

Not Parallel: The tutorial covers how to **identify clauses**, **correct common errors**, and **proofreading for errors**.

Parallel: The tutorial covers how to **identify clauses**, **correct common errors**, and **proofread for errors**.

Bulleted items should be parallel.

Not Parallel:

The master gardener talked about these topics:

- compost
- wildflowers
- eradicating pests
- irrigation

Parallel:

The master gardener talked about these topics:

- compost
- wildflowers
- pests
- irrigation

Using Active Voice

In a sentence using **active voice,** the subject of the sentence performs the action expressed by the verb.

The girl **threw** the ball.
I **ate** three apples yesterday.

In a sentence using **passive voice,** the subject of the sentence receives the action expressed by the verb.

The ball **was thrown**.
Three apples **were eaten** yesterday.

	Active	Passive
Simple Present	Acme **ships** the widgets to many clients.	Widgets **are shipped** to many clients.
Present Progressive	The chef **is cooking** the beets.	The beets **are being cooked.**
Simple Past	I **mailed** a letter last Friday.	A letter **was mailed** last Friday.
Past Progressive	The principal **was making** announcements at the assembly.	Announcements **were being made** at the assembly.
Future	The president **will make** decisions.	Decisions **will be made** by the president.
Present Perfect	Kelli **has made** the appointment.	The appointment **has been made.**
Past Perfect	They **had baked** muffins for us.	Muffins **had been baked** for us.
Future Perfect	By Tuesday, we **will have completed** this project.	By Tuesday, this project **will have been completed.**

The active voice is more vigorous and direct. There are times when passive voice is useful or appropriate—for instance, when you want to be diplomatic and avoid naming names, or when you want to emphasize the recipient of the action. However, generally, you should use active voice most of the time. Avoid unnecessary shifts in voice.

Part 4: Mechanics

Capitalization

Capitalize the first word of a sentence.

> Do you have my schedule?

Capitalize the pronoun *I*.

> When I sneeze, I try not to do so loudly.

Capitalize proper nouns (the names of specific people, places, organizations, and things).

Dreiser Company	Brooklyn Bridge
Supreme Court	Cleveland, Ohio
Indian Ocean	Federal Trade Commission

Capitalize proper names of family members.

> I sent cookies to Grandma but not to Uncle Joe.
> What did Father say?

Lowercase words for family members when they are preceded by *a, an, the,* or a possessive pronoun.

> Carina is an aunt now.
> I sent cookies to our grandmothers but not our uncles.
> What did your father say?

Capitalize the names of specific deities, religious figures, and holy books.

God	Abraham
the Virgin Mary	Shiva
the Bible	Buddha
Mercury	Zeus
the Torah	the Koran

Exception: Do not capitalize the nonspecific use of the word *god*.

> The Greek gods seem almost human at times.

Capitalize titles preceding names but not titles that follow names.

> What do you think of Mayor Nagin?
> I voted for Cecilia Guerra, the mayor of Nettontown.

Capitalize directions that are used as names of parts of the country.

> The Rogers family has lived in the South for several generations.

Note: Do not capitalize directions when they are not used as names.

> We are heading south next week.

Capitalize days of the week, months of the year, and holidays.

Easter	Monday
January	September
Friday	Thanksgiving

Capitalize the names of seasons only when they are part of a proper noun.

Brentwood Fall Festival
2016 Summer Olympics

Capitalize the names of countries, nationalities, and specific languages.

Paraguay	Russia
Spanish	Russian

Capitalize the first word in a sentence that is a direct quotation.

George Saunders said, "Grief is the bill that comes due for love."

Capitalize the first, last, and all important words in titles of literary and artistic works.
Do not capitalize short prepositions or the articles *a*, *an*, and *the* unless used as the first word of the title.

The Catcher in the Rye
"Nothing Gold Can Stay"
Starry Night

Capitalize the names of members of national, political, racial, social, civic, and athletic groups.

New Orleans Saints	Republicans
African Americans	Phi Beta Kappan
Austin Mavericks	Japanese

Capitalize historical periods and major events.

Edwardian Era	Boston Tea Party
Great Depression	Louisiana World Exposition

Note: Do not capitalize names of centuries.

sixteenth century
first century

Capitalize trademarked brand names.

Pepsi	IBM
Toyota	Nintendo

Punctuating Sentences
Here are basic sentence patterns and how they are punctuated.

Simple Sentence
This pattern is an example of a simple sentence:

Independent clause [.]
We went on an urban hike downtown.

Compound Sentence with a Comma and Coordinating Conjunction
This pattern is an example of a compound sentence with a coordinating conjunction:

Independent clause [,] **coordinating conjunction** *independent clause* [.]

These are the coordinating conjunctions: *and*, *but*, *for*, *or*, *nor*, *so*, *yet*. Note that *then* is not a coordinating conjunction and cannot be used with a comma to separate independent clauses.

> We went on an urban hike downtown, and we took notes on the world around us.

Compound Sentence with a Semicolon

This pattern is an example of a compound sentence with a semicolon:

> *Independent clause* [;] *independent clause* [.]

We went on an urban hike downtown; we took notes on the world around us.

Compound Sentence with a Conjunctive Adverb

This pattern is an example of a compound sentence with a conjunctive adverb.

> *Independent clause* [;] **conjunctive adverb** [,] *independent clause* [.]

These are examples of conjunctive adverbs: *also*, *consequently*, *however*, *moreover*, *therefore*, *thus*.

> We went on an urban hike downtown; **also**, we took notes on the world around us.

Complex Sentence Beginning with a Dependent Clause

This pattern is an example of a complex sentence. It begins with a subordinating conjunction and a subordinate (dependent) clause.

> **Subordinating conjunction** *dependent clause* [,] *independent clause* [.]

These are examples of subordinating conjunctions: *after*, *although*, *as*, *as if*, *because*, *before*, *if*, *since*, *until*, *when*, *while*.

> When we went on an urban hike downtown, we took notes on the world around us.

Complex Sentence Beginning with an Independent Clause

This pattern is an example of a complex sentence beginning with an independent clause.

> *Independent clause* **subordinating conjunction** *dependent clause* [.]
> We took notes on the world around us while we were on an urban hike downtown.

Independent Clause with an Embedded Nonessential Phrase or Clause

This pattern includes an independent clause with an embedded nonessential clause or phrase. A nonessential clause or phrase can be removed without changing the basic meaning of the sentence or making it ungrammatical. The nonessential clause or phrase provides "extra" information, but the sentence can stand alone without it.

> *First part of independent clause* [,] **nonessential clause or phrase** [,] *rest of the independent clause* [.]
> We took notes, some serious and some humorous, on the world around us.
> We took notes, which we used later in reports, on the world around us.

Independent Clause with an Embedded Essential Phrase or Clause

This pattern includes an independent clause with an embedded essential clause or phrase. An essential clause or phrase cannot be removed without changing the basic meaning of the sentence.

First part of an independent clause essential clause or phrase rest of the independent clause [.]
The next hike that we will take will go along Main Street.
The next hike through downtown will go along Main Street.

Commas

Commas are often used between grammatical elements and have many conventional uses.
Here are essential rules for comma use.

Use a comma with a coordinating conjunction **to join two independent clauses** (*and, but, or, for, nor, so, yet*).

> Rain fell last weekend, but this weekend should be sunny.

Use a comma after an **introductory verbal phrase or an introductory adverb clause**.

> To see the meteors, you should go where there is less light pollution.
> Watching the meteors, we felt both excited and sleepy.
> Before we left, we packed extra snacks.

Use a comma after a long **introductory prepositional phrase** or after more than one prepositional phrase.

> By one o'clock in the morning, we were getting cold.

Use a comma after one short **introductory prepositional phrase** if needed for clarity or readability.

> In December, 17 meteors streaked above me as I watched. [Without the comma, it looks at first as if the sentence contains the date *December 17*.]

Use a comma to separate **items in a series.** For logic and consistency, it is helpful to include a final comma (called the serial comma, or Oxford comma) before the conjunction; however, it is usually not incorrect to omit it.

> The trail was long, dusty, and arduous.
> I like to read novels by George Eliot, Charles Dickens, and E. M. Forster.
> They invited my parents, Frank, and Peggy. [Note that without the serial comma, it would be unclear whether two or four people were invited.]

Use a comma to set off **nonessential phrases and clauses**.

> My hen, a Rhode Island Red, lays several eggs each week.
> Russell Hoban's novel *Riddley Walker*, which I am reading, is fascinating.

Use a comma between **coordinate adjectives** (adjectives that have equal weight and that can be reordered in the sentence).

> He turned in a concise, well-written essay.

If you cannot change the order of the adjectives without making the sentence sound awkward or unidiomatic, you may not need commas.

> His skateboard is the big green one. [You wouldn't say "green big one."]
> The routine involves an easy high kick. [You wouldn't say "high easy kick."]

Use a comma after a **transitional word or phrase**, such as *however, therefore, nonetheless, also, otherwise, finally, instead, thus, of course, above all, for example, in other words, as a result, on the other hand, in conclusion, in addition*.

> Nonetheless, we will proceed as planned.
> Otherwise, we will be stranded here without our phones.

Use a comma to set off **direct quotations and speech tags**.

"Hey," Roy said, "I will be taking photos at the gallery reception."
Emily replied, "I hope you get good pictures of Katherine and Alan."

Use commas to set off **items in a date**.

She was born on October 27, 1962.
That was due on Friday, April 12, 2013, but was turned in late.

Use commas to set off **thousands, millions, billions**, and so on.

27,000,000

Use commas to set off **personal titles and suffixes**. Note that in running text, a comma follows the title or suffix.

Please welcome Michael Davidson, M.D., to the stage.
We studied Martin Luther King, Jr., and his accomplishments.

Use a comma to separate a **city name** from a state or country name. In running text, a comma follows the state or country name.

I am from Salisbury, England, and she is from Edinburgh, Scotland.
I ordered copies from a bookstore in Philadelphia, Pennsylvania, but they haven't arrived.

Semicolons

Use a semicolon to **join two independent clauses** when the second clause restates the first or when the two clauses are closely related.

If you can arrive early, I will appreciate it; we'll have to set up the sound system.

Use a semicolon to join two independent clauses when the second clause begins with a conjunctive adverb, such as *however, therefore, moreover, furthermore, thus, meanwhile, nonetheless,* or *otherwise,* or a transition, such as *in fact, for example, that is, for instance, in addition, in other words, on the other hand,* or *even so.*

The technician has already left; however, I think I have her cell number.

Use a semicolon to join items in a series when the items themselves include commas.

My favorite cities are London, England; Dublin, Ireland; and Chicago, Illinois.

Colons

Use a colon to join two independent clauses when you want to emphasize the second clause.

I'll ask you again: Would you please return the shirt you borrowed?

Use a colon after an independent clause when it introduces a list, a quotation, an appositive, or other idea directly related to the independent clause.

We need supplies for the party: ice, beverages, cups, and snacks.
This is Nelson's favorite quotation by George Eliot: "What do we live for, if it is not to make life less difficult for each other?"
Tasha has an idea for the perfect classroom pet: a turtle.

Use a colon after the greeting of a business letter.

To Whom It May Concern:

Use a colon to separate hours and minutes.

12:00 p.m.

Use a colon to separate the chapter and verse in a Biblical reference.

I John 4:7

Parentheses

Parentheses are used to set off explanatory content, especially if it is tangential.
Use parentheses to set off nonessential, or nonrestrictive, information such as dates,
clarifying information, or sources, from a sentence.

David Foster Wallace (1962–2008) wrote both fiction and nonfiction.
You can find us at 1802 Quentin Street (just behind Compson Middle School).

Use parentheses to enclose literary citations or explanations of acronyms.

The Wired Northwest (Hirt, 2012) details the electrification of the Northwest.
The scientists at NIH (National Institutes of Health) will issue a report.

Brackets

Brackets are used to clarify the meaning of quoted material.

The biologist explained, "We were dismayed to find that it [the mantis shrimp] was capable of
breaking the glass of the aquarium."
Dr. Carlisle replied, "The reform bill of the [eighteen-]thirties was in some ways problematic."

Quotation Marks

Use quotation marks to enclose direct quotations. Note that commas and periods are
placed inside closing quotation marks, while colons and semicolons are placed outside.
The placement of question and exclamation marks depends on meaning.

Monique asked, "What time does the plane land?" and Jay replied, "Right at noon."
Monique said, "I'll bring the car"; Jay replied, "Great! "
Did Jay really say, "I'm sure the plane will be late"?

Use quotation marks to indicate that a word is jargon, slang, or a new word,
or is used ironically.

That's what is known as a "culture capture."
She raised an eyebrow at this "fair" decision but did not object.

Use quotation marks around the titles of short poems, songs, short stories, magazine or
newspaper articles, essays, speeches, chapters, short films, and episodes of television or
radio programs.

"Nothing Gold Can Stay," by Robert Frost
"Dizzy," by Tommy Roe
"City Council to Reconsider Redevelopment Plan," an article in the newspaper

Italics

Italicize the titles of magazines, books, newspapers, films, television programs, long poems, plays, operas, music albums, works of art, and individual spacecraft, trains, planes, or ships.

> *TIME*
> *Julius Caesar* by William Shakespeare
> *Starry Night* by Vincent van Gogh
> *Enterprise* (space shuttle)

Italicize foreign words and phrases.

> *C'est la vie* means "That's life."

Italicize a word or phrase to add emphasis. (This should be done sparingly.)

> I said we'd be there *late*, not *at eight*.

Italicize words referred to as words, letters referred to as letters, or numbers referred to as numbers.

> The word *curfew* comes from the French. It means "cover fire" and refers to the time of day when medieval families would bank their fires and go to bed.

> Are those *0*'s, *8*'s, or *o*'s?

Hyphens

Use a hyphen to divide a word at the end of a line, if necessary. Break words only between syllables.

> splen-did
> heart-felt
> class-i-fi-ca-tion

For line breaks, divide already hyphenated words only at the hyphen:

> half-
> dollar
> many-
> sided

Use a hyphen to join two or more words serving as a single adjective before a noun.

> hand-dipped chocolates
> well-loved book

However, when compound modifiers come after a noun, they are often not hyphenated:

> The chocolates were hand dipped.
> The book was well loved.

Use a hyphen between tens and ones in compound numbers.

> twenty-seven
> one hundred forty-four

Use a hyphen with the prefixes *ex–* (meaning former), *self–*, *all–*, and *half–*, and with the suffix *–elect*.

> ex-wife
> self-critical
> all-inclusive

half-life
president-elect

Use a hyphen between a prefix and a capitalized word

mid-October
anti-American
pre-Reformation

Use a hyphen between figures and letters.

T-shirt
mid-1900s

Dashes

En dashes (–) are used between sequential numbers, such as page ranges and date ranges.

Chapters 1–3 are due tomorrow.
The show is on stage September 20–27.

Em dashes (—) are used to set off nonrestrictive or parenthetical information or to emphasize text. Dashes can be used to show pauses or breaks in thought. They are more emphatic than commas or parentheses.

Two of the plays—*Macbeth* and *Guest by Courtesy*—are Jamie's favorites.
If you peek over the edge—watch your footing—you can see far into the canyon.
There is room in the van for six people—not sixteen.

Use a dash to set off an appositive phrase that already includes commas.

Three cats—Penny, Clytie, and Penguin—are in the front room.

Apostrophes

The apostrophe is used

- to form possessives of nouns
- to show the omission of letters in contractions
- to indicate plurals of certain lowercase letters

Possessives of Nouns

There are several rules for making the possessive forms of nouns.

Add an apostrophe and –s to

- the singular form of a word (even if it already ends in –s)
  a dog**'s** collar
  Mr. Rogers**'s** pocket watch
- plural forms that do not end in –s
  those women**'s** books
  these sheep**'s** vaccinations
- the end of compound words
  attorney-general**'s** money
  president-elect**'s** agenda
- the last name of two in a pair to show joint possession
  Ben and Max**'s** wagon
- both names in a pair to show individual possession
  Ben**'s** and Max**'s** backpacks

Add just an apostrophe to plural nouns that end in –s

four trees' leaves
the Smiths' new house

Don't use apostrophes to make pronouns possessive or to make nouns plural.

Possessive pronouns: *his, her, hers, its, my, your, yours, our, ours, their, theirs*
Incorrect: That book is her's.
Correct: That book is **hers**.
Incorrect: Is that it's box?
Correct: Is that **its** box?
Incorrect: That book is your's.
Correct: That book is **yours**.

Contractions

Apostrophes are used in contractions to show where one or more letters or numbers have been omitted.

doesn't = does not
we're = we are
should've = should have
'70s = 1970s

Ellipses

Use an ellipsis, three spaced periods (. . .), to show where text is left out of a quoted passage.

"Four score and seven years ago our fathers brought forth on this continent a new nation . . . dedicated to the proposition that all men are created equal."

Use an ellipsis to show a pause or break in thought.

It's just that . . . I don't know . . . maybe you're right.

Resources

SpringBoard Learning Strategies

READING STRATEGIES

STRATEGY	DEFINITION	PURPOSE
Chunking the Text	Breaking the text into smaller, manageable units of sense (e.g., words, sentences, paragraphs, whole text) by numbering, separating phrases, drawing boxes	To reduce the intimidation factor when encountering long words, sentences, or whole texts; to increase comprehension of difficult or challenging text
Close Reading	Accessing small chunks of text to read, reread, mark, and annotate key passages, word-for-word, sentence-by-sentence, and line-by-line	To develop comprehensive understanding by engaging in one or more focused readings of a text
Diffusing	Reading a passage, noting unfamiliar words, discovering meaning of unfamiliar words using context clues, dictionaries, and/or thesauruses, and replacing unfamiliar words with familiar ones	To facilitate a close reading of text, the use of resources, an understanding of synonyms, and increased comprehension of text
Double-Entry Journal	Creating a two-column journal (also called Dialectical Journal) with a student-selected passage in one column and the student's response in the second column (e.g., asking questions of the text, forming personal responses, interpreting the text, reflecting on the process of making meaning of the text)	To assist in note-taking and organizing key textual elements and responses noted during reading in order to generate textual support that can be incorporated into a piece of writing at a later time
Graphic Organizer	Using a visual representation for the organization of information from the text	To facilitate increased comprehension and discussion
KWHL Chart	Setting up discussion that allows students to activate prior knowledge by answering "What do I know?"; sets a purpose by answering "What do I want to know?"; helps preview a task by answering "How will I learn it?"; and reflects on new knowledge by answering "What have I learned?"	To organize thinking, access prior knowledge, and reflect on learning to increase comprehension and engagement
Marking the Text	Selecting text by highlighting, underlining, and/or annotating for specific components, such as main idea, imagery, literary devices, and so on	To focus reading for specific purposes, such as author's craft, and to organize information from selections; to facilitate reexamination of a text
Metacognitive Markers	Responding to text with a system of cueing marks where students use a ? for questions about the text; a ! for reactions related to the text; and an * for comments ,about the text and underline to signal key ideas	To track responses to texts and use those responses as a point of departure for talking or writing about texts
OPTIC	**O** (Overview): Write notes on what the visual appears to be about. **P** (Parts): Zoom in on the parts of the visual and describe any elements or details that seem important. **T** (Title): Highlight the words of the title of the visual (if one is available). **I** (Interrelationships): Use the title as the theory and the parts of the visual as clues to detect and specify how the elements of the graphic are related.	To analyze graphic and visual images as forms of text

STRATEGY	DEFINITION	PURPOSE
OPTIC (continued)	**C** (Conclusion); Draw a conclusion about the visual as a whole. What does the visual mean? Summarize the message of the visual in one or two sentences.	
Predicting	Making guesses about the text by using the title and pictures and/or thinking ahead about events which may occur based on evidence in the text	To help students become actively involved, interested, and mentally prepared to understand ideas
Previewing	Examining a text's structure, features, layout, format, questions, directions, prior to reading	To gain familiarity with the text, make connections to the text, and extend prior knowledge to set a purpose for reading
QHT	Expanding prior knowledge of vocabulary words by marking words with a Q, H, or T (Q signals words students do not know; H signals words students have heard and might be able to identify; T signals words students know well enough to teach to their peers)	To allow students to build on their prior knowledge of words, to provide a forum for peer teaching and learning of new words, and to serve as a prereading exercise to aid in comprehension
Questioning the Text* The AP Vertical Teams Guide for English (109–112)	Developing levels of questions about text; that is, literal, interpretive, and universal questions that prompt deeper thinking about a text	To engage more actively with texts, read with greater purpose and focus, and ultimately answer questions to gain greater insight into the text; helps students to comprehend and interpret
Paraphrasing	Restating in one's own words the essential information expressed in a text, whether it be narration, dialogue, or informational text	To encourage and facilitate comprehension of challenging text.
RAFT	Primarily used to generate new text, this strategy can also be used to analyze a text by examining the role of the speaker (R), the intended audience (A), the format of the text (F), and the topic of the text (T).	To initiate reader response; to facilitate an analysis of a text to gain focus prior to creating a new text
Rereading	Encountering the same text with more than one reading.	To identify additional details; to clarify meaning and/or reinforce comprehension of texts
SIFT* The AP Vertical Teams Guide for English (17–20)	Analyzing a fictional text by examining stylistic elements, especially symbol, images, and figures of speech in order to show how all work together to reveal tone and theme	To focus and facilitate an analysis of a fictional text by examining the title and text for symbolism, identifying images and sensory details, analyzing figurative language and identifying how all these elements reveal tone and theme
Skimming/Scanning	Skimming by rapid or superficial reading of a text to form an overall impression or to obtain a general understanding of the material; scanning focuses on key words, phrases, or specific details and provides speedy recognition of information	To quickly form an overall impression prior to an in-depth study of a text; to answer specific questions or quickly locate targeted information or detail in a text
SMELL* The AP Vertical Teams Guide for English (138-139)	Analyzing a persuasive speech or essay by asking five essential questions: • Sender-receiver relationship—What is the sender-receiver relationship? Who are the images and language meant to attract? Describe the speaker of the text. • Message—What is the message? Summarize the statement made in the text.	To analyze a persuasive speech or essay by focusing on five essential questions

STRATEGY	DEFINITION	PURPOSE
SMELL* (continued)	• Emotional Strategies—What is the desired effect? • Logical Strategies—What logic is operating? How does it (or its absence) affect the message? Consider the logic of the images as well as the words. • Language—What does the language of the text describe? How does it affect the meaning and effectiveness of the writing? Consider the language of the images as well as the words.	
SOAPSTone*	Analyzing text by discussing and identifying Speaker, Occasion, Audience, Purpose, Subject, and Tone	To facilitate the analysis of specific elements of non-fiction literary and informational texts and show the relationship among the elements to an understanding of the whole
Summarizing	Giving a brief statement of the main points or essential information expressed in a text, whether it be narration, dialogue, or informational text	To facilitate comprehension and recall of a text
Think Aloud	Talking through a difficult passage or task by using a form of metacognition whereby the reader expresses how he/she has made sense of the text	To reflect on how readers make meaning of challenging texts and to facilitate discussion
TP-CASTT* The AP Vertical Teams Guide for English (94–99)	Analyzing a poetic text by identifying and discussing Title, Paraphrase, Connotation, Attitude, Shift, Theme, and Title again	To facilitate the analysis of specific elements of a literary text, especially poetry. To show how the elements work together to create meaning
Visualizing	Forming a picture (mentally and/or literally) while reading a text	To increase reading comprehension and promote active engagement with text
Word Maps	Using a clearly defined graphic organizer such as concept circles or word webs to identify and reinforce word meanings	To provide a visual tool for identifying and remembering multiple aspects of words and word meanings

*Delineates AP strategy

WRITING STRATEGIES

STRATEGY	DEFINITION	PURPOSE
Adding	Making conscious choices to enhance a text by adding additional words, phrases, sentences, or ideas	To refine and clarify the writer's thoughts during revision and/or drafting
Brainstorming	Using a flexible but deliberate process of listing multiple ideas in a short period of time without excluding any idea from the preliminary list	To generate ideas, concepts, or key words that provide a focus and/or establish organization as part of the prewriting or revision process
Deleting	Providing clarity and cohesiveness for a text by eliminating words, phrases, sentences, or ideas	To refine and clarify the writer's thoughts during revision and/or drafting
Drafting	Composing a text in its initial form	To incorporate brainstormed or initial ideas into a written format

STRATEGY	DEFINITION	PURPOSE
Free writing	Write freely without constraints in order to capture thinking and convey the writer's purpose	To refine and clarify the writer's thoughts, spark new ideas, and/or generate content during revision and/or drafting
Generating Questions	Clarifying and developing ideas by asking questions of the draft. May be part of self-editing or peer editing	To clarify and develop ideas in a draft; used during drafting and as part of writer response
Graphic Organizer	Organizing ideas and information visually (e.g., Venn diagrams, flowcharts, cluster maps)	To provide a visual system for organizing multiple ideas, details, and/or textual support to be included in a piece of writing
Looping	After free writing, one section of a text is circled to promote elaboration or the generation of new ideas for that section. This process is repeated to further develop ideas from the newly generated segments	To refine and clarify the writer's thoughts, spark new ideas, and/or generate new content during revision and/or drafting
Mapping	Creating a graphic organizer that serves as a visual representation of the organizational plan for a written text	To generate ideas, concepts, or key words that provide a focus and/or establish organization during the prewriting, drafting, or revision process
Marking the Draft	Interacting with the draft version of a piece of writing by highlighting, underlining, color-coding, and annotating to indicate revision ideas	To encourage focused, reflective thinking about revising drafts
Note-taking	Making notes about ideas in response to text or discussions; one form is the double-entry journal in which textual evidence is recorded on the left side and personal commentary about the meaning of the evidence on the other side.	To assist in organizing key textual elements and responses noted during reading in order to generate textual support that can be incorporated into a piece of writing at a later time. Note-taking is also a reading and listening strategy.
Outlining	Using a system of numerals and letters in order to identify topics and supporting details and ensure an appropriate balance of ideas.	To generate ideas, concepts, or key words that provide a focus and/or establish organization prior to writing an initial draft and/or during the revision process
Quickwrite	Writing for a short, specific amount of time in response to a prompt provided	To generate multiple ideas in a quick fashion that could be turned into longer pieces of writing at a later time (May be considered as part of the drafting process)
RAFT	Generating a new text and/or transforming a text by identifying and manipulating its component parts of Role, Audience, Format, and Topic	To generate a new text by identifying the main elements of a text during the prewriting and drafting stages of the writing process
Rearranging	Selecting components of a text and moving them to another place within the text and/or modifying the order in which the author's ideas are presented	To refine and clarify the writer's thoughts during revision and/or drafting
Self-Editing/Peer Editing	Working individually or with a partner to examine a text closely in order to identify areas that might need to be corrected for grammar, punctuation, spelling	To provide a systematic process for editing a written text to ensure correctness of identified components such as conventions of standard English

STRATEGY	DEFINITION	PURPOSE
Sharing and Responding	Communicating with another person or a small group of peers who respond to a piece of writing as focused readers (not necessarily as evaluators)	To make suggestions for improvement to the work of others and/or to receive appropriate and relevant feedback on the writer's own work, used during the drafting and revision process
Sketching	Drawing or sketching ideas or ordering of ideas. Includes storyboarding, visualizing	To generate and/or clarify ideas by visualizing them. May be part of prewriting
Substituting / Replacing	Replacing original words or phrases in a text with new words or phrases that achieve the desired effect	To refine and clarify the writer's thoughts during revision and/or drafting
TWIST* The AP Vertical Teams Guide for English (167–174)	Arriving at a thesis statement that incorporates the following literary elements: tone, word choice (diction), imagery, style and theme	To craft an interpretive thesis in response to a prompt about a text
Webbing	Developing a graphic organizer that consists of a series of circles connected with lines to indicate relationships among ideas	To generate ideas, concepts, or key words that provide a focus and/or establish organization prior to writing an initial draft and/or during the revision process
Writer's Checklist	Using a co-constructed checklist (that could be written on a bookmark and/or displayed on the wall) in order to look for specific features of a writing text and check for accuracy	To focus on key areas of the writing process so that the writer can effectively revise a draft and correct mistake
Writing Groups	A type of discussion group devoted to sharing and responding of student work	To facilitate a collaborative approach to generating ideas for and revising writing.

SPEAKING AND LISTENING STRATEGIES

STRATEGY	DEFINITION	PURPOSE
Choral Reading	Reading text lines aloud in student groups and/or individually to present an interpretation	To develop fluency; differentiate between the reading of statements and questions; practice phrasing, pacing, and reading dialogue; show how a character's emotions are captured through vocal stress and intonation
Note-taking	Creating a record of information while listening to a speaker or reading a text	To facilitate active listening or close reading ; to record and organize ideas that assist in processing information
Oral Reading	Reading aloud one's own text or the texts of others (e.g., echo reading, choral reading, paired readings)	To share one's own work or the work of others; build fluency and increase confidence in presenting to a group
Rehearsal	Encouraging multiple practices of a piece of text prior to a performance	To provide students with an opportunity to clarify the meaning of a text prior to a performance as they refine the use of dramatic conventions (e.g., gestures, vocal interpretations, facial expressions)
Role Playing	Assuming the role or persona of a character	To develop the voice, emotions, and mannerisms of a character to facilitate improved comprehension of a text

COLLABORATIVE STRATEGIES

STRATEGY	DEFINITION	PURPOSE
Discussion Groups	Engaging in an interactive, small group discussion, often with an assigned role; to consider a topic, text or question	To gain new understanding of or insight into a text from multiple perspectives
Think-Pair-Share	Pairing with a peer to share ideas; before sharing ideas and discussion with a larger group	To construct meaning about a topic or question; to test thinking in relation to the ideas of others; to prepare for a discussion with a larger group

Glossary / Glosario

A

active-voice verbs: a verb form indicating that the subject performs the action

verbos en voz activa: forma verbal que indica que el sujeto realiza la acción

advertising techniques: specific methods used in print, graphics, or videos to persuade people to buy a product or use a service

técnicas publicitarias: métodos específicos usados en impresos, gráfica o videos para persuadir a las personas a comprar un producto o usar un servicio

alliteration: the repetition of initial consonant sounds in words that are close together

aliteración: repetición de sonidos consonánticos iniciales en palabras cercanas

allusion: a reference made to a well-known person, event, or place from history, music, art, or another literary work

alusión: referencia a una persona, evento o lugar muy conocidos de la historia, música, arte u otra obra literaria

analogy: a comparison between two things for the purpose of drawing conclusions on one based on its similarities to the other

analogía: comparación entre dos cosas con el propósito de sacar conclusiones sobre las semejanzas que una cosa tiene a otra

anaphora: the repetition of the same word or group of words at the beginning of two or more clauses or lines

anáfora: repetición de la misma palabra o grupo de palabras al comienzo de una o más cláusulas o versos

anecdotal evidence: evidence based on personal accounts of incidents

evidencia anecdótica: evidencia basada en relatos personales de los hechos

annotated bibliography: a list of sources used in research along with comments or summaries about each source

bibliografía anotada: lista de fuentes utilizadas en la investigación, junto con comentarios o resúmenes acerca de cada fuente

antagonist: the character who opposes or struggles again the main character

antagonista: personaje que se opone o lucha contra el personaje principal

aphorism: a short statement expressing an opinion or general truth

aforismo: afirmación corta que expresa una opinión o verdad general

archetypal criticism: examining literature based on its symbols and patterns

critica de arquetipos: examinación de la literature basada en símbolos y diseño

archetypes: universal symbols—images, characters, motifs, or patterns—that recur in myths, art, and literature throughout the world

arquetipos: símbolos universales—imágenes, personajes, motivos o patrones—reiterativos en los mitos, el arte y la literatura alrededor del mundo

archival footage: film footage taken from another, previously recorded, source

cortometraje de archivo: fragmento de película tomada de otra fuente grabada previamente

argument: a form of writing that presents a particular opinion or idea and supports it with evidence

argumento: forma de redacción que presenta una opinión o idea particular y la apoya con evidencia

argumentation: the structure of an argument includes the *hook* (quotation, example, or idea that catches readers' attention), *claim* (the opinion or thesis statement), *support* (evidence in the form of facts, statistics, examples, anecdotes, or expert opinions), *concession* (the writer's admission that the other side of the argument has a valid point), *refutation* (a well-reasoned denial of an opponent's point, based on solid evidence), and *call to action* (an inspired request of readers)

argumentación: la estructura de una argumentación incluye el *gancho* (cita, ejemplo o idea que capta la atención del lector), *afirmación* (declaración de opinión o tesis), *apoyo* (evidencia en forma de hechos, estadísticas, ejemplos, anécdotas u opiniones de expertos), *concesión* (admisión por parte del escritor de que la otra parte del debate tiene un punto válido), *refutación* (negación bien razonada de una opinión del oponente, basada en evidencia sólida) y *llamado a la acción* (petición inspirada de lectores)

argument by analogy: a comparison of two similar situations, implying that the outcome of one will resemble the outcome of the other

argumento por analogía: comparación de dos situaciones semejantes, infiriendo que el resultado de será parecido al resultado de la otra

artistic license: the practice of rewording dialogue, alteration of language, or reordering of the plot of a text created by another artist

licencia artística: la costumbre de reformular un diálogo, aliteración de palabras, o arreglo de la trama de un texto creado por otro artista

aside: a short speech spoken by an actor directly to the audience and unheard by other actors on stage
aparte: alocución breve dicha por un actor directamente al público y que no escuchan los demás actores que están en el escenario

assonance: the repetition of similar vowel sounds in accented syllables, followed by different consonant sounds, in words that are close together
asonancia: repetición de sonidos vocálicos similares en sílabas acentuadas, seguida de diferentes sonidos consonánticos, en palabras que están cercanas

audience: the intended readers, listeners, or viewers of specific types of written, spoken, or visual texts
público: lectores objetivo, oyentes o espectadores de tipos específicos de textos escritos, hablados o visuales

audience analysis: determining the characteristics and knowledge of the people who will read a work or hear a speech
análisis del público: determinar las características y conocimiento de las personas que leen una obra o escuchan un discurso

author's purpose: the specific reason or reasons for the writing; what the author hopes to accomplish
propósito del autor: razón específica para escribir; lo que el autor espera lograr

autobiography: an account written by a person about his or her own life
autobiografía: narración de una vida escrita por el propio sujeto del relato

B

balanced sentence: a sentence that presents ideas of equal weight in similar grammatical forms to emphasize the similarity or difference between the ideas
oración balanceada: oración que representa ideas de igual peso en formas gramaticales similares para enfatizar la semejanza o diferencia entre las ideas

bias: an inclination or mental leaning for or against something that prevents impartial judgment
sesgo: inclinación o tendencia mental a favor o en contra de algo, lo que impide una opinión imparcial

bibliography: a list of the sources used for research
bibliografía: lista de fuentes primarias en la preparación de un texto

biography: a description or account of someone else's life or significant events from that person's life written by another person
biografía: descripción o narración de la vida de una persona o los sucesos importantes de su vida escritos por otra persona

blank verse: unrhymed verse
verso libre: verso que no tiene rima

blocking: in drama, the way actors position themselves in relation to one another, the audience, and the objects on the stage
bloqueo: en drama, el modo en que los actores se sitúan entre sí, con el público y los objetos en el escenario

book review: a formal assessment or examination of a book
reseña de libro: evaluación o examinación formal de un libro

C

cacophonous: harsh, unpleasant sounds
cacofónico: sonidos molestos y desagradables

call to action: a restatement of the claim and what the writer wants the reader to do
llamado a la acción: repetición de la afirmación y lo que el escritor quiere que el lector responda

caricature: a visual or verbal representation in which characteristics or traits are exaggerated or distorted for emphasis
caricatura: representación visual o verbal en la que las características o rasgos se exageran o se distorsionan para dar énfasis

catalog poem: a poem that uses repetition and variation in the creation of a list, or catalog, of objects or desires or plans or memories
lista en poema: poema que usa repetición y variación en la creación de una lista o catálogo, de objetos o deseos o planes o memorias

cause: an action, event, or situation that brings about a particular result
causa: acción, suceso o situación que produce un resultado particular

censor: to examine materials for objectionable content
censurar: examinar materiales por contenido desagradable

censorship: the act of suppressing public speech or publication of materials deemed to be offensive by the censor
censura: acto de suprimir un discurso público o publicación de materiales considerados ofensivos por un censor

challenge: to oppose or refute a statement that has been made
poner en duda: oponerse a algo o refutar una declaración que alguien ha hecho

characterization: the methods a writer uses to develop characters
caracterización: métodos que usa un escritor para desarrollar personajes

characters: people, animals, or imaginary creatures that take part in the action of a story. A short story usually centers on a *main character*, but may also contain one or more *minor characters*, who are not as complex, but whose thoughts, words, or actions move the plot along. A character who is *dynamic* changes in response to the events of the narrative; a character who is *static* remains the same throughout the narrative. A *round* character is fully developed—he or she shows a variety of traits; a *flat* character is one-dimensional, usually showing only one trait.

personajes: personas, animales o criaturas imaginarias que participan en la acción de un cuento. Un cuento corto normalmente se centra en un *personaje principal*, pero puede también contener uno o más *personajes secundarios*, que no son tan complejos, pero cuyos pensamientos, palabras o acciones hacen avanzar la trama. Un personaje que es *dinámico* cambia según los eventos del relato; un personaje que es *estático* permanece igual a lo largo del relato. Un personaje *complejo* está completamente desarrollado: muestra una diversidad de rasgos; un personaje *simple* es unidimensional, mostrando normalmente sólo un rasgo.

character sketch: a brief description of a literary character
reseña del personaje: breve descripción de un personaje literario

chorus: in traditional or classic drama, a group of performers who speak as one and comment on the action of the play
coro: en el drama tradicional o clásico, grupo de actores que hablan al unísono y comentan la acción de la obra teatral

cinematic elements: the features of cinema—movies, film, video—that contribute to its form and structure: *angles* (the view from which the image is shot), *framing* (how a scene is structured), *lighting* (the type of lighting used to light a scene), *mise en scène* (the composition, setting, or staging of an image, or a scene in a film), and *sound* (the sound effects and music accompanying each scene)
elementos cinematográficos: las características del cine—películas, filmaciones, video—que contribuyen a darle forma y estructura: *angulación* (vista desde la cual se toma la imagen), *encuadre* (cómo se estructura una escena), iluminación (tipo de *iluminación* que se usa para una escena), y *montaje* (composición, ambiente o escenificación de una imagen o escena en una película), y *sonido* (efectos sonoros y música que acompañan cada escena)

cinematic techniques: the methods a director uses to communicate meaning and to evoke particular emotional responses from viewers
técnicas cinematográficas: métodos que emplea un director para comunicar un significado y evocar cierta respuesta emocional de los videntes

claim: a position statement (or thesis) that asserts an idea or makes an argument for a specific position
afirmación: declaración de opinión (o tesis) que asevera una idea o establece un debate hacia una posición específica

cliché: an overused expression or idea
cliché: expresión o idea que se usa en exceso

climax: the point at which the action reaches its peak; the point of greatest interest or suspense in a story; the turning point at which the outcome of a conflict is decided
clímax: punto en el que la acción alcanza su punto culminante; punto de mayor interés en un cuento; punto de inflexión en el que se decide el resultado del conflicto

coherence: the quality of unity or logical connection among ideas; the clear and orderly presentation of ideas in a paragraph or essay
coherencia: calidad de unidad o relación lógica entre las ideas; presentación clara y ordenada de las ideas en un párrafo o ensayo

commentary: in an expository essay or paragraph, the explanation of the importance or relevance of supporting detail and the way the details support the larger analysis
comentario: ensayo o párrafo expositivo, explicación de la importancia o relevancia de los detalles de apoyo, y la manera en que los detalles apoyan el análisis principal

complementary: combining two or more elements in ways that enhance both
complementario: combinar dos o más elementos de una manera que mejora los dos

complex character: a character that has multiple or conflicting motivations
personaje complejo: personaje que tiene motivaciones multiples o conflictivas

complex sentence: a sentence containing one independent clause and one or more subordinate clauses
oración compleja: oración que contiene una cláusula independiente y una o más cláusulas subordinadas

complications: the events in a plot that develop a conflict; the complications move the plot forward in its rising action
complicaciones: sucesos de una trama que desarrollan el conflicto; las complicaciones hacen avanzar la trama en su acción ascendente

compound sentence: a sentence containing two independent clauses
oración compuesta: oración que contiene dos cláusulas independientes

concession: an admission in an argument that the opposing side has valid points
concesión: admitir en un debate que el lado opositor tiene opiniones válidas

concluding statement: a statement that follows from and supports the claim made in an argument
declaración concluyente: declaración que sigue de la afirmación, o la apoya, en un argumento

conflict: a struggle or problem in a story. An *internal conflict* occurs when a character struggles between opposing needs or desires or emotions within his or her own mind. An *external conflict* occurs when a character struggles against an outside force. This force may be another character, a societal expectation, or something in the physical world.
conflicto: lucha o problema en un cuento. Un *conflicto interno* ocurre cuando un personaje lucha entre necesidades o deseos o emociones que se contraponen dentro de su mente. Un *conflicto externo* ocurre cuando un personaje lucha contra una fuerza externa. Esta fuerza puede ser otro personaje, una expectativa social o algo del mundo físico.

connotation: the associations and emotional overtones attached to a word beyond its literal definition or denotation; a connotation may be positive, negative, or neutral
connotación: asociaciones y alusiones emocionales unidas a una palabra más allá de su definición literal o denotación; una connotación puede ser positiva, negativa, o neutra

consonance: the repetition of final consonant sounds in stressed syllables with different vowel sounds
consonancia: repetición de sonidos consonánticos finales en sílabas acentuadas con diferentes sonidos vocálicos

context: the circumstances or conditions in which something takes place
contexto: circunstancias o condiciones en las que algo ocurre

conventions: standard features, practices, and forms associated with the way something is usually done
convenciones: prácticas y formas usuales asociadas con las costumbres de hacer algo

counterclaim: a position taken by someone with an opposing viewpoint
contrarreclamación: posición que toma una persona con un punto de vista contrario

couplet: two consecutive lines of verse with end rhyme; a couplet usually expresses a complete unit of thought
copla: dos líneas de versos consecutivos con rima final; una copla normalmente expresa una unidad de pensamiento completa

credibility: the quality of being trusted or believed
credibilidad: calidad de ser confiable o creíble

critical lens: a particular identifiable perspective as in Reader Response Criticism, Cultural Criticism, etc., through which a text can be analyzed and interpreted
ojo crítico: punto de vista particular identificable como por ejemplo Teoría de la recepción, Crítica sociocultural, etc., por medio del que se puede analizar e interpretar un texto

cultural conflict: a struggle that occurs when people with different cultural expectations or attitudes interact
conflicto cultural: lucha que ocurre cuando interactúan personas con diferentes expectativas o actitudes culturales

cultural criticism: analyzing text based on elements of culture and how they affect one's perceptions and understanding of texts
crítica cultural: analizar un texto basándose en elementos culturales y como ellos afectan la percepción y la comprensión de textos

culture: the shared set of arts, ideas, skills, institutions, customs, attitude, values, and achievements that characterize a group of people, and that are passed on or taught to succeeding generations
cultura: conjunto de artes, ideas, destrezas, instituciones, costumbres, actitud, valores y logros compartidos que caracterizan a un grupo de personas, y que se transfieren o enseñan a las generaciones siguientes

cumulative (or loose) sentence: a sentence in which the main clause comes first, followed by subordinate structures or clauses
oración acumulativa (o frases sueltas): oración cuya cláusula principal viene primero, seguida de estructuras o cláusulas subordinadas

D

deductive reasoning: a process of using general information from which to draw a specific conclusion
razonamiento deductivo: proceso en que se usa información general para sacar una conclusión específica

defend: to support a statement that has been made
defender: dar apoyo a una declaración que alguien ha hecho

denotation: the literal definition of a word
denotación: significado literal de una palabra

detail: a specific fact, observation, or incident; any of the small pieces or parts that make up something else
detalle: hecho, observación o incidente específico; cualquiera de las pequeñas piezas o partes que constituyen otra cosa

dialect: the distinctive language, including the sounds, spelling, grammar, and diction, of a specific group or class of people
dialecto: lenguaje distintivo, incluyendo sonidos, ortografía, gramática y dicción, de un grupo o clase específico de personas

dialogue: the words spoken by characters in a narrative or film
diálogo: palabras que dicen los personajes en un relato o película

dialogue tags: the phrases that attribute a quotation to the speaker, for example, *she said* or *he bellowed*
marcas del diálogo: frases que atribuyen la cita de un hablante, por ejemplo, *dijo ella* o *bramó él.*

diction: the writer's choice of words; a stylistic element that helps convey voice and tone
dicción: selección de palabras por parte del escritor; elemento estilístico que ayuda a transmitir voz y tono

diegetic sound: any sound that can logically be heard by characters on screen
sonido diegético: sonidos lógicos que los personajes pueden oír en una escena en la pantalla

direct characterization: specific information about a character provided by the narrator or author
caracterización directa: información específica sobre un personaje creada por un narrador o autor

discourse: the language or speech used in a particular context or subject
discurso: lenguaje o habla usada en un contexto o tema en particular

documentary or nonfiction film: a genre of filmmaking that is based on factual events, using photographs, video footage, and interviews
documental o película de no-ficción: género cinematográfico que realiza un registro visual de sucesos basados en hechos por medio del uso de fotografías, registro en videos y entrevistas

dominant group: a more powerful group that may perceive another group as marginalized or subordinate
grupo dominante: un grupo más poderoso que puede percebir a otro grupo como maginado o subordinado

drama: a play written for stage, radio, film, or television, usually about a serious topic or situation
drama: obra teatral escrita para representar en un escenario, radio, cine o televisión, normalmente sobre un tema o situación seria

dramatic irony: a form of irony in which the reader or audience knows more about the circumstances or future events than the characters within the scene
ironía dramática: una forma de la ironía en que los lectores o el público sabe más sobre las circunstancias o sucesos futuros que los personajes en la escena

dramaturge: a member of an acting company who helps the director and actors make informed decisions about the performance by researching information relevant to the play and its context
dramaturgo: socio de una compañía teatral que ayuda al director y a los actores tomar decisiones informadas sobre la interpretación investigando información relevante a la obra teatral y su contexto

dynamic (or round) character: in literature, one who changes in response to the events of a narrative
personaje dinámico: en la literatura, un personaje que cambia debido a los sucesos de una narrativa

E

editorial: an article in a newspaper or magazine expressing the opinion of its editor or publisher
editorial: artículo de periódico o revista, que expresa la opinión de su editor

effect: the result or influence of using a specific literary or cinematic device; a result produced by a cause
efecto: resultado o influencia de usar un recurso literario o cinematográfico específico; resultado o producto de una causa

elaborate: expand on or add information or detail about a point and thus to develop the point more fully
elaborar: extender o agregar información o detalles sobre un asunto, y asi desarrollar el asunto de manera más completa

empirical evidence: evidence based on experiences and direct observation through research
evidencia empírica: evidencia basada en experiencias y en la observación directa por medio de la investigación

emulate: imitate an original work
emular: imitar una obra original

enfranchisement: having the rights of citizenship, such as the right to vote
emancipación: tener los derechos de la ciudananía, tales como el derecho al voto

epigram: a short witty saying
epigrama: dicho corto e ingenioso

epigraph: a phrase, quotation, or poem that is set at the beginning of a document or component
epígrafe: frase, cita, o poema que aparece al comienzo de un documento o componente

epithet: a descriptive word or phrase used in place of or along with a name
epíteto: palabra o frase descriptiva usada en lugar de o junto con un nombre

ethos: (ethical appeal) a rhetorical appeal that focuses on ethics, or the character or qualifications of the speaker
ethos: (recurso ético) recurso retórico centrado en la ética o en el carácter o capacidades del orador

euphonious: a harmonious or pleasing sound
eufónico: un sonido armonioso y agradable

evaluate: make a judgment from an analysis about the value or worth of the information, idea, or object
evaluar: dar una opinión basándose en un análisis sobre el valor o mérito de la información, idea, u objeto

evidence: the information that supports or proves an idea or claim; forms of evidence include facts, statistics (numerical facts), expert opinions, examples, and anecdotes; *see also* anecdotal, empirical, and logical evidence
evidencia: información que apoya o prueba una idea o afirmación; formas de evidencia incluyen hechos, estadística (datos numéricos), opiniones de expertos, ejemplos y anécdotas; *ver también* evidencia anecdótica, empírica y lógica

exaggeration: representing something as larger, better, or worse than it really is
exageración: representar algo como más grande, mejor o peor que lo que realmente es

exemplification: to define by example by showing specific, relevant examples that fit a writer's definition of a topic or concept
ejemplificación: definir por ejemplo mostrando ejemplos específicos y relevantes que se ajustan a la definición de un tema o concepto del escritor

explicit theme: a theme that is clearly stated by the writer
tema explícito: tema que está claramente establecido por el escritor

exposition: events that give a reader background information needed to understand a story (characters are introduced, the setting is described, and the conflict begins to unfold)

exposición: sucesos que dan al lector los antecedentes necesarios para comprender un cuento. Durante la exposición, se presentan los personajes, se describe el ambiente y se comienza a revelar el conflicto.

expository writing: a form of writing whose purpose is to explain, describe, or give information about a topic in order to inform a reader

escrito expositivo: forma de la escritura cuyo propósito es explicar, describir o dar información sobre un tema para informar al lector

extended metaphor: a metaphor that extends over several lines or throughout an entire poem

metáfora extendida: metáfora que se extiende por varios versos o a través de un poema completo

external coherence: unity or logical connection between paragraphs with effective transitions and transitional devices

coherencia externa: unidad o conexión lógica entre párrafos con transiciones efectivas y recursos transitionales

F

fallacy: a false or misleading argument

falacia: argumento o poema falso o engañoso

falling action: the events in a play, story, or novel that follow the climax, or moment of greatest suspense, and lead to the resolution

acción descendente: sucesos de una obra teatral, cuento o novela posteriores al clímax, o momento de mayor suspenso, y que conllevan a la resolución

feminist criticism: focuses on relationships between genders and examines a text based on the patterns of thought, behavior, values, enfranchisement, and power in relations between and within the sexes

crítica feminista: se enfoca en la relación entre los sexos y examina un texto basándose en el diseño de pensamiento, comportamiento, valores, emancipación, y poder en las relaciones entre los sexos

figurative language: imaginative language or figures of speech not meant to be taken literally

lenguaje figurativo: lenguaje imaginativo o figuras retóricas que no pretenden ser tomados literalmente; el lenguaje figurativo usa figuras literarias

film techniques: the methods a director uses to communicate meaning and to evoke particular emotional responses in viewers

técnicas cinematográficas: metodos que usa un director en la comunicación del significado y evocar una respuesta emocional específica en los videntes

fixed form: a form of poetry in which the length and pattern are determined by established usage of tradition, such as a sonnet

forma fija: forma de poesía en la que la longitud y el patrón están determinados por el uso de la tradición, como un soneto

flashback: an interruption in the sequence of events to relate events that occurred in the past

flashback: interrupción en la secuencia de los sucesos para relatar sucesos ocurridos en el pasado

flat (or static) character: a character who is uncomplicated and stays the same without changing or growing during the story

personaje estático: personaje no complicado que permanence del mismo caracter y que no cambia a lo largo de una historia

foil: a character whose actions or thoughts are juxtaposed against those of a major character in order to highlight key attributes of the major character

antagonista: personaje cuyas acciones o pensamientos se yuxtaponen a los de un personaje principal con el fin de destacar atributos clave del personaje principal

folk tale: a story without a known author that has been preserved through oral retellings

cuento folclórico: cuento sin autor conocido que se ha conservado por medio de relatos orales

footage: literally, a length of film; the expression is still used to refer to digital video clips

metraje: literalmente, la longitud de una película; la expresión aún se usa para referirse a video clips digitales

foreshadowing: the use of hints or clues in a narrative to suggest future action

presagio: uso de claves o pistas en un relato para sugerir una acción futura

form: the particular structure or organization of a work

forma: estructura o organización particular de una obra

free verse: poetry without a fixed pattern of meter and rhyme

verso libre: poesía que no sigue ningún patrón, ritmo o rima regular

G

genre: a kind or style of literature or art, each with its own specific characteristics. For example, poetry, short story, and novel are literary genres. Painting and sculpture are artistic genres.

género: tipo o estilo de literatura o arte, cada uno con sus propias características específicas. Por ejemplo, la poesía, el cuento corto y la novela son géneros literarios. La pintura y la escultura son géneros artísticos.

genre conventions: the essential features and format that characterize a specific genre

convenciones genéricas: caractcrísticas básicas y el formato que caracterizan un género específico

graphic novel: a book-length narrative, or story, in the form of a comic strip rather than words

novela gráfica: narrativa o cuento del largo de un libro, en forma de tira cómica más que palabras

graphics: images or text used to provide information on screen
gráfica: imágenes o texto que se usa para dar información en pantalla

H

hamartia: a tragic hero's fatal flaw; an ingrained character trait that causes a hero to make decisions that ultimately lead to his or her death or downfall
hamartia: error fatal de un héroe trágico; característica propia de un personaje que causa que un héroe tome decisiones que finalmente llevan a su muerte o caída

hero: the main character or protagonist of a play, with whom audiences become emotionally invested
héroe: personaje principal o protagonista de una obra teatral, con el que el público se involucra emocionalmente

historical context: the circumstances or conditions in which something takes place
contexto historico: circuntancias o condiciones en las cuales algo sucede o pasa

hook: an interesting quotation, anecdote, or example at the beginning of a piece of writing that grabs the reader's attention
gancho: cita, anécdota o ejemplo interesante al comienzo de un escrito, que capta la atención del lector

Horatian satire: satire that pokes fun at human foibles and folly with a witty, gentle, even indulgent tone
sátira de Horacio: sátira en que se burla de las debilidades y locuras con un tono suave, ingenioso, hasta indulgente

humor: the quality of being amusing
humor: calidad de ser divertido

hyperbole: exaggeration used to suggest strong emotion or create a comic effect
hipérbole: exageración que se usa para sugerir una emoción fuerte o crear un efecto cómico

I

iamb: a metrical foot that consists of an unstressed syllable followed by a stressed syllable
yambo: pie métrico que consta de una sílaba átona seguida de una sílaba acentuada

iambic pentameter: a rhythmic pattern of five feet (or units) of one unstressed syllable followed by a stressed syllable
pentámetro yámbico: patrón rítmico de cinco pies (o unidades) de una sílaba átona seguida de una sílaba acentuada

image: a word or phrase that appeals to one of more of the five senses and creates a picture
imagen: palabra o frase que apela a uno o más de los cinco sentido y crea un cuadro

imagery: the verbal expression of sensory experience; descriptive or figurative language used to create word pictures; imagery is created by details that appeal to one or more of the five senses
imaginería: lenguaje descriptivo o figurativo utilizado para crear imágenes verbales; la imaginería es creada por detalles que apelan a uno o más de los cinco sentidos

imperialism: a policy of extending the rule or influence of a country over other countries or colonies
imperialismo: política de extender el reino o influencia de un país sobre otros paises o colonias

implied theme: a theme that is understood through the writer's diction, language construction, and use of literary devices
tema implícito: tema que se entiende a través de la dicción del escritor, construcción lingüística y uso de recursos literarios

indirect characterization: a narrator's or author's development of a character through the character's interactions with others, thoughts about circumstances, or speaking his or her thoughts aloud
caracterización indirecta: el desarrollo de un personaje según un narrador o autor por las interacciones del personaje con otros, pensamientos sobre las circunstancias, o su habilidad de enunciar sus pensamientos en voz alta

inductive reasoning: a process of looking at individual facts to draw a general conclusion
razonamiento inductivo: proceso de observación de hechos individuales para sacar una conclusión general

inference: a conclusion about ideas or information not directly stated
inferencia: conclusión sobre las ideas o información no presentadas directamente

interior monologue: a literary device in which a character's internal emotions and thoughts are presented
monólogo interior: recurso literario en el que se presentan las emociones internas y pensamientos de un personaje

interpretation: the act of making meaning from something, such as a text
interpretación: acto de interpretar un significado de algo, tal como un texto

internal coherence: unity or logical connection within paragraphs
coherencia interna: unidad o conexión lógica entre párrafos

irony: a literary device that exploits readers' expectations; irony occurs when what is expected turns out to be quite different from what actually happens. *Dramatic irony* is a form of irony in which the reader or audience knows more about the circumstances or future events in a story than the characters within it; *verbal irony* occurs when a speaker or narrator says one thing while meaning the opposite; *situational irony* occurs when an event contradicts the expectations of the characters or the reader.

ironía: recurso literario que explota las expectativas de los lectores; la ironía ocurre cuando lo que se espera resulta ser bastante diferente de lo que realmente ocurre. La *ironía dramática* es una forma de ironía en la que el lector o la audiencia saben más acerca de las circunstancias o sucesos futuros de un cuento que los personajes del mismo; la *ironía verbal* ocurre cuando un orador o narrador dice una cosa queriendo decir lo contrario; la *ironía situacional* ocurre cuando un suceso contradice las expectativas de los personajes o del lector.

J

justice: the quality of being reasonable and fair in the administration of the law; the ideal of rightness or fairness
justicia: calidad de ser razonable e imparcial en la administración de la ley; ideal de rectitud o equidad

Juvenalian satire: satire that denounces, sometimes harshly, human vice and error in dignified and solemn tones
sátira de Juvenal: sátira de denuncia, a veces con aspereza, los vicios y errores humanos con tonos dignos y solemnes

juxtaposition: the arrangement of two or more things for the purpose of comparison
yuxtaposición: ordenamiento de dos o más cosas con el objeto de compararlas

L

lining out: the process of creating line breaks to add shape and meaning in free verse poetry
llamada y respuesta: proceso de crear rupturas de lineas para dar forma y significado en la poesía del verso libre

literal language: the exact meanings, or denotations, of words
lenguaje literal: los signficados y denotaciones exactos de las palabras

literary theory: attempts to establish principles for interpreting and evaluating literary texts
teoría literaria: intento de establecer principios para interpretar y evaluar textos literarios

logical evidence: evidence based on facts and a clear rationale
evidencia lógica: evidencia basada en hechos y una clara fundamentación

logos: (logical appeal) a rhetorical appeal that uses factual evidence and logic to appeal to the audience's sense of reason
logos: (apelación lógica) apelación retórica que usa la evidencia factual y la lógica para apelar al sentido de la razón

M

main idea: a statement (often one sentence) that summarizes the key details of a text
idea principal: declaración (con frecuencia una oración) que resume los detalles claves de un texto

marginalize: to relegate or confine a person to a lower or outer limit
marginar: relegar or confinar a una persona a un límite bajo o ajeno

Marxist criticism: viewing a text through the perspective that economics provides the foundation for all social, political, and ideological reality
crítica marxista: ver un text a través de la perspectiva en que la economía proporciona la fundación de toda realidad social, política, e ideológica

media: collectively refers to the organizations that communicate information to the public
medios de comunicación: colectivamente refiere a las organizaciones que comunican información al público

media channel: a method an organization uses to communicate such as radio, television, website, newspaper, or magazine
canales mediaticos: método que usa una organización en la comunicación como radio, televisión, sitios de web, periódico, o revista

metacognition: the ability to know and be aware of one's own thought processes; self-reflection
metacognición: capacidad de conocer y estar consciente de los propios procesos del pensamiento; introspección

metaphor: a comparison between two unlike things in which one thing is spoken of as if it were another, for example, the moon was a crisp white cracker
metáfora: comparación entre dos cosas diferentes en la que se habla de una cosa como si fuera otra, por ejemplo, la luna era una galletita blanca crujiente

meter: a pattern of stressed and unstressed syllables in poetry
métrica: patrón de sílabas acentuadas y átonas en poesía

mise-en-scène: the composition, or setting, of a stage
puesta en escena: la composición o el lugar de un escenario

monologue: a dramatic speech delivered by a single character in a play
monólogo: discurso dramático que hace un solo personaje en una obra teatral

montage: a composite picture that is created by bringing together a number of images and arranging them to create a connected whole
montaje: cuadro compuesto que se crea al reunir un número de imágenes y que al organizarlas se crea un todo relacionado

mood: the atmosphere or general feeling in a literary work
carácter: atmósfera o sentimiento general en una obra literaria

motif: a recurrent image, symbol, theme, character type, subject, or narrative detail that becomes a unifying element in an artistic work or text
motivo: imagen, símbolo, tema, tipo de personaje, tema o detalle narrativo recurrente que se convierte en un elemento unificador en una obra artística

musical (or sound) device: the use of sound to convey and reinforce the meaning or experience of poetry
aparatos musicales: uso del sonido para transmitir y reforzar el significado o experiencia de la poesía

myth: a traditional story that explains the actions of gods or heroes or the origins of the elements of nature
mito: cuento tradicional que explica las acciones de dioses o héroes, o los orígenes de los elementos de la naturaleza

N

narration: the act of telling a story
narración: acto de contar un cuento

narrative: a story about a series of events that includes character development, plot structure, and theme; can be a work of fiction or nonfiction
narrativa: narración sobre una serie de sucesos que incluye el desarrollo de personajes, estructora del argumento, y el tema; puede ser una obra de ficción o no ficción

narrative pacing: the speed at which a narrative moves
compás de la narrativa: la rapidez en que una narrativa pasa

narrator: the person telling the story
narrador: persona que cuenta una historia

non-diegetic sound: voice-overs and commentary; sounds that do not come from the action on screen
sonido no diegético: voces y comentarios superpuestos; sonidos que no provienen de la acción en pantalla.

O

objective: based on factual information
objetivo: basado en información de hechos

objective tone: a tone that is more clinical and that is not influenced by emotion
tono objetivo: tono que es mas aséptico y que no se deja influir por la emoción

objectivity: the representation of facts or ideas without injecting personal feelings or biases
objetividad: representación de los hechos o ideas sin agregar sentimientos o prejuicios personales

ode: a lyric poem expressing feelings or thoughts of a speaker, often celebrating a person, event, or a thing
oda: poema lírico que expresa sentimientos o pensamientos de un orador, que frecuentemente celebra a una persona, suceso o cosa

onomatopoeia: words whose sound suggest their meaning
onomatopeya: palabras cuyo sonido sugiere su significado

oral interpretation: a planned oral reading that expresses the meaning of a written text
interpretación oral: lectura oral planeada que interpreta el signficado de un text escrito

oral tradition: the passing down of stories, tales, proverbs, and other culturally important stories and ideas through oral retellings
tradición oral: traspaso de historias, cuentos, proverbios y otras historias de importancia cultural por medio de relatos orales

oxymoron: words that appear to contradict each other; for example, cold fire
oxímoron: palabras que parecen contradecirse mutuamente; por ejemplo, fuego frío

P

parallel structure (parallelism): refers to a grammatical or structural similarity between sentences or parts of a sentence, so that elements of equal importance are equally developed and similarly phrased for emphasis
estructura paralela (paralelismo): se refiere a una similitud gramatical o estructural entre oraciones o partes de una oración, de modo que los elementos de igual importancia se desarrollen por igual y se expresen de manera similar para dar énfasis

paraphrase: to briefly restate ideas from another source in one's own words
parafrasear: volver a presentar las ideas de otra fuente en nuestras propias palabras

parenthetical citations: used for citing sources directly in an essay
citas parentéticas: usadas en citas de fuentes primarias en un ensayo

paradox: a statement that contains two seemingly incompatible points
paradoja: declaración que contiene dos asuntos aparentemente incompatibles

parody: a literary or artistic work that imitates the characteristic style of an author or a work for comic effect or ridicule
parodia: obra literaria o artística que imita el estilo característico de un autor o una obra para dar un efecto cómico o ridículo

passive-voice verbs: verb form in which the subject receives the action; the passive voice consists of a form of the verb *be* plus a past participle of the verb
verbos en voz pasiva: forma verbal en la que el sujeto recibe la acción; la voz pasiva se forma con el verbo *ser* más el participio pasado de un verbo

pathos: (emotional appeal) a rhetorical appeal to the reader's or listener's senses or emotions
pathos: (apelación emocional) apelación retórica a los sentidos o emociones de los lectores u oyentes

patriarchal: a society in which the male is head of the household and holds authority over women and children
patriarcal: sociedad en que el varón es jefe del hogar en el cual mantiene autoridad sobre las mujeres y niños

perception: one person's interpretation or sensory or conceptual information
percepción: interpretación de una persona en cuanto a información sensorial o conceptual

periodic sentence: a sentence that makes sense only when the end of the sentence is reached, that is, when the main clause comes last
oración periódica: oración que tiene sentido sólo cuando se llega al final de la oración, es decir, cuando la cláusula principal viene al final

persona: the voice assumed by a writer to express ideas or beliefs that may not be his or her own
personaje: voz que asume un escritor para expresar ideas o creencias que pueden no ser las propias

personification: a figure of speech that gives human qualities to an animal, object, or idea
personificación: figura literaria que da características humanas a un animal, objeto o idea

perspective: a way of looking at the world or a mental concept about things or events, one that judges relationships within or among things or events
perspectiva: manera de visualizar el mundo o concepto mental de las cosas o sucesos, que juzga las relaciones dentro o entre cosas o sucesos

persuasive argument: an argument that convinces readers to accept or believe a writer's perspective on a topic
argumento persuasivo: argumento que convence a los lectores a aceptar o creer en la perspectiva de un escritor acerca de un tema

photo essay: a collection of photographic images that reveal the author's perspective on a subject
ensayo fotográfico: recolección de imágenes fotográficas que revelan la perspectiva del autor acerca de un tema

plagiarism: the unattributed use of another writer's words or ideas
plagio: usar como propias las palabras o ideas de otro escritor

plot: the sequence of related events that make up a story or novel
trama: secuencia de sucesos relacionados que conforman un cuento o novela

poetic structure: the organization of words, lines, and images as well as ideas
estructura poética: organización de las palabras, versos e imágenes, así como también de las ideas

point of view: the perspective from which a narrative is told, that is, first person, third-person limited, or third-person omniscient
punto de vista: perspectiva desde la cual se cuenta un relato, es decir, primera persona, tercera persona limitada o tercera persona omnisciente

precept: a rule, instruction, or principle that guides a person's actions and/or moral behavior

precepto: regla, instrucción o principio que guía las acciones de una persona y/o conducta moral de alguien

primary footage: film footage shot by the filmmaker for the text at hand
metraje principal: filmación hecha por el cineasta para el texto que tiene a mano

primary source: an original document containing firsthand information about a subject
fuente primaria: documento original que contiene información de primera mano acerca de un tema

prologue: the introduction or preface to a literary work
prólogo: introducción o prefacio de una obra literaria

prose: ordinary written or spoken language, using sentences and paragraphs, without deliberate or regular meter or rhyme; not poetry or song
prosa: forma común del lenguaje escrito o hablado, usando oraciones y párrafos, sin métrica o rima deliberada o regular; ni poesía ni canción

protagonist: the central character in a work of literature, the one who is involved in the main conflict in the plot
protagonista: personaje central de una obra literaria, el que participa en el conflicto principal de la trama

proverb: a short saying about a general truth
proverbio: dicho corto sobre una verdad general

Q

qualify: to consider to what extent a statement is true or untrue
calificar: consider hasta qué punto una declaración es verdadera o falsa

quatrain: a four-line stanza in a poem
cuarteta: en un poema, estrofa de cuatro versos

R

reader response criticism: analyzing a text based on the reader's own experiences, social ethics, moral values, and general views of the world
crítica de reacción del lector: análisis de un texto basado en las experiencias, ética social, valores, y percepciones generales del mundo

reasoning: the thinking or logic used to make a claim in an argument
razonamiento: pensamiento o lógica que se usa para hacer una afirmación en un argumento

refrain: a regularly repeated line or group of lines in a poem or song, usually at the end of a stanza
estribillo: verso o grupo de versos que se repiten con regularidad en un poema o canción, normalmente al final de una estrofa

refutation: the reasoning used to disprove an opposing point
refutación: razonamiento que se usa para rechazar una opinión contraria

reliability: the extent to which a source provides good quality and trustworthy information
confiabilidad: grado en el que una fuente da información confiable y de buena calidad

renaissance: a rebirth or revival
renacimiento: un volver a nacer o una reanimación

repetition: the use of any element of language—a sound, a word, a phrase, a line, or a stanza—more than once
repetición: uso de cualquier elemento del lenguaje—un sonido, una palabra, una frase, un verso o una estrofa—más de una vez

resolution (denouement): the end of a play, story, or novel in which the main conflict is finally resolved
resolución (desenlace): final de una obra teatral, cuento o novela, en el que el conflicto principal finalmente se resuelve

résumé: a document that outlines a person's skills, education, and work history
currículum vitae: documento que resume las destrezas, educación y experiencia laboral de una persona

rhetoric: the art of using words to persuade in writing or speaking
retórica: arte de usar las palabras para persuadir por escrito o de manera hablada

rhetorical appeals: the use of emotional, ethical, and logical arguments to persuade in writing or speaking
recursos retóricos: uso de argumentos emocionales, éticos y lógicos para persuadir por escrito o de manera hablada

rhetorical context: the subject, purpose, audience, occasion, or situation in which writing occurs
contexto retórico: sujeto, propósito, audiencia, ocasión o situación en que ocurre el escrito

rhetorical devices: specific techniques used in writing or speaking to create a literary effect or enhance effectiveness
dispositivos retóricos: técnicas específicas que se usan al escribir o al hablar para crear un efecto literario o mejorar la efectividad

rhetorical question: a question that is asked for effect or one for which the answer is obvious
pregunta retórica: pregunta hecha para producir un efecto o cuya respuesta es obvia

rhyme: the repetition of sounds at the ends of words
rima: repetición de sonidos al final de las palabras

rhyme scheme: a consistent pattern of rhyme throughout a poem
esquema de la rima: patrón consistente de una rima a lo largo de un poema

rhythm: the pattern of stressed and unstressed syllables in spoken or written language, especially in poetry
ritmo: patrón de sílabas acentuadas y no acentuadas en lenguaje hablado o escrito, especialmente en poesía

rising action: the movement of a plot toward a climax or moment of greatest excitement; the rising action is fueled by the characters' responses to the conflict
acción ascendente: movimiento de una trama hacia el clímax o momento de mayor emoción; la acción ascendente es impulsada por las reacciones de los personajes ante el conflicto

round (or dynamic) character: a character who evolves and grows in the story and has a complex personality
personaje dinámico: personaje que evoluciona y crece en la historia y que tiene una personalidad compleja

S

satire: a manner of writing that mocks social conventions, actions, or attitudes with wit and humor
sátira: manera de escribir en que se burla de convenciones sociales, acciones, o actitudes con ingenio y humor

scenario: an outline, a brief account, a script, or a synopsis of a proposed series of events
escenario: bosquejo, relato breve, libreto o sinopsis de una serie de sucesos propuestos

secondary audience: a group that may receive a message intended for a target audience
audiencia secundaria: grupo que puede recibir un mensaje orientado a una audiencia específica

secondary source: discussion about or commentary on a primary source; the key feature of a secondary source is that it offers an interpretation of information gathered from primary sources
fuente secundaria: discusión o comentario acerca de una fuente primaria; la característica clave de una fuente secundaria es que ofrece una interpretación de la información recopilada en las fuentes primarias

sensory details: details that appeal to or evoke one or more of the five senses—sight, sound, smell, taste, and touch
detalles sensoriales: detalles que apelan o evocan uno o más de los cinco sentidos—vista, oído, gusto, olfato, y tacto

sensory images: images that appeal to the reader's senses—sight, sound, smell, taste, and touch
imágenes sensoriales: imágenes que apelan a los sentidos del lector—vista, oído, olfato, gusto, y tacto

sequence of events: the order in which things happen in a story
secuencia de eventos: orden en que los sucesos de una historia pasan:

setting: the time and place in which a story happens
ambiente: tiempo y lugar en el que ocurre un relato

simile: a comparison of two different things or ideas using the words *like* or *as*, for example, the moon was as white as milk
símil: comparación entre dos o más cosas o ideas diferentes usando las palabras *como* o *tan*, por ejemplo, la luna estaba tan blanca como la leche

situational irony: occurs when an event contradicts the expectations of the characters or the reader
ironía situacional: ocurre cuando un evento contradice las espectativas de los personajes o el lector

slanters: rhetorical devices used to present the subject in a biased way
soslayo: recursos retóricos para presentar el tema de modo sesgado

slogan: a short, catchy phrase used for advertising by a business, club, or political party
eslogan: frase corta y tendenciosa que usa como publicidad para un negocio, club o partido político

social commentary: an expression of an opinion with the goal of promoting change by appealing to a sense of justice
comentario social: expresión de una opinión con el objeto de promover el cambio al apelar a un sentido de justicia

soliloquy: a long speech delivered by an actor alone on the stage representing his or her internal thoughts
soliloquio: discurso largo realizado por un actor sobre el escenario que representa sus pensamientos internos

sonnet: a fourteen-line lyric poem, usually written in iambic pentameter and following a strict pattern of rhyme
soneto: poema lírico de catorce versos, normalmente escrito en un pentámetro yámbico y que sigue un patrón de rima estricto

speaker: the imaginary voice or persona of the writer or author
orador: voz o persona imaginaria del escritor o autor

stage directions: instructions written into the script of a play that indicate stage actions, movements of performers, or production requirements
direcciones escénicas: instrucciones escritas en un guión o drama que indican acción, movimiento de actors, o requisitos de la producción

stakeholder: a person motivated or affected by a course of action
participante: persona motivada o afectada por el curso de una acción

stanza: a group of lines, usually similar in length and pattern, that form a unit within a poem
estrofa: grupo de versos, normalmente similares en longitud y patrón, que forman una unidad dentro de un poema

static (or flat) character: a character who remains the same throughout a narrative
personaje estático: personaje que no cambia a lo largo de una narrativa

stereotype: an oversimplified, generalized conception, opinion, and/or image about particular groups of people
estereotipo: concepto generalizado, opinión y/o imagen demasiado simplificada acerca de grupos específicos de personas

stichomythia: in drama, the delivery of dialogue in a rapid, fast-paced manner, with actors speaking emotionally and leaving very little time between speakers
esticomitia: en el drama, es la rendición del diálogo de una manera rápida con actores que hablan con emoción, dejando espacio muy breve entre los hablantes

storyboard: a tool to show images and sequencing for the purpose of visualizing a film or a story
guión gráfico: método de mostrar imágenes y secuencias con el propósito de visualizar una película o historia

strategize: planning the actions one will take to complete a task
estrategizar: planear las acciones de uno para complir una tarea

structure: the way a literary work is organized; the arrangement of the parts in a literary work
estructura: manera en que la obra literaria está organizada; disposición de las partes en una obra literaria

style: the distinctive way a writer uses language, characterized by elements of diction, syntax, imagery, and so on
estilo: manera distintiva en que un escritor usa el lenguaje, caracterizada por elementos de dicción, sintaxis, lenguaje figurado, etc.

subculture: a smaller subsection of a culture, for example, within the culture of a high school may be many subcultures
subcultura: subsección más pequeña de una cultura, por ejemplo, dentro de la cultura de una escuela secundaria puede haber muchas subculturas

subjective tone: a tone that is obviously influenced by the author's feelings or emotions
tono subjetivo: tono obviamente influído por los sentimientos o emociones del autor

subjectivity: based on one's personal point of view, opinion, or values
subjetividad: en base en nuestro punto de vista, opinión o valores personales

subordinate: a person or group that is perceived as having a lower social or economic status
subordinado: persona o grupo percibido de ser de rango social o estado económico bajo

subplot: a secondary or side story that supports the main plot and usually involves minor characters
argumento secundario: una historia secundaria o periférica que apoya el argumento principal y que suele involucrar a personajes secundarios o menores

subtext: the underlying or implicit meaning in dialogue or the implied relationship between characters in a book, movie, play, or film; the subtext of a work is not explicitly stated
subtexto: significado subyacente o implícito en el diálogo o la relación implícita entre los personajes de un libro, película, u obra teatral. El subtexto de una obra no se establece de manera explícita.

survey: a method of collecting data from a group of people; it can be written, such as a print or online questionnaire, or oral, such as an in-person interview

encuesta: método para recolectar datos de un grupo de personas; puede ser escrita, como un impreso o cuestionario en línea, u oral, como en una entrevista personal

symbol: anything (object, animal, event, person, or place) that represents itself but also stands for something else on a figurative level

símbolo: cualquier cosa (objeto, animal, evento, persona o lugar) que se representa a sí misma, pero también representa otra cosa a nivel figurativo

symbolic: serving as a symbol; involving the use of symbols or symbolism

simbólico: que sirve como símbolo; que implica el uso de símbolos o simbolismo

synecdoche: a figure of speech in which a part is used to represent the whole or vice versa

sinécdoque: figura retórica en que una parte se usa para representar el todo, o vice-versa

syntax: the arrangement of words and the order of grammatical elements in a sentence; the way in which words are put together to make meaningful elements such as phrases, clauses, and sentences

sintaxis: disposición de las palabras y orden de los elementos gramaticales en una oración; manera en que las palabras se juntan para formar elementos significativos como frases, cláusulas y oraciones

synthesis: the act of combining ideas from different sources to create, express, or support a new idea

síntesis: acto de combinar ideas de diferentes fuentes para crear, expresar o apoyar una nueva idea

T

target audience: the intended group for which a work is designed to appeal or reach

público objetivo: grupo al que se pretende apelar o llegar con una obra

textual commentary: explanations about the significance or importance of supporting details or examples in an analysis

comentario textual: explicaciones acerca de la importancia de los detalles que tienen apoyo o ejemplos en un análisis

textual evidence: the details, quotations, and examples from a text that support the analysis or argument presented

evidencia textual: detalles, citas, y ejemplos de un texto que apoyan el análisis o la argumentación presentada

theatrical elements: elements used by dramatists and directors to tell a story on stage. Elements include *costumes* (the clothing worn by actors to express their characters), *makeup* (cosmetics used to change actors' appearances and express their characters), *props* (objects used to help set the scene, advance a plot, and make a story realistic), *set* (the place where the action takes place, as suggested by objects, such as furniture, placed on a stage), and *acting choices* (gestures, movements, staging, and vocal techniques actors use to convey their characters and tell a story).

elementos teatrales: elementos utilizados por los dramaturgos y directores para contar una historia en el escenario. Los elementos incluyen *vestuario* (ropa que usan los actores para expresar sus personajes), *maquillaje* (cosméticos que se usan para cambiar la apariencia de los actores y expresar sus personajes), *elementos* (objetos que se usan para ayudar a montar la escena, avanzar la trama y crear una historia realista), *plató* (lugar donde tiene lugar la acción, según lo sugieren los objetos, como muebles, colocados sobre un escenario), y *opciones de actuación* (gestos, movimientos, representación y técnicas vocales que se usan para transmitir sus personajes y narrar una historia).

thematic statement: an interpretive statement articulating the central meaning or message of a text

oración temática: afirmación interpretativa que articula el significado o mensaje central de un texto

theme: a writer's central idea or main message about life; *see also* explicit theme, implied theme

tema: idea central o mensaje principal acerca de la vida de un escritor; *véase también* tema explícito, tema implícito

thesis: the main idea or point of an essay or article; in an argumentative essay the thesis is the writer's position on an issue

tesis: idea o punto principal de un ensayo o artículo; en un ensayo argumentativo, la tesis es la opinión del autor acerca de un tema

tone: a writer's or speaker's attitude toward a subject, character, or audience

tono: actitud de un escritor u orador acerca de un tema

topic sentence: a sentence that states the main idea of a paragraph; in an essay, the topic sentence also makes a point that supports the thesis statement

oración principal: oración que establece la idea principal de un párrafo; en un ensayo, la oración principal también establece una proposición que apoya el enunciado de la tesis

tragedy: a dramatic play that tells the story of a character, usually of a noble class, who meets an untimely and unhappy death or downfall, often because of a specific character flaw or twist of fate

tragedia: obra teatral dramática que cuenta la historia de un personaje, normalmente de origen noble, que encuentra una muerte o caída imprevista o infeliz, con frecuencia debido a un defecto específico del personaje o una vuelta del destino

tragic hero: an archetypal hero based on the Greek concept of tragedy; the tragic hero has a flaw that makes him or her vulnerable to downfall or death

héroe trágico: héroe arquetípico basado en el concepto griego de la tragedia; el héroe trágico tiene un defecto que lo hace vulnerable a la caída o a la muerte

transcript: a written copy of a conversation that takes place between two or more people
transcripción: copia escrita de una conversación que sucede entre dos o más personas

U

understatement: the representation of something as smaller or less significant than it really is; the opposite of exaggeration or hyperbole
subestimación: representación de algo como más pequeño o menos importante de lo que realmente es; lo opuesto a la exageración o hipérbole

V

valid: believable or truthful
válido: creíble o verídico

validity: the quality of truth or accuracy in a source
validez: calidad de verdad o precisión en una fuente

verbal irony: occurs when a speaker or narrator says one thing while meaning the opposite
ironía verbal: ocurre cuando un hablante o narrador dice una cosa mientras quiere decir lo opuesto

verify: to prove or confirm that something is true
verificar: probar o confirmar que algo es verdadero

vignette: a picture or visual or a brief descriptive literary piece
viñeta: ilustración o representación visual o pieza literaria descriptiva breve

visual delivery: the way a performer on stage interprets plot, character, and conflict through movement, gestures, and facial expressions
presentación visual: manera en que un actor en un escenario interpreta trama, carácter, y conflicto a través de movimiento, gestos, y expresiones de la cara

visual rhetoric: an argument or points made by visuals such as photographs or by other visual features of a text
retórica visual: argumentos o asuntos representados en visuales como fotos u otros rasgos visuales de un texto

vocal delivery: the way words are expressed on stage through volume, pitch, rate or speed of speech, pauses, pronunciation, and articulation
presentación vocal: manera en que se expresan las palabras en el escenario, por medio del volumen, tono, rapidez o velocidad del discurso, pausas, pronunciación y articulación

voice: the way a writer or speaker uses words and tone to express ideas as well as his or her persona or personality
voz: manera en que el escritor u orador usa las palabras y el tono para expresar ideas, así como también su personaje o personalidad

Word Map

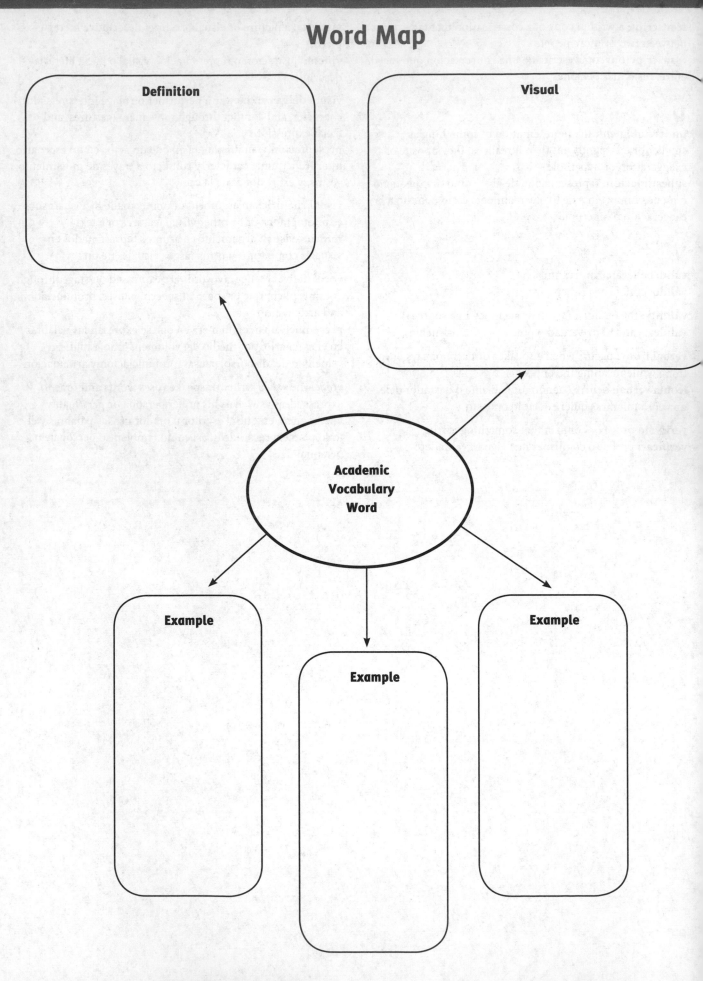

Definition

Visual

Academic Vocabulary Word

Example

Example

Example

Editor's / Writer's Checklist

Organizational Elements

	Does your title express the topic and engage the reader?
	Do you have an engaging hook or lead to open your essay?
	Do you end your introductory paragraph with a thesis statement that states an opinion on a topic and suggests an organization?
	Do you have topic sentences that relate to the thesis statement?
	Do your body paragraphs contain detail and commentary to support your topic sentences?
	Do you include transitions to link ideas?
	Do your body paragraphs contain concluding sentences that also act as transitional statements to the next paragraph?
	Have you ended your essay with a strong conclusion that comments on the significance of your thesis ideas?

Sentence Elements

	Have you revised to make sure all sentences are complete sentences?
	Do your sentences contain vivid verbs and descriptive adjectives when appropriate?
	Is the verb tense of your writing consistent? Do the subject and verb agree?
	Is pronoun use appropriate and consistent?
	Is parallel structure used to advantage and when appropriate?
	Do you vary sentence beginnings? Have you started sentences with a subordinate clause?
	Are your sentence types (simple, compound, complex) and lengths varied for interest and emphasis?
	Have you tried to include figurative and sensory language for effect?
	Have you used appositives when appropriate?
	Have you checked punctuation use for correctness, especially for appositives, complex sentences and parallel structure?
	Have you incorporated and punctuated quoted material correctly?

SOAPSTone:

SOAPSTone	Analysis	Textual Support
Speaker: What does the reader know about the writer?		
Occasion: What are the circumstances surrounding this text?		
Audience: Who is the target audience?		
Purpose: Why did the author write this text?		
Subject: What is the topic?		
Tone: What is the author's tone, or attitude?		

SOAPSTone:

SOAPSTone	Analysis	Textual Support
S		
O		
A		
P		
S		
Tone		

TP-CASTT Analysis

Poem Title:

Author:

Title: Make a Prediction. What do you think the title means before you read the poem?

Paraphrase: Translate the poem in your own words. What is the poem about? Rephrase difficult sections word for word.

Connotation: Look beyond the literal meaning of key words and images to their associations.

Attitude: What is the speaker's attitude? What is the author's attitude? How does the author feel about the speaker, about other characters, about the subject?

Shifts: Where do the shifts in tone, setting, voice, etc., occur? Look for time and place, keywords, punctuation, stanza divisions, changes in length or rhyme, and sentence structure. What is the purpose of each shift? How do they contribute to effect and meaning?

Title: Reexamine the title. What do you think it means now in the context of the poem?

Theme: Think of the literal and metaphorical layers of the poem. Then determine the overall theme. The theme must be written in a complete sentence.

TP-CASTT

Poem Title:

Author:

T		
P		
C		
A		
S		
T		
T		

SMELL

Sender-Receiver Relationship - Who are the senders and receivers of the message, and what is their relationship (consider what different audiences the text may be addressing).

Message - What is a literal summary of the content? What is the meaning/significance of this information?

Emotional Strategies - What emotional appeals (*pathos*) are included? What seems to be their desired effect?

Logical Strategies - What logical arguments/appeals (*logos*) are included? What is their effect?

Language - What specific language is used to support the message? How does it affect the text's effectiveness? Consider both images and actual words.

Speaker, 39, 43, 44, 65, 116, 191, 232, 233, 281, 287, 371

Stanza, 262, 274, 276, 291, 293

Style, 88, 93, 94, 95, 129, 130, 274, 276, 277, 295, 297, 299, 308, 311, 315, 37

Subplot, 217, 221

Subtext, 358, 359, 360

Symbol(ism), 88, 90, 96, 97, 98, 103, 104, 112, 119, 125, 126, 131, 222, 230, 268, 278, 293, 331, 354, 356

Synecdoche, 264

Syntax, 11, 14, 30, 32, 38, 94, 120, 129, 130, 131, 141, 232

Tableau, 326

Thematic statement, 105, 112, 125, 220, 221, 238, 274, 286, 292, 300

Theme, 40, 90, 98, 104, 105, 115, 125, 131, 133, 163, 203, 207, 219, 223, 226, 228, 231, 239, 240, 248, 249, 268, 277, 284, 286, 300, 311, 331, 354, 356, 357, 380

Tone, 14, 30, 35, 43, 44, 98, 104, 111, 129, 130, 131, 136, 138, 141, 142, 148, 191, 204, 210, 232, 242, 268, 274, 277, 287, 295, 296, 297, 311, 331, 356, 371, 374

Tragedy, 324, 325

Transcript, 45, 49

Visual prompt, 1, 85, 103, 169, 251, 276, 317

Voice, 5, 11, 14, 22, 23, 28, 30, 31, 38, 39, 40, 43, 44, 51, 54, 93, 94, 232, 275

Reading Skills

Annotating the text, 7, 28, 31, 45, 94, 97, 203, 210, 224, 242, 249, 284, 297, 308

Chunking the text, 327, 329, 346, 349, 354, 357, 382

Close reading, 96, 106, 136, 138, 149, 150, 151, 154, 157, 160, 217, 222, 228, 230, 235, 248, 272

Compare and contrast, 125

Connecting to the text, 224
   text-to-self, 212, 219
   text-to text, 212, 219
   text-to-world, 212, 219

Independent Reading Link, 4, 29, 56, 88, 95, 105, 113, 122, 125, 128, 172, 175, 193, 254, 286, 297, 310, 320, 366

Inferring, 5, 6, 11, 14, 21, 32, 38, 40, 41, 51, 192, 214, 217, 224, 230, 243, 330, 331, 356, 363

Interpreting graphs and tables, 64

Levels of questions, 106, 118, 125, 147, 200, 219, 220, 221, 272, 284, 286

Main idea, 133, 135

Making meaning, 327

Marking the text, 8, 12, 13, 14, 16, 28, 32, 41, 43, 50, 51, 66, 70, 71, 77, 94, 96, 98, 100, 115, 116, 122, 137, 138, 176, 186, 191, 192, 194, 204, 207, 209, 214, 217, 221, 222, 224, 228, 243, 256, 257, 259, 275, 278, 279, 280, 284, 287, 289, 291, 297, 321, 324, 335, 341, 348, 354, 370, 376, 386, 387, 388, 394, 399

Note-taking, 8, 144, 145, 151, 154, 157, 184, 223, 229, 233, 237, 327, 333, 351, 359, 363, 382, 400

Paraphrase, 292, 300, 327, 329, 346, 354

Poetry mixer, 255

Predicting, 96, 115, 117, 124, 148, 149, 206, 207, 214, 217, 222, 224, 300

Questioning the text, 147

Read aloud, 28, 96, 256, 257, 262, 273, 274, 284, 324, 327, 346, 348, 349, 354, 357, 360, 379

Rereading, 43, 96, 100, 112, 124, 229, 256, 272, 275, 284, 297, 323, 348

Scanning, 122, 178, 299, 327, 355

SIFT(symbol, images, figurative language, and tone/theme) strategy, 104, 125, 284, 286, 331

Sketching, 119, 210, 231, 334, 347, 354, 362

Skimming, 192, 224, 299, 327, 355

SMELL strategy, 71, 72, 236, 397

SOAPSTone strategy, 43, 186, 191, 370, 371

Socratic Seminar, 238

Summarizing, 8, 50, 130, 133, 184, 194, 218, 260, 263, 274, 323, 358

TP-CASTT analysis, 284, 286, 297, 300

Venn diagram, 131, 332

Visualizing, 119, 210, 231, 267, 327, 357, 362

Writing Skills

Analogy, 60, 61, 62, 73
   figurative, 61
   literal, 61

Analytical paragraph, 165

Analytical statement, 152, 153, 155, 158, 159, 160, 161, 165, 274

Annotated bibliography, 194, 197, 201, 339

Annotating the text, 51, 214, 248

Argument, 57, 65, 66, 77, 82, 83, 243, 366, 374, 395, 399, 400, 402, 403

Audience, 38, 65, 73, 74, 76, 77, 190

Audience analysis, 200, 201

Background information, 78, 79

Bibliography, 194

Brainstorming, 38, 53, 89, 96, 131, 173, 196, 211, 228, 248, 310, 312, 324, 337, 353

Call to action, 57, 76, 82, 233, 392, 399, 403

Claim, 57, 58, 62, 64, 68, 72, 75, 76, 77, 78, 79, 81, 83, 143, 158, 159, 161, 165, 187, 233, 244, 245, 246, 374, 375, 379, 381, 382, 386, 387, 388, 392, 393, 396, 399, 400, 403

Closure statement, 158, 159, 161, 165, 166

Commentary, 104, 155, 156, 158, 159, 161, 165, 167, 175, 185, 193, 194, 201, 211, 213, 214, 217, 226, 231, 247, 248, 320, 331, 341, 349, 352, 364, 375, 379, 381

Compare and contrast, 163, 231, 332, 341

Concluding statement, 24, 233, 392, 399, 400, 403

Conclusion, 27, 28, 54, 57, 76, 82, 126, 167, 221, 229, 248, 249, 313, 314

Counterclaim (concession), 57, 77, 78, 82, 83, 233, 246, 382, 386, 387, 388, 392, 393, 398, 399, 400, 403

Description, 51, 54

Details, 5, 31, 51, 113, 126, 132, 135, 164, 194, 195

Double-entry journal, 8, 11, 162

Drafting, 25, 30, 54, 83, 126, 167, 249, 293, 315, 403

Editing, 54, 83, 126, 167, 293, 403

Embedded Assessment, 54, 83, 126, 167, 201, 249, 293, 315, 364
   unpacking, 4, 56, 88, 128, 172, 203, 254, 295, 320, 366

Essays
   analytical, 128, 152, 165, 167
   argumentative, 366, 403
   literary analysis, 203, 221, 240, 248, 249, 295, 313
   persuasive, 83
   synthesis, 403

Evidence, 57, 58, 62, 65, 72, 73, 75, 76, 77, 81, 82, 83, 125, 156, 159, 161, 187, 188, 201, 233, 245, 366, 368, 374, 375, 376, 381, 382, 387, 388, 393, 394, 396, 399, 400, 403

Media Skills

Index of Authors and Titles

Credits

"Spotlight" from *Speak* by Laurie Halse Anderson. Copyright © 1999 by Laurie Halse Anderson. Reprinted by permission of Farrar, Straus and Giroux, LLC.

"Marigolds" by Eugenia Collier. Originally published in *Negro Digest*, November 1969. Reappeared in *Breeder and Other Stories* by Eugenia Collier, Black Classic Press, 1994. Used by permission of the author.

From *Always Running—LaVida Loca, Gang Days in L.A.* by Luis J. Rodriguez. (Curbstone Press, 1993) Reprinted with permission of Curbstone Press. Distributed by Consortium.

"'Race' Politics" from *Poems Across the Pavement* by Luis J. Rodriguez. Copyright © 1998 by Luis J. Rodriguez. Published by Tia Chucha Press. By permission of Susan Bergholz Literary Services, New York, NY and Lamy, NM. All rights reserved.

"WMDs" by Brian O'Connor *Men's Fitness*. Copyright © Weider Publications, LLC, a subsidiary of American Media, Inc. All rights reserved.

"Chuck Liddell" by Steve Yaccino *U.S. News & World Report* (August 21, 2008). Copyright © 2008 U. S. News & World Report LP.

"Editorial: An Early Start on College" from *Minneapolis Star Tribune* (January 14, 2012). Copyright © 2012 StarTribune.

"Why College Isn't for Everyone" by Richard Vedder *Bloomberg Business Week* (April 9, 2012). Copyright © 2012 Bloomberg L.P.

"Actually College Is Very Much Worth It" by Andrew J. Rotherham *TIME* (May 19, 2011). Copyright © 2011 Time Inc.

"The Stolen Party" by Liliana Heker © 1982, which appeared in *Other Fires: Short Fiction by Latin American Women*, edited and translated by Alberto Manguel © 1985. Reprinted by permission of Westwood Creative Artists Ltd.

From *Charlie and the Chocolate Factory* by Roald Dahl, copyright © 1964, renewed 1992 by Roald Dahl Nominee Limited. Used by permission of Alfred A. Knopf, an imprint of Random House Children's Books, a division of Random House, Inc.

"Jim Crow: Shorthand for Separation" by Rick Edmonds. Reproduced from *Forum*, the magazine of the Florida Humanities Council, an affiliate of the National Endowment for the Humanities.

"Letter from Birmingham Jail" by Martin Luther King, Jr. Reprinted by arrangement with The Heirs to the Estate of Martin Luther King, Jr. c/o Writers House as agent for the proprietor New York, NY. Copyright 1963 Dr. Martin Luther King, Jr.; copyright renewed 1991 Coretta Scott King.

"Civil Rights Timeline" from CNN.com. Copyright © 2007 Cable News Network.

From *Scout, Atticus & Boo: A Celebration of To Kill a Mockingbird* by Mary McDonagh Murphy. Copyright © 2010 by Mary McDonagh Murphy. HarperCollins Publishers.

From *To Kill a Mockingbird* by Harper Lee. Copyright © 1960 by Harper Lee. Foreword copyright © 1993 by Harper Lee. Reprinted by permission of HarperCollins Publishers.

From *In Defense of To Kill a Mockingbird* by Nicholas. J. Karolides, Lee Burress, and John M. Keam, 1993, Scarecrow Press. Used by permission.

"Poetry" from *Selected Poems of Pablo Neruda*, translated by Alastair Reid, edited by Nathaniel Tarn and published by Jonathan Cape. Reprinted by permission of The Random House Group Ltd.

From *Poemcrazy* by Susan G. Wooldridge, copyright © 1996 Susan G. Wooldridge. Used by permission of Crown Publishers, a division of Random House, Inc.

"Nikki Rosa" from *Black Feeling, Black Talk, Black Judgment* by Nikki Giovanni. Copyright © 1968, 1970 by Nikki Giovanni. Reproduced by permission of HarperCollins Publishers.

"We Real Cool" by Gwendolyn Brooks. Reprinted by consent of Brooks Permissions.

"Fast Break" from *Wild Gratitude* by Edward Hirsch, copyright © 1985 by Edward Hirsch. Used by permission of Alfred A.Knopf, a division of Random House, Inc.

"Identity" by Julio Noboa Polanco. Used by permission of the author.

"Ego Tripping" from *The Selected Poems of Nikki Giovanni* by Nikki Giovanni. Compilation copyright © 1996 by Nikki Giovanni. Reproduced by permission of HarperCollins Publishers.

"Hanging Fire" from *The Collected Poems of Audre Lorde* by Audre Lorde. Copyright © 1978 by Audre Lorde. Used by permission of W. W. Norton & Company, Inc.

Image Credits